Multidisciplinary Organizational Training of Human Capital in the Digital Age

Edgar Oliver Cardoso Espinosa
Instituto Politécnico Nacional, Mexico

IGI Global
Scientific Publishing
Publishing Tomorrow's Research Today

Vice President of Editorial Melissa Wagner
Director of Acquisitions Mikaela Felty
Director of Book Development Jocelynn Hessler
Production Manager Mike Brehm
Cover Design Phillip Shickler

Published in the United States of America by
IGI Global Scientific Publishing
701 East Chocolate Avenue
Hershey, PA, 17033, USA
Tel: 717-533-8845
Fax: 717-533-7115
Website: https://www.igi-global.com E-mail: cust@igi-global.com

Library of Congress Cataloging-in-Publication Data

Names: Cardoso Espinosa, Edgar Oliver, 1973- editor.
Title: Multidisciplinary organizational training of human capital in the digital age / [edited by] Edgar Oliver Cardoso Espinosa, Instituo Politécnico Nacional, Mexico.
Description: Hershey, PA : IGI Global Scientific Publishing, [2025] | Includes bibliographical references (pages 307-346) and index. | Summary: "The main objective of the publication is to provide research or empirical studies with a multidisciplinary vision of the formation of human capital for organizations and its relationship with leadership as a strategic factor for the management of organizational change"-- Provided by publisher.
Identifiers: LCCN 2024055951 (print) | LCCN 2024055952 (ebook) | ISBN 9798369370865 (hardcover) | ISBN 9798369370902 (paperback) | ISBN 9798369370872 (ebook)
Subjects: LCSH: Business enterprises--Technological innovations. | Organizational change. | Technological innovations--Management.
Classification: LCC HD45 .M863 2025 (print) | LCC HD45 (ebook) | DDC 658.4/06--dc23/eng/20250205
LC record available at https://lccn.loc.gov/2024055951
LC ebook record available at https://lccn.loc.gov/2024055952

British Cataloguing in Publication Data
A Cataloguing in Publication record for this book is available from the British Library.

Table of Contents

Detailed Table of Contents

Abstract The objective of this research is to analyze the characteristics of leadership in educational organizations for digital transformation as well as those challenges that school leaders face in carrying out the reinforcement and use of technological tools for the formation of highly prepared human capital as well as implementing technology in the management of the educational center to meet the objectives. Derived from the multiple changes left by the pandemic, one of them was undoubtedly the way to lead an educational center and at the same time, implement digital tools to improve educational processes. Therefore, school leadership plays an important role in this transformation of the digital age for the success and achievement of institutional objectives. However, it is necessary that both leaders and other members of the educational center be prepared on how to use these tools.

This chapter explores the challenges and opportunities facing educational leaders in the context of the digital transformation of educational organisations. As digital technologies reshape the educational landscape, digital leadership emerges as a core competency to guide institutions into the future. This text examines the evolution of the concept of digital leadership, its current applications in education, and the essential competencies that leaders need to develop, such as advanced digital literacy, change management, and pedagogical innovation. Ethical and equity challenges arising from technological implementation are highlighted, including the digital divide and resistance to change, as well as opportunities for pedagogical innovation and the development of digital and soft skills. In addition, the chapter offers strategies for effective digital leadership including ongoing training, fostering an innovative organisational culture, and building collaborative and supportive networks

This chapter has generated a series of compilations of ideas related to digital communication and the formation of human capital in contemporary societies, including the new challenges faced by the individual with the emergence of Artificial Intelligence applied in society and the impact that concerns the classification of truthful information in professionalization. Not making a criticism, but presenting a series of concepts to motivate the reader to generate their own criteria towards the new innovation trends of 2030. The importance of education facing the responsibility of granting the transmission of quality knowledge and accompanied by moral-ethical practices, are a series of topics that the global contexts take up in order to meet the new needs, which have growth initiative in the training of specialists and individuals who select the staff that will open solid paths in the collaborative work at the institutional level, giving an opportunity to new generations of graduates to take advantage and apply the knowledge.

This chapter explores digital leadership in the context of organizational digital transformation. It examines the evolving role of leaders in the digital age, highlighting core competencies such as visionary thinking, data-driven decision-making, and fostering innovation. The chapter discusses strategies for developing digital leadership capabilities, theoretical implications of digital leadership, and ethical considerations in the digital realm. It also addresses practical implications, including improved innovation, employee engagement, and organizational agility. The chapter concludes by identifying future research avenues, emphasizing the need for longitudinal studies, industry-specific research, and exploration of ethical dimensions in digital leadership. Throughout, it underscores the critical role of digital leadership in navigating technological change and driving organizational success.

In this chapter proposed by the authors, the importance of strengthening inclusive skills in teachers through agile change management is essential to meet the current challenges in higher education. This requires a leadership committed to equity and inclusion, capable of guiding its educational community towards a future where diversity is considered a valuable asset in the educational process. Agile change in education is crucial to adapt to the diverse needs of students in an ever-changing educational environment. Committed leadership that fosters creativity and supports teachers in adopting inclusive practices is essential to ensure accessible and equitable education for all. Agile change management focuses on a continuous process of learning and adaptation, involving all educational stakeholders and promoting a culture of openness and flexibility. This strategy allows inclusion to become a dynamic and sustainable process, constantly adjusting to improve in response to emerging needs and ensuring that diversity is valued as an asset within the educational system.

One of the most representative impacts on the development of human capital is the reduced use of paper, thus generating a culture of sustainability in processes as everything is archived digitally. This leads to more feasibility in the use of digital resources, speed, document location, and information security. However, these new alternatives can create a knowledge gap in the use of technological tools. One of the most representative impacts on the development of human capital is the reduced use of paper, thus generating a culture of sustainability in processes as everything is archived digitally. This leads to more feasibility in the use of digital resources, speed, document location, and information security. However, these new alternatives can create a knowledge gap in the use of technological tools. The development of technological inclusion for all involved is necessary; this inclusion must be structured with a well-planned action plan to close the gaps in information lag or the use of technological resources.

The main objective of this research is to analyze institutional management in the context of educational organizations, with the aim of facilitating a significant change in their organizational environment. Special emphasis is placed on the relationship between education and sustainable development, recognizing the need for educational institutions to align themselves with principles that promote a sustainable future. Therefore, the use of learning ecologies is proposed as a tool to promote quality education that is linked to the demands of sustainable development, in addition to creating students who become agents of change for their communities, thus promoting sustainable and conscious development.

The situation that concerns Mexico in the educational domain aims to leave behind those barriers that prevent the intercultural growth and development among managers, teachers, students and parents, which for many years was relegated by political, economic and social situations. Likewise, it has been identified that in order to achieve the goals set and obtain as a result a quality, inclusive, equitable, fair, empathetic and resilient education; first of all, it is necessary to recognize that a leader is the key to carry out diverse actions in favor of inclusive and intercultural education; Through his actions, skills and strategies, he tests a management profile that allows to generate within the educational institute under his charge, an optimal, comfortable, inclusive, respectful, free environment, among others; achieving that the staff and school community, have the certainty that they will be guided and accompanied during the academic process being the beginning of a collaborative work and proactive construction with the educational population.

Preface

Social changes have generated transformations in both organizations and citizens. This panorama implies considering diversity, equity and inclusion in the academic training and professional performance of people.

For its part, education is constantly changing and adapting for new generations in order to achieve successful development of the skills required to interact in an environment of uncertainty and information generation due to the advancement of technological tools. Thus, digital transformation in organizations requires digital leadership to align their mission, vision, human capital, strategies and culture to become a sustainable organization.

In this sense, organizational transformation is successful when practices based on the formation of inclusive and digital human capital are incorporated, where leadership is the strategic factor that influences the implementation of organizational change management.

Based on the above, it is relevant that the educational sector investigates the changes in the formation of human capital in the 19th century to design, implement and evaluate training processes on the development of the appropriate professional skills for successful organizational development. Likewise, it is important to train leadership oriented towards the development of communication skills, conflict management, emotional intelligence, service, inclusiveness and digital intelligence to achieve significant and sustainable changes in the organization.

The main objective of the publication is to provide research or empirical studies with a multidisciplinary vision of the formation of human capital for organizations and its relationship with leadership as a strategic factor for the management of organizational change in the digital age.

The main contributions of the book are current scientific studies about human capital, providing a conceptual, theoretical and empirical framework for research focused on the development of human capital in relation to leadership, leadership styles, management in organizations and the promotion of competencies to develop an organizational transformation such as communication, collaboration, creativity and innovation, digital, inclusion and social justice. It also includes studies on curricular and educational evaluation processes focused on the levels of development of competencies, redesign and updating of educational programs and even proposals on evaluation instruments.

It should be noted that the process carried out for the preparation of the present included the following phases by the editor: 1) Submission of book proposal describing the coverage and importance of the topic for its evaluation by the Advisory Board of the Editorial IGI Global; 2) Selection of the evaluation committee; 3) Invitation at the international level of chapter proposals; 4) Conducting double blind review and judgment for each proposal by at least two evaluators; 5) Sending to the authors the reviews of each evaluator for compliance; 6) Compilation and organization of the chapters that met the evaluation and format criteria and 7) Preparation of the final work.

The structure of this book is organized into twelve chapters.

Here is a brief description of each of the chapters:

In the Chapter 1 titled "Ethical Leadership in The Postcovid Era for Educational Organizations" has as objective analyze the characteristics of organizational commitment and affective states to carry out an ethical leadership required in educational centers in the post covid era.

Chapter 2, "Distributed leadership in educational training," discusses the challenges and opportunities facing educational leaders in the context of the digital transformation of educational organizations. As digital technologies transform the educational landscape, digital leadership emerges as a core competency to guide institutions into the future. This text examines the evolution of the concept of digital leadership, its current applications in education, and the essential competencies that leaders need to develop, such as advanced digital literacy, change management, and pedagogical innovation. Ethical and equity challenges arising from technological implementation are highlighted, including the digital divide and resistance to change, as well as opportunities for pedagogical innovation and the development of digital and soft skills. In addition, the chapter offers strategies for effective digital leadership, including ongoing training, fostering an innovative organizational culture, and creating collaborative and supportive networks.

Chapter 3, entitled "Digital Communication in Human Capital Formation", aims to present a series of compilations of ideas related to digital communication and human capital formation in contemporary societies, including the new challenges faced by individuals with the emergence of Artificial Intelligence applied to society and the impact on the classification of truthful information in professionalization. The aim is not to criticize, but to present a series of concepts to motivate the reader to generate their own criteria for the new innovation trends of 2030. The importance of education in the face of the responsibility of providing the transmission of quality knowledge accompanied by ethical and moral practices are a series of topics that global contexts take up again to meet new needs, which have an initiative to grow in the training of specialists and individuals who select the personnel who will open solid paths in collaborative work at an institutional level, giving the opportunity to new generations of graduates to take advantage of and apply knowledge.

In chapter 4 with the theme "Digital Leadership in Organizations for Digital Transformation" examines digital leadership in the context of organizational digital transformation. The changing role of leaders in the digital age is examined, highlighting core competencies such as visionary thinking, data-driven decision making, and fostering innovation. The chapter discusses strategies for developing digital leadership capabilities, the theoretical implications of digital leadership, and ethical considerations in the digital realm. Practical implications such as enhancing innovation, employee engagement, and organizational agility are also addressed. The chapter concludes by identifying future research directions, emphasizing the need for longitudinal studies, industry-specific research, and exploring the ethical dimensions of digital leadership. Throughout the chapter, the critical role of digital leadership in coping with technological change and driving organizational success is underscored.

Chapter 5, entitled "Leadership challenges to strengthen inclusive teacher skills through agile change management in higher education", raises the importance of strengthening inclusive skills in teachers through agile change management, which is essential to address the current challenges of higher education. This requires leadership committed to equity and inclusion, capable of guiding its educational community towards a future where diversity is considered a valuable asset in the educational process. Agile change in education is crucial to adapt to the diverse needs of students in a constantly changing educational environment. Committed leadership that fosters creativity and supports teachers in adopting inclusive practices is essential to ensure accessible and equitable education for all. Agile change management focuses on a continuous process of learning and adaptation, involving all educational actors and promoting a culture of openness and flexibility. This strategy allows inclusion to become a dynamic and sustainable process, constantly adjusting to improve in response to emerging needs and ensuring that diversity is valued as an asset within the educational system.

Chapter 6, entitled "Personal Motivation for Digital Inclusion in Human Capital within Organizations," focuses on promoting a culture of sustainability in the development of human capital. One of the most significant impacts on the development of human capital is the reduction in the use of paper, thus generating a culture of sustainability in the processes by archiving everything digitally. This leads to greater feasibility in the use of digital resources, speed, location of documents, and information security. However, these new alternatives can create a knowledge gap in the use of technological tools. The development of technological inclusion of all those involved is necessary; this inclusion must be structured with a well-planned action plan to close the gaps in information lag or use of technological resources.

In Chapter 7, entitled "Managing Organizational Change in Education for Sustainable Development: Sustainable education in the era of digital transformation", the main objective of this research is to analyze institutional management in the context of educational organizations, with the aim of facilitating a significant change in their organizational environment. Special emphasis is placed on the relationship between education and sustainable development, recognizing the need for educational institutions to align themselves with principles that promote a sustainable future. Therefore, the use of learning ecologies is proposed as a tool to promote quality education that is linked to the demands of sustainable development, in addition to training students to become agents of change for their communities, thus promoting sustainable and conscious development.

In it Chapter 8 entitled "Professional training in Tourism through Hybrid Learning in relation to target 4.c of Sustainable Development Goal 4 Quality Education". The objective of this research is to identify the characteristics of the training of tourism professionals through hybrid learning derived from the health contingency caused by COVID -19 and the relationship between goal 4.c of SDG 4, with the purpose of proposing a scheme of tools used by teachers for the development of tourism professional competencies. Likewise, a scheme of the competencies that a professional in the tourism sector should acquire and develop in higher education institutions is proposed.

Chapter 9, entitled "Digital skills in the formation of human capital for tourism activity", aims to outline a proposal for digital skills necessary for the formation of human capital in the tourism industry based on the educational theory for the development of skills. The chapter addresses issues related to the conceptualization of tourism and the industries that make up the activity, the concepts and classification of digital skills with global parameters, the formation of human capital and the vision of UN Tourism for the digitalization of the sector; with the purpose of specifying, based on the list of tourism industries, the skills oriented to the development of digital skills. The result raises the confluence of digital skills with Knowledge, Know-How, Transversal Skills and Being Skills; emphasizing the Skills Know-How and Use specialized software for the tourism industry with the specification of the Tourism Industries and specialized software for common use.

Chapter 10, "Matrix for Assessing Key Competences", focuses on competency-based teaching and establishes the possibility of organizing learning content into meaningful units, solving one problem at a time, with strong interrelations between its components. Therefore, competency-based assessment within its multiple components has advantages, allowing competencies to be assessed through criteria, indicators and performance levels using different assessment instruments. The problem identified is that there are no instruments to measure achievements in key competencies, generic competencies or soft skills. Once the key competencies have been identified according to the graduate profile, criteria, indicators and performance levels are developed that will be the origin of the proposal for a competency matrix or rubric.

Chapter 11, "Programmer Profile in Terms of Job Vacancies Compared to University Vocational Training," aims to analyze the requirements requested by IT consultancies when hiring a programmer, in order to obtain a technical profile for a software developer in 2024. The methodology used was a comparative evaluation of the web platforms where companies publish the vacancies they request; filters were used to determine only those that corresponded to software developer positions in Mexico City. Likewise, a matrix was made by platform to compare the academic degree, years of experience, and technical knowledge requested by IT consultancies. As part of the results, it was found that companies are looking for programmers with specific technical knowledge in programming languages, web programming, databases, interfaces, software architecture, web and mobile applications, as well as some soft skills: communication, teamwork, and proactivity.

Chapter 12 "Challenges in the formation of human capital at the postgraduate level in the digital era" aims to analyze the main challenges of training human capital at the postgraduate level in the digital age in order to determine the main skills to be developed by students. Postgraduate studies are the educational level aimed at developing professional skills of human capital. that allows them to be independent professionals prepared to perform effectively and efficiently in a digital world. The challenges that the Fourth Industrial Revolution has established for the educational system: Incorporation of technological impact in academic training; formulation of proposals to innovate in training processes ; generation of knowledge based on social innovation. Students who access the postgraduate level need to acquire skills that allow them to adapt to a work environment in constant technological evolution, in addition to acquiring both technical knowledge and relevant social skills. Digital leadership has become a become a strategic factor for organizational success in the era of technological transformation

Therefore, this book contributes from a multidisciplinary perspective on the state of research regarding the formation of human capital in the digital age, which is why it constitutes a valuable resource to be used by academics, researchers, educational leaders, business leaders, students, consultants, universities and professionals.

The target audience is academics, researchers, educational leaders, business leaders, students, consultants, universities and professionals. The book will also be used as one of the references to be used in the training of postgraduate students.

Edgar Oliver Cardoso Espinosa

Instituto Politécnico Nacional, Mexico

Acknowledgment

The editor would like to acknowledge the help of all the people involved in this project and, more specifically, to the authors and reviewers that took part in the review process. Without their support, this book would not have become a reality.

First, the editor would like to thank each one of the authors for their contributions. Our sincere gratitude goes to the chapters authors who contributed their time and expertise to this book.

Second, the editor wishes to acknowledge the valuable contributions of the reviewers regarding the improvement of quality, coherence, and content presentation of chapters. Most of the authors also served as referees; we highly appreciate their double task.

Third, the editor thanks the Instituto Politécnico Nacional for promoting scientific and technological research. Specifically, the topic of this book came from the SIP project number 20240865,

Fourth, to the graduate students for their interest in strengthening their academic training at the Instituto Politécnico Nacional.

Edgar Oliver Cardoso Espinosa
Instituto Politécnico Nacional, Mexico

Chapter 1

Challenges of Leadership in Educational Organizations for Digital Transformation:

Influence of the Transformational Era on Education

Marlett Jasmin Blas Rivera
https://orcid.org/0000-0002-0237-9718
Instituto Politécnico Nacional, Mexico

ABSTRACT

Abstract The objective of this research is to analyze the characteristics of leadership in educational organizations for digital transformation as well as those challenges that school leaders face in carrying out the reinforcement and use of technological tools for the formation of highly prepared human capital as well as implementing technology in the management of the educational center to meet the objectives. Derived from the multiple changes left by the pandemic, one of them was undoubtedly the way to lead an educational center and at the same time, implement digital tools to improve educational processes. Therefore, school leadership plays an important role in this transformation of the digital age for the success and achievement of institutional objectives. However, it is necessary that both leaders and other members of the educational center be prepared on how to use these tools.

DOI: 10.4018/979-8-3693-7086-5.ch001

INTRODUCTION

The pandemic caused changes in different sectors and in the specific case of this research, in the education part, since various technological tools had to be used to continue with distance education as well as the administrative processes of each educational center in each country.

Therefore, this health crisis shows the digital gap at different school levels while in the post-covid era, it is necessary to continue using these digital tools to improve procedures in educational centers and to train human talent using technology and innovation, which will be required in the future work world.

In addition, each school leader needs adequate preparation to connect the management part, that is, the strategic part and management through technology, allowing to promote said innovation in all the processes of the institute, which will allow the achievement of the objectives of the educational center.

In an environment as changing as it is today in our society, not only human talent has to adapt, develop new techniques and update itself to play its role in the best way. However, in the case of organizations, they must also adapt to the needs that are being generated in society from these new digital trends.

This way, educational centers serve as the place where human capital is trained and instructed so that it has the necessary tools to face the vicissitudes of the environment, and with greater importance those higher education institutes, since it is the academic degree where students choose a place to work, or in a few cases, to continue their academic career.

According to INEGI (2023), only 8 out of every 100 students who enter university manage to finish it. This graduation rate, or "percentage of university graduates in Mexico," is extremely low, and if the challenges left by the pandemic coupled with the development of artificial intelligence are considered, this becomes an even greater challenge.

Therefore, educational organizations must be led by trained school leaders, who are updated according to the needs of the environment, as is the case today in the digital age. In addition, for Martín (2016), it is necessary to work from a traditional methodology to an innovative one, since in the education part, work must be done by projects (different modalities): the teacher sets out a work guide and the students acquire knowledge and develop skills by themselves, so the contents are transversal and involve several areas of knowledge and allow a global and integrative understanding, also cooperative and group work: students explore the contents, process them and solve them in collaboration, sharing learning in the group and self-assessment and co-assessment: not only results are evaluated, but also the process and progress of learning with self-criticism (individual and group) so that schoolchildren are more aware of their development.

Also, for Bellamy, (2021), reflecting on distance education first brings us closer to the idea of how education is currently thought of, the contents and skills that must be learned and developed, but these do not make sense if education is not first clarified in our context (currently). In addition to reflecting and delving into how to educate, considering both the present situation and, especially, the future, since educating is a word that must be written in the future as an opportunity for development.

Meanwhile, for Ruiz-Coberlla (2023) in this situation of demand for education, of its recognition for everyone throughout life, of the emergence of continuous technological innovations, distance education is also present. And, especially, during these last years in which, due to the COVID-19 health emergency, the physical closure of educational institutions has been imposed, being replaced, suddenly, by distance learning actions supported, for the most part, by digital devices and resources.

This distance teaching-learning modality, already consolidated in the 1960s, is a good reference to raise this question and reflect on its role in the panorama of educational offering in this emerging scenario. This means that we are reviewing the concept of 'distance education' and are going into it in greater depth compared to other training proposals inserted in virtuality, better assessing what it can offer to a large part of society.

Meantime, the objective of this study is to address leadership in educational management through digital transformation, where these agents of change become a digital leader, which requires the development of digital skills that allow combining technology with the processes of the educational center in order to optimize resources and times so that there is greater fluidity in information and the implemented strategies are quickly modified to achieve institutional objectives.

Besides, this study will address issues related to digital leadership in educational management, and digital leadership as a key factor to promote technology in educational organizations as well as the development of digital skills, the creation of a digital culture and finally the challenges for the transition to the digital age in educational institutions.

Digital Leadership in Educational Management

The concept of leadership has changed over time. In essence, it is the capacity and ability that a person must know how to lead people and match their vision with that of the rest of the work team, with the objective of meeting the goals established in the educational center.

Now, with the various changes that the digital age has brought, it is not enough just to have new technological tools; today, the development and training of a new generation of human talent as well as new models for working are required. In other words, it is necessary for school leaders to integrate and, above all, connect with the new digital generation, who are the natives in this transformation.

Further, digital leadership requires the development of new competencies, skills and processes. It faces challenges where its work team must deliver results based on the use of technologies, knowledge of data analysis and information processing, and, above all, automation.

It should be noted that the digital leader must be the first to set the example, therefore he is responsible for knowing the use of digital tools and at the same time creating a new leadership style, where the work scenario is dominated by technology driven by the vision of the digital leader.

In addition, for the European School of Excellence (2024) indicated that various leaders have faced the challenge of re-teaching their work team on how to optimize the performance of equipment and systems both remotely and in person, as well as having knowledge to transfer information and maintain stable communications, therefore a digital leader needs to be involved in all the information and the use of technology that will be necessary to carry out innovative management.

Meanwhile, technology is evolving and to face the challenges of this advance it is necessary that both school leaders and the rest of the members of the educational center have the capacity for adaptation and flexibility.

Likewise, developing leadership in the digital age leads to new opportunities to enhance the use of technology for various approaches such as monitoring strategies and data analysis, responding to the abrupt changes of this globalized world and obtaining better performance from each of the members of the educational organization regardless of the modality, hybrid, in-person and remote.

However, it is necessary for a leader to adapt to the digital age, since today's generations are mostly native in the use of digital tools and devices and if these digital leaders do not have these skills, it generates little confidence and credibility and would be negative for the organization.

Consequently, it is necessary to promote digital leadership to generate innovation, since organizations require the ability to respond immediately to abrupt changes in digital transformation; to encourage creativity, that is, to solve problems supported by the use of available technology, which generates new ideas and strategies and helps in the formation of new models and solutions, which also encourages teamwork, leading to the exchange of ideas and knowledge to achieve institutional objectives.

Digital leadership as a Key Factor to Drive Digital Transformation and Innovation in Organizations

Likewise, organizations today depend largely on their ability to adapt, especially in digital transformation, where they must take advantage of the advantages offered by technology, since in this context, adapting to a new leadership style and new teaching-learning models, the development of digital leadership is of vital importance, which will be a determining factor in achieving the desired results.

Therefore, for Cegos (2023) digital leadership is a management approach where its main objective is to take advantage of all technological tools to maintain a constant evolution in the processes of the educational organization. Now, it must be considered that a digital leader has to develop virtual communication skills, since it is essential to lead digital environments and promote effective collaboration.

In addition, a digital leader has the knowledge to use technology and new work models to their advantage. The goal is for the organization to be in constant innovation and to promote organizational growth and success. For this to be achieved in the best way, it is necessary for said change agent to take on various activities that promote change and success from the technological environment, such as:

- Maintaining a strategic vision: developing a clear vision and designing digital strategies to maintain constant evolution.
- Change management: guiding the educational center towards digital transformation through motivation, empathy and teamwork.
- Promoting innovation: Creating an environment that promotes the generation of ideas and solutions to position the organization as a benchmark for educational centers.
- Promoting the development of digital talent: training the entire work team to develop digital skills, recognizing their achievements to obtain a team in constant training and adaptation to the various changes in the globalized world in the digital age.

Besides, digital transformation offers a wide range of benefits for organizations in any field. In the case of educational centers, operational efficiency will be improved by automating activities and this leads to the streamlining of bureaucratic processes that end up affecting teachers, since they not only have to plan their class activities but also must fulfill their role as administrator, so this generates an extra effort for them, and thanks to technology these processes would be streamlined.

Moreover, organizations adapt more easily to the various changes in a globalized world and would encourage assertive decision-making, since using technology will help to have immediate and timely information to keep up with the new needs required by companies and society in general, as well as the creation of new management strategies, which will be specific for each educational center according to its demands.

Thus, for RECLA (2024), organizations must integrate technological tools in the educational field, becoming a priority especially in those institutions that are training human talent to face the challenges of the 21st century. Therefore, it is important to adopt educational strategies based on the digital age, and not only to incorporate electronic devices for learning, whether online or in the classroom, they must maximize the potential of each student. Therefore, digital leaders must understand that technology is a means that will allow them to complement and enrich theoretical-practical knowledge and prepare students for the uncertain and dynamic future.

It should be noted that implementing educational strategies in the digital transformation and for them to be effective, it is necessary that they adapt to the different educational levels while considering the needs of each educational institution. Therefore, these strategies seek to integrate technology into the educational process and improve the quality of teaching to train increasingly digitalized human talent, ensuring that they acquire the skills required for the future.

Based on the above, digital strategies have to focus on making the most of the technological platforms that are available to form dynamic and collaborative learning environments, such as the use of online communication and collaboration applications such as: Microsoft Teams, Google Classroom, social networks (Facebook, Tik Tok, X and Instagram) that allow student participation by promoting continuous and contextual learning as well as teamwork to carry out projects.

There are also applications such as Canvas, Blackboard that allow the creation of virtual classrooms, and access to study materials, delivery of assignments and feedback, which promotes equitable and inclusive learning.

Therefore, implementing technology in the educational field presents various challenges that must be addressed with clearly designed strategies. Therefore, it is necessary to improve infrastructure programs that improve connectivity and close the digital gap, as well as plans and programs for training both digital leaders and the rest of the members of the educational center, especially teachers, who will be the ones to measure the learning performance of students in the use of technology. Before continuing, it is worth taking a brief look at the concept of what a leader is: their leadership and the changes that have occurred throughout history leading up to what a digital leader would be today.

Connotations of the Leader and Leadership in Educational Centers

It should be remembered that in relation to leadership theories, for Bolman and Terrence (1995) the word leader, which is more than a thousand years old, refers to the subject who leads people, providing them with help and security, reducing the fear of uncertainty. For its part, the Royal Spanish Academy RAE (2014) defines the word "leader" as the person who directs or leads one or more people while "leadership" is the actions of the leader's activities.

From a general perspective, intermediate leadership is identified as one of the most important, according to the situation experienced during 2020, and as will be observed in some research such as that of Díaz et al. (2021); McLeod (2020) and Rigby et al. (2020), school leaders managed the decision-making process for teachers to use both the digital tools and the teaching methods they believed most convenient, according to the options of each educational system in each country that they had agreed upon.

Additionally, as described by Cifuentes-Medina et al. (2020), a leader always goes hand in hand with his leadership, which translates into human behavior that arises naturally and by instinct, with the manifestation of a boss who was enough of his strategies to carry out the survival of his own. Therefore, a leader is recognized as that person who guides, directs, commands, heads and directs his work team to achieve the desired objective.

Therefore, for the Ministry of Education of Chile [MINEDUC] 2019 through its document "School leadership: Recognizing the types of leadership", it indicated the following:

School leaders are the first people who are at the head of an institution and are identified through the development of a shared vision and for the benefit of their schools through a process of influence that allows them to achieve the desired objectives, as well as articulating and sharing this vision that they have at every opportunity that is presented to them (p. 196).

However, the pandemic shows that a leader does not only have to apply a single style or model of leadership, he or she has to use one or the other or several at the same time, according to the context in which he or she is living and in this way move to updated models, in accordance with the structure of each educational organization that allows improving both administrative and teaching-learning processes for organizational success.

Now, for Blas-Rivera et al. (2023) Although there are various investigations focused on school leaders, innovative studies are required that focus on the needs of the current context. Therefore, it is important that school leaders are updating themselves to leave behind traditional models (such as authoritarian, democratic and laissez faire, to name a few), which, although they worked in the past, now need to be renewed to face social transformations.

This scenario is clearly manifested in the changes implemented in various educational institutions in response to the pandemic. At this juncture, deficiencies in the training and capacity building of some school leaders were revealed. In other words, these change agents were not prepared to face such a disruptive situation that affected both nationally and internationally. Suddenly, they found themselves in the position of having to develop crisis strategies without having previously experienced a situation of such magnitude. In addition, the rapid response by governments and educational systems to not interrupt education around the world put these school leaders in the spotlight, as their decisions had a direct impact on student performance.

Additionally, it is essential to reiterate the importance of ongoing training for school leaders. This training process must be constant, based on study, training and experience, and must be adapted and updated in response to changes in the educational environment. By incorporating these key characteristics into the training of educational leaders, qualified personnel can be counted on to lead educational institutions. This implies the need to develop flexible leadership processes in the educational system, which strengthen the ability to analyze and understand the environment, and which facilitate organizational adaptation to effectively deal with threats and opportunities (Robles et al., 2013).

In addition, the evolution of school leadership, from the adoption of styles previously more common in the business field and their adaptation to the educational context. Subsequently, various leadership models were developed, taking as a reference the principles of educational systems.

Therefore, the need arises to adapt the various traditional leadership styles and models. In some cases, it may be relevant to preserve the essence of these, such as the democratic style that promotes participation and collaborative decision-making with the work team. However, the pandemic has made it clear that a leader should not cling to a single leadership style or model.

Instead, he or she must be able to apply different styles or models depending on the context in which he or she finds himself or herself. This involves the transition to more up-to-date leadership models, adapted to the structure of each educational organization, with the aim of improving both administrative and teaching-learning processes to achieve organizational success.

During the pandemic, some leadership models were implemented and adapted, such as the adaptive-transformational (focused on virtual learning), the crisis-based, the authentic, the service-based, and the intermediate. These models played a fundamental role in the support provided by school leaders during the management of the covid-19 crisis, allowing the continuity of distance education.

This is how the leaders of some universities chose to address the health crisis according to their training, skills, knowledge and experiences. This involved adopting different leadership styles and models and combining methods, plans and strategies to achieve the goal of training the next generation of professionals. Thus, the importance of teachers at this educational level was highlighted and work was done to improve communication and the relationship with these key actors, although greater participation of teachers in management and decision-making at the management level is still required, with the hope that this will develop in the post-covid era.

In this perspective, during the pandemic, the joint effort of all the main actors in educational organizations will be observed to keep teaching-learning ongoing, without neglecting the health aspect. According to documented studies, health became a factor that impacted the academic and work performance of some members of the educational community at this level (Torres et al., 2021).

Meanwhile, for an adequate development of school leadership in the post-pandemic era, the training of school leaders oriented to the digital age is required, as seen in Figure 1. It is necessary for these change agents to become digital leaders. This will allow significant advances in the learning of each of the main actors in the educational center and at the same time achieve institutional objectives with the support of technology.

Figure 1. Transformation of educational management in the digital age

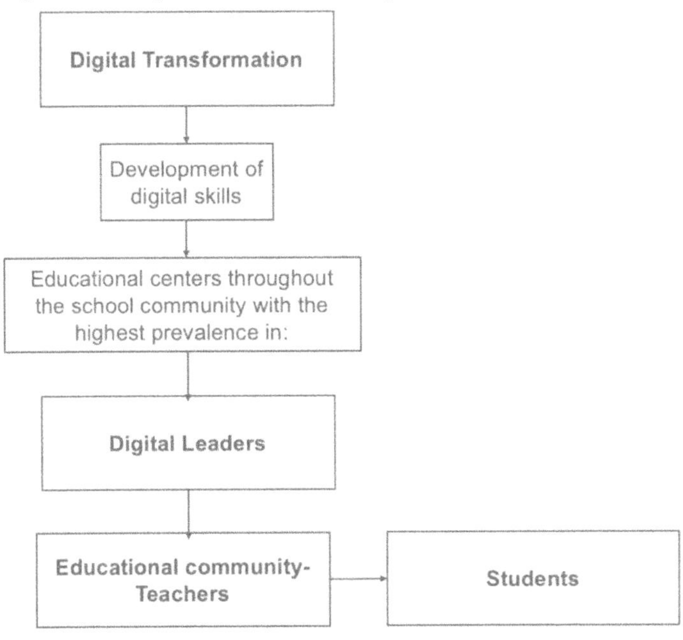

Note: Own elaboration.

Continuing with "Figure 1.", the global approach of this study is presented, which addresses as its main topic the digital transformation in education and the development that must be promoted towards all members of the educational center to achieve digital innovation in said institute, emphasizing a new style of leadership and allowing continuous training and innovation starting from the change agents who have to become a digital leader.

Further, for Blas-Rivera (2023), it is essential to reflect on the effects that the pandemic has had on education globally focusing on the positive changes that have occurred. We must pay attention to the actions and resources that were successfully implemented in educational organizations, since they represent a starting point for the development and innovation of teaching processes and methods that have become obsolete in many schools. It can finally be said that the pandemic revealed these deficiencies and allowed their transformation.

Although they are still adapting to the new normal in the post-covid era, these changes have opened the door to more effective and up-to-date education. Now, in the particular case of school leaders in Higher Education Institutions in Mexico (HEI), it is necessary to make a clarification, since there is a difference with respect to other change agents at different educational levels, since this leader has to transmit their principles of well-being to each person who works at the institute as well as the processes and methods of each educational center and in some way watch over society in general, exercising synergy in each member of the university. and with greater emphasis on the participation of the teaching role, since it is crucial, when standing in front of the group and taking on the role of trainer for the training of human talent that has the tools to face the challenges in the world of work and in society.

Transformation from the Digital Age to Education

For Ruiz-Cordella (2023) the difference between distance education and face-to-face teaching is that educator and learners do not share simultaneously in the same setting. This is solved with emerging technologies that facilitate synchronous interaction. However, the most significant thing in this new context is that, despite this temporal simultaneity, the linear space-time sequentially is broken, enabling interactions and communication proposals that were previously unthinkable, therefore, it is necessary to reflect on technology and the action it develops.

Now, returning to the fact that during the pandemic the use of technological tools was promoted and this caused changes in the way of working and learning, thus accelerating the digital age and as explained by the Organization for Economic Cooperation and Development [OECD], (2019) "education has not been at the forefront of digitalization", although the information and communications technology (ICT) infrastructure is present in many schools.

From this perspective, the digital era in education has been made evident thanks to the COVID-19 pandemic, so leaders in charge of educational centers as well as the education system in each country have to think about the future and not limit themselves to the "traditional", they have to employ the use of technologies and, as is the case today, use Artificial Intelligence as a complement to education, and not take it as a threat. Since the use of these technological tools will be, in the not-too-distant future, part of learning for students and in general for society. However, as McCarthy et al. (2023) mention, strategies in education must include technology as part of continuous improvement, and to achieve this it is necessary to clarify the concepts of these, and where the objective of digital transformation for school leaders is to provide a basis on which to build a shared vision and emphasize that digital transformation is about more than just technological innovation, as Chávez (2022) mentions, education in this digital age must be considered a tool that responds to the objectives of the educational system, to achieve quality education for all, a more personalized education that allows young people to make the most of their talent, that serves as a channel to achieve inclusiveness and reduce inequalities.

Below are some concepts that are related, but it is necessary to identify their ambiguities, such as innovation, which is a new way of doing things, which implies new ways of thinking, we speak of a world in which collaboration, connection, adaptation, flexibility, data-based technology, transparency, diversity, openness, innovation and agility are defining characteristics.

On the other hand, digital innovation can be expressed as the use of digital technology in the "concerted orchestration of new products, new processes, new services, new platforms or even new business models in a given context" (Hinings et al., 2018, p. 52) such as online tutoring and distance learning in education (McCarthy et al., 2023).

In the case of Digital Transformation, by its acronym in English DT or DX, it is described by Hinings et al. (2018) as "the combined effects of various digital innovations that generate new actors (and constellations of actors), structures, practices, values, and beliefs that change, threaten, replace, or complement the existing rules of the game within organizations, ecosystems, industries, or fields" (p. 53). Therefore, this digital transformation is an "extended process of change that can have multiple objectives, while innovation focuses on the moment of invention and the implementation of that invention" (Gobble, 2018, p. 57).

Therefore, members of educational centers must develop processes and strategies aimed at digital age systems, to respond to the challenges brought by the current environment. Human talent must be trained with the social, emotional, and technological skills that are necessary to perform in a dynamic society.

The best practices for success suggested by the survey include leadership, capacity building, worker empowerment, updating tools, and communication (McKinsey & Company, 2018). Therefore, today's society lives in an environment in which digital technologies have been imposed for evolution and development in various areas and where educational institutions through their objective of human capital training must adapt and update to this current educational model and guide students towards the knowledge society.

In addition, applying leadership in the digital age will develop educational processes and strategies based on analysis, reflection and action in a society that demands a different educational system and according to the needs where the transformation has to take into account various factors that affect the development of competencies in school leadership and lead and manage the relationship between university education and professional competencies, the significant elements that configure the culture and the organizational climate towards the development of digital and social competencies.

All the above, focused on the changes that stand out in the development of educational interventions aimed at the comprehensive improvement of all the main actors in the organization, mainly students, and encourage participation in the training process and promote their commitment to the entire community, trying to offer comprehensive and ethical training.

The impact of the COVID-19 pandemic on the acceleration of digital transformation in Higher Education

As seen today, it is evident that digital transformation is at a decisive strategic moment for the organization and in the development of its medium and long-term objectives. Therefore, digital transformation includes changes related to the key foundations of institutional design derived from teaching, research, projection and management, and the development of these aspects with the improvement and optimization of tangible and intangible operations, among which the use of information and communication technologies (ICT) in education stands out through virtual teaching, robotics and artificial intelligence.

Besides, developing digital skills, knowing how to use them in the best way, the amount of information provided by the current digital environment, that is, digital analysis is essential and complementary for school leaders and teachers to guide, optimize and strengthen the quality of education and move towards the knowledge society.

Accordingly, the impact that digital transformation has had on education at a national and international level shows that it is necessary:

- New educational models: which maintain flexible learning, as was the case during the pandemic with online and hybrid education, which allows students to learn at their own pace and anywhere. Personalization of learning is also important, since technologies allow content and activities to be adapted to individual needs and collaborative learning is achieved by facilitating interaction between students and teachers, fostering autonomy, problem solving and teamwork. distance learning.

- Changes in the role of the school leader: Mainly, it requires the development of digital skills, critical and creative thinking as well as encouraging autonomy in the rest of the members of the educational center, especially in teachers who will transmit these skills to the students.

Changes in School Leadership Post-Pandemic for the use of Digital Transformation

School leaders had to quickly adapt to a new environment and take on more complex roles to ensure the continuity of teaching and learning processes. Some changes that were observed after the pandemic in relation to the use of digital transformation were:

- Digital Strategic Vision: School leaders need to develop a clear vision for how to integrate technology into every aspect of the institution, beyond an emergent response to a crisis.
- Investment in infrastructure: A significant investment is required in technological equipment, connectivity and staff training. In this case, it is desirable to start with the educational leader who helps the teachers and in turn can transmit knowledge to the students.
- Collaboration with experts: Education leaders need to partner with education technology experts to design innovative, customized solutions.

It should be noted that any educational proposal, whether face-to-face or distance, may become obsolete if it is not capable of responding to individual and social needs and interests, if it is not capable of being designed with pedagogical criteria, which logically include the technological advances present in the different contexts in which we live. If it is not capable of humanizing these actions by facilitating each person's learning of the necessary skills to achieve the best of themselves, which, ultimately, is capable of self-determining their life. If it is not capable of facilitating their future.

Consequently, derived from the 2020 pandemic, there were important changes in educational management both in study plans and programs as well as in the way of learning, however, these challenges evidenced the lack of training of some school leaders as well as teachers and This allowed the first step to the digital age, where each of the members of the educational organization began their training in digital skills, emphasizing each of the educational leaders who are the ones who have the control and responsibility of maintaining an updated and integrated team as shown in Figure 2 and then transmit this knowledge to the rest of the members and continue with the teaching-learning of the students who will be the precursors in the digital transformation.

Figure 2. School leadership in digital transformation

Note: Own elaboration.

According to "Figure 2." School leaders are agents of change capable of transforming their educational institutions into innovative and equitable learning environments, and for this it is essential that they develop a set of digital skills that allow them to lead the digital transformation of education, maintaining a vision of innovation to achieve the objectives of the institute.

Digital Skills in School Leaders

For UNESCO (2019), digital competencies are skills and knowledge necessary for the critical and reflective use of technologies and communication. These include searching, selecting, evaluating and using digital information, communicating remotely, solving problems remotely and using digital software and applications for the production and creation of content.

Now, the digital transformation has redefined the role of educational leaders internationally after the pandemic, and therefore, it is no longer enough to have a basic command of technological tools, a deep understanding of how to integrate technology into educational processes and how to lead the change towards a more innovative and equitable education is required.

Besides, a clear vision is required on how technology can transform the institution and develop a strategic plan to achieve the objectives. s. Likewise, changes in culture, effectively communicating the importance of digital transformation for the institute.

- It is important that in this digital age, training for the use of these technological tools is crucial, they must be handled fluently, that is, have a mastery of these technological skills, and at the same time, stay up to date especially on technological trends such as AI, continuous learning, virtual reality among others.

It is necessary that, along with the use of this technology, critical and creative thinking, innovation and adaptability continue to develop, where complex problems are identified and resolved with the implementation of these software. are. In addition, the impact of technology on learning has been evaluated with the SAMR model (substitution, expansion, modification and redefinition) by Puentedura (2014), which has shown that the use of digital technologies can transform the way in which teaching and learning is done in education.

Among the main technological tools integrated into education, some are identified by Kapp (2012); Dávila-Cervantes (2014); Islas and Carranza (2017); Amador et al, (2023); Pazmay-Pazmay (2023):

- Educational simulations: allow students to learn in an active and exploratory way, which is especially useful for learning science, and foster the ability to interact with interfaces and manage technological tools.
- Online learning platforms: foster the ability to collaborate online and participate in virtual learning communities, along with the use of technological tools for knowledge management.
- Digital learning ecosystems: promote the ability to collaborate in digital environments, the ability to access and evaluate information online, and to learn autonomously in virtual environments.
- Gamification: In the educational context, it can be a useful strategy to encourage motivation and learning. In addition to navigating in virtual environments, it encourages interaction with game interfaces and the application of logical and critical thinking.

Furthermore, active learning approaches, such as problem-based learning and project-based learning (PBL), have been shown to be effective in promoting the development of digital skills in university students. At the same time, social media and virtual classrooms should be used to promote teamwork, communication, motivation and automation through technological projects, to develop the skills required in the future for both organizations and the knowledge society.

Besides, for Martín (2016) digital education is essential for the development of the principles of desirable learning, and if these tools are applied properly, it will be found that ICTs imply new evaluation methods, since not only content is evaluated but also digital skills.

To acquire and put these contents into practice, ICTs allow the development of autonomous work, research capacity, information processing, collaborative work, communication, among others.

In the case of teachers, a new role of the teacher and their training will be created, since they will become a guide in the learning process and must be fully aware of the resources that will help the student achieve their learning objective; therefore, they must have a lot of theoretical and practical knowledge, master the sources of information and the flows and strategies of searches and interaction on the contents.

Networking, with many points of information and criticism, allows the student to think and interact with problems or contents, from various sources, develop their own content in an exercise of synthesis, abstraction and contrast.

Challenges in Digital Transformation

Despite the use of technology, there are still challenges that school leaders have to overcome for their educational organization, such as resistance to change, lack of resources and the digital divide, where each government and educational system in each country has to develop strategies that allow each student to have access to online education and, most importantly, data security, since the increased use of these technological tools also increases cases of cybersecurity attacks, since all the data that is recorded online can be compromised and end up on illegal platforms and misused. In the case of training school leaders, training programs dedicated to the development of digital skills are necessary, where opportunities are offered for leaders to put the acquired skills into practice but in real situations and through their shared experiences with other leaders and stay up to date.

According to Chávez-Márquez et al. (2023), the importance of using these tools responsibly and critically is highlighted, considering ethical, legal and information security aspects; In addition, it is stressed that these digital tools should not replace face-to-face teaching but rather complement it, since face-to-face interaction is essential for comprehensive learning. a l. The accelerated and dynamic development of educational innovations in the use of digital tools and technologies reaffirms the importance of acquiring digital competencies and soft skills, which every profession must possess. a l.

Likewise, the incorporation of digital skills generated with the use of technological tools and the introduction of educational innovations such as simulations, social networks, educational games, b-learning platforms and artificial intelligence in the university context, are crucial to equip students with the necessary skills to s. These skills are not limited only to technical skills, but also encompass critical competencies such as analytical thinking, problem solving and communication in digital environments. e s.

Therefore, higher education must maintain constant adaptation to meet changing technological and labor demands. e s. The implementation of innovations in education, such as the adoption of cutting-edge technology, the offering of online courses, and the adaptation of learning according to individual needs, has the potential to improve the quality of university education and to promote participation and success of students.

Developing a Digital Culture in Educational Management

To maintain an innovative educational system, it is necessary to develop new skills in the digital transformation environment, which is why staff training is important, that is, a school leader must seek support either through the educational system, government or private companies, to offer continuing education programs so that teachers acquire the digital skills necessary to use technological tools effectively.

Furthermore, it is important to promote a digital culture, that is, a leader must create a learning environment that values innovation and experimentation with new technologies. Also, the promotion of collaborative learning, encouraging teamwork and collaboration between school leaders and teachers to share experiences and resources.

At the same time, educational leaders must support teachers in the creation of meaningful and personalized learning experiences that use digital technologies effectively, for which a continuous evaluation of pedagogical practices is suggested to identify what works and what needs to be improved, in addition to promoting educational research to generate knowledge about the effective application of technologies in the classroom.

In addition, the school leader must guarantee access to devices and connectivity for all students in the institute so that they can continue their education online or in a hybrid manner. And, just like teachers, students require programs for the development of digital skills, which must be taught by teachers or, where appropriate, external personnel who have the knowledge to use the different technological tools.

However, it is necessary for each person in charge of an educational center to be an example for the rest of its members, so these agents of change require continuous training to adapt to the changes that exist today. In this case, as seen in Figure 3, it is necessary for them to take training that keeps them up to date on the skills and abilities required for digital transformation in education.

Figure 3. Leadership in digital transformation for teaching-learning

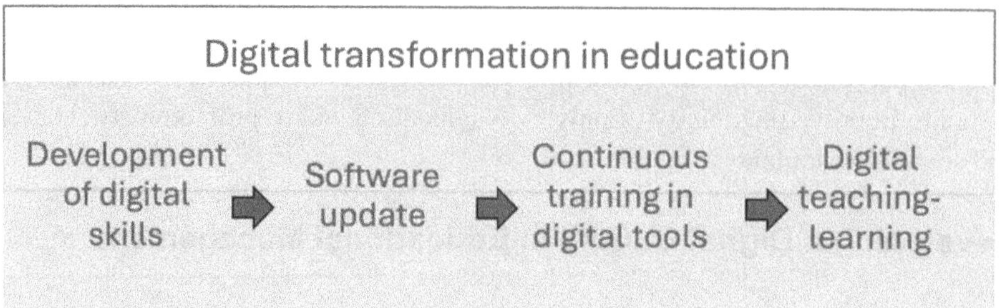

Note: Own elaboration.

As seen in "Figure 3.", each school leader is required to maintain continuous training in digital tools, which will allow the development of digital skills, which must be transferred to the rest of the members of the institute, mainly to teachers who in turn will provide digital teaching-learning to students.

CONCLUSION

In summary, school leadership during the pandemic was an important factor in continuing distance education and is crucial for the success of implementing digital transformation in educational institutions. Since school leaders are agents of change who inspire, empower, influence and guide the entire educational community towards the adoption of new technologies. Since, starting from the need to have a strategic vision, the ability to adapt and the development of skills to foster collaboration, these skills are essential to overcome the challenges and take advantage of the opportunities offered by digital transformation.

Now, this digital transformation in educational organizations demands that leaders have to be prepared, trained and constantly updated, since this continuous training is necessary for development in topics such as educational technology, digital pedagogy and transformational leadership is essential for these leaders to design and implement innovative projects that respond to the needs of students in the 21st century. Therefore, maintaining effective school leadership will become a driver of change that drives the continuous improvement of educational processes.

Besides, school leadership plays a crucial role in training students for an increasingly digitalized future, so it is necessary to promote the development of digital skills, critical thinking, creativity, school leaders contributing to students being active human capital and agents of change for society. Since digital transformation, which is driven by visionary leadership, opens new opportunities to personalize learning, promote collaboration and prepare students for the challenges of the future world of work.

Therefore, we are facing a new scenario in which school leaders are primarily tasked with reinventing educational design according to the demands of the context in which we live. It is not about including the latest digital devices and applications in the learning process. This is not the issue, since what is essential in education is the person, not the technology. If the objective is to facilitate inclusive and quality education for all throughout life, as stated in the fourth Sustainable Development Goal, to shape an increasingly uncertain and volatile future in digitally mediated environments, it is urgent to reflect, debate, and delve deeper into the key skills that need to be developed in students so that they are able to face their future: self-regulation, critical and reflective thinking, proactive citizen participation, among others.

However, it is necessary that both leaders and other members of the educational center be prepared on how to use these tools, in addition to maintaining continuous training and in the case of teachers and students, focusing on technological and pedagogical issues, since this will allow the formation of highly trained human capital that has all the tools to face the challenges of the future work world.

This is how some important points are analyzed from the concept of what a leader is and what leadership is in educational centers; the transformation of the digital era to education; the impact of the COVID-19 pandemic on the acceleration of digital transformation in Higher Education; the changes in school leadership post pandemic for the use of digital transformation as well as the digital skills required in school leaders and some challenges in digital transformation and pedagogy in digital transformation. And, especially, during these last years in which, due to the COVID-19 health emergency, the physical closure of educational institutions has been imposed, being replaced, suddenly, by distance learning actions supported, for the most part, by digital devices and resources.

FUTURE DIRECTIONS OF RESEARCH

For future studies, it is suggested to analyze the relationship and influence of leadership style on the success of the implementation of educational technologies, the impact of AI on leadership and school management, based on quantitative research to determine the dimensions involved and to what extent they are involved in the implementation of technological management, and for qualitative research it is suggested that it be based on the development of a digital culture, since it is the same people who are going to make these changes, it is necessary to know their testimonies in order to move to a digital model, in addition to helping school leaders promote collaboration with all members of the institute for a digital environment, address the challenges or barriers that school leaders perceive for the adoption of emerging technologies in their educational centers, even the ethical implications associated with the use of digital transformation are suggested, which leads to social responsibility, as well as the role that social networks play in the development of learning in both teachers and students.

REFERENCES

Amador, M., Torres, G., & Lagunes, D. (2023). Problem based learning for the development of competencies in students. *Revisión sistemática de literatura.RECEIN*, 15(59), 131–166. DOI: 10.26457/recein.v15i59.3491

Bellamy, F. X. (2021). Transmission crisis and innovation fever. *Teoría de la Educación.Revista Interuniversitaria*, 33(2), 1–10. DOI: 10.14201/teri.25407

Blas-Rivera, M. J., Cardoso-Espinosa, E. O., & Nava-Meléndez, E. D. (2023). School leadership models during the pandemic to face the post-covid era. *Revista Iberoamericana para la Investigación y el Desarrollo Educativo RIDE*, 14(27), e571. DOI: 10.23913/ride.v14i27.1713

Bolman, L., & Terrence, E. (1995). *Leadership perspectives considered by Bolman and Deal.* Recuperado de https://www.redalyc.org/pdf/993/99326637004.pdf

Cegos (2023). *Liderazgo digital, clave para el éxito en la era digital.* Recovered from https://www.cegoslatam.com/actualidades/liderazgo-digital

Chávez, N. (2022). Education for Digital Transformation. Recovered from https://www.ift.org.mx/transformacion-digital/blog/educacion-para-la-transformacion-digital

Chávez-Márquez, I., Ordóñez, A., & Flores, C. (2023). Digital skills in university students through educational innovations: A review of current literature. *Apertura (Guadalajara, Jal.)*, 15(2), 74–87. DOI: 10.32870/Ap.v15n2.2398

Cifuentes-Medina, E., González-Pulido, W., & González-Pulido, A. (2020). Effects of school leadership on learning. *Revista Panorama*, 14(26), 78–93. DOI: 10.15765/pnrm.v14i26.1482

Dávila-Cervantes, A. (2014). Simulation in medical education. *Investigación en Educación Médica*, 3(10), 100–105. DOI: 10.1016/S2007-5057(14)72733-4

Díaz, J., Ledesma, M., Tito, J., & Díaz, L. (2021). Leadership skills in a context of health emergency, COVID-19 in Peru. *Revista Venezolana de Gerencia*, 26(5), 505–519.

Escuela Europea de Excelencia. (2024). *Liderazgo digital: adaptándose a la era de la tecnología.* Recovered from https://www.escuelaeuropeaexcelencia.com/2024/07/liderazgo-digital-adaptandose-a-la-era-de-la-tecnologia/

Gobble, M. (2018). Digital strategy and digital transformation. *Research Technology Management*, 61(5), 66–71. DOI: 10.1080/08956308.2018.1495969

Hinings, B., Gegenhuber, T., & Greenwood, R. (2018). Digital innovation and transformation: An institutional perspective. *Information and Organization*, 28(1), 52–56. DOI: 10.1016/j.infoandorg.2018.02.004

INEGI. (2023). *Students enrolled, graduates and holders of higher education degrees at the bachelor's level of normal, university and technological education of the school modality by territorial demarcation and field of academic training. Retrievedfrom*https://www.inegi.org.mx/app/cuadroentidad/CDMX/2018/06/6_18

Islas, C., & Carranza, M. (2017). Digital ecosystems and their manifestation in learning: Literature analysis. *RED*, (55), 1–13. DOI: 10.6018/red/55/9

Kapp, K. M. (2012). *The gamification of learning and instruction: Game-based methods and strategies for training and education*. John Wiley & Sons. Recovered from https://www.wiley.com/enushe+Gamification+of+Learning+and+Instruction%3A+Game+based+Methods+and+Strategies+for+Training+and+Education-p-9781118191989

McCarthy, A., Maor, D., McConney, A., & Cavanaugh, C. (2023). Digital transformation in education: Critical components for leaders of system change. *Social Sciences & Humanities Open*, 8(1), 100479. DOI: 10.1016/j.ssaho.2023.100479

McKinsey & Company. (2018). McKinsey, Company Unlocking success in digital transformations. Recovered from https://www.mckinsey.com/capabilities/people-and-organizational-performance/our-insights/unlocking-success-in-digital-transformations

McLeod, S. (2020). Rising to the challenge and looking ahead: School leadership during the pandemic. *Journal UCEA*, 61(2), 17–19.

McLeod, S., & Dulsky, S. (2021). Resilience, Reorientation, and Reinvention: School Leadership During the Early Months of the COVID-19 Pandemic. *Frontiers in Education*, 6, 637075. DOI: 10.3389/feduc.2021.637075

Ministerio de Educación de Chile [MINEDUC]. (2019). Guía de Herramientas para el desarrollo de recursos personales en equipos directivos. Herramienta 2. *Liderazgo escolar: reconociendo tipos de liderazgo. División de Educación General, 2*(9.1), 196. https://hdl.handle.net/20.500.12365/14511

OECD. (2019). *Future of education and skills 2030*. https://www.oecd.org/education/2030-project/

OECD. (2019). *Going digital: Shaping policies, improving lives*. OECD Publishing., DOI: 10.1787/9789264312012-

Pazmay-Pazmay, D. (2023). Plataformas virtuales y fomento del aprendizaje con sentido en la educación superior. *Revista Científica FIPCAEC*, 8(1), 411–425. DOI: 10.23857/fipcaec.v8i1

RAE. (2014). *Liderazgo*. Recuperado de https://dirae.es/palabras/liderazgo

Rigby, J., Forman, S., Foster, L., Kazemi, E., & Clancey, S. (2020). *Promising District Leadership Practices for Transformative Change in the Context of COVID-19*. https://education.uw.edu/sites/default/files/pdf/Promising-Leadership-Practices-Brief.pdf

Robles, V., Contreras, F., Barbosa-Ramírez, D., & Juárez, F. (2013). Liderazgo en directivos colombianos vs. mexicanos. Un estudio comparativo. *Revista Investigación y Desarrollo, 21*(2), 395-418. https://www.redalyc.org/articulo.oa?id=26828939004

Torres, A., Pérez, L., López, A., & Toro, J. (2021). Política educativa implementada a partir de la emergencia sanitaria por COVID-19 en el nivel de educación superior. *Revista Docencia Politécnica, 2*(6), 25-39. https://www.ipn.mx/assets/files/innovacion/docs/docencia-politecnica/docencia-politecnica-6/Politica-educativa-implementada-a-partir-de-la-emergencia-sanitaria-por-COVID-19-en-el-nivel-de-educacion-superior%20.pdf

ADDITIONAL READING

Alenezi, M. (2023). Digital learning and digital institution in higher education. *Education Sciences*, 13(1), 88. DOI: 10.3390/educsci13010088

Kraus, K., Kraus, N., Nikiforov, P., Pochenchuk, G., & Babukh, I. (2021). Information and digital development of higher education in the conditions of innovatyzation economy of Ukraine. *WSEAS Transactions on Environment and Development*, 17(64), 659–671. DOI: 10.37394/232015.2021.17.64

Lefort, A. (2018). *Consejos para introducir la tecnología en el aula*. Recovered from https://www.teamnet.com.mx/blog/consejos-para-introducir-la-tecnologia-en-el-aula

Matveeva, S. V., Akatova, N. S., Shcherbakov, Y. I., & Filinova, N. V. (2020). Digitalization of higher education and professional development of educators: Technologies and new opportunities. *Amazonia Investiga*, 9(29), 77–86. DOI: 10.34069/AI/2020.29.05.10

Mohamed Hashim, M. A., Tlemsani, I., & Matthews, R. (2022). Higher education strategy in digital transformation. *Education and Information Technologies*, 27(3), 3171–3195. DOI: 10.1007/s10639-021-10739-1 PMID: 34539217

Rodríguez-Abitia, G., & Bribiesca-Correa, G. (2021). Assessing digital transformation in universities. *Future Internet*, 13(2), 52. DOI: 10.3390/fi13020052

Ruiz-Corbella, M. (2023). Repensar la educación a distancia en la era digital. *Estudios Pedagógicos (Valdivia)*, 49(1), 237–253. DOI: 10.4067/s0718-07052023000100237

Treviño, R. (2024). *Nueve dimensiones que sirven como guía para universidades que buscan implementar un modelo de educación digital.* Recovered from https://conecta.tec.mx/es/noticias/nacional/educacion/tec-presenta-guia-para-implementar-educacion-digital-en-universidades

Vlados, C., & Chatzinikolaou, D. (2021). Evolutionary transformation of the global system and the COVID-19 pandemic: The search for a new development trajectory. *The Cyprus Review*, 33(1), 127–166. https://papers.ssrn.com/abstract=3964657

Vuchkovski, D., Zalaznik, M., Mitręga, M., & Pfajfar, G. (2023). A look at the future of work: The digital transformation of teams from conventional to virtual. *Journal of Business Research*, 163(113912), 113912. DOI: 10.1016/j.jbusres.2023.113912

KEY TERMS AND DEFINITIONS

Digital competence: It is defined as the critical and safe use of Information Society Technologies for work, leisure and communication. It involves a set of knowledge, skills, attitudes and strategies that are required for the use of digital media and information and communication technologies.

Digital culture: All the practices, values and knowledge related to the use of digital technologies, making the most of them to carry out various activities and make them more optimal.

Digital education: All human, technological and material resources dedicated to learning knowledge and skills that integrate digital uses for the training of human talent duly trained in technological skills.

Digital leader: is the person who has the skills and abilities to lead the members of an organization and promotes the use of technology to streamline processes and better manage all the resources of the institution.

Digital transformation: the implementation of new technologies, talents and processes to remain competitive in a constantly changing technological landscape.

Chapter 2
Challenges and Opportunities for Digital Leadership in the Transformation of Educational Organisations:
Developing Digital, Soft, Intercultural, and Inclusive Skills

Sandra Viridiana Cortés Ruiz
Instituto Politécnico Nacional, Mexico

Silvia Daniella Pérez Muñoz
https://orcid.org/0009-0004-8984-0520
Instituto Politécnico Nacional, Mexico

ABSTRACT

This chapter explores the challenges and opportunities facing educational leaders in the context of the digital transformation of educational organisations. As digital technologies reshape the educational landscape, digital leadership emerges as a core competency to guide institutions into the future. This text examines the evolution of the concept of digital leadership, its current applications in education, and the essential competencies that leaders need to develop, such as advanced digital literacy, change management, and pedagogical innovation. Ethical and equity challenges arising from technological implementation are highlighted, including the digital divide

DOI: 10.4018/979-8-3693-7086-5.ch002

and resistance to change, as well as opportunities for pedagogical innovation and the development of digital and soft skills. In addition, the chapter offers strategies for effective digital leadership including ongoing training, fostering an innovative organisational culture, and building collaborative and supportive networks

INTRODUCTION

Digital transformation has reshaped the reality in which we live, affecting not only the way we work, interact and consume, but also how we learn and teach. This process, which began slowly in the mid-1990s, has reached a turning point in recent years, with technology becoming a fundamental pillar of virtually all sectors of society. In education, the digital transformation has brought with it a number of challenges and opportunities that require adaptive and committed leadership. Rather than just the incorporation of technological devices and platforms, the digital shift in education represents a profound structural and cultural transformation that impacts pedagogical methods, classroom dynamics and educational management.

The COVID-19 pandemic, which began in 2020, unexpectedly and massively accelerated this digitization in education. In a matter of weeks, educational institutions around the world were forced to migrate to a distance learning model, facing a lack of infrastructure, the digital divide and limited technological skills preparation of students and teachers. According to Amankwah-Amoah, Khan, Wood and Knight (2021), the pandemic acted as a catalyst for digitization, highlighting both the shortcomings and potential of technology in education. These authors note that the global health crisis drove a "great acceleration" of digitization in various sectors, and education was no exception. Despite the challenges, the pandemic revealed the importance of technology in ensuring educational continuity and, at the same time, highlighted the urgent need for leadership capable of guiding this transformation in an ethical and inclusive manner.

In this context of rapid change, digital leadership has become an essential competence for those who manage educational institutions and for teachers who interact directly with students. However, digital leadership should not be understood solely as a technical skill or a skill in the use of devices and platforms. The true essence of digital leadership lies in its holistic approach, combining technical competence with an ethical and humanistic vision. This leadership involves not only the ability to incorporate technology effectively, but also a commitment to building an inclusive, accessible and equitable educational environment, where technology is used to serve all learners and does not become a factor of exclusion or inequality.

The central aim of this chapter argues that digital leadership is much more than a set of technological skills; it is a transformative approach that requires a combination of digital competencies, ethical sensitivity and an inclusive perspective. Such leadership must be able to understand and apply the principles of technology in ways that benefit the entire education community, not just those with privileged access to technological resources. In this sense, digital leaders in education must be architects of a learning space that leverages digital tools to enhance students' academic and personal development, ensuring that everyone has the opportunity to participate in and benefit from technological advances.

To inform this holistic view of digital leadership in education, this chapter is underpinned by a theoretical review methodology. This qualitative research approach focuses on the analysis and synthesis of existing literature and theories to develop an in-depth and systematic understanding of a particular topic. Unlike other methods that seek primary data through surveys or experiments, the theoretical review is based on the collection, analysis and critical reflection of information already published in academia, in order to explore concepts, identify relationships and illuminate the underlying dynamics around digital leadership in educational contexts.

According to Grant and Booth (2009), the theoretical review aims to analyze and synthesize previous theories, methods and findings to provide an interpretative structure of existing knowledge on the topic of study. This type of review helps to clarify concepts, identify gaps in knowledge, and can propose new directions for future research, especially in complex and multifaceted fields such as digital leadership in education, where approaches to digital transformation, educational ethics and inclusion studies converge.

1. Background to Digital Leadership

In the era of technological transformation, digital leadership has emerged as a fundamental concept that redefines how organizations operate and thrive in an increasingly complex technological environment. The term digital leadership began to emerge in the early 2000s, in parallel with the rapid digitization of business processes and the increasing integration of the internet into the corporate environment. However, it was not until the 2010s that the concept gained significant relevance in both academic literature and business practices.

Therefore, one of the first to address this issue was George Westerman, who, along with his colleagues at the Massachusetts Institute of Technology (MIT), investigated how companies were undertaking digital transformation. His work *"Leading Digital: Turning Technology into Business Transformation"* is considered one of the pillars that established the foundations of digital leadership, highlighting how companies use technology to transform their business models and gain competitive advantages (Westerman et al., 2014).

Simultaneously, global consultancies such as McKinsey and Deloitte contributed to the development of digital leadership by publishing reports highlighting the importance of digital transformation and the crucial role of leadership in facilitating this process. These publications helped popularize the concept in business, identifying the need for leaders capable of guiding their organizations through digital change with clear vision and strategic adaptability.

A number of leaders and academics have also played a crucial role in conceptualizing and promoting digital leadership. Satya Nadella, for example, has been a transformative figure since taking over as CEO of Microsoft in 2014. His approach has been recognized for leading the company's digital transformation, promoting a culture of innovation, openness and organizational agility that has positioned Microsoft as a model of effective digital leadership (Heskett,2022). Similarly, Erik Brynjolfsson and Andrew McAfee of MIT have extensively researched the impact of digital technologies on business and the economy, providing a deep understanding of how these technologies are reshaping leadership and management in the digital age.

On the other hand, Charlene Li (2010), founder of *Altimeter Group*, has been an influential voice in the discussion on digital leadership, especially in the context of social media and organizational transformation. Notably, Li's work has significantly influenced the evolution of digital leadership within education: during the rise of Massive Open Online Courses (MOOCs) and the mass adoption of learning management systems between 2010 and 2015, Li developed leadership frameworks applicable to digital environments, which were implemented by various educational institutions. His book *Open Leadership* provided educational leaders with effective strategies for navigating an increasingly connected and open world. His emphasis on using data to guide leadership decisions synchronized with the growing importance of analytics in education (Li & Solis, 2013).

Consequently, in recent years, conceptions of digital leadership have evolved to capture the complexity and dynamism of today's world. Kane (2019) describe digital leadership as *"the ability to create a clear vision for digital transformation, inspire and align people around that vision, and execute the strategy in an agile and adaptive way"*. This highlights the importance of a strategic vision and the ability to implement it in an ever-changing digital environment, where adaptability and precision in action are critical.

Imran et al. (2020) elaborate on this idea by defining digital leadership as *"a process of social influence mediated by advanced information technologies to produce changes in attitudes, feelings, thoughts, behaviors and performance"*. This highlights the central role that technologies play in leadership, transforming not only the tools used, but also the internal dynamics of organizations.

Consequently, this type of leadership has become crucial in an increasingly digital world, where the ability to adapt and learn continuously is vital. According to Colbert et. al. (2016), successful digital leaders are those who can manage uncertainty and ambiguity, as the digital environment is always changing. The ability to manage change is key, because the implementation of new technologies not only affects the tools that are employed, but also profoundly transforms the culture of an organization and the way things are done (Kane et al., 2019).

1.1 The Current State of Digital Leadership in Education

Educational leaders who thrive in this digital domain share certain characteristics: they have a clear vision for using technology to enhance teaching and learning processes; they are committed to ongoing professional development in educational technology; they foster an environment that encourages experimentation with new digital tools; and they collaborate with other leaders and key stakeholders to share effective practices and resources.

In addition, the COVID-19 pandemic has highlighted the need for agile and adaptive leadership. Fernandez and Shaw (2020) note that academic leaders who have successfully managed this challenge did so by communicating clearly and frequently, empowering other team members to lead, promoting ongoing collaboration, making data-informed decisions, and showing empathy and emotional support. These elements have been essential to maintaining cohesion and educational advancement in a digital environment.

Alongside these transformations, research by Raza et al. (2021) highlights that the success of online learning depends not only on technological infrastructure, but also on psychological and motivational factors. Students' self-efficacy, intrinsic motivation and engagement are significant indicators of academic performance in digital environments. This finding implies that educational leaders need to implement strategies that maintain student motivation, provide psychological and emotional support, and design online learning experiences that foster interaction and engagement.

However, the pandemic has also revealed profound disparities in the implementation of digital technologies in education, revealing a significant digital divide. Sánchez-Cruzado et al. (2021) emphasize the urgent need to improve the digital literacy of teachers, who often lack the necessary skills to integrate technology into their pedagogical practices. This challenge is critical in the post-COVID-19 context, where digital skills training must be practical, contextualized and aligned with the specific needs of each discipline.

Looking beyond the immediate challenges, Darling-Hammond et al. (2020) propose a broader vision for "reinventing schooling". They suggest closing the digital divide, strengthening distance and blended learning, redesigning schools to strengthen relationships, and emphasizing equity and inclusion. However, Williamson et al. (2020) warn that this accelerated digitization requires a critical approach. Over-adoption of commercial platforms and mass collection of student data could lead to over-reliance on these technologies and ignore fundamental issues of educational equity and quality.

Consequently, in higher education, artificial intelligence (AI) is transforming learning. For as mentioned, Zawacki-Richter et al. (2019) identify various applications of AI, from administrative support services to intelligent tutoring systems and adaptive content management tools. However, Popenici and Kerr (2017) highlight the ethical and pedagogical challenges of this technological integration, emphasizing the need for a reflective approach that avoids perpetuating biases and dehumanizing the educational process.

On the other hand, Marín et al. (2022) emphasize the importance of building resilience in education systems, promoting equity, inclusion, and international collaboration. Sá and Serpa (2020) consider the COVID-19 crisis as an opportunity for sustainable development in education, fostering pedagogical innovation, flexibility in teaching models and the meaningful integration of digital technologies.

2. KEY COMPETENCES OF DIGITAL LEADERSHIP IN EDUCATION

Digital leadership in education is based on a set of key competences that enable leaders not only to manage technology, but also to transform it into a meaningful tool for holistic educational development. Three competencies stand out in this context: advanced digital literacy, strategic vision and adaptability. Each of these skills not only facilitates the implementation of technological tools, but also promotes ethical and adaptive leadership capable of responding to changing educational needs in an era of constant digital transformation.

This kind of vision enables leaders to anticipate technological change and prepare for it proactively. In education, a strategic vision means understanding technology as a resource to significantly improve teaching and learning, not simply as a functional tool. With this vision, digital leaders are able to set long-term goals that harness the potential of technology in a coherent and sustainable way. For example, a leader with a strategic vision not only implements online learning platforms to facilitate distance education, but also uses them to develop collaborative and digital competences in students, ensuring that these skills will be useful to them in a professional future. .

Strategic vision also enables digital leaders to address emerging challenges, such as privacy and data security in digital learning environments. By maintaining a long-term perspective, leaders can prevent these issues and develop data protection and data management policies that ensure a safe learning environment. This vision is especially valuable in a context where technology is rapidly changing and raises new ethical and operational implications.

On the other hand, adaptability emerges as an essential competence for digital leadership in education. This attribute enables leaders to respond effectively to constant and rapid changes in technology, adjusting their strategies and approaches to meet new challenges and capitalize on emerging opportunities. Adaptability also implies a willingness to continuously learn and re-evaluate practices, enabling leaders to adjust their plans and policies to maintain the institution's relevance and effectiveness in an evolving digital environment. Adaptability becomes a crucial advantage during times of crisis, as evidenced by the COVID-19 pandemic, where leaders' ability to shift quickly to a digital teaching model was critical to educational continuity. Adaptive leaders not only respond to change, but anticipate it, planning proactive solutions that enable their institutions to stay at the forefront of innovation.

Digital influence in educational management is a fundamental aspect of digital leadership, as it facilitates the building of a culture of learning and collaboration through digital media. Avolio et al. (2014) describe "e-leadership" as a model in which leaders use digital tools to connect, motivate and guide their teams. In the educational context, this digital influence not only affects leadership relationships, but also extends to communication with students, parents and the wider community.

2.1 Challenges of Digital Leadership In Education

In the information age, where technology encompasses every aspect of our existence, educational leadership is at a critical inflection point. Educational leaders in the 21st century face a constantly evolving digital landscape, which demands not only continuous adaptation, but also a profound reconceptualization of what it means to lead in this new context (Hargreaves & Fullan, 2020). Today's educational leaders are required to possess a unique set of competencies that enable them to manage the complex digital landscape, the essential competencies for digital leaders in education include:

2.1.1 Strategic Vision for Technology Integration

Alongside digital literacy, strategic vision is an essential competence that defines digital leadership. Kane (2019) stresses that digital leadership is not just a technical issue, but requires an inspiring, strategic and adaptive vision. Therefore, technology integration in education goes beyond the simple adoption of digital tools; it requires a strategic vision that enables educational leaders to discern the opportunities that digital technology offers to enrich teaching and learning processes. This vision requires setting clear goals and communicating a perspective that can inspire and mobilize the entire educational community towards meaningful transformation. As Fullan (2020) suggests, an effective vision in this context not only incorporates technology but creates an environment in which both teachers and students thrive in an increasingly digital world.

It is essential to understand this vision holistically, encompassing much more than the introduction of new technologies. It is about profoundly reviewing and re-thinking pedagogical methods, the professional development of educators, student engagement and the technological infrastructure needed to support these changes. Johnson et al. (2022) point out that a truly effective vision must be in harmony with the educational mission of the institution, recognizing that technology is not an end in itself, but a means to enhance teaching and learning. This approach requires leadership that not only manages technology resources but is also able to guide an integration that keeps the educational purpose at the center.

In order to develop a sound strategic vision, it is therefore essential to first understand the educational context through a thorough analysis of the needs of students and teachers, the existing technological infrastructure, the digital skills of staff and the resources available. As mentioned by Salmon (2021), this diagnosis allows for setting priorities and designing strategies that respond to the identified gaps, maximizing opportunities for all members of the educational organization.

Therefore, the vision must be underpinned by clear and measurable objectives that align technology with learning goals. These goals range from increasing student engagement through more interactive learning environments to developing 21st century skills such as critical thinking and collaboration. Kozma (2019) stresses the importance of these goals being achievable and attuned to the skills that both educators and students need to develop to meet the challenges of the digital age.

2.1.2 Advanced Digital Literacy

Advanced digital literacy, at its core, goes beyond the mere ability to operate technological tools. Rather, it is presented as a form of cognition, a way of perceiving and interacting with an increasingly evolved world. As Beetham (2021) points out, this literacy is a language of its own, a medium through which digital leaders not only communicate, but also imagine the transformative possibilities that technology brings to education.

This digital language therefore demands a fluency that transcends mere technical competence. It demands a deep understanding of how emerging technologies are reshaping knowledge and learning scenarios. Consequently, Mishra and Koehler (2023), in their analysis of Technological and Pedagogical Content Knowledge (TPACK), argue that digitally literate leaders must be able to create a complex network where technology, pedagogy and content are interwoven in a coherent and meaningful way.

For this reason, a leader's ability to navigate the vast world of data and information that floods educational institutions is another manifestation of this advanced literacy. Moreover, Williamson (2022) argues that leaders act as *'data miners'*, extracting valuable insights from the infinite information generated by digital educational platforms. This skill goes beyond the use of data analysis tools; it also requires deep wisdom to interpret this information in ways that enrich teaching and learning processes.

Therefore, beyond data management, advanced digital literacy encompasses the realm of ethics and social responsibility. In an environment where AI and algorithms play an increasing role in educational decision-making, leaders need to cultivate *"critical algorithmic awareness"* (Selwyn, 2021). This awareness involves not only understanding how these technologies work, but also questioning their ethical and social implications, ensuring that they are used to foster equity and inclusion, rather than deepen existing inequalities.

Furthermore, this literacy is reflected in the leader's ability to promote a culture of innovation and experimentation within their organizations. Fullan (2020), in his reflection on *'leadership for change',* suggests that digitally literate leaders create environments where creativity and a willingness to take calculated risks are core values. This involves not only providing the necessary tools and resources, but also fostering a mindset of continuous growth and learning throughout the education community.

At the same time, at the heart of this literacy lies an intriguing paradox: as a leader becomes more digitally competent, the more aware he or she becomes of the importance of the human in education. Hargreaves (2023), in his reflection on *'human-centered digital leadership'*, argues that the real skill in digital literacy lies in the ability to use technology to extend and enrich, rather than replace, human connections and experiences in the educational process.

Similarly, this type of literacy also includes mastery of digital communication and collaboration. In a context where virtual meetings and online communities have become the norm, digital leaders are experts in the art of digital presence. This involves not only managing digital communication platforms, but also knowing how to cultivate meaningful relationships and promote effective collaboration in virtual environments.

2.1.3 Digital Influence on Educational Management

The concept of digital leadership also encompasses the role of digital influence in educational management. Avolio et al. (2014) propose the term 'e-leadership' to describe a model in which leaders use digital tools to connect, motivate and guide their teams. In education, this digital influence is not only limited to leadership relationships, but also extends to communication with students, parents and the wider community. Digital influence allows leaders to establish an online presence that strengthens the identity of the institution and facilitates closer and more transparent interaction with the educational community.

Digital influence in education management is also reflected in the ability of leaders to foster a culture of continuous learning and collaboration. Through digital platforms and support networks, leaders can facilitate collaboration among teachers and promote a culture of innovation that inspires the entire education community to actively participate in the digital transformation process. In addition, digital influence strengthens the sense of community, allowing leaders to stay connected to their teams, understand their needs and provide real-time support. This ability to positively influence the educational environment through digital means is an essential extension of digital leadership in today's context.

2.1.4 Change and Innovation Management

Change management, in the context of digital educational leadership, transcends the implementation of new technologies or methodologies. In other words, it is, in essence, about leading a profound transformation in the culture and ethos of educational institutions. Importantly, there is a need to create a sense of shared leadership amidst the complexity of digital change. From this perspective, the effective digital leader acts as an architect of coherence, aligning visions, strategies and practices into a cohesive and adaptive whole (Fullan and Quinn 2023).

However, this process of alignment and transformation requires an acute sensitivity to human dynamics and a deep understanding of the natural resistances to change - the importance of creating a sense of exigency that inspires rather than threatens. In digital education, this demand stems from an awareness of a rapidly changing world, where today's skills and knowledge are quickly becoming obsolete. The effective digital leader therefore cultivates this awareness, guiding the exciting possibilities that digital transformation offers to enhance learning and broaden the reach of education.

Consequently, the intersection of change management and innovation in digital educational leadership gives rise to a fascinating dynamic. On the one hand, the leader strives to maintain the stability and continuity necessary for the effective functioning of the institution. On the other hand, it fosters the creative disruption necessary for innovation. Heifetz et al. (2024), in their exploration of adaptive leadership in the digital age, describe this balance as a *"dance on the edge of chaos"*. Thus, the effective digital leader learns to move gracefully between these extremes, creating a safe space for experimentation while maintaining a sense of direction and purpose.

In this sense, the concept of *"sustainable innovation"* emerges as a crucial guiding principle. Thus, Hargreaves and O'Connor (2022) argue that the most effective innovation is not necessarily the most radical or disruptive, but one that can be sustained and scaled through robust collaborative networks. The effective digital leader therefore not only generates innovative ideas, but also creates the ecosystems necessary to nurture and sustain these innovations over time.

Equally important, managing change and innovation in digital educational leadership also involves a fundamental rethink of the power and decision-making structures within educational organizations. Harris and Jones (2023) argue that the traditional hierarchical model of leadership is often inadequate to meet the complex challenges of digital transformation. Instead, they propose a distributed leadership model, where authority and responsibility are shared more broadly across the organization.

This distributed approach recognizes that the expertise and creativity needed for digital innovation often resides at various levels of the organization. Thus, the role of the digital leader evolves into that of a facilitator and catalyst, creating the conditions for innovation to flourish from all corners of the educational institution. This requires a subtle ability to foster autonomy and initiative, while maintaining a sense of direction and organizational cohesion.

In this process, therefore, the digital leader becomes a cultural translator, able to bridge different visions of the educational future. This skill of cultural translation becomes particularly crucial in an increasingly globalized and diverse educational world. As for innovation in digital educational leadership, it also involves a fundamental reconsideration of learning spaces and times. Selwyn and Facer (2021) argue that the traditional boundaries between the classroom and the outside world, between study time and leisure time, become increasingly permeable in the digital age. In this way, the innovative digital leader re-imagines the educational institution not as a bounded physical place, but as a learning ecosystem that extends beyond the walls of the classroom and classroom hours.

Importantly, this expansion of educational space and time presents significant challenges, but also exciting opportunities. Luckin et al. (2024), mention that emerging technologies such as virtual and augmented reality, AI and the Internet of Things offer unprecedented possibilities for creating immersive and adaptive learning environments. Consequently, the effective digital leader leverages these opportunities to create richer, more personalized, and relevant learning experiences.

On the other hand, change management and innovation in digital educational leadership also involves a profound reconsideration of the nature of knowledge and learning. Siemens and Downes (2023), in their update of *"the theory of connectivism"*, argue that in a world where information is at the click of a button, the role of education evolves from the transmission of knowledge to the development of critical thinking skills, creativity and lifelong learning. The effective digital leader therefore fosters a culture of questioning and exploration, where learning is seen as a continuous process of discovery and knowledge creation.

2.1.5 Understanding Digital Pedagogy

Digital pedagogy, at its deepest core, is not simply an adaptation of analogue educational practices to the digital environment; it is, in fact, a transformative paradigm that challenges deeply entrenched conceptions of what it means to know, to teach and to learn. This approach invites us to reconsider the nature of knowledge, to rethink the role of the educator and to redefine the dynamics of learning as a whole. In this sense, Laurillard (2023) argues that digital pedagogy arises from the ability to design learning experiences that make optimal use of digital tools, not as an end in themselves, but as a means to enrich understanding and critical thinking.

Therefore, the educational leader transcends the role of mere facilitator of content to become a builder of experiences. This builder not only integrates technology, pedagogy and disciplinary content, but does so in a fluid and harmonious way, building a coherent and meaningful whole. Thus, digital pedagogy is presented not only as a tool for the transmission of knowledge, but also as an opportunity to rethink education from a more inclusive and humanistic perspective.

However, this integration is not a simple or linear process; it is a complex process that demands a deep understanding of how digital technologies not only transform the means of delivery of educational content, but also the very nature of that content and the ways in which learners relate to it. Consequently, this new vision of digital pedagogy invites a rethinking of traditional roles within the educational process. In the digital learning ecosystem, rigid hierarchies between educator and learner are blurred, giving way to more dynamic, horizontal and collaborative relationships.

From this perspective, understanding digital pedagogy also involves an appreciation of the new forms of literacy emerging in the digital environment. Jenkins et al. (2024), argue that the skills of navigating and creating digital content have become as fundamental in the 21st century as reading and writing were in previous centuries. The forward-thinking educational leader recognizes the need to integrate these new literacies into the curriculum, not as isolated competencies, but as essential components of every discipline and subject area. In the same vein, digital pedagogy introduces new challenges and opportunities in terms of assessment and feedback.

2.2 The Skills Gap and the Challenge of Digital Leadership

The Global Digital Skills Gap Report (UNESCO, 2024) reveals an alarming reality: only 37% of education leaders globally consider themselves fully prepared to lead the digital transformation of their institutions. This statistic not only underscores the magnitude of the challenge, but also highlights the urgency of fundamentally rethinking how leaders are prepared and supported in the digital age.

Furthermore, the Technology Horizon in Education report (Johnson et al., 2024) projects that, in the next five years, more than 60% of educational institutions will incorporate some form of AI into their teaching and management processes. This situation raises profound questions about how educational leaders not only keep up with these technologies, but also develop the wisdom to implement them ethically and effectively.

Consequently, another critical aspect of the skills gap lies in the ability of leaders to manage the ethical and equity complexities that arise with the digitization of education. Unequal access to technology, concerns about data privacy and the potential for technology to exacerbate existing inequalities are challenges that require not only technical expertise, but also a deep understanding of social justice and ethics.

In turn, the skills gap extends to leaders' ability to rethink learning spaces and times in the digital age. With the proliferation of hybrid and flexible learning environments, digital educational leaders are challenged to design and manage educational experiences that transcend the traditional constraints of the physical classroom.

2.3 Resistance to Change

Resistance to change emerges as a significant challenge for digital leaders seeking to transform their institutions. This resistance, far from being a mere obstacle, reveals itself as a complex and multifaceted phenomenon, rooted in both human psychology and organizational structures.

From this perspective, the sources of resistance to change in educational institutions are diverse and often interconnected. Fullan and Quinn (2023) identify fear of the unknown as one of the main barriers. This fear manifests itself in educators' anxiety that their skills will become obsolete or that their authority in the classroom will be diminished by technology. Similarly, Hargreaves and O'Connor (2022) point out that institutional inertia, rooted in years of tradition and established practice, acts as a powerful brake on change.

This is compounded by a perceived loss of professional identity. As Biesta (2023) argues, many educators see digitalization as a threat to their traditional role as gatekeepers of knowledge and facilitators of learning. This perception is intertwined with broader concerns about the dehumanization of education and the loss of meaningful interpersonal connections in increasingly technology-mediated learning environments.

In the face of these challenges, managing and mitigating resilience requires a nuanced and multidimensional approach. Kotter (2023) proposes a model of change that emphasizes creating and building a shared vision. In the educational context, this involves clearly communicating how digital transformation is not only essential for institutional survival, but also for improving the quality and relevance of the education offered.

In parallel, Senge et al. (2024) advocate the creation of learning organizations where change is seen as a continuous process of growth and adaptation, rather than as a series of disruptive events. This approach suggests fostering a culture of experimentation and critical reflection, where mistakes are seen as learning opportunities rather than failures.

On the other hand, training and professional development play a crucial role in mitigating resistance. As Darling-Hammond (2023) points out, this training encompasses not only technical skills, but also pedagogical and reflective competencies that enable digital leaders to integrate technology meaningfully into their practice. Mentoring programs and communities of practice emerge as effective strategies to provide continuous and personalized support during the change process.

To understand this process of digital transformation in education, consideration of the Hegelian dialectic offers a valuable philosophical lens. The thesis of traditional education and the antithesis of technological innovation are not seen as irreconcilable forces, but as elements of a broader process of educational evolution. The synthesis that emerges from this tension is not a simple combination of old and new, but a fundamental reconfiguration of educational practice that respects tradition while embracing the transformative possibilities of technology.

2.4 Infrastructure and Resources

In today's world, the digital transformation of educational organizations is not a process that can be reduced to simply implementing technologies. It is a profound journey that involves a reflection on the infrastructures and resources needed to sustain this transition. Technological infrastructure and financial resources emerge as essential pillars in this process, but their limitations often present significant challenges for leaders trying to guide their institutions through this profound and multifaceted change.

From this perspective, the assessment of these limitations reveals a complex picture. According to a recent UNESCO study (2024), 68% of educational institutions in developing countries lack the basic technological infrastructure to implement effective digital learning solutions. This gap includes not only the lack of adequate hardware and software, but also the absence of reliable and high-speed connectivity, fundamental elements in the era of online and hybrid learning.

In turn, financial constraints further complicate this situation. Williamson (2023) highlights that many institutions face limited or shrinking budgets, making it difficult to invest in advanced educational technology. This economic context challenges leaders to make difficult strategic choices, prioritizing some areas of technology development over others, often at the expense of comprehensive digital transformation.

On the other hand, an emerging strategy is the adoption of Infrastructure-as-a-Service (IaaS) and Software-as-a-Service (SaaS) models. As Selwyn (2023) argues, these models allow educational institutions to access advanced technologies without the need for large upfront investments in infrastructure. However, this approach also raises questions about dependence on external providers and the sovereignty of educational data, which invites further reflection on the risks and benefits involved.

In addition, inter-institutional collaboration emerges as another promising solution. Hargreaves and O'Connor (2023) describe successful cases where educational institutions share technological resources and expertise, creating economies of scale and communities of practice that benefit all participants. This collaborative approach not only optimizes resources, but also fosters innovation and knowledge sharing.

Similarly, the implementation of open source technologies and open educational resources (OER) offers another avenue to overcome resource constraints. Wiley and Hilton (2024) argue that these resources not only reduce costs, but also promote a culture of sharing and collaboration. At a deeper level, reflection on the relationship between technology and humanity, inspired by Heidegger's ideas on technology, invites critical consideration of the role of technology in education. Heidegger warns against the danger of perceiving technology as simply an instrument, suggesting that this view blinds us to the ways in which technology shapes our understanding of the world and ourselves.

In education, this Heideggerian perspective invites us to question how decisions about technological infrastructure and resources shape the very nature of education. As Biesta (2023) points out, the passive adoption of educational technologies risks reducing education to a mere process of information transmission, losing sight of its crucial role in the formation of critical and engaged human beings.

3. PEDAGOGICAL INNOVATION

Pedagogical innovation, as a driver of educational change, finds itself in a dilemma with the advent of digital technologies. This phenomenon radically transforms previous conceptions of the ways of teaching and learning. With the emergence of virtual and augmented reality, a new frontier for pedagogical innovation is opening up. Bailenson (2024) describes how these technologies are revolutionizing fields such as medical education, allowing students to practice complex procedures in safe and controlled environments. Beyond simulation, these tools offer the possibility of transcendent educational experiences, such as virtual tours of historical sites or explorations of the cosmos, fusing learning with adventure and discovery.

In this context, game-based learning and gamification represent another fruitful area for innovation. Kapp and Defelice (2023) argue that these approaches not only increase student motivation and engagement, but also promote the development of complex skills such as problem solving and strategic thinking. The integration of playful elements in learning resonates with Dewey's (1995) vision of education as an active and meaningful experience.

Thus, technology-supported pedagogical practices abound in today's educational scenario. A notable example is the flipped classroom model, where technology facilitates the delivery of content outside the classroom, freeing up class time for interactive and problem-solving activities. Bergmann and Sams (2024) report significant improvements in student performance and engagement in flipped learning environments, especially when combined with active learning strategies.

Another example is the use of digital collaboration platforms for global projects. Zhao (2023) describes initiatives in which students from different parts of the world collaborate on research projects, using synchronous and asynchronous communication tools. These experiences not only develop technical and collaborative skills, but also foster intercultural understanding and global citizenship.

In addition, learning analytics emerges as another promising pedagogical practice. Siemens and Long (2024) illustrate how educational data analytics enables educators to identify learning patterns, anticipate challenges and provide timely interventions. This real-time responsiveness transforms classroom dynamics, enabling more proactive teaching geared to individual student needs.

In a profound sense, technological innovation in education aligns with John Dewey's (1995) ideas about experiential learning and democratic education. Dewey's vision of education as a continuous reconstruction of experience is amplified in the digital environment, where active learning is no longer confined to the walls of the classroom. Digital technologies, when implemented with a sound educational philosophy, democratize access to knowledge and encourage participation in the learning process.

In this vein, Biesta (2023) points out that true pedagogical innovation lies not simply in the adoption of new tools, but in the creation of spaces where students can experiment, reflect and build knowledge collaboratively. Dewey's concept of education as life finds new relevance in the digital age. Emerging technologies blur the boundaries between formal and informal learning, creating opportunities for continuous and contextualized learning.

3.1. Digital and Soft Skills Development

Today, the development of digital and soft skills is emerging as an educational imperative shaping the landscape of learning and professional preparation. This dual approach opens up an unprecedented opportunity for digital leadership, challenging traditional conceptions of the curriculum and the purpose of education. It is not just about adding technical competences to the educational repertoire, but about thinking about how these skills are integrated into the holistic education of individuals.

From this perspective, effective integration of these skills into the curriculum requires a comprehensive and strategic approach. Beetham and Sharpe (2023) propose that a successful model involves the seamless merging of digital competencies with soft skills in all aspects of learning. This integration is not limited to specific technology courses, but permeates all disciplines, creating an educational ecosystem where the digital and the human coexist and reinforce each other.

In addition, the creation of digital makerspaces within educational institutions represents another innovative approach. Halverson and Sheridan (2023) argue that these environments foster creativity, problem solving and adaptability as students experiment with emerging technologies such as 3D printing or robotics. These spaces become incubators of innovation, where digital and soft skills are developed in a context of experimentation and hands-on learning.

Likewise, gamification and games are presented as another powerful strategy for integrated skills development. Deterding et al. (2024) illustrate how game elements in educational contexts not only increase motivation and engagement, but also provide a productive ground for the development of skills such as decision-making, time management and resilience, all of which are essential in the digital environment.

Thus, the benefits of these skills for students' future careers are diverse and profound. A recent study by the World Economic Forum (2024) projects that, by 2030, more than 50% of jobs will require a sophisticated combination of digital and soft skills. The ability to work in complex digital environments, along with skills such as empathy, adaptability and systems thinking, is emerging as the new paradigm for employability.

Beyond employability, these skills prepare students for an ever-changing world. Harari (2023) observes that, in an era where technical knowledge is rapidly becoming obsolete, the ability to learn, unlearn and relearn becomes the most valuable competence. Soft skills, in this context, act as an anchor, enabling individuals to adapt and thrive in the midst of technological and social uncertainty.

Reflecting on the role of soft skills in integral human development, we find resonance in the philosophy of Maslow and Rogers. Maslow's pyramid of needs, reinterpreted in the digital context by Nussbaum (2024), suggests that digital skills satisfy needs for security and belonging in the modern world, while soft skills are crucial for self-fulfilment and transcendence.

In this sense, Rogers' theory of personal growth and the actualizing tendency takes on new relevance in the digital age. As Turkle (2023) argues, technology, when used with awareness and purpose, can amplify our capacity for self-reflection and genuine connection with others. Soft skills, in this context, become the steppingstone that connects the digital self with essential humanity.

Moreover, the development of these skills aligns with Rogers' vision of person-centered education. In a digital world, the ability to empathize, collaborate and communicate effectively becomes even more crucial. Therefore, digital leadership is not limited to facilitating the acquisition of technical skills, but also seeks to cultivate an environment where students explore and develop their full human potential. This educational vision transcends mere preparation for the labor market and aspires to the formation of ethical, reflective, and engaged digital citizens.

3.2. Promoting Interculturality and Inclusion

The promotion of interculturality and inclusion emerges as an ethical and pragmatic imperative, offering significant opportunities for digital leadership in transforming educational organizations. This approach not only enriches the social canvas of learning, but also prepares students for a globally interconnected and diverse world, where mutual understanding and intercultural collaboration become essential.

In this sense, programs and policies that foster an intercultural and inclusive educational environment are being reinvented in the digital age. According to Banks (2023), online learning platforms open up new possibilities for creating truly global educational spaces. These platforms facilitate collaboration between learners from different cultural backgrounds, transcending geographical barriers and fostering authentic intercultural dialogue.

An innovative example of this approach is the *"Global Virtual Exchange Program"* implemented by the University of California, Berkeley. This program, described by Lee and Guth (2024), uses advanced communication technologies to connect students from different countries in collaborative projects. Participants not only develop intercultural competences, but also acquire crucial digital skills for the 21st century, thus integrating the digital with the human in the educational process.

Furthermore, the integration of virtual reality in intercultural education emerges as another promising strategy. Bailenson (2023) explains how virtual reality experiences allow students to walk in the shoes of others, fostering empathy and intercultural understanding in a visceral and profound way. These immersive experiences challenge stereotypes and promote a genuine appreciation of cultural diversity, expanding students' ability to connect with different perspectives.

Similarly, AI is playing a crucial role in promoting inclusion. A notable success story is the adaptive tutoring system developed by Carnegie Mellon University. Aleven et al. (2024) note that this system uses AI to personalize learning by adapting to the individual needs of students, including those with diverse abilities and cultural backgrounds. This approach allows for a more equitable education, where each student finds a learning space suited to his or her characteristics and potential.

From another perspective, the consideration of the philosophy of intercultural dialogue and social justice, inspired by the work of Paulo Freire and Martha Nussbaum, takes on new relevance in the digital context. Freire's vision of education as a practice of freedom is echoed in the democratizing possibilities of digital technologies. As Giroux (2023) argues, digital tools, when used critically, have the potential to challenge existing power structures and foster a critical consciousness in learners.

4. STRATEGIES FOR EFFECTIVE DIGITAL LEADERSHIP

In an environment where digital technologies permeate every aspect of education, it is essential that digital leaders maintain an updated and expanded view of the competencies needed to successfully navigate this complex landscape. Therefore, to address this need, the design of continuing education programs for educational leaders must start from a thorough analysis of the specific needs of each institution.

As Rodríguez-Molina (2021) points out, these programs should cover not only technical aspects, but also soft skills such as effective communication, empathy and resilience, all of which are crucial in the exercise of digital leadership. The structure of these programs needs to be flexible and adaptive, allowing leaders to combine their training with their day-to-day responsibilities, creating a learning environment that adapts to the dynamic challenges of the educational context.

Likewise, constant updating in digital competences appears as an inescapable requirement for contemporary educational leaders. Gutiérrez-Pérez (2020) suggests that mastery of digital tools and platforms is just the beginning; leaders need to develop a deep understanding of how these technologies transform teaching-learning processes. This approach involves being in tune with the latest trends and research in the field, actively participating in professional networks and communities of practice that nurture a culture of shared and continuous learning.

Likewise, the continuous education and training of educational leaders is understood as a process of self-realization and self-improvement. Nietzsche (1886/2003) conceived education as a means to achieve greatness of soul, a state of constant growth and evolution. In this sense, leaders who engage in lifelong learning embark on a journey of discovery and transformation, challenging their own limits and expanding their horizons. This quest for greatness is not about a mastery of power, but a deep commitment to continuous improvement and self-knowledge.

Furthermore, Foucault (1994) invites us to rethink the role of knowledge in power relations. In the context of digital leadership, the acquisition of new skills and knowledge can be seen as a form of empowerment, enabling leaders to challenge traditional structures and bring about significant change in their organizations. However, Foucault also warns that this power carries with it an ethical responsibility; knowledge and skills must be used in the service of the common good, not as tools of control or domination.

4.1. Innovative Organizational Culture

In the process of digital transformation of educational organizations, organizational culture is fundamental to fostering innovation and change. Organizational culture is not just a set of norms and practices, but an interplay of values and aspirations of the entire education community.

Promoting an innovative organizational culture therefore implies a paradigm shift in the conception of learning and teaching. It is a call to challenge the established, to question traditional methodologies and to open up to the possibilities offered by the digital age. In this sense, leadership plays a crucial role in creating spaces where ideas flow freely, and experimentation is valued. To encourage the participation of all members of the educational community, it is essential to implement mechanisms that democratize innovation, such as the creation of collaborative digital platforms, the organization of educational hackathons and the implementation of recognition systems that celebrate innovative initiatives. Fullan (2020) suggests that sustainable innovation in education requires a systemic approach that engages students, teachers, administrators and families in an ongoing dialogue about the future of education.

From an existentialist perspective, innovative organizational culture takes on a profoundly human dimension. Sartre's ideas on freedom and responsibility resonate in this context, reminding us that each member of the educational organization is the architect of his or her own destiny and, by extension, of the collective destiny of the institution. Freedom, in this sense, is not only the absence of restrictions, but the capacity to imagine and create new educational realities. Kierkegaard, for his part, stresses the importance of authenticity and personal commitment in the pursuit of innovation. In the educational context, this translates into the need for each individual to embrace their unique role in the process of digital transformation, recognizing that true innovation is born out of passion and personal conviction.

4.2. Collaboration and Support Networks

Building collaborative networks between educational institutions to share resources and best practices has become a crucial strategy in the digital age. These strategic alliances broaden the reach, enrich the perspectives, and optimize the resources of educational organizations. As Siemens (2021) points out in his theory of connectivism, learning in the digital age is not limited to individuals, but extends to the networks and connections they form.

An outstanding example of effective collaboration at the local level is the "Escuelas en Red" project in Barcelona, Spain, which connects schools in different districts, fostering the exchange of pedagogical experiences and technological resources. The result has been a significant improvement in educational quality and greater equity in access to digital resources (Castells, 2022). At the international level, the European Union's eTwinning program illustrates the power of cross-border collaboration. This platform connects more than 900,000 teachers from 43 countries, enabling them to develop collaborative projects and share innovative practices. According to a study by Vuorikari et al. (2020), participating teachers report a significant increase in their digital competences and increased motivation to innovate in their pedagogical practices.

Moreover, the philosophy behind these collaborative networks is in tune with Pyotr Kropotkin's ideas on mutual aid. Kropotkin argued that cooperation, rather than competition, was the main driver of evolutionary progress. Transposing this concept to the field of education, one can envision an ecosystem where institutions thrive through synergistic collaboration (Dugatkin, 2019).

This cooperative approach is intertwined with complex systems theory, which invites consideration of educational organizations as interconnected entities within a larger system. Morin (2020) argues that the inherent complexity of educational systems requires a comprehensive and collaborative approach to address modern challenges.

Accordingly, Hargreaves and O'Connor (2018) propose the concept of collaborative professionalism, which suggests that the role of the leader is to cultivate a culture of trust and openness that allows for the free flow of ideas and resources. In this way, solidarity in education manifests itself not only in the sharing of material resources, but also in the joint construction of knowledge. Open source platforms such as edX and Coursera represent tangible examples of how collaboration can democratize access to quality education on a global scale (Deimann and Farrow, 2021).

It is important to recognize that effective collaboration in the digital age does not emerge spontaneously, but that a robust technological infrastructure and, more importantly, an open mind and a willingness to share and learn from others is crucial.

Senge (2020) argues that successful educational organizations of the future harness the enthusiasm and learning capacity of people at all levels of the organization.

For all these reasons, the digital transformation of educational organizations seen through collaboration and support networks is not simply a technological process, but a revolution in the conception of learning and knowledge. It calls for transcending institutional and disciplinary boundaries, cultivating an ethic of intellectual solidarity and recognizing that, in the age of complexity, no institution is an island.

5. ETHICAL AND SUSTAINABILITY CONSIDERATIONS

Ethical reflection on privacy and individual autonomy in the educational context connects with the ideas of both classical and contemporary thinkers. Bentham's concept of the panopticon, originally conceived as an architectural design for penal institutions, takes on new relevance in the age of digital surveillance. The pervasiveness of technology in educational institutions raises the question: Is an educational panopticon being created where students and educators are constantly observed and evaluated?

On the other hand, Rawls' theory of justice invites consideration of how to design privacy and security systems if one did not know where one stood in the educational ecosystem. This veil of ignorance prompts the creation of policies that equitably protect all members of the educational community, from the most vulnerable students to the administrators with the greatest access to data (Rawls, 1999). In this sense, digital leadership faces the challenge of balancing technological innovation with the protection of individual rights and freedoms. Floridi (2023) argues for the need to develop an information ethic that recognizes the personal value of privacy and autonomy in the formation of identities and relationships in the digital space.

These ethical considerations have profound implications that go beyond institutional politics, affecting how we conceptualize education and the role of technology in it. Is it possible to foster an open and collaborative learning environment while maintaining rigorous privacy protections? How do we reconcile the potential of learning analytics to improve educational outcomes with students' right to informational self-determination?

Consequently, these questions lead to consider alternative models of data governance in education. Initiatives such as MyData for Education propose a user-centred approach, where students and educators have control over their personal data and decide how and when to share it (Kärkkäinen & Vincent-Lancrin, 2023). This approach not only protects privacy, but also empowers individuals as active agents in their educational journey.

Therefore, the sustainability of digital leadership in transforming educational organizations depends, to a large extent, on their ability to address these ethical issues in a proactive and reflective manner. It is not simply a matter of complying with regulations, but of cultivating an organizational culture that fundamentally values privacy and security as essential components of ethical and human-centered education.

CONCLUSION

In the landscape of the digital transformation of educational organizations, a crucial figure emerges: the digital leader. This concept, far from being a mere technological label, embodies a convergence of skills, virtues and responsibilities that challenge our traditional conceptions of leadership and education.

The notion of the digital leader therefore invites deep reflection on the nature of leadership in the information age. What does it mean to be a leader in a world where technology increasingly mediates our interactions and learning processes? This question goes back to the roots of ethical philosophy, in particular the Aristotelian conception of virtue.

Aristotle, in his *Nicomachean Ethics,* proposes that virtue is a habit that is cultivated through constant practice. In the context of digital leadership, this suggests that the virtues of leadership are not innate or acquired simply through technical knowledge but are developed through reflective experience and deliberate action in the digital environment.

From this perspective, the digital leader cultivates a set of virtues that allow him or her to navigate the complex technological-educational ecosystem wisely and ethically. These virtues include digital prudence - the ability to discern the appropriate use of technology in different educational contexts; digital justice - a commitment to equity in access to and use of technological resources; digital temperance - moderation in the implementation of technological solutions; and digital fortitude - resilience in the face of the challenges and failures inherent in technological innovation.

This perspective leads us to consider the notion of buen vivir in the digital context. The concept of buen vivir, rooted in indigenous Latin American philosophies and reinterpreted by contemporary thinkers such as Acosta (2020), offers a holistic view of well-being that transcends mere technological progress. For the digital leader, this involves cultivating an approach that not only seeks efficiency and innovation, but also promotes harmony between technology, the educational community and the wider environment.

The digital leader, in this vision, is an agent of transformation who integrates the possibilities of technology with the core values of education and holistic human development. Selwyn (2023) points out that true digital leadership is not about imposing technological solutions, but about facilitating a critical and constructive dialogue about the role of technology in education; therefore, this approach requires the development of skills that go beyond technical competence. The effective digital leader cultivates soft skills such as empathy, intercultural communication and emotional intelligence, crucial for navigating the complex human landscapes that underlie any technological transformation.

Moreover, the digital leader acts as a bridge between different worlds: that of technology and that of pedagogy, that of innovation and that of educational tradition, the global and the local. This capacity for synthesis and mediation becomes especially important in an increasingly diverse and interconnected educational context, and inclusivity emerges as another fundamental virtue of the digital leader. In a world where technology can both widen and exacerbate existing inequalities, the digital leader takes responsibility for ensuring that digital transformation is a process that empowers all members of the education community. This involves not only providing access to technology, but also cultivating the skills necessary for its meaningful use.

The concept of the digital leader then also invites us to rethink the nature of power and authority in educational organizations. In an environment where knowledge is increasingly distributed and innovation often emerges from the ground up, the digital leader acts more as a facilitator and catalyst than as a traditional manager.

Ultimately, the concept of the digital leader in the transformation of educational organizations invites deep reflection on the very purpose of education in the digital age. How do we reconcile the transformative possibilities of technology with the humanistic values that have been the foundation of education? How do we cultivate leaders who are not only competent in the use of digital tools, but also wise in their application for the common good?

Future Projections

Digital leadership in education represents a fundamental transformation in the way academic institutions are managed and organized. This adaptation not only involves the implementation of technologies, but also the ability of leaders to respond to the challenges and opportunities that digitalization brings. In order to explore the impact of this leadership in education in greater depth, it is important to propose studies that, using qualitative, quantitative or mixed methodologies, provide a detailed understanding of how digital leadership influences different aspects of the educational environment. The following research proposals explore key areas of this phenomenon, with the aim of contributing to the development of more inclusive, adaptive and effective educational practices.

First, a qualitative study on the role of digital leadership in the organizational culture of educational institutions could provide detailed insight into how digital leaders influence the culture of collaboration and innovation within their organizations. This research could take the form of in-depth interviews with managers, teachers, and administrative staff, allowing for an in-depth analysis of how the use of technology impacts on work dynamics and perceptions of the educational environment. The aim would be to understand how digital leaders foster an innovative and collaborative organizational culture, as well as to explore how educational staff perceive these changes in their daily work. As a qualitative study, it is suggested to use semi-structured interviews and thematic analysis to identify key trends and perceptions, which would contribute to building an interpretative framework on the cultural elements that define a digitally advanced institution.

REFERENCES

Acosta, A. (2020). *El Buen Vivir: Sumak Kawsay una oportunidad para imaginar otros mundos*. Icaria.

Ahmad, S., & Wahid, N. A. (2019). Digital leadership, social media competence, and decision-making quality among school leaders in Malaysia. *International Journal of Leadership in Education*, 22(3), 333–348. DOI: 10.1080/13603124.2018.1450998

Aleven, V.. (2024). *AI-adaptive tutoring in educational diversity*. Carnegie Mellon University.

Aleven, V., McLaughlin, E., Glenn, R. M., & Koedinger, K. R. (2016). Intelligent tutoring systems. *International Journal of Artificial Intelligence in Education*, 26(1), 150–166.

Amankwah-Amoah, J., Khan, Z., Wood, G., & Knight, G. (2021). COVID-19 and digitalization: The great acceleration. *Journal of Business Research*, 136, 602–611. DOI: 10.1016/j.jbusres.2021.08.011 PMID: 34538980

Aristóteles. (1999). *Ética a Nicómaco (Trans. de A. Zozaya)*. Ediciones Akal.

Avolio, B. J., & Kahai, S. (2003). Adding the "e" to e-leadership: How it may impact your leadership. *Organizational Dynamics*, 31(4), 325–338. DOI: 10.1016/S0090-2616(02)00133-X

Avolio, B. J., Sosik, J. J., Kahai, S., & Baker, B. (2014). E-leadership: Re-examining transformations in leadership source and transmission. *The Leadership Quarterly*, 25(1), 105–131. DOI: 10.1016/j.leaqua.2013.11.003

Bailenson, J. (2018). *Experience on Demand: What Virtual Reality Is, How It Works, and What It Can Do*. W. W. Norton & Company.

Bailenson, J. (2023). Virtual reality in education: Promises and pitfalls. *Harvard Educational Review*, 93(2), 145–170.

Banks, J. A. (2007). *Educating Citizens in a Multicultural Society*. Teachers College Press.

Banks, J. A. (2023). *Diversity, Equity, and Inclusion in Digital Education*. Teachers College Press.

Benkler, Y. (2021). *The Wealth of Networks: How Social Production Transforms Markets and Freedom* (2nd ed.). Yale University Press.

Bergmann, J., & Sams, A. (2024). *Flipped Learning: Gateway to Student Engagement* (3rd ed.). International Society for Technology in Education.

Biesta, G. (2022). *World-Centered Education: A View for the Present*. Routledge.

Biesta, G. (2023). *The Beautiful Risk of Education* (2nd ed.). Routledge.

Brynjolfsson, E., & McAfee, A. (2014). *The Second Machine Age: Work, Progress, and Prosperity in a Time of Brilliant Technologies*. W. W. Norton & Company.

Castells, M. (2021). *The Rise of the Network Society* (3rd ed.). Wiley-Blackwell.

Castells, M. (2022). Digital education networks: A case study of Barcelona's "Schools in Network" project. *Journal of Education Policy*, 37(3), 321–340.

Christensen, C. M., Horn, M. B., & Johnson, C. W. (2016). *Disrupting Class: How Disruptive Innovation Will Change the Way the World Learns*. McGraw-Hill Education.

Colbert, A., Yee, N., & George, G. (2016). The digital workforce and the workplace of the future: Implications for organizational behavior. *The Academy of Management Perspectives*, 30(3), 1–17. DOI: 10.5465/amp.2015.0072

Cope, B., & Kalantzis, M. (2024). *e-Learning Ecologies: Principles for New Learning and Assessment*. Routledge.

Couldry, N.. (2024). Digital storytelling as a tool for intercultural understanding: Lessons from the UNESCO Intercultural Digital Narratives Project. *International Journal of Cultural Studies*, 27(2), 178–195.

Czerniewicz, L. (2022). *Open Education in the Global South: Stories from the Field*. MIT Press.

Darling-Hammond, L. (2023). *Powerful Teacher Education: Lessons from Exemplary Programs* (2nd ed.). Jossey-Bass.

Darling-Hammond, L.. (2020). *Restarting and Reinventing School: Learning in the Time of COVID and Beyond*. Learning Policy Institute.

Deimann, M., & Farrow, R. (2021). Democratising education with open educational resources: A critical look at MOOCs and open education. *Distance Education*, 42(2), 235–251.

Deterding, S.. (2024). Gamification in education: What, how, why bother? *Educational Researcher*, 53(3), 178–189.

Dewey, J. (1995). *Democracia y educación: una introducción a la filosofía de la educación*. Ediciones Morata.

Dugatkin, L. A. (2019). *The Prince of Evolution: Peter Kropotkin's Adventures in Science and Politics*. University of Chicago Press.

Dweck, C., & Yeager, D. S. (2023). *Mindset: The New Psychology of Success* (Updated edition). Random House.

Earl, L., & Fullan, M. (2023). *Using Data for School Improvement* (3rd ed.). Corwin.

Fernández, E., & Shaw, G. P. (2020). Academic leadership in a time of crisis: The coronavirus and COVID-19. *Journal of Leadership Studies*, 14(1), 39–45. DOI: 10.1002/jls.21684

Floridi, L. (2022). *The Ethics of Digital Ethics*. Oxford University Press.

Floridi, L. (2023). *The Philosophy of Information* (2nd ed.). Oxford University Press.

Foucault, M. (1994). *The Order of Things: An Archaeology of the Human Sciences*. Vintage.

Fullan, M. (2020). *Leading in a Culture of Change* (2nd ed.). Jossey-Bass.

Fullan, M., & Quinn, J. (2016). *Coherence: The Right Drivers in Action for Schools, Districts, and Systems*. Corwin Press.

García-Peñalvo, F. J. (2024). Digital transformation in education: Challenges and opportunities. *International Journal of Educational Technology in Higher Education*, 21(1), 1–18.

Giroux, H. A. (2023). *Critical Digital Pedagogy: A Reader*. Bloomsbury Academic.

Gümüş, S., & Beyhan, Ö. (2023). School principals as digital leaders: Challenges and opportunities. *International Journal of Educational Leadership and Management*, 11(2), 156–174. DOI: 10.17583/ijelm.2023.12345

Halverson, E. R., & Sheridan, K. (2023). The maker movement in education. *Harvard Educational Review*, 93(4), 495–528. DOI: 10.17763/haer.84.4.34j1g68140382063

Harari, Y. N. (2018). *21 Lessons for the 21st Century*. Spiegel & Grau.

Hargreaves, A. (2023). *Digital Leadership for Human-Centered Education*. Teachers College Press.

Hargreaves, A., & Fullan, M. (2020). *Professional Capital: Transforming Teaching in Every School* (2nd ed.). Teachers College Press.

Hargreaves, A., & O'Connor, M. T. (2018). *Collaborative Professionalism: When Teaching Together Means Learning for All*. Corwin.

Hargreaves, A., & O'Connor, M. T. (2022). *Leading Collaborative Professionalism*. Corwin.

Harris, A., & Jones, M. (2023). *Distributed Leadership in Digital Contexts*. Routledge.

Heifetz, R.. (2024). *The Practice of Adaptive Leadership: Tools and Tactics for Changing Your Organization and the World* (2nd ed.). Harvard Business Review Press.

Heskett, J. (2022). *Win from Within: Build Organizational Culture for Competitive Advantage*. Columbia University Press. DOI: 10.7312/hesk20300

Ito, M.. (2024). *Connected Learning: An Agenda for Research and Design*. Digital Media and Learning Research Hub.

Jenkins, H.. (2024). *Participatory Culture in a Networked Era* (2nd ed.). Polity.

Johnson, L.. (2024). *NMC Horizon Report: Higher Education Edition*. The New Media Consortium.

Kärkkäinen, K., & Vincent-Lancrin, S. (2023). *Trustworthy artificial intelligence (AI) in education: Promises and challenges*. OECD Publishing.

Kotter, J. P. (2023). *Leading Change* (2nd ed.). Harvard Business Review Press.

Kozma, R. B. (2019). *Transforming Education: The Power of ICT Policies*. UNESCO.

Larjovuori, R. L.. (2023). Digital leadership: Leveraging digital technologies for organizational value creation. *Journal of Management Development*, 42(4), 256–270.

Larmer, J.. (2024). *Project-Based Learning: Your Field Guide to Real-World Projects in the Digital Age* (3rd ed.). Buck Institute for Education.

Lee, L., & Guth, S. (2024). Virtual exchange as a tool for developing intercultural competence: A case study of the Global Virtual Exchange Program. *Language Learning & Technology*, 28(2), 10–30.

Li, C. (2010). *Open Leadership: How Social Technology Can Transform the Way You Lead*. Jossey-Bass.

Li, C., & Solis, B. (2013). *The Seven Success Factors of Social Business Strategy*. Jossey-Bass.

Livari, N.. (2020). Digital transformation of everyday life: How COVID-19 pandemic transformed the basic education of the young generation and why information management research should care? *International Journal of Information Management, 55*, 102183. DOI: 10.1016/j.ijinfomgt.2020.102183 PMID: 32836640

Looi, C. K., & Wong, L. H. (2023). *Seamless Learning in the Age of Connectivity* (2nd ed.). Springer.

Luckin, R.. (2023). *Intelligence Unleashed: An Argument for AI in Education* (2nd ed.). Pearson.

Luckin, R.. (2024). *Enhancing Learning and Teaching with Technology: What the Research Says* (2nd ed.). UCL IOE Press.

Marín, V. I.. (2022). Emergency remote teaching in higher education: Mapping the first global online semester. *International Journal of Educational Technology in Higher Education*, 19(1), 1–24. PMID: 35013716

Mishra, P., & Koehler, M. J. (2023). *Technological Pedagogical Content Knowledge: A Framework for Teacher Knowledge in a Digital Age* (2nd ed.). Teachers College Press.

Morin, E. (2020). *Seven Complex Lessons in Education for the Future*. UNESCO.

Nietzsche, F. (2003). *Beyond Good and Evil: Prelude to a Philosophy of the Future*. Penguin Classics. (Original work published 1886)

Noddings, N. (2024). *Philosophy of Education* (5th ed.). Routledge.

Nussbaum, M. C. (2024). *Creating Capabilities: The Human Development Approach* (2nd ed.). Belknap Press.

O'Neil, C. (2022). *Weapons of Math Destruction: How Big Data Increases Inequality and Threatens Democracy* (Updated edition). Crown.

OCDE. (2023). *OECD Skills Outlook 2023: The State of Global Education*. OECD Publishing.

OCDE. (2024). *Education at a Glance 2024: OECD Indicators*. OECD Publishing.

Piderit, S. K. (2023). *Rethinking Resistance and Recognizing Ambivalence: A Multidimensional View of Attitudes Toward an Organizational Change* (2nd ed.). Academy of Management Review.

Popenici, S. A., & Kerr, S. (2017). Exploring the impact of artificial intelligence on teaching and learning in higher education. *Research and Practice in Technology Enhanced Learning*, 12(1), 22. DOI: 10.1186/s41039-017-0062-8 PMID: 30595727

Prinsloo, P. (2023). Student privacy self-management: Implications for learning analytics. *LAK '23: Proceedings of the 13th International Conference on Learning Analytics and Knowledge.*

Prinsloo, P., & Slade, S. (2024). *Student Privacy in Learning Analytics: An Ethical Perspective.* Routledge.

Rapanta, C., Botturi, L., Goodyear, P., Guàrdia, L., & Koole, M. (2020). Online university teaching during and after the Covid-19 crisis: Refocusing teacher presence and learning activity. *Postdigital Science and Education*, 2(3), 923–945. DOI: 10.1007/s42438-020-00155-y

Raza, S. A.. (2021). Factors affecting the adoption of online teaching in higher education institutions: The perspective of faculty members. *International Journal of Educational Management*, 35(5), 1050–1067.

Reich, J. (2023). *Failure to Disrupt: Why Technology Alone Can't Transform Education.* Harvard University Press.

Rodríguez-Molina, G. (2021). Digital leadership in schools: Exploring the relationship between digital competence and leadership. *Computers & Education*, 167, 104221.

Rose, D. H., & Meyer, A. (2023). *Universal Design for Learning: Theory and Practice* (2nd ed.). CAST Professional Publishing.

Sá, M. J., & Serpa, S. (2020). The COVID-19 pandemic as an opportunity to foster the sustainable development of teaching in higher education. *Sustainability (Basel)*, 12(20), 8525. DOI: 10.3390/su12208525

Salmon, G. (2021). *E-Moderating: The Key to Online Teaching and Learning* (4th ed.). Routledge.

Sánchez-Cruzado, C.. (2021). Digital competence in higher education faculty: Systematic literature review. *International Journal of Educational Technology in Higher Education*, 18(1), 1–21.

Schein, E. H. (2024). *Organizational Culture and Leadership* (6th ed.). Jossey-Bass.

Schrum, L., & Levin, B. B. (2021). *Leading 21st-Century Schools: Harnessing Technology for Engagement and Achievement* (3rd ed.). Corwin.

Selwyn, N. (2021). *Digital technology and the futures of education: Towards 'non-stupid' optimism.* UNESCO.

Selwyn, N. (2023). Should Robots Replace Teachers? AI and the Future of Education. *Polity.*

Selwyn, N. (2024). *Education and Technology: Key Issues and Debates* (4th ed.). Bloomsbury Academic.

Selwyn, N., & Facer, K. (2023). *Digital technology and the futures of education: Towards 'non-stupid' optimism*. UNESCO.

Selwyn, N., & Facer, K. (2024). *The Ethics of Educational Technology*. Routledge.

Senge, P., ... (2024). *Schools That Learn: A Fifth Discipline Fieldbook for Educators, Parents, and Everyone Who Cares About Education* (Updated and revised ed.). Crown Business.

Senge, P. M. (2020). *The Fifth Discipline: The Art and Practice of the Learning Organization* (Revised and updated ed.). Currency.

Senge, P. M., & Schein, E. H. (2023). *Organizational Learning and Leadership for the Digital Age*. MIT Press.

Siemens, G. (2021). Learning analytics and educational data mining: Towards communication and collaboration. *LAK '21: Proceedings of the 11th International Conference on Learning Analytics and Knowledge*.

Siemens, G., & Baker, R. S. (2023). *Learning Analytics Handbook*. Society for Learning Analytics Research.

Siemens, G., & Downes, S. (2023). *Connectivism: A Learning Theory for the Digital Age* (2nd ed.). Athabasca University Press.

Siemens, G., & Long, P. (2024). Penetrating the fog: Analytics in learning and education. *EDUCAUSE Review*.

Spillane, J. P., & Diamond, J. B. (2023). *Distributed Leadership in Practice* (2nd ed.). Teachers College Press.

Turkle, S. (2023). *Reclaiming Conversation: The Power of Talk in a Digital Age* (2nd ed.). Penguin Books.

UNESCO. (2023). *Global Education Monitoring Report 2023*. UNESCO.

UNESCO. (2024). *Global Report on Digital Skills Gap*. UNESCO.

Van Dijk, J. A. (2023). *The Digital Divide* (2nd ed.). Polity.

Van Dijk, J. A. (2024). *The Network Society* (5th ed.).

Voogt, J., & Knezek, G. (2022). *International Handbook of Information Technology in Primary and Secondary Education* (2nd ed.). Springer.

Vuorikari, R.. (2020). eTwinning in the time of COVID-19: Agents of change in European schools. *European Journal of Education*, 55(4), 572–587.

Warschauer, M. (2021). *Technology and Social Inclusion: Rethinking the Digital Divide* (2nd ed.). MIT Press.

Warschauer, M. (2022). *Learning in the Cloud: How (and Why) to Transform Schools with Digital Media*. Teachers College Press.

Wenger, E., & Traynor, B. (2023). *Learning to Make a Difference: Value Creation in Social Learning Spaces*. Cambridge University Press.

Wiley, D., & Hilton, J. L.III. (2024). *Open Educational Resources: Foundations and Futures*. EdTech Books.

Williamson, B. (2022). *Big Data in Education: The Digital Future of Learning Policy and Practice*. SAGE Publications.

Williamson, B. (2023). *Datafication of Education*. Routledge.

Williamson, B. (2024). *Learning Analytics Futures*. Routledge.

Williamson, B., Eynon, R., & Potter, J. (2020). Pandemic politics, pedagogies, and practices: Digital technologies and distance education during the coronavirus emergency. *Learning, Media and Technology*, 45(2), 107–114. DOI: 10.1080/17439884.2020.1761641

Williamson, B., & Macfadyen, L. P. (2023). *Critical Perspectives on Learning Analytics*. Routledge.

World Economic Forum. (2024). *The Future of Jobs Report 2024*. World Economic Forum.

Zawacki-Richter, O., Marín, V. I., Bond, M., & Gouverneur, F. (2019). Systematic review of research on artificial intelligence applications in higher education – where are the educators? *International Journal of Educational Technology in Higher Education*, 16(1), 39. DOI: 10.1186/s41239-019-0171-0

Zhao, Y. (2021). *World Class Learners: Educating Creative and Entrepreneurial Students*. Corwin.

Zhao, Y. (2023). *Reach for Greatness: Personalizable Education for All Children*. Corwin.

Zhao, Y. (2024). *What Works May Hurt: Side Effects in Education*. Teachers College Press.

Zhao, Y., & Lei, J. (2023). *Teaching for innovation fatigue: Understanding and addressing burnout in educational technology integration*. Teachers College Press.

Zhao, Y., & Watterston, J. (2024). *Making Schools Work: A Vision for Innovation in Education*. Routledge.

Chapter 3

Digital Communication in Human Capital Formation

José Enrique Trejo
Instituto Politécnico Nacional, Mexico

ABSTRACT

This chapter has generated a series of compilations of ideas related to digital communication and the formation of human capital in contemporary societies, including the new challenges faced by the individual with the emergence of Artificial Intelligence applied in society and the impact that concerns the classification of truthful information in professionalization. Not making a criticism, but presenting a series of concepts to motivate the reader to generate their own criteria towards the new innovation trends of 2030. The importance of education facing the responsibility of granting the transmission of quality knowledge and accompanied by moral-ethical practices, are a series of topics that the global contexts take up in order to meet the new needs, which have growth initiative in the training of specialists and individuals who select the staff that will open solid paths in the collaborative work at the institutional level, giving an opportunity to new generations of graduates to take advantage and apply the knowledge.

A bibliographic review of authors that includes descriptive sections of the trends in research, and of public opinion in pages that are commonly accessible, just to find possible contrasts of the theories, thus. Including communication as a classic practice but revealing that it maintains an ease of adaptation in the different ways that are mentioned below, and describing the paths that are relevant in the hierarchical functionality in the structures of work teams, understanding formal and informal communication for optimal management of productivity. Culturally, the media is only linked in written and television media, but it is a reality that we are always in contact with it, from personal to professional relationships, just in order to solve problems.

DOI: 10.4018/979-8-3693-7086-5.ch003

FROM COMMUNICATION TO OPERABILITY

The changes in the organizational systems during the evolution of the human being, have been the product of innumerable conceptions or interpretations of the relationship of the individual with the environment, so that this phenomenon is able to be functional from the basic origins of these social connections for the operation of society is relevant to mention the importance of communication in everyday life from the understanding of classical theories to those that in practice are in a process of change in real time.

Why is communication an important part of human life? Generally, this aspect is detailed with the description of the functionality of the message, but, it is not very common to take up the need to express it. Since ancient times, when human beings face a hostile world which presents daily life as a survival challenge, they are forced to interact with groups to address the problems that are in constant motion, thus accompanying the creation of strategies and techniques that will prevail for generations, just alluding to the empirical transmission of knowledge.

Communication is usually so complex that depending on the human perception together with the geographic location, it triggers an infinity of forms, pictograms and figures to generate a message, thus proving the basis or beginnings of different types of languages, writings and forms of expression, which use a physical medium so that they can be reproduced and eventually codified. Acceptance by a community makes it evolve into a system of codes that represent a society that, with the passage of time, is part of the culture that describes a place or group of people.

As soon as language, writing and the medium of dissemination are accepted, changes in styles of expression become commonplace; this suggests the level of mastery of the base message so that it can be modified. Establishing a clear and concise message is important to begin to solve the new challenges of contemporary society; however, these skills are currently acquired in such early stages of basic schooling that they are only refined over time.

The challenges in the contemporary age do not necessarily describe a more complex difficulty than in the prehistoric stages of society's history. The difference lies in the accumulation of empirical knowledge in order to address needs more quickly. A community arises from a regional, state, and countrywide community; however, institutions also function in a mini ecosystem, which sets goals, coexistence and operational norms, not far from our collaborative role in daily life.

The formation of human capital, a way to make responsible the first stages of the acquisition of knowledge that has already been obtained from empirical and scientific knowledge, is a fundamental part to reinforce the operational systems of institutions and companies at a global level, not only to meet the needs derived from the economic interest, but also the cultural and collaborative growth as the development of the human being trying to improve the environment and its relationship with others.

The new digital era has revolutionized the world of communication during its evolution since the 1980s, this phenomenon has found a way to accelerate the processes of elaboration and manufacture of products, including services to contain the messages necessary to complete the receiver/emitter cycle, the creation of such products also contemplate the training of specialized human beings to attend tasks from the pre-university and professional stages, all with the intention that quality prevails in the different productive branches of society.

The Azienda Comunale Elettricità e Acque (2018)or internationally known Electricity and Water Municipal Utility with its headquarters in Rome, Italy, is an organization specialized in the consolidation of multi-operational networks in the fields of energy, productivity and government development. It raises the importance of leadership in the axis of acquiring new talents in order to place them in the points that need to be addressed in the short and long term, so three levels of attention are proposed, in which the community indirectly is a participant in the whole global process.

The first is called the execution level, in which the organizational chart put in the head of the project the action of leader and second the action of the members, under a project management style of which is proposed from the first level is when the actions will begin to emerge in stage, the main derives from the idea and then the future execution that gives the name of the overall strategy. Each understands its participatory nature, the leader in decision making under the actions of the members who fulfill the function of attending to common tasks.

The second level in the communication cycle involves the coordination of a training section. The first described by the organization is the stage of promoting the necessary skills that need to be integrated into the values, objectives and means of publication. The promoters function as a first filter to reach new talents, however, the human capital development managers are the ones who lay the foundations of the so-called "skills", and who in the future will develop the necessary psychometric, profiling, and interviewing parameters.

Within the same stage, the relevance of the trainer is mentioned once the individuals capable of performing the tasks required by the company have been selected. In this area, the participation of the promoters is not necessary and, indirectly, the developers of human capital will be aware of the evolution of those trained, once the new elements are integrated, it is not necessarily synonymous that they should not be evaluated during their stay in the company, which originates the importance of internal or external audits.

Finally, there is a circle where all the actors must have a direct communication system and it is called "the vision", in this step the changes and confrontations with the new challenges posed by modernity are proposed, including this initiative towards the future, taking into account the human, technical and monetary capital. The strategic blackboard is an evaluation system where everyone participates in order to decipher the functional departments and propose institutional modifications.

Figure 1. Execution model (Azienda Comunale Elettricità e Acque, 2018)

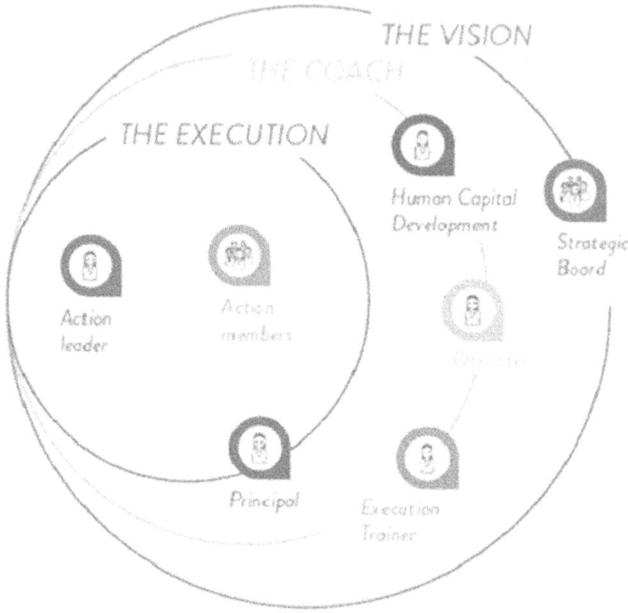

The execution of the model proposed by ACECA, is a design that is considered functional in its context, and that is applied in similar situations, but it is necessary to emphasize that not every organization must follow the same steps in order to obtain the necessary personnel to perform the daily activities.

Avalos (2016) describes the importance of internal communication, very different from the external contact in the example described above but agreeing that everything starts from a theoretical model that is previously modified and has its own objectives. The emission of the message is important because from there originates the meaning of what is being described, adding that the reception is an even more complex situation because external factors will be part of the final result of the intention.

In organizational communication, there are three models that describe how communication works within systems that represent institutions, companies, teams where human groups must coordinate to achieve objectives. These three models that represent the communication process are called: linear, interaction (interactional) and transactional. The process of how communication occurs is represented in the following theoretical models. It should be noted that these models describe the communication process and its elements, but do not define what communication is or where it occurs.

The first model described by the author is the linear model, traditionally known as unidirectional in the classical theories of communication, it originates from the need of the human being to deliver a message without the capacity of the receiver to reply, in its execution the ideas can be basic or complex depending on the physical, semantic, and psychological state of the originator. In its application it is not the best option in organizational systems as it is very limited and lacks context.

A second model is the interactional one in which the receiver is already an active part of the conversation, it behaves as two participants, and the answers are always contemplated as a feedback method with the purpose of confirming if the sender's intention is the original one from the output. Elements of context and points of specialization are added, as can be seen the process becomes more complex and determines a more focused intention of the message. All are senders and all are receivers.

Therefore, the last one proposed is the transactional model that works in a similar way as the interactional one, except that the number of participants is greater than two and the messages flow in different directions with the intention of having multiple feedbacks. Thus, different communication channels are used, for example: written, digital, verbal, acoustic broadcast, among others. The number of participants, depending on the specialty, will be able to share experiences and solutions to the problems raised in real time.

Figure 2. Models of the communication process (Avalos, 2016)

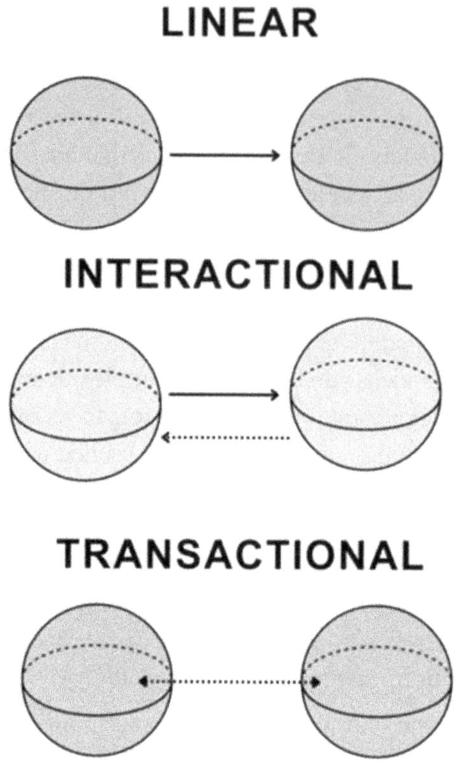

How are the communication models applicable to a real organizational problem? It is not difficult to address a simple situation in which help is required from the various channels proposed by the author, starting with the usual problem in a common organizational chart between the directorates and sub-directorates, which implies a conflict with the personnel in charge of the sub-bosses when they do not obtain the desired results from the higher management, and in which the participation of other areas is not accepted in order to find the solution. A linear and closed communication system is detected.

Detecting communication problems is relatively easy, experience will be a factor that will help to raise awareness when attention is needed in a certain productive area, however, not everyone has the ability to develop this skill to the maximum, generally experts in organizational communication are responsible for developing internal strategies capable of positioning the human capital and that together collaborate in harmony.

The communicative language and the formation of human capital coexist with a series of factors that are classifiable, which entails the external and internal, the former refers to all the things that are of interest to the organization to achieve the objective and determines human relations with other institutions, therefore, have a type of language depending on the design of the message and matters the hierarchy of the apostille, formality plays a key role even to determine the status and personality of the organization.

External communication is something that is commonly learned empirically, trial and error, so it is normal to experience it from even childhood, when cultural values are instilled to learn to respect the hierarchy of the relative older than us and watching for two possible ways, the look that society has on us and also, the position of the person to whom the message is addressed. Something very different from what concerns the internal, which can be more complex when making an introspection and own evaluation to be able to determine the identity, and that has for objective to analyze the following phenomena.

Sordo (2023) has compiled a series of effects that are produced or are intuited by the lack of communication in a contemporary organization, in which different actors are reflected who in practice are pursuing the same objective and all derived from the selection of human capital. In principle, such problems should not occur when a selection filter has already been carried out on the specialists, but it is alluded to emphasize that sometimes the theoretical processes do not behave in the same way when they are already part of a social environment, where opinions, experiences and work styles converge.

The first point pointed out by the author is the beginning of work conflicts that are usually represented by discussions without common agreements, so that the psychological and personality factor are confronted overcoming the barriers of the common goal, when everyone is involved in it, it is expected that the work environment is hostile and there are negative attitudes to collaborative work. Sometimes the origin of the conflict comes from the upper management, directors and administrators; it is at that moment where attention should be paid to training methods in human rights and human perspective.

A second sign is the lack of commitment in the communication systems, sometimes produced by not respecting the hierarchical channels or ignoring the messages designated to attend a specific area, and even not having the necessary discretion in matters classified by the organization. It is necessary to instill values of trust to prevent employees from feeling outside the company and to determine their identity as soon as possible, the result of which will be reflected in productivity.

Returning to the identity of the individual, if this is not formed in the time designated for it, there will be a stage of demotivation, which is the third section mentioned by the author. This step is considered the first step to attract potentially serious problems at the operational level, the lack of impetus and goals is a topic that involves psychology, and that raises many questions about whether the results are really being obtained or if it is really worth working for the organization.

The organization's responsibilities are housed from the introduction of the entity's principles. During the human capital assessment stage, it is important to clarify internal and external business processes, which are very different from communication. The fourth sign of poor communication indicates that ignoring them increases the likelihood of direct conflict and a lack of understanding of the designation of responsibilities. Also, this includes the company's operating margins and action manuals. Not knowing the processes is basically never having understood the institution as an equivalent to working with a blindfold on.

In a fifth point, mention is made of the decrease in productivity. Linked to the lack of communication, no commitment and demotivation, these results begin to denote the deficiency of teamwork, so that not only an objective is not achieved, but future goals that have no chance of being achieved are already taken into account due to a series of aspects originated in the leader's decisions. Decreasing productivity is the index of making radical changes in the organizational charts, perhaps starting from the analysis of the type of leadership or subordinations in their work style.

The difficulties in the flow of information are obvious, the communication channels are totally broken and there is a tendency to design new ones with the rotation of personnel, being an indicator of having to carry out external evaluations to be able to analyze the capacities of the operative personnel, if not, there is the option of the strategic change of work by teams or called changes of templates. If the above two points are ignored, a serious consequence is that the people being served will begin to notice the flaws in the organizational system.

As it can be observed, there are different factors that act and depend on the phenomenon of communication, it is advocated on the importance of the formation of human capital conscious of developing such capacities at present, taking up the technological channels that are now part of the daily life of the human being and that simplify the transmission of messages, but that do not solve all the problems, it is a matter of initiative and collective work in the new perception of society.

Organizations can host different disciplines, and collaborate with information and communication technologies, traditionally, the digital era is linked to careers that use their own tools for the design of audiovisual materials or that converge in branches of engineering, however, no one is exempt from having to operate under the use of the same and can be reflected in a paper from the University of Medical Sciences Cienfuegos of Cuba, Molina et al., (2015) came to the conclusion of the operational margin of the tools.

The usefulness of technology depends on who develops, manages and controls it and what interests it serves. It is the way it is used that determines the consequences on the social and individual level, forms that are in turn culturally determined, since they depend on how the world is conceived, human relations, production relations, values and assumptions that guide and regulate the activity.

Regulating the activity of the media is a practice that originates in political regulations, organizational standards and learning that during the process of professional training, universities are increasingly opting to make learning cycles based on information technologies, but accessibility will be a challenge as long as there is no democratization of hardware with the high costs that represent the equipment in some regions of the world due to excessive import and export costs.

University education faces new challenges as the decades go by, the complexity of attending to the entire educational offer is almost impossible to solve one hundred percent in real time, taking into account professionalization as one of the fundamental aspects in the generation of human capital and that in erroneously only the culture of generational change is based, perhaps, by way of excusing the lack of resources that can be reached in the future working stages of the graduates. It is not only to mention the deficiencies, but to address them and apply real practices that in the future will provide the qualities that exploit the tools of communication.

Orozco et al., (2019) describes university education as a solid basis for conceiving generational change, and how national problems are addressed first in order to face the opening with the phenomenon of globalization, together with ethical values and good practices. Emphasizing that the educational models are considered in designs with an international focus and thus maintaining a spirit of taking up the experiences of other regions, being applicable in specific contexts.

The social responsibility of universities has been to promote educational models that are centered on Ethics as the guiding axis of professional training and the generation of good citizens. That is why the new educational models seek to resolve the dilemma between training professionals with a nationalistic approach or professionals who think globally but are able to address local problems.

Addressing basic problems coincides with the precept of the formation of human capital, for this we seek the links of collaborative individuals and find the ideal channels of communication, train new generations with ethical and moral principles will help to find stability, not only in organizations and institutions, but also in the society in which they develop. If we analyze the responsibility of universities from this point of view, we find that education is the universal axis of social construction and it is their obligation to offer quality education, accessible and with a variable offer in the different fields in order to achieve the proposed objectives.

Whether in universities, in the media or even in political discourse, the concept was used abusively and irresponsibly, making citizens believe that by participating in this process we would one day enter the first world; that we would have the same capabilities to compete with the best in the world. Students were told in the classrooms that in the "global world" they would have to compete against North Americans, Europeans or Japanese; as if all citizens of the world and of all nationalities were going to compete in the same labor market.

A second quote from the authors invites reflection and advocates that operating systems of any kind are already influenced by the effects of accelerated globalization with the implementation of digital technology, countries with higher rates of development are those that took advantage of the implementation in their institutions, however, it invites contexts such as Latin America to consider training to maintain the spirit of innovation and finding alternative solutions in the training of human capital.

Training is a complex process for the productive activity, when the stage is not taken with reality in the need, it is counterproductive and, instead of benefiting the development, it would be navigating without own course, without morality and identity. Today's manager establishes the attitude of those who follow him, establishes trust and elaborates strategies that procure human values with the needs, all without forgetting the objectives that are set, for this it is necessary to surround himself with personnel that have the same natural and not forced principles.

The competitiveness of the graduates of the educational centers have the theoretical knowledge to face the problems of the XXI century, the approaches derived from technology call to maintain the culture of updating and that the individual is aware of differentiating when a communication channel is used in leisure spaces and at what times it is applicable to generate campaigns to promote skills, solve problems and strengthen internal-external collaboration.

One of the models proposed for the generation of knowledge that involves communication as the basis of its proposal is constructivism, Maldonado, (2007) Maldonado (2007) is in charge of linking this effect with the acquisition of new ideas in important stages and that for the present text are applicable to the university level, inferring that teaching practices have a direct and indirect responsibility, perhaps the study plans are ideal, but if at the moment of transferring knowledge to the student it is only based on repetition it will be something that will affect in the future to develop professionally.

These structures are responsible for acquiring new information through two basic processes: assimilation and accommodation. This suggests that learning does not consist in memorizing information but in the assimilation or incorporation of information into schemas that have information previously organized into patterns, as well as cognitive functions that adjust or accommodate new and previously acquired information.

Collaborative work in constructivist practices has visions that depend on the type of leadership applied; the triggering question is: What is being built, for whom is it being built, and for what purpose? The morality of the actions of the head of the group will find the answers and, based on ethics, will make others part of the gain, whether in the areas of experience, technical or economic knowledge. Institutional progress is not exempt from personal interest and the manifestation of nonconformities within the work groups, it is alluded to understand the nature of the collectivity as a society as it is commonly known.

The work of institutional communication has benefits that are subdivided into different specialized areas, it is inferred that being able to consolidate that part at the local level will naturally make that other departments can access greater productivity and that issues such as accessibility have a reliable environment in the development of their activities. Riofrio, (2018) describes the advantages.

These guidelines are essential for organizations to keep abreast of trends and innovation in products and services. It is important to mention that communication is central to the organizational culture and climate, factors of notable influence in strengthening the values and beliefs of both internal and external audiences who create, promote and maintain the image of a company or institution. The problem lies in the fact that several institutions have not believed it pertinent to channel communication and strengthen it with departments or professionals destined to manage it in a strategic manner.

Knowing the environments in which the institution develops will allow you to compare its context and apply new knowledge, accompanied by trends in the development of its specialization. The new information channels that are called informal, also play a clear role in the transformation of the identity that is applicable in external communication, can be glimpsed with the new companies in how they adapt their content to have a closer approach with the new generations.

The new practices of young graduates is to base most of their time in perfecting the use of digital tools, be in contact with new content and even create them for fun, it is a new trend in the formation of human capital, capture new talent and take advantage of the nature of learning of new generations and create new proposals in communication.

Perspectives of Communicative Practice in Training.

Once the basic outlines of communication in the training of future professionals have been outlined, it is important to address the challenges that we all face every day with technological progress, it is not an assumption to think that Artificial Intelligence is already solving some problems in the acquisition of knowledge, but at the same time complicating the classic practices in the verification of information, and of course, analyze how companies that offer such services give us these tools with or without ethical purposes, it all depends on the vision of the user.

In the second decade of the 21st century, the effects of new technologies and the internet of things are beginning to be noticed, the implementation of Artificial Intelligence has created a series of unsafe environments that challenge the morality of users, plagiarism and the superficial review of sources have come to light worldwide with executives of important organizations in governments and institutions. Communication is such a complex issue that humans are exposed to develop skills to interact with technology and not make the mistakes that are being unveiled.

The challenges in the formation of human capital begin with morality and ethics, finding a balance before being able to apply any technology to the methodologies and work techniques, the teacher's responsibility is to raise awareness so that students learn to differentiate between right and wrong. Once these bases are established, find the link with the area of professional specialization and delimit the legal margins that govern good practices, annexing those that are internal to the institution.

A second plane of interaction is to understand the applicable nature of internal communication, to establish the hierarchy and directionality described in the first chapter, and, little by little, to link operational responsibilities with professional ethics. The elements that are already collaborating will find a solution in the methods of updating or training of personnel, so that they can be in force with the new generations and reinforce the work environment. To realize the cycle, it is invited to first develop communication in the transmission of knowledge and make the potential of the interested party applicable to the institutional values with a motive to innovate. Yang et al., (2016) makes a brief mention of the objectives to be pursued with such a phenomenon.

However, those who say so sometimes overlook the fact that the construction of knowledge as a process that allows the subject to capture the properties or characteristics of the object, read data, information that are transformed into an image or representation, does not occur in individual isolation. It is through the act of human and social interaction where it finds its synthesis and possibility of objectifying the active capacity of a subject that can orient itself towards the object, perceive it, experience it, value it, reason it, manipulate it, imagine it and represent it, and in this way learn it and develop the skills to assume it, know how to do things with it and transform it.

Finding the benefits of communication training will make the human's creative sense develop, and on their own, they will start to build new paths in the way of expressing an idea that has as a format different options, even, raising problems and easy to observe solutions will be a great addition to the work system, speeding up the processes and nurturing confidence in the collaborators. As already mentioned, the ethical values accompanied by the structure will make the work environment more humane and understanding of the needs of the collaborative staff.

Humanism is one of the trends at a global level, creating a place in the agenda of the new global regulations or at least in western societies that belong to international organizations, and adapting increasingly comfortable spaces for communication sciences, being inclusive with the new generations and with the objective that everyone has a voice in society in a dignified manner. However, a contrary position exists in terms that the power of the media is a very big responsibility, the individual who is endowed with directing internal communication is susceptible to dominate what involves the system and with personal intentions that are not part of the general objectives of the community. Tapia, (n.d.) integrates moral responsibilities and complements the ideal position of the human being.

This means moving away from the pride of wanting to dominate nature. Of wanting to make use of it and exhaust it for the benefit of a single species, as if that were possible without exhausting itself. Without ending its own existence. And this secular humanism will be the most powerful dike against the fundamentalist waves that are already hitting hard. It will also become a constant contribution in the search for new value-based answers that will restore human beings' confidence. It will give him hope and make him think that happiness is possible, and to dream of it, a just dream.

Happiness as an indication of what are considered good practices is not a concept that only applies to the individual who is not related to the collective, it also includes work teams with constant results, a happy society is productive and as long as the rights studied in the capital formation stage are respected, everything will go well. Time will be the most important challenge to conceive modifications that encourage the construction of new ways in the internal regulation, and why not? Also the national and internal regulation of the university formation centers.

Problem solving is not the only method for proposing new routes, questioning the nature of the work and criticism will accompany complementing that identity that has been sought, avoiding ego-centric circles and functioning interdisciplinary groups, all being specialists in one area and with the ability to respond, even if it is not their initial position designated in company with the new technologies of the digital age.

Mental health and Communication in Human Capital Formation

Once the possible problems that the lack of communication originates have been raised, the individual, as a thinking being, also has a series of impacts that have repercussions on his formation process, including mental health and under what conditions technology is a relevant part of it. The use of applications in the digital era has modified the social behaviors of human beings and the relationships they form in their daily lives. If analyzed from the classic interactions between two people without any work relationship, negative and positive behavioral factors are identified, and if these resources are applied in the world of work, they become more complex to classify.

In the professional field, personal interests tend to be a barrier in modern communication, inferring political, economic and growth aspects, which may or may not be compatible with the other members of the group at an operational level and which create an impact on the emotional stability of others. It is alluded to that the future professional has the ability to take care of his mental health when he joins the labor field and always, keeping informed of what his rights are, there are plenty of data and information available on the regulations at work at national and international level, and that with the access of the new digital era.

Mingote & Núñez (2011)(2011), mention the high levels of emotional destabilization and suffering that can be found in any work environment, which must be addressed firstly by the worker, and secondly, by the help of the work centers for which he/she operates. With a prevalence of 32.6%, it is indicated that one third of the people will suffer some disorder at a global level and that only a small portion of them have the resources to be able to face it.

There are numerous and important reasons why we should pay attention to mental health problems at work. The increase in their frequency, the effects on the health of workers, as well as the interaction with the work organization, increasing absenteeism with a significant cost both human and economic. The total costs of an illness include not only direct and indirect costs, but also the so-called intangible costs, which include the suffering experienced by the patient and his or her family. The potential lost by people with a given disorder, often marginalized from economic, cultural and social life, cannot be quantified in economic terms but constitutes an unacceptable cost, given the preventive and therapeutic possibilities currently available.

The phenomenon involves different actors, from the social and organizational interaction of the institution, to the personal aspects of the employee. Without even retaking the relationship with digital communication, the situation tends to be described in an ephemeral way, because it is understood that this has always existed without the need to use technologies, but one thing is certain, if it is retaken from the interaction of social networks and learning resources, the situation will only become more complicated if you do not have the ability to understand the environment, just as in the phenomenon of the COVID-19 pandemic, which generated millions of job losses globally. The lack of training in the communicative culture in the past generations of graduates, hindered the ability to adapt in the working life of transmission category channels such as Zoom, Microsoft Teams and Google

Meet, making it impossible for companies to operate remotely and demonstrating certain skills of workers, students and managers.

Companies like Google, have solved the ways of human training for their workers, creating a training platform in different disciplines, being accessible to all public and part of the Google For Education program. The difference is that workers will take the skills they need to strengthen, such as communication, digital, entrepreneurial business, among others. The possibility that the content is in MOOC formats, helps to avoid the need for presence and does not affect the personal activities of the human being, and thus obtaining more comprehensive environments in mental health.

Carrazana (2002)Carrazana (2002), relates mental health with the social development of the individual and the ailments that affect the productive capacity, companies that tend to work in teams have the responsibility to integrate the interests of the personnel to ensure the implementation of common objectives, the reaching of agreements and avoid confrontations, communication will be the ideal channel in the formation of competencies to create harmony.

In this sense, mental health has to do with everyone's daily life, it refers to the way in which everyone relates to general activities in the community; it comprises the way in which everyone harmonizes their desires, wishes, abilities, ideals, feelings and moral values with the requirements to cope with the demands of life. Mental health depends on: how one feels about oneself, how one feels about other people, and how one responds to the demands of life.

The author suggests that human beings tend to develop levels of empathy and sympathy for the people with whom they develop in everyday life, including work and personal scenarios, so a balance is sought between introspection of one's own mental health to find solutions to daily problems in order to focus on short and long term goals. The formation of the conscience begins from the first stages of life and that it is possible to attend the conception of the new generations in a globalized world. The mental problems of a generation are not the same as those of today.

To close this section, we declare the intention of associating in future sociological studies communication as the axis of the worker's mental health, and that a failure in this may mean the appearance of problems in the future at a personal, social and operational level in the new institutions that are governed by an increasingly competitive and strict market. It is invited to prioritize research work that relates health with the formation of human capital, and the influences that have the technologies that impact directly in a positive and negative way, in order to ensure and protect the rights of the worker.

CONCLUSION

Human capital is one of the factors that institutes society from the historical and anthropological context, the way in which its participation is conceived to generate new possibilities of knowledge application are completely linked to the context in which it develops and therefore interferes with the tools that it designs to address the problems it faces for the purpose of personal or individual growth.

Finding the balance between moral and ethical practices, define the identity of the group and make reject or accept the ideals, not all seek to agree, being a natural cycle, being a supporter is to have initiative that does not oppose change and despite the effects are positive or negative, allude to the democratic teachings that are sought in the collective.

The new challenges faced by education increasingly involve a series of sub-themes that allude to the complex, modern agendas seek to reinforce trends on accessibility, development and humanism, but are policies that address these problems really being generated without any personal or economic interest? Democracy does not only involve issues of participation, as it is colloquially known in the election of a manager or representative, but also acquires properties in the environments of resource accessibility and affordability in the same opportunities.

To participate is also to be part of a society with the same possibilities of growth; however, the first stages of the conformation of collaborative work begin with the formation of specialties in the work and academic environment. Technological capital is not a replacement tool, or not until at least a response time superior to that of human brain capacity is designed. It happens that what helps the individual not to be surpassed by machines is logical and emotional reasoning.

It is inferred that the use of digital environments have the ability to enhance human work, and thus cut operational time problems, not necessarily wearing out the individual, but accelerating those processes that were previously classified in impossible tasks or that took more effort invested, among these complex systems communication and its multiple channels described above. Valuing the training of adequate personnel includes personalities that know how to select new elements in their institutions and that provide the opportunity for professional growth.

It is sought that students who have factors in their favor to specialize do so in a critical, honest and moral way, defining the values that will be of help in such changing times towards the trends of 2030, a decade that will have the benefits of the democratization of communication and that will undoubtedly be a new niche of innovation in digital postmodernism. The challenge will be to learn to classify sources so that the message designs are with reality and not to link disinformation, it is necessary to know how to use the lines of communication safely, and always watching over the human practice of knowledge transmission in the formation of human capital.

REFERENCES

Avalos, C. (2016). *How does communication work?* Vivir Es Aprender.

Azienda Comunale Elettricità e Acque. (2018). Human capital development and communications. *Human Capital Development and Communications.*http://sostenibilita2018.gruppo.acea.it/en/relation-whit-stakeholders/personnel/human-capital-development-and-communications

Carrazana, V. (2002). The concept of mental health in humanistic-existential psychology. *AJAYU Órgano de Difusión Del Departamento de Psicología*, 1, 19.

Maldonado, M. (2007). Collaborative work in the university classroom. *Laurus Revista de Educación*, 13, 263–278.

Mingote, C., & Núñez, C. (2011). Importance of mental health in labour health management: A shared liability. *Medicina y Seguridad del Trabajo*, 57, 24.

Molina, M., Lian, R., Garcés, R., Rojas, Y., Dulzaides, M., & Selín, M. (2015). The Communication Process Mediated by Information Technologies. Advantages and Disadvantages in Various Spheres of Social Life. *University of Medical Sciences*, 13. http://scielo.sld.cu/pdf/ms/v13n4/ms04413.pdf. http://scielo.sld.cu/pdf/ms/v13n4/ms04413.pdf

Orozco, J., Nuñes, P., & Orozco, M. (2019). The challenges of Mexico's higher education in the 21st century. *InterSedes*, 20, 11. https://www.scielo.sa.cr/scielo.php?script=sci_arttext&pid=S2215-24582019000100076

Riofrio, E. (2018). Communication in institutional development. *Universidad Técnica Particular de Loja*, 1.

Sordo, I. (2023). *8 signs of poor communication in your company and how to reverse them*. Hubspot.

Tapia, W. (n.d.). Media and humanism. *Universidad La República*, 1. https://periodismo.uchile.cl/asepecs/ponencias/3pwturep.htm

Yang, Y., Saladrigas, H., & Torres, D. (2016). The process of the communication in the step of knowledge. A theoretic analysis of your behavior as from two typical models. *University of Havana, 8.*

Chapter 4
Digital Leadership in Organizations for Digital Transformation

Martin Sposato
https://orcid.org/0000-0001-9260-9961
Zayed University, UAE

ABSTRACT

This chapter explores digital leadership in the context of organizational digital transformation. It examines the evolving role of leaders in the digital age, highlighting core competencies such as visionary thinking, data-driven decision-making, and fostering innovation. The chapter discusses strategies for developing digital leadership capabilities, theoretical implications of digital leadership, and ethical considerations in the digital realm. It also addresses practical implications, including improved innovation, employee engagement, and organizational agility. The chapter concludes by identifying future research avenues, emphasizing the need for longitudinal studies, industry-specific research, and exploration of ethical dimensions in digital leadership. Throughout, it underscores the critical role of digital leadership in navigating technological change and driving organizational success.

INTRODUCTION

In the rapidly evolving landscape of the 21st century, challenges and opportunities presented by digital transformation are being grappled with by organizations across all sectors. This profound shift in the way businesses are operated, communications are conducted, and value is delivered to customers has been determined to be a critical factor in organizational success and longevity (Vial, 2019). Digital transformation is

DOI: 10.4018/979-8-3693-7086-5.ch004

encompassed not only by the adoption of new technologies but also by the reimagining of business processes, customer experiences, and organizational cultures by which the potential of digital innovations can be fully leveraged (Fitzgerald et al., 2014). As this complex terrain is being navigated by organizations, the role of leadership has been made increasingly pivotal. Traditional leadership approaches, while still valued, are often found to be insufficient when the unique challenges posed by digital disruption and the pace of technological change are addressed (Cortellazzo et al., 2019). By this development, the concept of digital leadership has been given rise to, which is characterized as a multifaceted approach by which technological literacy, strategic vision, and the ability to drive organizational change in a digital context are combined (El Sawy et al., 2016).

The evolving landscape of digital leadership in organizations undergoing digital transformation is explored in this chapter. The core competencies required of digital leaders will be examined, strategies for developing these capabilities will be investigated, and the theoretical underpinnings by which effective digital leadership practices are informed will be analyzed. Additionally, the ethical considerations that are raised in the digital age will be delved into, and the practical implications of implementing digital leadership strategies will be discussed. Through a comprehensive analysis of digital leadership, readers will be equipped with the knowledge and insights by which the complexities of digital transformation can be successfully navigated. Furthermore, digital leadership in different global contexts will be expanded upon, as cultural factors by which leadership practices and digital adoption rates across regions are influenced must be recognized. As is noted by Sposato (2019) in his work on paternalistic leadership in China, effective leadership in global contexts must be informed by cultural nuances. The specifics of key digital technologies by which the leadership landscape is being shaped will also be explored, such as artificial intelligence, blockchain, and the Internet of Things. In this exploration, an analysis will be included of how business models and leadership practices across industries are being reshaped by these technologies.

The multifaceted dimensions of digital leadership in organizational transformation are systematically explored in this chapter. The evolving role of leaders in the digital age is first examined, after which core digital leadership competencies are analyzed, including visionary thinking, data-driven decision-making, and innovation fostering. Strategies for developing digital leadership capabilities through training programs, mentoring, and experiential learning are then delved into. Theoretical frameworks by which digital leadership practices are underpinned are examined, followed by an in-depth discussion of ethical considerations in the digital realm, including algorithmic bias, privacy concerns, and cybersecurity. The chapter is concluded with practical implications for organizations, and crucial areas for future research are identified.

Several significant contributions to the field of digital leadership and organizational transformation are made by this chapter. First, a novel synthesis of traditional leadership theories and emerging digital competencies is provided, by which a comprehensive framework for understanding leadership in the digital age is offered. Second, a critical gap in the literature is addressed by the integration of ethical considerations with practical leadership strategies, through which leaders are provided with actionable guidance for responsible digital transformation. Third, valuable insights for global organizations are offered through the chapter's analysis of cultural nuances in digital leadership, particularly as drawn from research on paternalistic leadership in different contexts. Finally, this chapter serves as both a theoretical foundation and practical guide for scholars and practitioners by whom digital leadership capabilities in their organizations are being advanced, achieved through the identification of specific areas for future research and the presentation of real-world applications.

The Evolving Role of Leaders in the Digital Age

The digital age has ushered in a new era of business, characterized by rapid technological advancements, shifting consumer expectations, and unprecedented levels of connectivity. This dynamic environment has presented significant challenges to traditional leadership styles and organizational structures (Kane et al., 2019). Leaders who once relied primarily on hierarchical decision-making processes and long-term strategic planning now find themselves navigating a landscape where agility, adaptability, and continuous innovation are paramount. Digital disruption has fundamentally altered the competitive landscape across industries, forcing organizations to rethink their business models and value propositions (Weill & Woerner, 2018). In this context, the role of leaders has evolved from that of strategic decision-makers to catalysts for organizational transformation. Digital leaders must not only possess a deep understanding of emerging technologies but also the ability to envision how these technologies can be leveraged to create value and drive competitive advantage (Schwarzmüller et al., 2018).

The shift towards digital leadership is characterized by several core competencies that distinguish it from traditional leadership approaches. First and foremost, digital leaders must exhibit visionary thinking and strategic planning for a digital future. This involves the ability to anticipate technological trends, identify potential disruptions, and chart a course that positions the organization for success in an increasingly digital world (Westerman et al., 2014). Digital leaders must be able to articulate a compelling vision of the organization's digital future and inspire their teams to work towards its realization. Fostering a culture of innovation and embracing change is another crucial aspect of digital leadership. In an environment where technological advancements can quickly render existing business models obsolete, organizations must cultivate a mindset of continuous innovation and adaptability (Candi et al., 2020). Digital leaders play a critical role in creating an organizational culture that encourages experimentation, tolerates calculated risks, and views failure as an opportunity for learning and growth.

Data-driven decision-making has become a hallmark of successful digital organizations, and digital leaders must be adept at leveraging technological tools to inform their strategic choices. This involves not only the ability to interpret complex data sets but also the capacity to translate data-driven insights into actionable strategies (McAfee & Brynjolfsson, 2012). Digital leaders must champion the use of analytics and data visualization tools throughout their organizations, fostering a culture of evidence-based decision-making at all levels. The fast-paced nature of digital transformation necessitates the development of agile and adaptable teams that are comfortable with continuous learning. Digital leaders must build and nurture teams that can quickly pivot in response to changing market conditions, technological advancements, or emerging customer needs (Holbeche, 2018). This requires a leadership approach that emphasizes flexibility, encourages skill development, and provides team members with the autonomy to make decisions and take ownership of their work.

Effective communication and collaboration across departments have become increasingly critical in the digital age. As organizations become more interconnected and interdependent, silos between departments can hinder innovation and impede the flow of information (Fitzgerald et al., 2014). Digital leaders must act as bridge-builders, facilitating cross-functional collaboration and ensuring that all parts of the organization are aligned in their digital transformation efforts. In the context of global leadership, digital leaders must be adept at navigating diverse cultural landscapes. Sposato (2021) highlights the importance of understanding cultural nuances in leadership practices, particularly in the context of paternalistic leadership in China. This underscores the need for digital leaders to adapt their approaches to different cultural contexts, ensuring that digital transformation initiatives are culturally sensitive and locally relevant.

Developing Digital Leadership Capabilities

As organizations recognize the importance of digital leadership in driving successful digital transformation, the development of these capabilities has become a strategic priority. Several strategies can be employed to foster digital leadership skills within organizations, ensuring that leaders at all levels are equipped to navigate the challenges of the digital age. Leadership training programs focused on digital literacy and technology adoption play a crucial role in developing digital leadership capabilities. These programs should go beyond basic technical skills to include strategic thinking about technology's role in business, understanding of emerging trends, and the ability to assess the potential impact of new technologies on organizational processes and customer experiences (Bonnet & Westerman, 2021). Such training programs can be delivered through a combination of formal coursework, hands-on workshops, and immersive experiences that expose leaders to cutting-edge technologies and digital business models.

Mentoring and coaching opportunities with experienced digital leaders can provide invaluable insights and guidance for those developing their digital leadership skills. By pairing emerging leaders with seasoned digital executives, organizations can facilitate the transfer of knowledge, best practices, and lessons learned from successful digital transformation initiatives (Petrucci & Rivera, 2018). These mentoring relationships can help bridge the gap between theoretical knowledge and practical application, providing aspiring digital leaders with real-world context and strategies for navigating complex digital challenges. Encouraging participation in conferences and workshops on digital transformation exposes leaders to a broader perspective on digital trends and best practices. These events provide opportunities for networking with peers, learning from industry experts, and gaining insights into how other organizations are approaching digital transformation (Kane et al., 2019). By actively participating in the wider digital transformation discourse, leaders can stay abreast of emerging technologies, innovative business models, and evolving customer expectations.

Creating a culture that values experimentation and risk-taking is essential for developing digital leadership capabilities throughout the organization. Digital leaders must model a mindset of continuous learning and adaptation, encouraging their teams to explore new ideas and approaches without fear of failure (Candi et al., 2020). This involves establishing safe spaces for experimentation, providing resources for innovation projects, and recognizing and rewarding creative problem-solving efforts. Moreover, organizations should consider the role of human resource management (HRM) strategies in developing digital leadership capabilities. Garcia-Carbonell et al. (2014) highlight the importance of aligning HRM practices with organizational strategy to enhance performance. In the context of digital leadership, this might involve designing recruitment, selection, and development processes that specifically target and nurture digital leadership competencies.

As digital technologies continue to evolve, the development of digital leadership capabilities must also adapt. ElSayary (2024) emphasizes the importance of integrating generative AI in active learning environments to enhance metacognition and technological skills. This approach can be applied to leadership development programs, creating more dynamic and personalized learning experiences for aspiring digital leaders. Furthermore, Sposato (2024) discusses the emerging trends in leadership training and development in the age of artificial intelligence. He highlights the potential of AI-powered tools to provide personalized leadership development experiences, real-time feedback, and data-driven insights into leadership performance. Organizations should consider incorporating these advanced technologies into their digital leadership development strategies to stay ahead of the curve.

Leadership Theories and Digital Transformation

The unique challenges posed by digital transformation have prompted a reexamination of traditional leadership theories and their applicability in the digital age. While no single leadership theory fully encompasses the complexities of digital leadership, several established frameworks offer valuable insights that can inform and shape effective digital leadership practices. Transformational leadership, with its emphasis on inspiring and motivating followers to embrace change, aligns well with the demands of digital transformation (Bass & Riggio, 2006). Digital leaders must articulate a compelling vision of the organization's digital future and inspire their teams to work towards its realization. By appealing to higher ideals and fostering a sense of shared purpose, transformational leaders can galvanize their organizations to overcome the challenges associated with digital disruption and embrace new ways of working (Cortellazzo et al., 2019). Servant leadership, which prioritizes the needs and well-being of employees, offers a valuable perspective for digital leaders navigating the human aspects of digital transformation. As organizations undergo significant changes, employees may experience uncertainty, stress, and resistance. Servant leaders focus on empowering their teams, providing support, and creating an environment where individuals can thrive amidst change (Eva et al., 2019). This approach can help build trust and commitment among employees, essential factors in successful digital transformation initiatives.

Participative leadership, characterized by involving employees in decision-making processes, can be particularly effective in the context of digital transformation. Given the complexity and rapid pace of technological change, leaders cannot be expected to have all the answers. By fostering a collaborative decision-making environment, digital leaders can tap into the collective knowledge and creativity of their teams, leading to more innovative solutions and greater buy-in for digital initiatives (Avolio & Gibbons, 2020). Authentic leadership, which emphasizes leading with transparency, integrity, and genuine passion, is crucial in building trust and credibility during times of significant organizational change. Digital leaders who demonstrate authenticity in their commitment to digital transformation and consistently align their actions with their stated values can inspire confidence and foster a sense of psychological safety among their teams (Avolio & Gardner, 2005). This is particularly important when navigating the ethical challenges and uncertainties that often accompany digital transformation efforts.

While these leadership theories offer valuable insights, effective digital leadership often requires a synthesis of multiple approaches. Digital leaders must be adaptive, drawing on different leadership styles as the situation demands. They must balance the visionary aspects of transformational leadership with the empathy and support emphasized in servant leadership, while also fostering collaboration and authenticity throughout the organization (Schwarzmüller et al., 2018). It is worth noting that leadership approaches may need to be adapted to different cultural contexts. For instance, Sposato (2019, 2021) discusses the concept of paternalistic leadership in China, highlighting the importance of understanding cultural nuances when implementing leadership strategies in a global context. This underscores the need for digital leaders to be culturally sensitive and adaptable in their approach, especially when leading digital transformation initiatives across diverse cultural settings.

Ethical Considerations in Digital Leadership

As organizations embrace digital transformation, they are confronted with a host of ethical challenges that require careful consideration and proactive management. Digital leaders play a crucial role in navigating these ethical dilemmas and ensuring that their organizations' digital initiatives align with ethical principles and societal values. One of the most pressing ethical concerns in the digital age is the potential for bias in algorithms and data-driven decision-making processes. As organizations increasingly rely on artificial intelligence and machine learning to inform strategic decisions, there is a risk of perpetuating or even amplifying existing biases (Bosco et al., 2015). Digital leaders must be vigilant in identifying and mitigating these biases, ensuring that their data-driven approaches do not lead to unfair or discriminatory outcomes. This involves not only technical considerations, such as auditing algorithms for bias, but also fostering a diverse and inclusive organizational culture that can help identify and challenge biased assumptions (Sánchez-Monedero et al., 2020). Employee privacy concerns in a digital workplace present another significant ethical challenge. As organizations adopt technologies that enable greater monitoring and data collection on employee activities, there is a tension between organizational interests in productivity and efficiency and individual rights to privacy (Ajunwa et al., 2017). Digital leaders must navigate this delicate balance, establishing clear policies and practices that protect employee privacy while also leveraging data to improve organizational performance.

This may involve implementing transparent data collection practices, obtaining informed consent from employees, and ensuring that data is used ethically and responsibly. Cybersecurity risks and data protection have become critical ethical concerns in the digital age. As organizations collect and store vast amounts of sensitive data, they bear a significant responsibility to protect this information from breaches and unauthorized access. Digital leaders must prioritize cybersecurity efforts, investing in robust security measures and fostering a culture of security awareness throughout the organization. This includes not only technical safeguards but also ethical considerations around data handling, storage, and sharing practices.

To address these and other ethical challenges, digital leaders must promote ethical practices and responsible technology use within their organizations. This involves developing and implementing comprehensive ethical frameworks that guide decision-making around digital initiatives (Floridi, 2018). Such frameworks should be grounded in core ethical principles such as transparency, fairness, accountability, and respect for individual rights. Digital leaders should also prioritize ethical considerations in the design and implementation of digital systems and processes. This may involve adopting principles of "ethics by design," where ethical considerations are integrated into the development process from the outset rather than being treated as an afterthought (Dignum, 2018). By embedding ethical considerations into the fabric of digital initiatives, organizations can build trust with stakeholders and mitigate potential risks.

Furthermore, digital leaders must foster a culture of ethical awareness and responsibility throughout their organizations. This involves providing ethics training for employees, creating channels for reporting ethical concerns, and demonstrating a commitment to ethical practices through their own actions and decisions (Treviño et al., 2014). By prioritizing ethics in digital transformation efforts, leaders can help ensure that their organizations harness the power of technology in ways that benefit both the business and society at large.

An emerging ethical consideration in the digital age is the use of artificial intelligence in recruitment and selection processes. Ore and Sposato (2022) highlight both the opportunities and risks associated with AI-driven recruitment, emphasizing the need for digital leaders to carefully consider the ethical implications of these technologies. This includes addressing potential biases in AI algorithms, ensuring transparency in the selection process, and maintaining a human touch in candidate interactions. López Jiménez et al. (2021) further emphasize the importance of developing robust codes of conduct in the digital environment, particularly in the context of corporate social responsibility and ethics. Digital leaders must ensure that these codes of conduct are comprehensive, regularly updated to reflect emerging digital challenges, and effectively communicated and enforced throughout the organization.

Practical Implications of Digital Leadership

The implementation of effective digital leadership strategies can yield significant practical benefits for organizations undergoing digital transformation. These benefits extend beyond mere technological adoption, encompassing improvements in innovation, employee engagement, organizational agility, and decision-making processes. One of the most significant practical implications of digital leadership is increased innovation and competitive advantage in the digital marketplace. By fostering a culture that embraces experimentation and calculated risk-taking, digital leaders can unleash the creative potential of their organizations (Candi et al., 2020). This results in the development of innovative products, services, and business models that can differentiate the organization in an increasingly crowded digital landscape. Moreover, by staying attuned to emerging technologies and market trends, digital leaders can help their organizations identify and capitalize on new opportunities before competitors (Kane et al., 2019).

Improved employee engagement and satisfaction in a dynamic work environment is another crucial outcome of effective digital leadership. By involving employees in the digital transformation process, providing opportunities for skill development, and creating a sense of shared purpose, digital leaders can foster higher levels of engagement and commitment (Cortellazzo et al., 2019). This is particularly important in the context of digital transformation, where the pace of change can be overwhelming for many employees. Digital leaders who prioritize communication, transparency, and employee well-being can create a work environment where individuals feel valued and motivated to contribute to the organization's digital future. Enhanced agility and adaptability to respond to changing market demands is a key practical benefit of digital leadership. In today's fast-paced business environment, organizations must be able to pivot quickly in response to new technologies, shifting customer expectations, or disruptive competitors (Holbeche, 2018). Digital leaders foster this agility by building flexible organizational structures, encouraging cross-functional collaboration, and empowering teams to make decisions quickly. This increased adaptability allows organizations to seize new opportunities and navigate challenges more effectively in the digital marketplace.

More efficient and data-driven decision-making for organizational success is another significant practical implication of digital leadership. By championing the use of advanced analytics and data visualization tools, digital leaders can help their organizations move away from intuition-based decision-making towards a more evidence-based approach (McAfee & Brynjolfsson, 2012). This leads to more informed strategic choices, improved resource allocation, and better alignment between organizational initiatives and market realities. Furthermore, by democratizing access to data and insights throughout the organization, digital leaders can empower employees at all levels to make more informed decisions in their day-to-day work. The practical benefits of digital leadership extend to improved customer experiences and relationships. Digital leaders who prioritize customer-centric innovation and leverage data to understand customer needs can help their organizations create more personalized, seamless, and valuable customer experiences across digital and physical touchpoints (Weill & Woerner, 2018). This focus on customer value can lead to increased customer loyalty, higher retention rates, and ultimately, improved business performance.

Finally, effective digital leadership can result in more resilient and future-ready organizations. By cultivating a mindset of continuous learning and adaptation, digital leaders prepare their organizations to navigate future disruptions and technological shifts (Bonnet & Westerman, 2021). This resilience is crucial in an era where the pace of technological change shows no signs of slowing, and organizations must be prepared to evolve continuously to remain competitive. Furthermore, digital leadership can facilitate more effective collaboration within and beyond organizational boundaries. Jiménez et al. (2021) discuss the importance of cooperation in the triple helix model of innovation, which involves interactions between academia, industry, and government. Digital leaders can leverage their technological expertise and strategic vision to foster these collaborative relationships, driving innovation and knowledge exchange across sectors.

In the context of human resource management, digital leadership has significant implications for recruitment and talent development. As Ore and Sposato (2022) point out, the use of AI in recruitment and selection processes presents both opportunities and risks. Digital leaders must navigate this landscape carefully, ensuring that AI-driven recruitment tools are used ethically and effectively. This includes addressing potential biases in AI algorithms and maintaining a balance between technological efficiency and human judgment in the hiring process. Moreover, digital leaders must be attuned to the changing nature of work and its impact on employee well-being. As remote and hybrid work models become more prevalent, leaders must adapt their strategies to maintain team cohesion, foster collaboration, and support employee mental health in virtual environments. This may involve implementing new digital tools for communication and project management, as well as developing policies that promote work-life balance in a digitally connected world.

Further Research Avenues

As the field of digital leadership continues to evolve, several areas warrant further research to deepen our understanding of its impact on organizations and to refine best practices for effective digital leadership. To advance this field systematically, several specific methodological approaches are recommended for investigating key aspects of digital leadership.

A critical area for future investigation is the effectiveness of digital leadership development programs across different organizational contexts. Using a mixed-methods approach, researchers should conduct longitudinal studies that combine quantitative assessments of leadership outcomes with qualitative insights from program participants. Quantitative metrics could track improvements in digital competencies, decision-making effectiveness, and organizational performance indicators, while qualitative interviews and case studies could provide deep insights into the learning experiences, challenges, and behavioral changes of developing digital leaders. This comprehensive approach would help organizations design more effective leadership development initiatives and better understand the return on investment in digital leadership training.

There is a pressing need for large-scale quantitative studies that establish clear metrics for measuring digital leadership effectiveness. Such research should employ sophisticated statistical analyses to examine the relationships between digital leadership practices and key organizational outcomes such as innovation rates, digital transformation success, employee engagement, and financial performance. Researchers should develop and validate standardized instruments for assessing digital leadership capabilities and their impact across different industries and organizational sizes. This quantitative approach would help establish evidence-based benchmarks and enable organizations to better evaluate and develop their digital leadership capabilities.

Future research should employ qualitative methodologies to explore how cultural factors influence digital leadership effectiveness in different global contexts. Through in-depth interviews, ethnographic studies, and detailed case analyses, researchers can examine how digital leaders navigate cultural nuances while implementing transformation initiatives across diverse geographical regions. This research is particularly important given the increasing globalization of digital transformation efforts and the need to understand how leadership approaches must be adapted to different cultural contexts while maintaining effectiveness in driving digital change.

A crucial area for future investigation is how digital leaders navigate ethical challenges in technology implementation and use. Using a mixed-methods approach, researchers should examine both the decision-making processes of digital leaders when faced with ethical dilemmas and the outcomes of their choices. Quantitative surveys could map patterns in ethical decision-making across different industries and contexts, while qualitative case studies could provide detailed insights into specific ethical challenges and their resolutions. This research would help develop more robust frameworks for ethical digital leadership and inform the development of guidelines for responsible technology adoption.

Future research should employ quantitative methodologies to examine the relationship between digital leadership capabilities and organizational resilience during times of disruption. Large-scale studies using advanced statistical analyses could investigate how different digital leadership styles and practices correlate with an organization's ability to adapt to technological changes, market disruptions, and crisis situations. This research should include the development of resilience metrics and examine data from organizations across different sectors and sizes. Such quantitative analysis would provide valuable insights into how digital leadership can enhance organizational adaptability and survival in an increasingly volatile business environment.

One critical area for future research is the long-term effectiveness of digital leadership practices. While many studies have examined the short-term impacts of digital leadership initiatives, there is a need for longitudinal research that tracks the outcomes of these practices over extended periods (Cortellazzo et al., 2019). Such studies could provide valuable insights into the sustainability of digital leadership approaches and their ability to drive lasting organizational transformation.

Another important avenue for research is the role of digital leadership in specific industries or business contexts. While general principles of digital leadership may apply across sectors, the nuances of implementing these practices likely vary depending on industry-specific challenges, regulatory environments, and technological landscapes (Vial, 2019). Comparative studies across different sectors could illuminate how digital leadership strategies can be tailored to maximize effectiveness in various contexts. The development of metrics to measure the success of digital leadership initiatives presents another crucial area for further research. While traditional leadership effectiveness measures may capture some aspects of digital leadership, there is a need for more specialized metrics that account for the unique challenges and outcomes associated with digital transformation (Kane et al., 2019). This could include measures of digital innovation, organizational agility, and the successful integration of digital technologies into business processes.

The impact of digital leadership on employee well-being and mental health is an increasingly important area for investigation. As digital transformation initiatives often involve significant changes to work processes and job roles, understanding how digital leadership practices affect employee stress levels, job satisfaction, and overall well-being is crucial (Rofcanin & Anand, 2020). This research could inform strategies for supporting employees through digital transformation and fostering a healthy, engaged workforce in the digital age. Further research is also needed on the ethical dimensions of digital leadership, particularly in light of emerging technologies such as artificial intelligence and the Internet of Things. As these technologies raise new ethical questions and challenges, understanding how digital leaders can effectively navigate these issues and promote responsible technology use is critical

(Floridi, 2018). This could include studies on ethical decision-making frameworks for digital leaders, strategies for embedding ethics into digital transformation initiatives, and approaches for balancing technological innovation with social responsibility.

The intersection of digital leadership and organizational culture presents another fertile area for research. While it's widely acknowledged that culture plays a crucial role in digital transformation success, more research is needed to understand how digital leaders can effectively shape and evolve organizational culture to support digital initiatives (Hartl & Hess, 2017). This could include studies on the cultural attributes that facilitate digital transformation, strategies for overcoming cultural resistance to change, and approaches for fostering a digital-first mindset throughout the organization.

Additionally, research into the development and nurturing of digital leadership talent could provide valuable insights for organizations seeking to build their digital leadership capabilities. This could include studies on effective training and development programs for digital leaders, strategies for identifying and nurturing digital leadership potential within organizations, and approaches for attracting and retaining top digital leadership talent in a competitive marketplace (Petrucci & Rivera, 2018). Furthermore, as digital transformation initiatives increasingly span organizational boundaries, research into digital leadership in the context of ecosystems and networks could yield important insights. This could include studies on how digital leaders can effectively collaborate across organizational boundaries, strategies for leading in platform-based business models, and approaches for fostering innovation in complex digital ecosystems (Tiwana, 2014).

In line with the critical management research perspective proposed by Kelemen and Rumens (2008), future studies should also examine the power dynamics and potential inequalities that may arise in the context of digital leadership. This could involve investigating how digital transformation initiatives impact different groups within organizations, and how digital leaders can ensure that the benefits of digital technologies are equitably distributed. Moreover, research on the gendered aspects of digital leadership could provide valuable insights. Building on the work of Jeffrey et al. (2015) on sexism in the workplace, studies could explore how gender biases may manifest in digital leadership roles and how organizations can promote more inclusive digital leadership practices.

CONCLUSION

The rise of digital technologies and the imperative for digital transformation have fundamentally altered the landscape of organizational leadership. Digital leaders today face a unique set of challenges and opportunities as they guide their organizations through the complexities of the digital age. This chapter has explored the multifaceted nature of digital leadership, examining its core competencies, strategies for development, theoretical underpinnings, ethical considerations, and practical implications. As we have seen, effective digital leadership goes beyond mere technological proficiency. It requires a combination of visionary thinking, strategic acumen, and the ability to foster a culture of innovation and continuous learning. Digital leaders must be adept at leveraging data-driven insights, building agile and adaptable teams, and facilitating collaboration across organizational boundaries. Moreover, they must navigate the ethical challenges posed by digital technologies, ensuring that their organizations' digital initiatives align with ethical principles and societal values.

The theoretical foundations of digital leadership draw from established leadership theories, including transformational, servant, participative, and authentic leadership. However, these theories must be adapted and synthesized to address the unique demands of digital transformation. Effective digital leaders must be flexible in their approach, drawing on different leadership styles as the situation demands while maintaining a consistent focus on driving digital innovation and organizational change. The practical implications of digital leadership are significant and far-reaching. Organizations that successfully implement digital leadership strategies can expect to see increased innovation, improved employee engagement, enhanced agility, and more efficient decision-making processes. These benefits translate into tangible competitive advantages in the digital marketplace, positioning organizations for long-term success in an increasingly digital world.

Looking ahead, the field of digital leadership presents numerous avenues for further research. From exploring the long-term effectiveness of digital leadership practices to developing specialized metrics for measuring digital leadership success, there is much work to be done in refining our understanding of this critical area. As digital technologies continue to evolve and new challenges emerge, the importance of effective digital leadership will only grow. In conclusion, digital leadership represents a critical capability for organizations navigating the complexities of digital transformation. By developing strong digital leadership capabilities, organizations can not only survive but thrive in the digital age, leveraging technological innovations to create value, drive growth, and make a positive impact on society. As we move further into the digital future, the role of digital leaders in shaping organizational success and societal progress will undoubtedly continue to expand and evolve.

REFERENCES

Ajunwa, I., Crawford, K., & Schultz, J. (2017). Limitless worker surveillance. *California Law Review*, 105, 735.

Avolio, B. J., & Gardner, W. L. (2005). Authentic leadership development: Getting to the root of positive forms of leadership. *The Leadership Quarterly*, 16(3), 315–338. DOI: 10.1016/j.leaqua.2005.03.001

Avolio, B. J., & Gibbons, T. C. (2020). Developing authentic leaders for the digital era. In Antonakis, J., & Day, D. V. (Eds.), *The Nature of Leadership* (3rd ed., pp. 474–494). SAGE Publications.

Bass, B. M., & Riggio, R. E. (2006). *Transformational leadership*. Psychology Press. DOI: 10.4324/9781410617095

Bonnet, D., & Westerman, G. (2021). The New Elements of Digital Transformation. *MIT Sloan Management Review*, 62(2), 82–89.

Bosco, F. A., Aguinis, H., Singh, K., Field, J. G., & Pierce, C. A. (2015). Correlational effect size benchmarks. *The Journal of Applied Psychology*, 100(2), 431–449. DOI: 10.1037/a0038047 PMID: 25314367

Candi, M., Melia, M., & Colurcio, M. (2020). Two birds with one stone: The quest for addressing both business goals and social needs with innovation. *Journal of Business Ethics*, 160(4), 1019–1033. DOI: 10.1007/s10551-018-3853-y

Cortellazzo, L., Bruni, E., & Zampieri, R. (2019). The role of leadership in a digitalized world: A review. *Frontiers in Psychology*, 10, 1938. DOI: 10.3389/fpsyg.2019.01938 PMID: 31507494

Dignum, V. (2018). Ethics in artificial intelligence: Introduction to the special issue. *Ethics and Information Technology*, 20(1), 1–3. DOI: 10.1007/s10676-018-9450-z

El Sawy, O. A., Kræmmergaard, P., Amsinck, H., & Vinther, A. L. (2016). How LEGO Built the Foundations and Enterprise Capabilities for Digital Leadership. *MIS Quarterly Executive*, 15(2).

ElSayary, A. (2024). Integrating Generative AI in Active Learning Environments: Enhancing Metacognition and Technological Skills. *Journal of Systemics, Cybernetics and Informatics*, 22(3), 34–37. DOI: 10.54808/JSCI.22.03.34

Eva, N., Robin, M., Sendjaya, S., van Dierendonck, D., & Liden, R. C. (2019). Servant leadership: A systematic review and call for future research. *The Leadership Quarterly*, 30(1), 111–132. DOI: 10.1016/j.leaqua.2018.07.004

Fitzgerald, M., Kruschwitz, N., Bonnet, D., & Welch, M. (2014). Embracing digital technology: A new strategic imperative. *MIT Sloan Management Review*, 55(2), 1.

Floridi, L. (2018). Soft ethics and the governance of the digital. *Philosophy & Technology*, 31(1), 1–8. DOI: 10.1007/s13347-018-0303-9 PMID: 30322997

Garcia-Carbonell, N., Martin-Alcazar, F., & Sanchez-Gardey, G. (2014). Understanding the HRM-performance link: A literature review on the HRM strategy formulation process. *International Journal of Business Administration*, 5(2), 71. DOI: 10.5430/ijba.v5n2p71

Hartl, E., & Hess, T. (2017). The role of cultural values for digital transformation: Insights from a Delphi study. *Twenty-third Americas Conference on Information Systems*, Boston.

Holbeche, L. (2018). *The agile organization: How to build an innovative, sustainable and resilient business*. Kogan Page Publishers.

Jeffrey, H. L., Beswick, E., & Meade, J. (2015). Learning and unlearning sexism in the workplace: Two important barriers prevent a more inclusive environment. *Human Resource Management International Digest*, 23(5), 18–20. DOI: 10.1108/HRMID-05-2015-0086

Jiménez, D. L., Dittmar, E. C., & Portillo, J. P. V. (2021). Cooperation and relationship in the triple helix model of innovation. *International Journal of Knowledge and Learning*, 14(1), 1–9. DOI: 10.1504/IJKL.2021.115025

Kane, G. C., Phillips, A. N., Copulsky, J. R., & Andrus, G. R. (2019). *The technology fallacy: How people are the real key to digital transformation*. MIT Press. DOI: 10.7551/mitpress/11661.001.0001

Kelemen, M. L., & Rumens, N. (2008). *An introduction to critical management research*. Sage. DOI: 10.4135/9780857024336

López Jiménez, D., Dittmar, E. C., & Vargas Portillo, J. P. (2021). New directions in corporate social responsibility and ethics: Codes of conduct in the digital environment. *Journal of Business Ethics*, •••, 1–11. DOI: 10.1007/s10551-021-04753-z

McAfee, A., & Brynjolfsson, E. (2012). Big data: The management revolution. *Harvard Business Review*, 90(10), 60–68. PMID: 23074865

Ore, O., & Sposato, M. (2022). Opportunities and risks of artificial intelligence in recruitment and selection. *The International Journal of Organizational Analysis*, 30(6), 1771–1782. DOI: 10.1108/IJOA-07-2020-2291

Petrucci, T., & Rivera, M. (2018). Leading growth through the digital leader. *Journal of Leadership Studies*, 12(3), 53–56. DOI: 10.1002/jls.21595

Rofcanin, Y., & Anand, S. (2020). Human Relations virtual special issue: Virtual working. *Human Relations*, 73(7), 1036–1041. DOI: 10.1177/0018726720926457

Sánchez-Monedero, J., Dencik, L., & Edwards, L. (2020). What does it mean to 'solve' the problem of discrimination in hiring? Social, technical and legal perspectives from the UK on automated hiring systems. In *Proceedings of the 2020 Conference on Fairness, Accountability, and Transparency* (pp. 458-468). DOI: 10.1145/3351095.3372849

Schwarzmüller, T., Brosi, P., Duman, D., & Welpe, I. M. (2018). How does the digital transformation affect organizations? Key themes of change in work design and leadership. *Management Review*, 29(2), 114–138.

Sposato, M. (2019). Understanding paternalistic leadership: How to work with Chinese leaders. *Development and Learning in Organizations*, 33(6), 19–21. DOI: 10.1108/DLO-12-2018-0169

Sposato, M. (2021). A critical perspective on gender and paternalistic leadership in China. *International Journal of Business Innovation and Research*, 24(3), 417–428. DOI: 10.1504/IJBIR.2021.113513

Sposato, M. (2024). Leadership training and development in the age of artificial intelligence. *Development and Learning in Organizations*, 38(4), 4–7. DOI: 10.1108/DLO-12-2023-0256

Tiwana, A. (2014). *Platform ecosystems: Aligning architecture, governance, and strategy*. Newnes. DOI: 10.1016/B978-0-12-408066-9.00001-1

Treviño, L. K., den Nieuwenboer, N. A., & Kish-Gephart, J. J. (2014). (Un)ethical behavior in organizations. *Annual Review of Psychology*, 65(1), 635–660. DOI: 10.1146/annurev-psych-113011-143745 PMID: 23834354

Vial, G. (2019). Understanding digital transformation: A review and a research agenda. *The Journal of Strategic Information Systems*, 28(2), 118–144. DOI: 10.1016/j.jsis.2019.01.003

Weill, P., & Woerner, S. L. (2018). *What's your digital business model?: Six questions to help you build the next-generation enterprise*. Harvard Business Press.

Westerman, G., Bonnet, D., & McAfee, A. (2014). *Leading digital: Turning technology into business transformation*. Harvard Business Press.

FURTHER READINGS

Aktürk, O. (2024). Evolution of Higher Education in the Social Sciences From Traditional Classrooms to AI-Driven Learning Environments. In *Enhancing Higher Education and Research With OpenAI Models* (pp. 1–36). IGI Global. DOI: 10.4018/979-8-3693-1666-5.ch001

Al Harrasi, N., El Din, M. S., & Al Balushi, B. (2021). Towards an Artificial Intelligence (AI)-Driven Government in Sultanate of Oman: Transforming and Augmenting Leadership Competencies. In Managerial Issues in Digital Transformation of Global Modern Corporations (pp. 244-256). IGI Global.

Altrogge, V. E., & Parks, R. L. (2021). Digital Leadership and Professional Development. In Shifting to Online Learning Through Faculty Collaborative Support (pp. 163-182). IGI Global. DOI: 10.4018/978-1-7998-6944-3.ch009

Hensellek, S. (2020). Digital leadership: A framework for successful leadership in the digital age. [JMME]. *Journal of Media Management and Entrepreneurship*, 2(1), 1–15. DOI: 10.4018/JMME.2020010104

Lakkshmanan, A., Amudhan, S., Gaikwad, S. M., & Tyagi, A. K. (2024). Further Research Opportunities and Challenges Towards AI-Driven Tools for Modern Generation. Impacts of Generative AI on Creativity in Higher Education, 69-100.

Pandey, J., Majumdarr, S., Hassan, Y., & Benuyenah, V. (2023). Role of digital leadership capability in shaping IT innovation: A digital agility perspective. [JGIM]. *Journal of Global Information Management*, 31(8), 1–20. DOI: 10.4018/JGIM.333168

Sandhu, K. (Ed.). (2019). *Leadership, management, and adoption techniques for digital service innovation.* IGI Global.

Sposato, M. (2025). Developing Digital Leadership Skills for AI-Driven Research Environments. In Impacts of Generative AI on the Future of Research and Education (pp. 235-254). IGI Global.

Srivastava, A. P., Yadav, M., Yadav, R., Singh, B., & Dewasiri, N. J. (2023). Exploring digital agility and digital transformation leadership: A mixed method study. [JGIM]. *Journal of Global Information Management*, 31(8), 1–23. DOI: 10.4018/JGIM.332861

Wang, V., & Berger, J. (2012). E-leadership in the digital age. In *Technology and its impact on educational leadership: Innovation and change* (pp. 1–10). IGI Global. DOI: 10.4018/978-1-4666-0062-1.ch001

KEY TERMS AND DEFINITIONS:

Cross-functional Collaboration: The practice of breaking down departmental silos to facilitate communication and teamwork across different organizational units, essential for successful digital transformation initiatives.

Digital Culture: An organizational environment that embraces experimentation, calculated risk-taking, continuous learning, and innovation, characterized by openness to technological change and digital ways of working.

Data-Driven Decision-Making: A leadership approach that emphasizes the use of analytics, data visualization tools, and empirical evidence to inform strategic choices and organizational decision-making processes, moving away from purely intuition-based decision-making.

Digital Ecosystem: A complex network of interconnected stakeholders, technologies, and processes that interact within and across organizational boundaries to create and deliver value in the digital age.

Digital Leadership: A multifaceted leadership approach that combines technological literacy, strategic vision, and the ability to drive organizational change in a digital context, focusing on leveraging digital innovations to create value and transform business processes.

Digital Leadership Capabilities: The core competencies required for effective leadership in the digital age, including visionary thinking, technological literacy, ability to foster innovation, strategic planning for digital futures, and skills in managing digital change initiatives.

Digital Resilienc: An organization's capacity to withstand, adapt to, and recover from digital disruptions while maintaining core operations and continuing to innovate and evolve in response to technological changes.

Digital Transformation: A comprehensive organizational change process that encompasses the adoption of new technologies, reimagining of business processes, customer experiences, and organizational cultures to fully leverage the potential of digital innovations.

Ethics by Design: An approach to digital transformation where ethical considerations are integrated into the development process from the beginning, rather than being treated as an afterthought, ensuring responsible technology use and protection of stakeholder interests.

Organizational Agility: The ability of an organization to quickly pivot and adapt in response to new technologies, shifting customer expectations, or disruptive competitors, enabled by flexible organizational structures and empowered decision-making.

Chapter 5
Leadership Challenges to Strengthen Inclusive Teacher Skills Through Agile Change Management in Higher Education

Mario Muñoz Mercado
https://orcid.org/0000-0001-5324-8200
Instituto Politécnico Nacional, Mexico

Cristina Cuevas Hoyos
https://orcid.org/0009-0001-1051-2443
Universidad de Sonora, Mexico

ABSTRACT

In this chapter proposed by the authors, the importance of strengthening inclusive skills in teachers through agile change management is essential to meet the current challenges in higher education. This requires a leadership committed to equity and inclusion, capable of guiding its educational community towards a future where diversity is considered a valuable asset in the educational process. Agile change in education is crucial to adapt to the diverse needs of students in an ever-changing educational environment. Committed leadership that fosters creativity and supports teachers in adopting inclusive practices is essential to ensure accessible and equitable education for all. Agile change management focuses on a continuous process of learning and adaptation, involving all educational stakeholders and promoting a

DOI: 10.4018/979-8-3693-7086-5.ch005

culture of openness and flexibility. This strategy allows inclusion to become a dynamic and sustainable process, constantly adjusting to improve in response to emerging needs and ensuring that diversity is valued as an asset within the educational system.

LEADERSHIP CHALLENGES TO STRENGTHEN INCLUSIVE TEACHER SKILLS THROUGH AGILE CHANGE MANAGEMENT IN HIGHER EDUCATION

The antecedents of leadership and management date back to early organizational efforts in ancient civilizations, where authority figures exercised control through clear hierarchies and command structures. Also, over time, the concept of leadership evolved from approaches based on innate power and authority to perspectives that recognize the importance of specific skills and characteristics in the leader.

During the 20th century, trait theory emerged as one of the first to formalize the study of leadership, focusing on individual qualities such as charisma, intelligence and confidence. However, later studies expanded this view by introducing the behavioral approach, focusing not only on who the leader is but also on what the leader does (Daft, 2021). This made it possible to consider leadership styles that adapt to different situations and team needs.

Towards the end of the 20th century and the beginning of the 21st century, the transformational leadership theory brought with it a more human and motivational vision, where the leader inspires, encourages innovation and promotes individual growth (Avolio & Yammarino, 2013).

Similarly, emotional intelligence and ethical principles gained relevance, highlighting the leader's ability to manage his or her emotions and relate effectively with others, while acting in accordance with solid ethical values.

These various stages and theories have been fundamental in developing a deeper understanding of leadership and management, recognizing that these processes not only influence the structure and direction of an organization, but also the well-being and motivation of its members.

This is why the study of leadership has evolved significantly, leaving behind the limited vision of innate traits and hierarchical authority to give way to a much broader and inclusive approach. It is for this reason that leadership today considers emotional, ethical and contextual factors. They are also considered essential to understanding and practicing leadership effectively. This evolution makes it easier for contemporary leaders to adjust their strategies, managing to respond with flexibility and agility to a dynamic environment in constant transformation (Northouse, 2021).

Thus, each phase and theory in this progression has provided key elements to enrich the understanding of leadership. The aforementioned research and references provide a solid foundation to explore in depth the various facets that shape this field today, allowing for a more complete and adaptive view of the role of a leader in different contexts.

Leadership is a fundamental aspect in any organization or group, as it implies the ability to influence others to achieve common goals. Moreover, leadership has existed since ancient times, its formal application in the context of today's organizations developed throughout the 19th and 20th century in the emergence of the first modern factories and companies to provide answers to the changing needs of management and direction in the constantly evolving business environment (Bass & Stogdill, 1990).

The purpose of this research chapter is to analyze the impact of different leadership styles in higher education settings on the development of inclusive skills among teachers. Therefore, identifying the most effective practices and strategies to foster leadership that enhances both the professional and personal growth of faculty. In addition, universities are increasingly in demand for students with disabilities.

In this sense, teachers do not have the necessary training to recognize, attend to and improve the educational trajectory of this population. It has also been pointed out that the older the teachers are, the less willing they are to implement alternative teaching strategies; they continue with the classical methods for teaching classes.

In the area of inclusion at the higher technical or bachelor's degree level, they are committed to promoting human rights as a fundamental precept of the institutional mission, so that no person is excluded from higher education for any reason (economic or social condition, gender, race, beliefs or age, disability, high disability, age, among other factors). In this sense, it is essential to have tools to diagnose the needs related to teacher training in inclusive skills.

Likewise, this study aims to improve the quality of teaching and learning in higher education institutions by understanding how leadership influences the development of inclusive skills in teachers. These competencies support inclusion through the improvement of educational environments, a crucial aspect that promotes human rights and the development of better roles of participation and belonging among the school community.

In this way, inclusion is considered feasible in the understanding as a process of constant social change innovating teaching and learning methods for all people, in which trained teachers will be able to design support strategies congruent to the particular needs of their students.

Among the main aspects that have been identified is the lack of reasonable accommodations in higher education, such as accessible infrastructure, both digital and physical, lack of guidelines for admission, so as to support the registration of applicants with disabilities, strategies to ensure permanence and graduation, lack of teacher training in inclusion processes, lack of accompaniment, Mexican sign language interpreters, support for the use of digital technologies. Therefore, these areas represent an opportunity for the development of these competencies in teachers.

This situation evidence change management as a channel for teachers to seek improvement in educational institutions, through training that facilitates the implementation of reasonable adjustments according to the needs of the student population, with positive impact on motivation, dedication and effort to feel integrated within the school environment.

Likewise, in order to establish these improvements, it is essential that higher education institutions consider agile change management in the strategies that are identified and required to be applied.

In such a way that the leaders in charge of implementing the strategic plan to improve the competencies related to inclusion in teachers are able to identify the challenges and opportunities that arise in their institutions. At the same time, to achieve the educational success of students and in meeting the organizational objectives outlined in their institutional development plans.

It is worth mentioning that leaders not only provide direction and guidance, but also inspire, motivate, and guide their followers towards success within the organization. In addition, leadership plays a crucial role in strengthening individual and collective skills in a work environment or in any area of life (Coleman, 2000; Kouzes & Posner, 2017).

In the case of this research, leadership focuses on change management orientation to induce greater teacher participation, and in turn decrease the resistance that occurs in most cases.

Therefore, effective leadership will help to make the change process easier, by influencing the leader on the importance of complying with the commitments established to improve inclusion in their schools, with adequate communication that makes visible the needs of teachers in their training in inclusive skills.

Likewise, fostering collaboration to achieve the goals and consolidate the changes that are achieved. And to translate the new forms of education into the organizational culture, including these aspects in measurement indicators within the development plans.

At the same time, the different leadership styles are identified and developed, which contribute to the achievement of these objectives since each one manages to be effective in different situations and contexts. It is important to highlight that a good leader is one who manages to adapt to the specific needs and challenges of his team or organization (Northouse, 2018).

In this way, it is able to build trust, foster personal and professional growth, and promote a positive and productive work environment. Thus, these aspects are imperative if we want to achieve a significant change in the teaching staff in higher education to support inclusion and grow together with the organizational culture, in the administrative processes, the paradigm shift and, above all, strengthen the union of students for the benefit of students with disabilities and their integration into the institution.

Finally, through leadership, it has the capacity to achieve effective implementation and application of policies that support inclusion, as well as the trajectory and timely graduation of all students at the higher education level. At the same time, this implies not only the design of clear and well-founded strategies, but also the ability to inspire and motivate the entire educational community to commit to these goals.

Likewise, strong, and empathetic leadership is fundamental to creating an environment in which each student feels valued and has the necessary tools to overcome the obstacles that may arise during their academic training. In addition, this leadership fosters collaboration and active participation of faculty, administrators, and students. Likewise, ensuring that inclusive policies are translated into concrete and sustainable practices that truly benefit the entire university community.

Leadership in Higher Education

The importance of leadership in higher education has become a topic of growing importance and relevance in recent decades. In a world characterized by rapid technological advances, economic and social changes. In addition, in a growing demand for quality education, higher education institutions face complex challenges that require effective leadership and management.

That is why leaders in this sector play a crucial role in shaping the future of universities and colleges, ensuring that they not only remain competitive and relevant, but are also engines of innovation, inclusion, and sustainable development.

Leadership in higher education encompasses a wide range of roles, from resource management and strategic planning to the promotion of high-quality research and teaching. These leaders are required to possess an unobstructed vision and the ability to inspire and guide their academic community toward the achievement of common goals. In addition, it is imperative to be prepared and equipped to navigate the complexities of the contemporary educational environment, which includes managing diversity, incorporating emerging technologies, and adapting to the changing demands of the labor market and society.

In this context, the ability of leaders to foster an inclusive and equitable environment is essential. Promoting diversity and inclusion not only enhances the educational experience for all students, but also enriches the academic community and prepares graduates to live and work in an increasingly globalized world.

Leadership in higher education is not limited to administration and management, but also involves creating a culture of collaboration, innovation, and excellence. Leaders need to be able to identify and seize opportunities, face, and overcome challenges, and make informed and ethical decisions that benefit the entire educational community.

Likewise, leadership in higher education is an essential component for the success and sustainability of academic institutions. Through effective leadership and strategic management, leaders consider transforming their institutions, promoting academic excellence, and preparing students to contribute meaningfully to society.

It is worth mentioning the contributions in the publication of Papeles de Economía Española (2024), which mentions the challenges of university education and the role of universities in higher education with quality for the future. In which crucial spaces for learning and social development are mentioned with changes in the contexts in which universities develop with pressures on financial budgets, geopolitical tensions, health, and climate emergencies. In addition, new technological advances in higher education and high quality university experiences in a globalized environment of great connectivity.

For this reason, recent changes are highlighted in the personnel profiles of the educational organization and in the development of continuous improvement in lifelong learning for students. Likewise, they adopt measures that guarantee residency in the face of disruptions and the capacity to adapt to changing environments in university development. In which challenges are generated in opportunities for growth and improvement of educational practices for the members of the educational organization and students.

Higher education with the constant changes in the technological revolution, have generated new alternative actors in university education in the implementation of online or virtual learning which has become an integral part of the educational system.

Thus, the importance of crucial leadership in the modern era, where many higher education organizations operate globally and rely on technology for their daily operations. In addition, effective communication through digital platforms, remote project management and adaptability to emerging technologies.

Inclusive Skills in Teachers

Inclusive skills in teachers represent an essential pillar in the transformation of the educational system towards a more equitable and accessible model. In a context where diversity in the classroom is increasingly evident, teachers need to be prepared not only to recognize the individual differences of their students, but also to respond to them effectively (Booth & Ainscow, 2011).

These skills encompass a wide range of competencies ranging from the ability to identify and understand the specific learning needs of each student, to the implementation of pedagogical strategies that allow all students to actively participate in the educational process.

Table 1 presents the main characteristics in the three fundamental dimensions for developing inclusive school environments, as mentioned in the "Index for Inclusion" by Booth & Ainscow (2011).

These dimensions (creating inclusive cultures, developing inclusive policies, and developing inclusive practices) are fundamental to the development of educational institutions that promote the participation and learning of all students, regardless of their differences. That is why each dimension is described in general terms and is accompanied by key elements detailing the actions and approaches needed to achieve true inclusion in the educational setting.

Table 1. Dimensions for developing learning and participation in schools

Dimension	Description	Key Elements
Creating Inclusive Cultures	Establish a school environment where all members of the community feel valued, respected, and have a sense of belonging. Diversity is seen as a strength, promotes collaboration and mutual support.	- Fostering positive relationships - Valuing diversity - Promoting a sense of community
Elaboration of Inclusive Policies	Development and adjustment of school policies that guarantee equity and inclusion for all students. These policies compensate for removing barriers, ensuring equal participation, and preventing discrimination.	- Review of existing policies - Development of new inclusive policies - Ensuring effective implementation
Development of Inclusive Practices	Adaptation of pedagogical and organizational practices that ensure that all students consider learning and actively participate in the classroom. It implies the use of flexible strategies that respond to the diversity of students.	- Adaptation of the curriculum - Differentiated teaching strategies - Inclusive assessment

Source: Own elaboration. Adapted *"Index for inclusion: Developing learning and participation in schools"*. Booth y Ainscow, 2011. Bristol: Centre for Studies on Inclusive Education (CSIE).

It is worth mentioning that all three dimensions provide a comprehensive framework for schools to develop and maintain inclusive environments. They also ensure that all students have the opportunity to participate fully in school life and reach their full potential in the educational organization.

Inclusive education is not just about integrating students with disabilities into regular classrooms, but about creating an environment where all forms of diversity are recognized and valued. This includes differences in cognitive abilities, learning styles, languages, cultures, gender, and socioeconomic situations. Teachers with inclusive skills are able to design and adapt their teaching so that all students feel valued and supported, developing their full potential (Florian & Black-Hawkins, 2011).

Inclusive pedagogy is an educational approach that seeks to integrate all students into the learning process, regardless of their individual differences or special needs. In addition, key aspects discussed in the article, including the definition of inclusive pedagogy, recommended pedagogical practices, challenges and opportunities associated with its implementation, examples of research in action, and the authors' main conclusions.

In analyzing how teachers manage to adopt inclusive pedagogical practices to address diversity in the classroom. Table 2 details the key concepts, recommended practices, challenges, and opportunities associated with the implementation of inclusive pedagogy. As well as the challenges and opportunities associated with implementing inclusive pedagogy provide an overview in transforming teaching to make it more equitable and accessible to all students.

Table 2. Inclusive pedagogical practices

Aspect	**Description**
Definition of Inclusive Pedagogy	Inclusive pedagogy seeks to create a learning environment accessible to all, without focusing on specific adaptation for students with special needs.
Inclusive Pedagogical Practices	Teaching methods that recognize and value the diversity of all students, integrating inclusive practices at the center of teaching.
Challenges and Opportunities	Challenges: Lack of resources and support. Opportunities: Improved learning for all students.
Research in Action	Case studies showing the successful implementation of inclusive pedagogies in schools, with concrete examples and lessons learned.

Source: Own elaboration. Adapted *"Exploring inclusive pedagogy"*. Florian y Black-Hawkins, 2011. British Educational Research Journal, 37(5), 813-828.

Inclusive pedagogical practices are essential to address diversity in the classroom, promoting an equitable and respectful learning environment for all. In addition, it implements teaching methods that recognize and value the diversity of all students in the classroom.

Likewise, rather than tailoring the curriculum specifically for students with special needs, these practices seek to integrate all students into the learning process in an equitable manner.

Inclusive practices are therefore considered to be at the core of teaching, which implies an initiative-taking approach to designing lessons, activities and assessments that are accessible and relevant to all students, regardless of their abilities or backgrounds. This requires teachers to adopt a flexible, creative mindset and work to remove barriers to learning, promoting an educational environment where all students are able to participate fully and reach their full potential.

In addition, these skills imply a commitment to continuous learning and self-criticism. Teachers have an obligation to be willing to reflect on their practices and seek new ways to improve inclusion in their classrooms. These may include the use of adaptive technology, diversification of assessment methods, collaboration with other education professionals, and active participation in professional learning communities.

Importance of Inclusive Skills

The inclusive ability is understood as the capacity of the institution together with all its members to carry out actions that allow making the necessary adjustments to eliminate the barriers that prevent full participation (Naranjo & Carrasco, 2022). Indeed, the ability is constituted from the continuous realization of effective practices that allow the integral development of students living with some life situation, an aspect that is part of the effective, which are those actions that serve as actions that allow the full participation of students, otherwise, the nature of the effective does not cover the need for inclusion (Fernandez, 2018).

Within the inclusion skills, the attitudinal situation of the teaching staff is shown as imperative (Sevilla et al., 2018), without these attitudes it will be difficult to develop the skills. A procedure for enabling inclusion strategies includes constant training, which allows the development of skills and competencies in the teaching staff for due attention to the community of members with some life condition (Hernández et al., 2018).

An indispensable skill to include the principle of communication is an indispensable tool for the execution of inclusion skills, as a fundamental principle for the realization of the adaptations that each student requires. In effect, the skill of inclusion is to go beyond the strategies provided in the literature and requires a great deal of willingness to make these adjustments (Mejía & Ullauri, 2022).

The realization of adaptations to facilitate the inclusion of students always requires communication skills and this is due to the great diversity of cases in which a person with a life situation lives, that is, several people with a similar life situation are able to present themselves and the strategies that are implemented are very different (Cuevas, 2023). Indeed, the main tool for inclusion is based on the flexibility of the classroom and institutional context.

By way of conclusion, inclusive skills are developed based on prior training through teacher training and the willingness of teachers to make their classroom social context more flexible, and through communication mechanisms to develop strategies that allow them to eliminate barriers that could impede the full participation of students.

Methods for Assessing and Developing Inclusive Skills

The methods to evaluate in inclusion topics are generally based on formative evaluation (Gutiérrez et al., 2019), that is, while the activities are being carried out during classroom time, feedback is questioned to verify the learning in the development of the subject, this method is very effective in the development of immediate adjustments that allow facilitating the participation of the student in question (Rodríguez et al., 2017). An amazingly effective method to continue promoting educational inclusion actions.

The evaluation mechanisms through projects are a clear example of agile management, since they allow adaptations to be made according to the needs of the context of the study developed by the students (Itati et al., 2021), so it is likely that evaluative goals can be established according to the needs requested by the social context of each student.

It is worth mentioning that methods for assessing and developing inclusive skills highlight the importance of a holistic and inclusive approach. It is crucial that assessments identify not only technical competencies, but also social, emotional, and cultural skills that promote inclusion. These methods are effective when they are adaptive and sensitive to individual differences, recognizing and valuing diverse forms of expression and learning.

In addition, inclusive skills development is aligned with continuous and reflective learning, promoting self-assessment and collaborative learning. Development programs are designed to foster empathy, cross-cultural understanding, and equity, providing individuals with the necessary tools to contribute to an inclusive environment.

Indeed, both the assessment and development of inclusive skills require a dynamic and contextualized approach, reflecting the diversity and complexity of today's social and work environments.

It therefore emphasizes the importance of an integrative approach that addresses technical competencies as well as social, emotional, and cultural skills to promote inclusion. These methods, adaptive and sensitive to individual differences, not only benefit the individual, but also drive cultural change in organizations and communities, fostering an environment where diversity is valued.

Inclusive assessment and skills development are conceived as continuous processes that not only seek individual growth, but also contribute to the strengthening of more equitable and sustainable collective environments. This approach stresses the importance of constant feedback and active participation, creating a cycle of learning and adaptation in the pursuit of inclusion.

Conceptual Development of Agile Change Management in IES.

Change is related to the transformation from one state to another, which within institutions is manifested through certain advantages and barriers, since for individuals it manages to feel overwhelmed or unstable, due to the fact that they are used to performing teaching functions in a routine manner. However, changes are dictated by the changing needs of the current environment and times (Le Grand & Deneckere, 2019).

According to Hasan et al., (2021), the Agile concept is understood as a ramification of lean thinking applied to the development of programs or products, i.e., lean is an innovative methodology to be efficient in both management and production processes of an organization. Agile has its origins in software development in the 90's, with a framework published by a team of programmers who created the *Manifiesto Ágil*[1]. Where agile is a combination of methods extracted from *Lean Management*[2], *Extreme Programming*[3]*y Scrum*[4]. This agile manifesto focuses primarily on project management for software development. Therefore, the purpose of the agile perspective is to improve the life cycle of a program, and to apply its foundation in other areas of business such as human resources. In this sense, agile does not only refer to a set of software techniques, but it is also considered a movement, an ideology, or a cause. As the first principle of the Agile Manifesto has been applied, "organizations must value people and their relationships over processes and tools".

Gandomani et al., (2013), the transition to agility has been a research topic to support this concept in organizations. Because the implementation of a change with the agile methodology is usually complex, that is why the conformation of work teams in charge of carrying out these activities must be people with a flexible mentality.

In such a way that they show willingness and readiness to create inclusive educational ecosystems. That is, that all areas of an educational institution adapt to the unique needs of students, through awareness, training and empowerment of all staff serving students. In this area it is crucial that teachers support flexible teaching and assessment methods adapted to the particular needs of students with disabilities.

According to Wiśniewska-Sałek (2021), there is a close relationship between the effectiveness of institutional processes and the relevance of subject content with the level of student satisfaction. So, the attitude and treatment that teachers provide to their students during the delivery of classes are determining factors in the acquisition of knowledge, especially for students with disabilities.

Inclusive Leadership

Leadership in educational organizations faces the challenge of integrating the main actions to create a work environment that fosters respect, tolerance, and appreciation of the needs of the educational community. It is essential to have quality training that reinforces the school culture, contributing to an inclusive and positive organizational climate.

The active participation of parents is crucial, as they play a key role in promoting and improving the participation of both students and the entire educational community. This collaboration among all members of the educational community strengthens the integral development of students and improves the overall school environment (Crisol et al., 2022).

In order to promote equality and social justice in educational institutions, it is crucial to have leadership that promotes inclusion and demonstrates a growing interest in improving diversity within the school environment. This implies that all the actors that make up the educational organization including: directors, administrative staff, and teachers. They are considered working together to achieve the objectives of the school mission in an efficient manner.

This collaborative approach ensures that each team member assumes his or her responsibilities and obligations in order to achieve academic success. Likewise, with a strong commitment to the school community it not only promotes identity and social development within the educational organization, but also ensures the creation of inclusive environments that value and respect diversity (Crisol et al., 2022).

Initially, the concept of inclusion has been linked to disability and special educational needs. However, in recent times, a growing involvement of students and families in the formulation of inclusive practices has been observed. This trend aims to promote awareness and encourage active community participation in the school setting (Sotomayor et al., 2020).

In addition, the concept of inclusion, as mentioned by Ossa et al., (2014). It emerges from a process that seeks to address the difficulties faced by people due to disabilities, poverty, gender, ethnicity, and other factors. This process has led to the implementation of significant structural changes through educational and social policies, as well as the adoption of new practices in the educational community.

Furthermore, these transformations seek not only equal opportunities, but also effective integration and respect for diversity, promoting an environment in which each individual is able to participate fully and benefit from the available resources.

By incorporating this concept into educational management, it promotes effective collaboration that boosts academic achievement and reduces dropout rates. This approach not only encourages students to develop their full potential, but also optimizes the school environment by addressing conflicts and fostering a culture of equitable participation. In this way, it strengthens the organizational fabric of the educational institution, contributing to a more inclusive and harmonious environment.

In this sense, inclusive leadership is based on collaborative and pedagogical leadership models. According to Murillo (2006), this style of leadership is considered among the most significant in educational management, as it seeks to foster the participatory collaboration of the entire school community through mutual commitment. Inclusive leadership not only promotes the active participation of all members of the educational community, but also focuses on creating an environment in which diverse voices and perspectives are valued and heard, thus contributing to a more equitable and effective management.

It is worth noting, as mentioned by the European Agency for Special Needs and Inclusive Education (2019), that a sense of belonging is built through the shared emotional connection between families and students. Therefore, inclusive leadership engages in involving the entire educational community, with educational leaders playing a crucial role in strengthening ties and reflecting on new strategies to include families in school decision making.

This need arises due to the disagreements and mutual distrust that manage to exist, as Okoko (2019) points out. Strengthening these relationships and establishing effective mechanisms for family participation that are in a position to contribute to a more collaborative and effective educational management, benefiting both students and the school community as a whole.

Likewise, educational leaders seek strategies to improve inclusive education through collaboration between institutions and the creation of co-responsibility channels (Crisol et al., 2022). As mentioned by Valdés (2018), which highlights that one of the greatest challenges in educational inclusion is to develop new leadership practices in school teams, which are key to building organizational cultures that truly integrate and value diversity.

To overcome this challenge, it is essential to promote leadership that fosters collaboration and empathy, as well as to invest in the continuous training of educational personnel to ensure the effectiveness and sustainability of inclusive practices.

The role of leaders and administrative staff in an educational organization is essential in building bridges between the work environment, the community, and families, ensuring that all work in harmony toward achieving common goals of academic success. Leaders are responsible for cultivating an environment in which every member of the educational community, including students, parents, teachers, and administrative staff, feels valued and committed to the organizational mission.

Inclusive leadership, as Collet-Sabé (2020) points out, emphasizes the importance of the active participation of parents in the educational process. This participation not only strengthens social ties within the community, but also contributes to the development of inclusive programs that integrate all members into the educational process. By involving parents and the community in general, it facilitates the creation of a supportive and collaborative environment, which enriches both the academic development of students and their socioemotional growth.

Therefore, the importance of collaboration between leaders, administrative staff, families, and the community are not only fundamental to achieving educational goals, but also promotes an environment of inclusion and support that benefits all members of the educational community.

To promote inclusion in student learning, it is essential that leaders in educational organizations adopt leadership practices that foster an inclusive environment. These leaders are obligated to focus on fostering active collaboration with parents and other educational institutions, as joint participation is crucial to the planning and evaluation of inclusive educational programs. This collaboration helps to ensure that the strategies implemented are aligned with the needs of all students and are effective in their application.

However, many educational organizations face economic difficulties due to the lack of material resources and services, which hinders the teaching-learning process, especially in contexts of educational inclusion. To address these challenges, it is necessary for leaders to implement leadership practices that optimize the distribution of available resources and services. This includes developing pedagogical strategies that maximize the impact of existing resources and seek innovative ways to overcome current constraints.

By integrating these leadership practices into pedagogical strategies, the quality of inclusive education is improved. This involves not only strengthening the leadership capacity of teachers, but also ensuring that service and resource distribution models are designed to support all students equitably. In this way, it contributes to creating a more inclusive educational environment, in which all students have the opportunities they need to reach their full potential.

Also, given that there is a paucity of research focused on analyzing how openness and community development benefit from leaders' inclusive practices, it is crucial to examine these issues in greater depth. Diversity is a central aspect, actively encouraging the participation of families and the entire educational community (Barrientos et al., 2016).

It is essential to foster an inclusive environment where each member gets to contribute and benefit from different perspectives and experiences. Collaboration among families, educators and other community stakeholders enriches the educational process and also helps build a more equitable, respectful community that values and celebrates individual differences.

Inclusive leadership not only has the potential to continuously improve educational practices but is also fundamental to the development of high quality educational organizations. Implementing an inclusive approach to school leadership contributes to the creation of a culture in which all students are recognized, valued, and cared for equitably. This inclusive environment fosters equality of opportunity, benefiting the entire educational community by ensuring that all members have access to the same opportunities for learning and development, regardless of their background or circumstances.

Adopting inclusive practices and promoting active family and community involvement not only improves the school environment, but also helps build a stronger support network, which enriches the educational experience for all students.

Previous Studies on Leadership and Inclusive Education

Inclusion is understood as the elimination of barriers that may prevent the participation of any person (Booth & Ainscow, 2015), according to the above, participation is understood as the possibility that any person has to feel part of their own being, acceptance by institutions and is recognized in such a way that is valued for their identity rather than focusing on their possible limitation (Sánchez et al., 2021), i.e. it has multidisciplinary aspects and axes that cut across the integrity of the person in their different spheres of life.

According to the above, educational inclusion is understood as the educational institution eliminates the barriers that prevent the participation of students from their first line of attention to the classroom, that is, from the beginning of the educational process to enter until the corresponding classes are taught (Cuevas, 2023), while inclusive practice is the action carried out by the educational community to eliminate possible barriers that prevent participation (Cuevas et al., 2022). Inclusive practices, as well as participation cover several dimensions, among these the socio-emotional, educational situations to those that impact with their professional and personal self-realization (Hoyos et al., 2021), so that the inclusive practice becomes an indispensable action towards the university community.

In recent decades, inclusive education has become a fundamental principle of education systems globally, reflecting a growing commitment to equity and respect for diversity in the classroom. Therefore, this approach seeks to ensure that all students, regardless of their abilities, ethnicity, gender, or any other characteristic, have access to quality education in environments that promote their full development. In this context, educational leadership plays a crucial role, as school leaders are responsible for implementing and sustaining inclusive practices that facilitate education for all.

It is worth mentioning that leadership in inclusive education involves not only the effective management of resources and the implementation of policies, but also the creation of a school culture that values diversity and encourages the participation of the entire educational community. Likewise, various leadership approaches, such as transformational, distributed, and ethical leadership, have proven to be effective in promoting inclusive practices, each providing different strategies to address the challenges presented by inclusive education (Ainscow, 2020).

It is worth mentioning, according to Ainscow (2020), the promotion of inclusion and equity in education depends not only on the adoption of adequate policies, but also on the capacity of educational leaders to transform those policies into effective practices within schools.

In addition, Ainscow stresses that one of the greatest challenges for school leaders is to create environments where diversity is valued and respected, which requires not only a commitment to social justice, but also an ability to mobilize and direct resources equitably. Thus, which highlights the importance of leadership that is able to recognize and address systemic barriers to inclusion and is willing to adopt innovative approaches to ensure that all students have an equal opportunity to succeed.

Implementation of Agile Management in Education

Some applications of agile management implementation were carried out by Echeverría et al., (2021), through SCRUM, which consists in the development of projects that benefit the contexts of the educational entities in the institutions, so that through the planning that arises, educational practices that the students execute in the company of the teaching staff, who build the strategy together, are tried to be built. Similar to this application is the research designed and applied by Audisio et al., (2021), which consisted in applying projects with the use of technological organizational tools that allowed generating greater efficiency in the activities from their beginning and end.

This last study is a clear example of the need for the application of technologies to assist the efforts made by students who manage to live with a different life situation. Indeed, technology has served as a means to facilitate the participation of students with disabilities (Godoy & Hidalgo, 2020), however, it has also been implemented in students from other cultures who are unfamiliar with many cultural situations, as well as some people who do not know the language of the institution they will attend (Quijada, 2021).

The relationship between agile management and inclusive practices is closely related, i.e., through the agile management method, strategies that allow the reduction of barriers that prevent the full participation of students are facilitated (Cuevas et al., 2022). Inclusion is a continuous effort that has the ability to achieve with the necessary adaptations to achieve academic and professional development, for which agile management is able to be taken as an effective means for the reduction of attitudinal barriers (Cobeñas & Grimaldi, 2021).

Lapicki & Terlato (2021) argue that an agile higher education institution is characterized by multidisciplinary teams that foster continuous learning. These teams, guided by committed leaders, seek to make informed decisions to ensure that students, staff, and other community members feel emotionally stable and committed to the institution's strategic goals. In this environment, bureaucracy is minimized, and response times are optimized to effectively address emerging problems and challenges, thus promoting greater adaptability and efficiency in educational management.

Likewise, in an agile educational organization, leadership focuses on guiding teams rather than imposing direct orders. This is achieved through questions that stimulate the analysis of the various situations faced by students with disabilities, favoring equitable and beneficial decision-making for the entire school community. Changes, therefore, are usually gradual and usually start from the middle and lower levels, with the support of those who are committed to the welfare of students with disabilities. It seeks to develop new educational strategies by asking questions, exchanging knowledge, and sharing experience, thus promoting a culture of collaboration and continuous adaptation.

Gallego (2023) argues that the model of educational inclusion requires significant transformations in all aspects of the educational system. This ranges from public policies and the adaptation of educational centers to curricular modification, the design of universal environments and content, and the collaboration and participation of families and the community. Thus, inclusion demands an integration between practices, policies, systems, and concepts. Aspects that are considered to be analyzed in order to make the necessary adjustments through the use of the agile change methodology.

The current curricula are still oriented to the promotion of average learning, i.e., they are not adjusted to the reality of educational institutions, where attention to multiculturalism, ethnic populations and people with disabilities has been left aside. For this reason, it is considered the application of innovative methodologies to support universities, especially teachers to be able to be at the forefront of the demands of contemporary education.

Thus, Hasan et al., (2021) propose removing barriers and adopting the principles of agile change where people's needs are prioritized over processes and administrative procedures. In this aspect, it is essential to involve students from vulnerable groups, as well as student societies, to carry out consultations and interviews, with the purpose of knowing in depth all the inconveniences they face during their entry to higher education institutions, during their school career and to provide better guidelines to ensure graduation and graduation. Table 3 shows the characteristic elements of an agile organization.

Table 3. Characteristics of agile organizations

In connection with	**Features**
Strategy	Shared vision and purpose. Identify opportunities for change more quickly.
Structure	Group of consolidated work teams, with practical and flexible governance.
Processes	Cycles of decision making, and continuous improvement oriented to action and aspects of higher value.
Persons	Prioritizing people, encouraging motivation and self-organization within teams. Service-based leadership, with effective communication and cohesion.
Technology	Inclusive architecture and constantly evolving systems.
Students	Higher value asset with incremental value.

Source: Own elaboration. Adapted *"Empresas ágiles - Cláves para sobrevivir a la complejidad del ambiente"*. Lapicki y Terlato, 2021. Documentos de Trabajo, 777, 1–30.

For educational institutions to implement the agile change approach to improve inclusion, it is essential that each of the characteristics listed in Table 3 align with the principles of inclusion and diversity. In terms of strategy, the institution is obligated to develop a shared vision that prioritizes inclusion and equity, quickly identifying opportunities to adapt programs and services to the needs of all students. Structurally, it is essential to have consolidated work teams, where governance is flexible and allows the participation of representatives from diverse student communities, ensuring that their voices are heard and considered in decision making.

In terms of processes, decision-making and continuous improvement that proceeds to focus on actions that generate the greatest positive impact for the most vulnerable students, ensuring that each change benefits everyone, leaving no one behind. In terms of people, it is crucial to prioritize the educational community, fostering motivation and self-organization in diverse teams, where leadership is based on service, promoting effective communication and cohesion between diverse groups.

Technology is considered to be inclusive, with systems that evolve to meet the needs of students with different abilities, ensuring accessibility and equity in the use of digital tools. Finally, considering students as the most valuable asset, it is necessary to recognize and enhance their diversity, implementing strategies that increase their value, not only in academic terms, but also in their personal and social development, ensuring that everyone has the same opportunities to thrive in an agile and inclusive educational environment.

It is worth mentioning, agile management facilitates the participation of the entire student body, serving as a valuable tool that is able to benefit especially vulnerable populations, by removing barriers that manage to prevent their full participation (Rodriguez, 2019). Therefore, the implementation of this management approach is extremely useful for both the student body and the faculty, promoting a more inclusive and accessible educational environment for all.

Familiar Challenges in Higher Education

Universities face global and contextual challenges in fulfilling their mission in educational organization and research. As a result, institutions face pressures on financial statement budgets with declining public funding and changes in enrollment, especially of international students, compounding these challenges.

Likewise, the tensions in the changes of governmental policies that are in constant geopolitical changes. In addition, in the constant changes of sanitary emergencies and climatic changes, as well as technological changes in constant evolution.

Universities need to diversify their revenue sources and adapt to modern technologies such as artificial intelligence and online courses. Growing student diversity and the demand for lifelong learning also require adjustments to traditional educational models. The COVID-19 pandemic highlighted the need for hybrid and online teaching, driving investment in technology and staff training.

In addition, political polarization, and misinformation present challenges to promoting media literacy and critical thinking. Universities must develop financial resilience and strategically adapt to these changes to remain relevant and effective. Therefore, meeting these challenges with innovation, inclusiveness and strategic planning will enable universities to continue their vital role in education and research.

In the field of higher education, several familiar challenges are faced that affect both students and institutions. Therefore, when addressing these challenges in higher education, they are analyzed from different perspectives:

1. **Access and Equity:** One of the greatest challenges is ensuring equitable access to higher education. Economic, geographic, and social barriers continue to limit access to universities for many students. The gap between different socioeconomic groups and regions is a persistent concern (Altbach & Peterson, 2023).

2. **Quality of Education:** Educational quality varies widely among institutions and programs. The lack of uniform standards and the rapidly changing needs of the labor market demand constant updating and improvement in curricula (Marginson, 2024).
3. **Technological Adaptation:** Integrating technology into the educational process is crucial but is often a challenge due to lack of adequate infrastructure and resistance to change by some teachers and administrators (Chen et al., 2023).
4. **Mental Health and Student Wellness:** Stress and anxiety among students are on the rise, affecting their academic performance and overall well-being. Universities are beginning to recognize the need to provide more support in these areas (Hicks et al., 2024).
5. **Financial Sustainability:** Rising educational costs and declining public funding are persistent problems that affect the sustainability of educational institutions and accessibility for students (Kuh, 2024).

Furthermore, today's challenges in higher education require a multidimensional approach and attention. To ensure equitable access, improve educational quality, adapt technology effectively, support student well-being and ensure financial sustainability, it is crucial that educational institutions, governments, and communities work closely together. Addressing these challenges will not only strengthen the education system but will also contribute to building a more skilled and resilient workforce to meet the challenges of the future. Joint reflection and action will be key to building a more inclusive and effective higher education system.

Leadership Challenges in Higher Education

Higher education faces a series of challenges that are transforming the academic landscape globally. Among the most significant is the integration of emerging technologies in teaching and learning processes. However, with digitalization increasingly present, universities are forced to rethink their pedagogical methods to incorporate tools such as online learning platforms, artificial intelligence and interactive resources that facilitate access to knowledge in a more efficient and personalized way.

This is why the current technological change is also accompanied by the need to manage the growing diversity in the classroom. Educational institutions face the challenge of creating inclusive environments that not only address cultural and linguistic differences, but also consider aspects such as disability and variability in learning abilities. Thus, promoting equity in higher education requires policies and practices that ensure that all students have equal opportunities for academic success.

In addition, another crucial challenge is the maintenance of high academic standards in a context of increasing demand for financial accessibility. The pressure to provide quality education is counterbalanced by the need to make higher education accessible to an increasingly large and diverse student population. This has led universities to explore alternative funding models, such as scholarships, grants, and cost-reducing distance learning programs.

Subsequently, institutions consider a preparation for a labor market that is constantly evolving. The skills required by employers are changing rapidly, driven by automation and globalization. As a result, universities face the challenge of designing academic programs that not only teach theoretical knowledge, but also develop practical and transferable skills. These include critical thinking skills, adaptability, and the ability to work in multicultural and multidisciplinary environments.

Notably, the article "Post-Pandemic Higher Education: Challenges and Opportunities" published by The Chronicle of Higher Education (2023) highlights how the pandemic has intensified these challenges. The global health crisis not only accelerated the adoption of educational technologies, but also underscored the importance of flexibility in educational models and the need to address the mental well-being of students. These aspects are now considered essential to the future design of higher education in an increasingly interconnected and complex world.

In this Table 4, we provide an overview of the challenges that universities face in the current environment and the types of solutions that are being implemented or explored to address them.

Table 4. Leadership challenges in universities

Challenge	**Description**	**Example**
Technological adaptation	Integrate digital tools, online platforms to improve teaching and learning.	Implementation of learning management systems (LMS) such as Moodle or Canvas.
Diversity and inclusion	Create inclusive environments that respect and value cultural, linguistic and skill differences.	Development of support programs for students with disabilities and resources in various languages.
Financial accessibility	Maintain educational quality while addressing economic barriers for students.	Offering scholarships, grants for low-income students and distance learning programs.
Preparation for the labor market	Adapt curricula to meet the changing demands of the labor market and develop transferable skills.	Inclusion of internship programs and soft skills training.

continued on following page

Table 4. Continued

Challenge	Description	Example
Mental well-being of students	Addressing the mental and emotional health of students, which has gained relevance in the post-pandemic context.	Implementation of counseling services and psychological support programs on campus.
Institutional sustainability	Addressing challenges related to funding, resources and ensuring long-term viability.	Optimization of resources and exploration of new sources of income, such as alliances with industry.

Source: Own elaboration. Adapted *"Post-pandemic higher education: Challenges and opportunities. The Chronicle of Higher Education"*. The Chronicle of Higher Education. (2023).

As such, the challenges facing universities today span a variety of critical areas, from integrating emerging technologies to ensuring inclusivity and supporting student mental health. The ability of institutions to adapt to address these challenges will be crucial to their future success and sustainability. Technological adaptation, diversity and inclusion, financial accessibility, labor market readiness, mental wellness, and institutional sustainability are interconnected elements that require a comprehensive and strategic approach. Therefore, universities that manage to balance these aspects will not only improve their educational quality but will also be better prepared to face the demands of an ever-changing world.

Emerging Perspectives: Discussions and Debates for the Future

In the current context, higher education faces the challenge of responding to an increasingly diverse and dynamic environment. Institutions must not only guarantee quality education, but also promote inclusion and equity in all their processes. In this sense, the role of leadership is fundamental to promote a change that allows teachers to develop inclusive skills and adapt in an agile way to the needs of students.

Inclusive leadership is essential to forge a culture of equity and respect, key elements for the success of any educational community. However, getting teachers to fully integrate these competencies involves overcoming challenges such as resistance to change, lack of specific training and the need to adapt pedagogical practices to diverse contexts.

Therefore, agile change management is presented as a strategic tool that facilitates adaptation and strengthens teachers' inclusive competencies. It also promotes a culture of continuous adaptation, flexibility and collaboration, aligned with the demands of an increasingly globalized and heterogeneous society. This approach allows teachers not only to adapt quickly to new teaching models, but also to feel supported by their leaders in the process of integrating inclusive practices into their daily work.

For this process to be successful, it is essential that leaders in higher education develop strategies that foster innovation, encourage commitment and foster an environment that is safe and open to change. This will not only strengthen the development of inclusive skills in teachers but will also contribute to building learning communities that value diversity and promote educational equity.

Therefore, inclusive leadership and agile change management are interdependent elements that, when applied together, can transform higher education into a more inclusive space that is prepared to face the challenges of a constantly evolving world.

Future Lines of Research

For the fulfillment and scope of the strategies that have been developed in this research, it is pertinent that HEIs design comprehensive monitoring systems through the evaluation of indicators both of school performance and of the aspects and conditions related to improving inclusion. In this sense, carrying out institutional and educational program self-evaluation processes represents an opportunity to find areas of opportunity in the search for a better leadership that, from the organizational structure, contributes to inclusion and respect for human rights, especially those of people with disabilities.

As pointed out by Márquez et al. (2020), self-evaluation through the exercise of responding to internal indicators, as well as those of external evaluation agencies, offers an effective tool to identify the key processes that have an impact on inclusion. It is also possible to compare with other HEIs and look at those actions and good practices that have been used to improve educational environments (infrastructure, curricula, inclusive culture).

In a complementary way, this work calls on Mexican HEIs to review how they are doing in terms of inclusion and equity, leadership and strategies to implement agile changes. Starting from the process of new admission to their institutions, the support offered to serve students with disabilities, also during their school career and extend research to the labor field. This is in order to guarantee higher education for this population and their insertion in the labor market (Wong & Robles, 2024).

Finally, it is essential that HEIs have an inclusion program that covers the legal framework related to the rights of persons with disabilities, including the interactions between the support areas that provide services to students with disabilities. In order to identify these processes and start with a plan to raise awareness among the school community on issues related to inclusion. The literature points out that there are very few educational institutions with formal inclusion programs. These actions endorse the commitment to comply with national regulations and policies in the continuous improvement of inclusive higher education.

CONCLUSION

Paľová & Vejačka (2023) stress that higher education has a responsibility to offer innovative training to students who will join the labor market in the future. It is not only considered to focus on the acquisition of technical skills, but also on strengthening students' competitiveness and fostering their autonomy in the learning process.

In the context of inclusive education, it is crucial that this innovative approach also considers the needs of students from diverse backgrounds and abilities. In supporting autonomy and competitiveness, it is essential that institutions provide an adapted environment where all students, including those with disabilities or from diverse cultures, can fully develop their potential and be prepared to face the challenges of the labor market with equal opportunities.

In this regard, Hasan et al., (2021) emphasize that agile transformation is no longer limited to software development; it has become a crucial necessity for companies to survive in a rapidly changing environment. Before the pandemic, 70% of companies were already adapting their work environments to become more agile. However, after the pandemic, which reshaped the business environment and promoted telecommuting, the global education system revealed the lack of strategies and changes needed to adapt online classes, both synchronously and asynchronously. In this context, it also became evident that student populations with specific needs were not receiving adequate attention.

Wiśniewska-Sałek (2021) emphasizes that agile change is based on flexible systems that improve the quality of teaching, meet expectations, and ensure continuity in educational improvement. This approach is reinforced through three key dimensions: strategic sensitivity, creation of emotional bonds among those involved, and leadership that supports change with the commitment of all members. Creativity and recognition are essential resources. In summary, developing agile change models in educational institutions responds to the needs of the contemporary market and the current global situation.

Change begins with awareness and strategic alignment toward the desired vision. Leading agility with an agile approach is critical to success. This involves fostering trust, collaboration, and self-organization within teams, creating an environment where experimentation is valued and encouraged. However, it is crucial to exercise caution, recognizing that each organization, like each individual, is unique. Adapting agility to the particularities of each context is essential for this methodology to work effectively. Thus, the true essence of agility lies in the ability to adapt and evolve continuously, adjusting to the specific needs and characteristics of each situation (Lapicki & Terlato, 2021).

The agile change approach to improving educational inclusion is especially relevant in today's context, where institutions are committed to adapting quickly to the diverse needs of students. By applying strategic sensitivity and fostering emotional bonds among all stakeholders, barriers to effective inclusion can be identified and addressed. Committed leadership that supports change and promotes creativity enables inclusive solutions to be not only implemented, but also sustainable over time. In this way, agile change becomes a powerful tool for transforming education, making it more accessible and equitable for all students, regardless of background or ability.

Likewise, leadership in higher education faces the crucial challenge of fostering an inclusive environment that values diversity and promotes equity. To achieve this, it is critical that educational leaders develop and strengthen inclusive skills in teachers, who are the direct agents of change in the classroom. Agile change management emerges as an effective strategy to address this challenge, allowing educational institutions to adapt quickly to the changing needs of their environment and to the demands of a more inclusive education..

Implementing agile change management involves engaging all educational stakeholders in a continuous process of learning and adaptation, where inclusive leadership plays a significant role. Leaders have an obligation to be able to inspire, motivate and empower teachers to adopt inclusive practices, thus ensuring that all students, regardless of their differences, have equal opportunities to gain experience and thrive.

In summary, strengthening inclusive skills in teachers through agile change management is not only possible, but necessary to meet the current challenges in higher education. This requires a leadership committed to equity and inclusion, capable of guiding its educational community towards a future where diversity is considered a valuable asset in the educational process.

Likewise, agile change in education is crucial to adapt to the diverse needs of students in a constantly evolving educational environment. Committed leadership that fosters creativity and supports teachers in adopting inclusive practices is essential to ensure accessible and equitable education for all.

Therefore, agile change management focuses on a continuous process of learning and adaptation. In addition, involving all educational actors, promoting a culture of openness and flexibility. This strategy allows inclusion to be a dynamic and sustainable process, constantly adjusting and improving in response to emerging needs, ensuring that diversity is valued as an asset within the educational system.

REFERENCES

Ainscow, M. (2020). Promoting inclusion and equity in education: Lessons from international experiences. *Prospects*, 49, 9–21. DOI: 10.1007/s11125-020-09495-8

Altbach, P. G., & Peterson, P. M. (2023). *Global Perspectives on Higher Education*. Routledge.

Audisio, M., Rueda, M., & Rodríguez, R. (2021). Uso de aplicaciones de gestión de proyectos como herramientas de apoyo, en espacios académicos de las instituciones de educación superior. *Revista Difusiones*, 21(2), 148–162.

Avolio, B. J., & Yammarino, F. J. (Eds.). (2013). Introduction to, and overview of, transformational and charismatic leadership. In *Transformational and charismatic leadership: The road ahead 10th anniversary edition* (pp. xxvii-xxxiii). Emerald Group Publishing Limited.Daft, R. L. (2021). *The Leadership Experience* (8a ed.). Cengage Learning. DOI: 10.1108/S1479-357120130000005005

Ballesteros, L. (2021). Implementación y práctica de scrum en la asignatura de formulación y evaluación de proyectos en la facultad de ciencias económicas y administrativas de la Universidad El Bosque. *Panorama*, 15(29), 7. DOI: 10.15765/pnrm.v15i29.2538

Barrientos, C., Silva, P. & Antúnez, S. (2016). El papel directivo y la promoción de la participación de las familias y la comunidad en las escuelas básicas. El caso de la Comuna de Panguipulli-Chile. REICE. *Revista Iberoamericana sobre Calidad. Eficacia y Cambio en Educación*,

Bass, B. M., & Stogdill, R. M. (1990). *Bass & Stogdill's Handbook of Leadership: Theory, Research, and Managerial Applications*. Free Press.

Booth, T., & Ainscow, M. (2005). *Index for inclusion*. Centre for Studies on Inclusive Education.

Booth, T., & Ainscow, M. (2011). Index for inclusion: Developing learning and participation in schools. Bristol: Centre for Studies on Inclusive Education (CSIE).

Chen, L., Johnson, D. J., & Smith, S. (2023). *Educational Technology in Higher Education: Current Trends and Future Directions*. Springer.

Cobeñas, P., & Grimaldi, V. (2021). Discusiones sobre inclusión educativa: una perspectiva desde la educación inclusiva. In Cobeñas, P., Grimaldi, V., Broitman, C., Sancha, I., & Escobar, M. (Eds.), *La enseñanza de las matemáticas a alumnos con discapacidad* (pp. 104–162). UDULP.

Collet-Sabe, J. (2020). Las relaciones entre la escuela y las familias desde una perspectiva democrática: Ejes de análisis y propuestas para la equidad. *Educar*, 56(1), 241–258. DOI: 10.5565/rev/educar.1012

Crisol, E., Romero, M.A., Burgos, A., & Sánchez, Y. (2022). Liderazgo inclusivo desde la perspectiva familiar en la Educación Obligatoria. *Revista de nuevos enfoques en investigación educativa*, 11 (2), 226-245. DOI: 10.7821/naer.2022.7.937

Cuevas, J. (2023). *Evaluación de un programa de formación docente hacia universitarios con discapacidad* [Tesis para obtener el grado de maestría]. Universidad de Sonora.

Cuevas, J., Hoyos, G., Quintana, O., Norzagaray, C., & Figueroa, C. (2022). Percepción de las funciones básicas de los estudiantes universitarios con discapacidad. *RIDE Revista Iberoamericana para la Investigación y el Desarrollo Educativo*, 13(25). Advance online publication. DOI: 10.23913/ride.v13i25.1369

Cuevas, J., Quintana, M., Figueroa, C., & Hoyos, G. (2022). Perfil de ingreso de estudiantes con discapacidad en la Universidad de Sonora. In Norzagaray, C., & Fraijo, J. (Eds.), *Inclusión educative de estudiantes con discapacidad en las instituciones de educación superior*. Fontamara.

Echeverría, F., León, M., Musso, L., & Pozo, E. (2021). SCRUMM como método ágil al aprendizaje dentro de cursos de estudiantes de maestría. *Revista Ibérica de Sistemas y Tecnologías de Información*, 47(1), 1–12.

European Agency for Special Needs and Inclusive Education. (2019). *Inclusive School Leadership: Exploring Policies Across Europe. Retrieved from*https://www.european-agency.org/resources/publications/inclusive-school-leadership-synthesis

Fernández, K. (2018). Programa de inclusion y equidad educative: Perspectiva docente. *Academia Journals*, 10(2), 608–612.

Florian, L., & Black-Hawkins, K. (2011). Exploring inclusive pedagogy. *British Educational Research Journal*, 37(5), 813–828. DOI: 10.1080/01411926.2010.501096

Gallego, E. M. (2023). Formación Docente Para La Educación Inclusiva en Instituciones Públicas Del Quindío. *Siglo Cero*, 54(4), 11–27. DOI: 10.14201/scero.31473

Gandomani, T. J., Zulzalil, H., Ghani, A. A. A., & Sultan, A. B. M. (2013). Towards comprehensive and disciplined change management strategy in agile transformation process. *Research Journal of Applied Sciences, Engineering and Technology*, 6(13), 2345–2351. DOI: 10.19026/rjaset.6.3706

Godoy, M., & Hidalgo, M. (2020). *Guía de accesibilidad digital para la docencia online*. Ediciones UVM.

Goleman, D. (2000). Leadership That Gets Results. *Harvard Business Review*, 78(2), 78–90.

Gutiérrez, M., Hernández, R., & Jenaro, C. (2019). Escala de evaluación de la inclusión (EEI) para centros y servicios para personas con discapacidad: Validación preliminar. *Revista Nacional e Internacional de Educación Inclusiva*, 12(1), 97–118.

Hasan, A. jafa, Fraij, J., & Várallyai, L. (2021). The Role of Agile Management in HRM Environment Change. Journal of Agricultural Informatics / Agrárinformatika Folyóirat, 12(2), 37–45. DOI: 10.17700/jai.2021.12.2.606

Hernandez, C., Fernández, M., Carrión, J., & Avilés, B. (2018). La inclusión educative en la Universidad de Minho. Percepciones y actitudes sobre el alumnado con discapacidad. *Revista Complutense de Educación.*, 30(4), 1097–1112. DOI: 10.5209/rced.60106

Hicks, T., Miller, M., & Young, R. (2024). *Mental Health and Wellbeing in Higher Education*. Palgrave Macmillan.

Hoyos, G., Salas, A., & Cuevas, J. (2021). *Percepción de universitarios sobre sus compañeros con discapacidad*. Editorial Académica Española.

Itati, S., Cardozo, G., & Alfonzo, P. (2021). Agilidad en el aprendizaje active: Propuesta en la asignatura modelos y simulación. Mendive. *Review of Education*, 19(2), 542–554.

Kouzes, J. M., & Posner, B. Z. (2017). *The Leadership Challenge: How to Make Extraordinary Things Happen in Organizations*. Wiley.

Kuh, G. D. (2024). *Financing Higher Education: Challenges and Solutions*. Jossey-Bass.

Lapicki, R. S., & Terlato, A. N. (2021). Empresas ágiles - Claves para sobrevivir a la complejidad del ambiente. *Documentos de Trabajo*, 777, 1–30.

Le Grand, T., & Deneckere, R. (2019). COOC: an agile change management method. In 2019 IEEE 21st Conference on Business Informatics (CBI) 2, pp. 28-37. IEEE. Doi: DOI: 10.1109/CBI.2019.10093

Marginson, S. (2024). *Higher Education and the Knowledge Economy*. Cambridge University Press.

Márquez, , Sandoval, M., Sánchez, S., Simón, C., Moriña, A., Morgado, B., Moreno-Medina, I., García, J. A., Díaz-Gandasegui, V., & Elizalde-San Miguel, B. (2020). Evaluación de la inclusión en educación superior mediante indicadores. *REICE. Revista Electrónica Iberoamericana sobre Calidad, Eficacia y Cambio en Educación*, 19(3), 39–59. DOI: 10.15366/reice2021.19.3.003

Mejía, P., & Ullauri, J. (2022). Actitudes de estudiates sobre el proceso inclusive de una persona Sorda en un contexto áulico Universitario, una experiencia inicial en la Universidad Nacional de Educación. *Revisma MAMAKUNA*, 19, 104–115.

Murillo, F. J. (2006). Una dirección escolar para el cambio: Del liderazgo transformacional al liderazgo distribuido. REICE. *Revista Electrónica Iberoamericana sobre Calidad, Eficacia y Cambio en Educación*, 4(4), 11–24. https://www.redalyc.org/articulo.oa?id=55140403

Naranjo, M. & Carrasco, A. (2022). Participación estudiantil e inclusión digital en la Universidad. Un studio en contextos iberoamericanos. Foro de educación, 20(1), 10-38.

Northouse, P. G. (2018). *Leadership: Theory and Practice*. Sage Publications.

Northouse, P. G. (2021). *Leadership: Theory and Practice* (9a ed.). SAGE Publications.

Okoko, J. M. (2019). Towards school leadership development: The essence of working with culturally and linguistically diverse newcomer families in Saskatchewan. *Research in Educational Administration & Leadership*, 4(2), 195–229. DOI: 10.30828/real/2019.2.1

Ordoñez, H., Escobar, A., Velandia, D., & Cobos, C. (2015). Business Processes as a Strategy to Improve Re-quirements Elicitation in Extreme Programming (XP). In *Memorias del VII Congreso de Telematica CITA*.

Ossa, C., Castro, F., Castañeda, M., & Castro, J. (2014). Cultura y liderazgo escolar: Factores claves para el desarrollo de la inclusión educativa. *Revista Electrónica. Actualidades Investigativas en Educación*, 14(3). Advance online publication. DOI: 10.15517/aie.v14i3.16157

Paľová, D., & Vejačka, M. (2023). Transformative Education with Agile Project Management and Project-Based Learning. *Ad Alta: Journal of Interdisciplinary Research*, 13(2), 197–206. DOI: 10.33543/j.1302.197206

Papeles de Economía Española. (2024). Desafíos y oportunidades para el futuro de la educación superior. Resúmenes ejecutivos (N.º 180). ISSN: 0210-9107

Quijada, K. (2021). Acciones afirmativas para la inclusion universitaria de estudiantes afrodescendientes e indígenas en Brasil, Colombia y México. *Ciencia y Cultura*, 46, 135–162.

Rodríguez, D. (2019). *Metodología ágil en la gestión de proyectos de medios educativos basados en las tecnologías de información para el SENA* [Tesis para obtener grado de maestría]. Universidad EAN.

Rodríguez, R., Rabassa, G., Salas, R., & Pardo, A. (2017). *Protocolo de identificación y evaluación del alumnado de altas capacidades en centros escolares.* Univesitat Santillana.

Rojas, R. A. (2023). La educación superior para el 2050. Desafíos y oportunidades para un futuro no tan lejano . Revista Educación Superior Y Sociedad (ESS), 35(1), 152-178. DOI: 10.54674/ess.v35i1.751

Sánchez, S., Simón, C., Moriña, A., Morgado, B., Moreno-Medina, I., García, J. A., Díaz-Gandasegui, V., & Elizalde, B. (2021). Evaluación de la inclusión en educación superior mediante indicadores. REICE. *Revista Electrónica Iberoamericana sobre Calidad, Eficacia y Cambio en Educación*, 19(3), 33–51. DOI: 10.15366/reice2021.19.3.003

Sevilla, D., Martín, M., & Jenaro, C. (2018). Actitud del docente hacia la educación inclusiva y hacia los estudiantes con necesidades educativas especiales. *Innovación Educativa (México, D.F.)*, 18(78), 115–142.

Sotomayor, P., Muñoz, J., Martínez, P., & Araya, A. (2020). Liderazgo, cultura y prácticas inclusivas desde la mirada de equipos directivos de establecimientos educativos. *Revista de Investigación en Comunicación y Desarrollo*, 11(1), 5–15. DOI: 10.33595/2226-1478.11.1.375

The Chronicle of Higher Education. (2023). *Post-pandemic higher education: Challenges and opportunities*. The Chronicle of Higher Education. https://www.chronicle.com/article/post-pandemic-higher-education-challenges-and-opportunities

Valdés, R., & Gómez-Hurtado, I. (2019). Competencias y prácticas de liderazgo escolar para la inclusión y la justicia social. *Perspectiva educativa.Formación de Profesores*, 58(2), 47–68. DOI: 10.4151/07189729

Wiśniewska-Sałek, A. (2021). Change Management: Agile Business Transformation in the Hybrid Education System Management. *Proceedings of the European Conference on Knowledge Management*, 821–829. https://doi.org/DOI: 10.34190/EKM.21.179

Wong, K. V., & Robles, D. R. (2024). Barreras que afronta el alumnado con discapacidad visual en los servicios de apoyo para la inclusión en educación superior en México. DOI: 10.1590/SciELOPreprints.7967

Zapata, J. C. M., & Yepes, P. D. E. (2024). Representation of some principles of the Agile Manifesto in the Semat Essence Kernel. *Scientia et Technica*, 29(1), 41–48. DOI: 10.22517/23447214.24241

Endnotes

1 The Agile Manifesto is a methodology developed in 2001 by 17 programmers led by Kent Beck. They improved the techniques for the creation of software, evolving the traditional methods of development (Zapata & Yepes, 2024).

2 The Lean Management philosophy originated in the 1990s in the Japanese automotive industry. Based on respect for people, it aims to offer solutions that simplify processes, services and bureaucratic administrative systems (Cano et al., 2022).

3 Extreme Programming refers to an agile methodology that encourages teamwork and facilitates constant feedback between the participants, whether they are customers or users interested in the project, and the development team (Ordoñez et al., 2015).

4 Scrum is a framework that allows people to face complex problems adaptively and deliver high-value products productively and creatively. Although it has been used mainly in the IT industry, in recent years it has found applications in other sectors, both private and public, including the education sector (Ballesteros, 2021).

Chapter 6
Personal Motivation for Digital Inclusion in Human Capital Within Organizations

Betzabe García Córdova
Instituto Politécnico Nacional, Mexico

ABSTRACT

One of the most representative impacts on the development of human capital is the reduced use of paper, thus generating a culture of sustainability in processes as everything is archived digitally. This leads to more feasibility in the use of digital resources, speed, document location, and information security. However, these new alternatives can create a knowledge gap in the use of technological tools. One of the most representative impacts on the development of human capital is the reduced use of paper, thus generating a culture of sustainability in processes as everything is archived digitally. This leads to more feasibility in the use of digital resources, speed, document location, and information security. However, these new alternatives can create a knowledge gap in the use of technological tools. The development of technological inclusion for all involved is necessary; this inclusion must be structured with a well-planned action plan to close the gaps in information lag or the use of technological resources.

DOI: 10.4018/979-8-3693-7086-5.ch006

INTRODUCTION

Currently, the skills that university students, school students or business organizations mainly possess are based on the management and development of new alternatives in a digital world. Technology, leadership and the components that make up the student or worker will complement the skills of future human capital, which requires experience and knowledge to integrate into a digital world and the environment will provide skills training to human personnel who are immersed in this phenomenon.

The Multidisciplinarity of human capital in the Digital Age, by covering the different disciplines united to direct or manage a project, focuses on the area of study and, for example: the training of human capital is a useful tool transferred to digital processes, that is, it has advantages from the formulation of strategies from a digital perspective, the development and creation of continuous improvement proposals that add value to the organization and the potentialization of resources, including first-hand human capital.

Chapter Objective

Personal motivation for digital inclusion in the human capital of organizations is a chapter whose main objective is for the reader to know in a broad, optimal, concise and coherent way the elements that revolve around the described topic, starting from the most basic needs of the human being to contextualize the environment of what personal motivation is, how it is achieved, how it is known, what elements surround it, up to the disciplines that are immersed, the regulations that govern the characteristics of international frameworks and everything related to digital inclusion.

Background

The lack of personal motivation for digital inclusion in human capital is a complex phenomenon with deep historical and sociological roots. Below are some of the most relevant antecedents.

Historical and Social factors:

Digital divide: Historically, access to digital technologies has been unequal, generating a digital divide that has made it difficult for certain population groups to be included. This has created a perception that technology is something foreign or inaccessible to many.

Accelerated technological change: The rapid evolution of technologies has generated a feeling of information overload and difficulty in keeping up. This can generate apathy and resistance to change in some people.

Job seniority: Workers with greater job seniority, accustomed to traditional work methods, may show greater resistance to adopting new technologies, especially if they do not perceive clear benefits in their daily performance.

Lack of formal education: Formal education that has not integrated digital skills across the board can create a gap in the knowledge and skills needed to use technologies effectively.

Fear of failure: Fear of making mistakes when using new technologies can lead to anxiety and demotivation, especially in people with low digital self-esteem.

Organizational Factors

Lack of training: Many organizations do not offer adequate training programs to develop the digital skills of their employees.

Resistance to change: Organizational changes, such as the implementation of new digital tools, can generate resistance and demotivation if not managed properly.

Lack of incentives: The absence of incentives or recognition for the use of technologies can decrease employee motivation.

Organizational culture: An organizational culture that does not value innovation and adaptation to change can make it difficult to adopt new technologies.

Individual Factors

Age: Age can influence the willingness to learn new technologies, as older people may be less familiar with them and have greater difficulty adapting.

Work experience: Previous work experience can shape attitudes toward new technologies.

Personality: Individual personality, such as openness to change or risk aversion, can influence motivation to learn new digital skills.

Perception of usefulness: If employees do not perceive a clear benefit in using new technologies for their daily work, they are less likely to be motivated to learn them.

The human being

Multidisciplinarity in Human Capital

Multidisciplinarity in human capital is a topic of growing relevance in the digital age, where the convergence of technologies and the rapid evolution of business demand professionals with diverse and complementary skills. Within this evolution are the contributions of important authors who throughout history according to:

Thomas H. Davenport: This renowned expert in knowledge management and business analytics has explored in depth how organizations can take advantage of the diversity of skills and perspectives to drive innovation and the resolution of complex problems.

On the other hand: Davenport highlights the importance of creating multidisciplinary teams that can integrate different disciplines to address the challenges of the 21st century.

Don Tapscott (2006): A pioneer in the study of the impact of emerging technologies on society and business, he has emphasized the need to develop a new type of leadership that can navigate an increasingly complex and connected world. In his works, he addresses the importance of collaboration and multidisciplinarity to drive digital transformation.

This digital transformation, due to the speed at which it has developed, makes it somewhat complex to ensure that all disciplines are known in some way by the same users, that is, to be aware of everything that emerging technologies and their multidisciplinarity imply.

On the other hand, according to: Linda Gratton (2005): Expert in the future of work, has investigated how organizations can develop the talent of their employees to adapt to a constantly changing work environment, highlighting the importance of the following elements:

Flexibility, adaptability,

the ability to learn throughout life and key skills for multidisciplinary professionals. Key elements and trends in multidisciplinarity in human capital are based on the following key concepts:

Design thinking: This user-centered methodology encourages collaboration between designers, engineers, researchers and other professionals to create innovative solutions to complex problems.

Agility: Agility implies the ability to adapt quickly to changes and to deliver value incrementally. Multidisciplinary teams are essential to adopt agile practices.

Artificial intelligence and automation: These technologies are transforming the world of work, creating new opportunities for collaboration between humans and machines. Multidisciplinary professionals can take advantage of these technologies to increase their productivity and creativity. Human capital is the most important resource in many companies and industries, and since we are dealing with human beings, it is necessary to have a relationship with disciplines such as: psychology, medicine, administration, sociology, anthropology, economics and social sciences. Human capital is a set of knowledge, skills and experiences of the workers of a company, which are mainly acquired through daily care and training. Below, the disciplines mentioned and their main use for the human factor are detailed:

Psychology: Psychology is a discipline that is used in the theoretical basis of human resources, which is responsible for the mental health of each of the workers,

Sociology as an organizational behavior that is based on disciplines related to human behavior and its development with the environment and society, involving actions such as: values exercised, civic values, rights and obligations of each person.

Anthropology: Studies the human being from his culture, his society, his behavior analyzing human reality.

Economy: Refers to the financial resources and knowledge of each of the collaborators to have financial education.

Social sciences: Studies human behavior in its different facets and roles with the society that surrounds it.

From a critical perspective, it is necessary to ask: Why is multidisciplinarity important? Below are some relevant characteristics of the answer to this question:

Innovation: Multidisciplinary teams can generate more creative and disruptive ideas by combining different perspectives and knowledge.

Complex problem solving: Complex problems often require a holistic view that can only be achieved through the collaboration of different disciplines.

Adaptability: The ability to adapt to a constantly changing work environment is essential for success in the digital age. Multidisciplinary professionals are more flexible and adaptable.

Challenges and Opportunities

Although multidisciplinarity offers numerous advantages, it also presents some challenges which require positive actions to achieve the necessary synergy in each of its interactions and thus achieve that human capital automatically achieves all its capabilities through:

Communication: Effective communication between professionals from different disciplines can be a challenge.

Team management: Managing multidisciplinary teams requires specific leadership skills.

Organizational culture: Organizational culture must encourage collaboration and diversity.

The use of technology has become a fundamental part of the daily life of the vast majority of people around the world, or current technological ones, however, the human being is more than a programming since it needs for survival and from the most basic activities of human survival, to the use of technology for the solution of current problems.

The human being, by the fact of being so, is programmed to develop basic skills of first necessity such as the psychological ones mentioned above, the distribution of time, assertiveness and personal motivation among many others which are found in the disciplines that relate to the human being, his capacities and his needs.

Personal motivation and human capital

Personal motivation in a person in all its areas and those that are broken down from them are the basis of the fundamental traits for the realization of the things that the human being wants to achieve and that has sufficient stimulation for the achievement of the activities or objectives that each person wants to achieve.

When these situations of the human being are raised, the foundations of life of the personality traits of each person are being reconsidered.

Each person who makes up the human capital department of a company or educational institution has personal needs, desires and wishes which are found in the personality of each of the employees. Among these is personal motivation which is defined:

Colloquially explained as the engine that drives each human being to carry out activities such as working, interacting or learning in a multidisciplinary way in different areas.

Various theories have emerged to explain what drives people to act and strive in their work roles.

Description of the Problem

The main problem identified and to promote awareness in organizations is that in each company each collaborator is a valuable element and that they use digital tools which, if not used correctly, always being in the same position or not having these tools for personal use and without prior training, it is perceived that workers can become demotivated by the indiscriminate use of technology or by the misuse of them due to not being familiar with the technology.

Historical Perspectives:

Theories of Scientific Administration: At the beginning of the 20th century, economic incentives were emphasized as the main motivator. It was believed that, by offering higher salaries or material rewards, workers would increase their productivity. School of Human Relations: In the 1920s, the importance of social relations at work was recognized. It was discovered that factors such as the sense of belonging, recognition and interpersonal relationships significantly influenced motivation. Maslow's Hierarchy of Needs: Proposed in the 1940s, this theory suggests that people have a hierarchy of needs that must be met in a specific order. From basic physiological needs to self-actualization, each level must be reached before the next becomes a motivator.

Modern Perspectives on Personal Motivation Exist According to Herzberg's Two-Factor Theory (1959): Distinguishes between hygiene factors (which prevent dissatisfaction, such as pay and working conditions) and motivational factors (which generate satisfaction, such as recognition and achievement).

Expectancy Theory: Suggests that motivation is influenced by a person's expectations about the outcomes of his or her effort.

Equity Theory: Is based on social comparison. People evaluate whether their contribution and reward are fair compared to others.

On the other hand, Herrera, Ramírez, Roa and Herrera (2004) indicate that motivation is one of the most important explanatory keys of human behavior with respect to the "why" of the behavior. That is, motivation represents what originally determines that the person initiates an action (activation), moves towards an objective (direction) and persists in achieving it (maintenance).

These The authors, after compiling the opinions of many others, formulated the following definition of motivation: we could understand it as a process that explains the initiation, direction, intensity and perseverance of behaviour aimed at achieving a goal, modulated by the perceptions that subjects have of themselves and by the tasks they have to face.

According to the explanations provided by Herrera et al. (2004), the historical evolution of the interpretation of motivation can be summarised as follows:

Between the 1920s and the mid-1960s, the subject of motivation was associated with experimental research into aspects such as motor behaviour, instinct and drive. During that period, the aim was to determine what leads an organism to restore its state of equilibrium or homeostasis, based on external factors that determine motivation, such as reinforcements.

After the 1960s, cognitive theories of motivation emerged, focusing on conscious experience, interest in performance motivation and its importance, along with achievements in personal life. For example, Atkinson's theory (cited by Herrera et al., 2004) establishes that performance motivation is determined by the value given to the goal and the expectations of achieving it, taking into account the characteristics of people with high or low need for performance, anxiety and internal control.

From the 1970s to the present, the trend is marked by cognitive theories, which highlight the importance of some of its constituent elements; among them, self-concept, as a central element of motivational theories. Different studies refer to aspects such as the role of causal attribution, perception of competence, perception of control, beliefs about ability and self-efficacy and learned helplessness, among others. According to: Pink D. (2021) "The Three Factors that Motivate Human Beings", One of the most representative impacts on the development of human capital is the reduction in the use of paper, fostering a culture of sustainability, since everything is filed digitally. This transition leads to greater feasibility in the use of digital resources, speed, accessibility.

Therefore, it is necessary to develop technological inclusion for all those involved. This inclusion must include planning an action plan to close the information deficiency gap or the use of technological resources now.

Behavioral Perspective

Those who agree with the use of incentives emphasize that they add interest and motivation to behavior, direct attention to appropriate behaviors and away from those considered inappropriate.

People usually perform behaviors with the aim of obtaining some benefit and avoiding or stopping those that lead to harm. For this approach, all behavior modification is basically done through reinforcements, rewards or avoiding or omitting that which is unpleasant.

To achieve a change in behavior, different methods can be applied, including reinforcement, extinction (not reinforcing a behavior), and punishment. Reinforcements can be positive or negative.

Positive reinforcements are used to increase the likelihood that an expected response will occur, so they can be said to be a reward.

The principle of positive reinforcement states that: "if in a given situation a person does something that is immediately followed by a positive reinforcer, that person is more likely to do the same thing again when faced with a similar situation" (Martín and Pear, cited by Naranjo, 2004, p. 41). Naranjo (2004) points out that there are several factors that must be taken into account to make effective use of positive reinforcement:

First, the behaviors to be reinforced must be specifically identified.

Second, appropriate motivators must be selected. Third, other aspects must be taken into account, such as the immediacy of the presentation of the reinforcement, deprivation and satiation, the amount of the reinforcement, and the novelty of the reinforcement. The reinforcer should be given immediately after the desired response is presented.

When the reinforcement is given immediately, the person can more easily identify the behaviors for which he or she receives the reinforcement and those for which he or she does not. Regarding deprivation and satiety, a reinforcer is considered ineffective if the person has not been deprived of it for some time. For example:

Offering a snack does not work as a reinforcer if the person has just eaten. In this case, there is a problem of satiety; that is, the reinforcer has been experienced so much that it stops fulfilling its function.

Novelty is another important aspect to consider in motivation to make reinforcements more effective.

In the extinction method, the behavior is not reinforced. According to Trechera (2005), the extinction of a behavior occurs when the reinforcing stimulus that sustains it is not presented. By not reinforcing the behavior, it will weaken, thus decreasing the probability of its repetition. In the punishment method, an aversive consequence is administered upon the appearance of a behavior. It is a way for the person to learn what he or she should not do, instead of what he or she should do. Azaroff and Mayer (cited by Naranjo, 2004) point out that:

Do not reward all people equally, reinforcements or rewards should be based on personal qualities and performance; be sure to tell the person what he or she must do to obtain the reinforcement.

"Tell the person what he or she is doing wrong"

Do not punish in the presence of other people, since public repression humiliates; likewise, be fair when granting a reward. García (2008) establishes differences between motivators and motivations, pointing out, on the one hand, that motivators are things that induce a person to achieve high performance; on the other hand, motivations are a reflection of the individual's desires, so motivators are the rewards or incentives already identified that increase the drive to satisfy those desires.

A motivator is something that powerfully influences a person's behavior. Similarly, differences are pointed out between motivation and satisfaction. Motivation refers to the drive and effort to achieve a goal, while satisfaction refers to the pleasure experienced once the goal is achieved. That is, motivation implies a drive towards a result, while satisfaction is the experience of the result.

It should be noted that the impact of digitalization is also immersed in the most widely used social networks worldwide, which also provide all kinds of information and digital tools for human beings. These networks promote inclusion by eliminating barriers with visual and auditory content, which also manages to impact mainly the human capital immersed in an organization. These same communication networks applied to specific objectives and the knowledge of their use are also indispensable for the fulfillment of organizational objectives.

The humanistic perspective emphasizes the person's ability to achieve their growth, their positive characteristics and the freedom to choose their destiny. The Theory of Needs is located within this perspective and includes the following:

Physiological needs: These are related to the human being as a biological being. They are the basic needs to sustain life. People need to satisfy certain basic needs in order to function, including: food, shelter and rest.

Security needs: These are those that lead a person to avoid physical risks, achieve stability, organize and structure the environment; that is, ensure survival.

Needs for love and belonging (social): As social beings, people experience the need to relate to others, to be accepted, to belong. They are related to the desire to receive affection from family, friends and partners.

Esteem needs: These are related to feeling good about oneself, to feeling like a worthy being with prestige. All people have a need for good self-evaluation, respect, and positive self-esteem, which also implies the esteem of other human beings.

The dissatisfaction of the needs indicated in this hierarchy has an important emotional impact, according to Bisquerra (2022). On the other hand, Valdés (2005) explains that Maslow discovered two additional needs experienced by those people who have satisfied the five mentioned above (very few people according to Trechera the author), which he called cognitive, they are: Need to know and understand the world around the person and nature. Need for aesthetic satisfaction, referring to the needs for beauty, symmetry and art in general and finally the:

Self-determination Theory: It emphasizes the importance of the basic psychological needs of autonomy, competence and relatedness for intrinsic motivation. These needs are a fundamental part of the importance of collaborating in the personal motivation of human capital, which can be achieved through:

Key Factors in Current Motivation:

Meaning: People look for jobs that have a purpose and that allow them to contribute to something bigger than themselves.

Development: The opportunity to learn new skills and grow professionally is highly valued.

Autonomy: The desire to have control over their work and make decisions.

Recognition: Recognition for achievements and feeling valued are fundamental.

Relationships: Positive relationships with colleagues and leaders are essential for well-being and motivation.

On the other hand, referring to training materials for workers, one of the most representative impacts on the formation of human capital today, among others, is the reduced use of paper, thus generating a culture of sustainability in the processes which directly impacts workers from the same perspective of how the company or educational institution changes the processes to evolve since everything is filed digitally, more feasibility in the use of digital resources, speed, location of documents and the protection of information, these actions directly impact human capital and feeling the constant positive changes, contribute directly or indirectly to the motivation of human capital.

Human Capital Management

Human capital management (HCM) is a strategic area within organizations that focuses on maximizing the potential of its employees. In essence, it is about managing and developing the people who make up the company to achieve organizational objectives.

Main Objectives of HCM:

Attract talent: Identify, recruit and select the best candidates for available positions.

Develop talent: Offer training, development and professional growth opportunities so that employees acquire new skills and knowledge.

Retain talent: Implement strategies to keep employees motivated and committed to the organization, avoiding staff turnover.

Improve performance: Establish performance evaluation systems and design incentive programs to boost productivity and quality of work.

Foster a positive organizational culture: Create a work environment where employees feel valued, respected and motivated.

Key and representative areas of HCM in human capital:

Recruitment and selection: Processes to find and hire the right candidates.

Organizational development: Design of training and skills development programs.

Compensation and benefits: Administration of salaries, bonuses, benefits and social benefits.

Labor relations: Management of relations between the company and employees, including collective bargaining and conflict resolution.

Performance Management: Individual and team performance assessment, goal setting, and feedback.

Succession Planning: Identifying and developing future leaders within the organization.

Importance of HCM:

Competitive Advantage: Organizations with effective human capital management have a competitive advantage by having highly trained and motivated employees.

Increased Productivity: Motivated and engaged employees are more productive and generate better results.

Reduced Staff Turnover: By investing in employee development and creating a positive work environment, talent loss is reduced.

Improved Corporate Image: Good human capital management contributes to building a positive image of the company as a good place to work.

Current Trends in HCM:

Digitalization: The implementation of technological tools to automate processes and improve talent management.

Employee Experience: The focus on creating positive experiences for employees at all stages of their relationship with the organization.

Skills Development: The emphasis on developing soft skills and digital competencies.

Diversity and inclusion: Promoting diversity in the workforce and creating inclusive work environments.

Remote and flexible work: Adapting to new ways of working in response to technological and social changes.

Human capital management is extremely important as it is a fundamental discipline for the success of any organization. By investing in their employees, companies can build highly motivated and committed teams that drive growth and innovation

Technological Tools

These are programs or applications that facilitate the completion of tasks, from the simplest to the most complex. These tools take advantage of technology to optimize processes, save time and resources, and improve efficiency in various areas. Likewise, they must be related to the tools used in each workplace corresponding to the procedures of each work area.

It is necessary to know what are technological tools?

They are programs or applications that facilitate the completion of tasks, from the simplest to the most complex. These tools take advantage of technology to optimize processes, save time and resources, and improve efficiency in various areas.

Types of technological tools:

There are a wide variety of technological tools, each designed for a specific purpose. Technological tools are indispensable in today's world. They allow us to work more efficiently, communicate more effectively, and access an unprecedented amount of information. Some examples are:

Word processors: Word, Google Docs (to create and edit documents).

Spreadsheets: Excel, Google Sheets (to organize and analyze numerical data).

Presentations: PowerPoint, Google Slides (to create slides and visual presentations).

Graphic design: Adobe Photoshop, Canva (to create images and designs).

Video editing: Adobe Premiere Pro, iMovie (to edit videos).

Communication: email, instant messaging, video conferencing (to keep in touch with other people).

Project management: Trello, Asana (to organize tasks and teams).

Cloud storage: Google Drive, Dropbox (to save files online).

Artificial intelligence: virtual assistants like Siri, Alexa (to perform tasks by voice).

Nowadays, in order to understand workers, it is necessary to know: What are technological tools for? Increase productivity: automating repetitive tasks and optimizing processes, all of these elements must be guided so that the worker is motivated in their use. In other words, personal motivation also enters directly or indirectly into the use of technological tools, it helps to:

Facilitate communication: connecting people from all over the world in real time, Access information: putting a huge amount of data at the click of a button, Create and share content: allowing creative expression and collaboration, Solve complex problems: offering analysis and simulation tools. Some of the main benefits of using technological tools are:

Greater efficiency: by automating tasks and optimizing processes,

Better communication: facilitating interaction and the exchange of information,

Access to information: putting a large amount of knowledge at the reach of everyone,

Development of skills: encouraging learning and creativity.

Innovation: driving the development of new solutions and products.

In the educational part: Online learning: platforms such as Coursera, edX (to access courses and training).

Technological tools must be provided by the company, to encourage workers it would also be important to have the flexibility of an informative talk on the use of said tools so that, in case of staff turnover, or the arrival of new workers, the same elements can collaborate in training how to use these tools in the workplace, as well as encourage and motivate workers or collaborators to work collaboratively or among peers. Digital inclusion

The various new technological alternatives already mentioned above can create a knowledge gap in the use of technological tools. The development of technological inclusion in all those involved is necessary. This inclusion must be formed with a plan of action to close this gap in information lag or in the use of technological resources. Some actions that can be proposed to achieve technological inclusion in the organization can be based on some of the problems or situations of digitalization:

Familiarization with digital media: training of human capital in the organization in updating, online training, reinforcement and updating of knowledge. The use of electronic devices is important, and such resources should exist within the organization, such as the Internet, the devices and their correct use.

Failures in technology: Do not create obstacles in training and development. Human capital must also be trained for technological contingencies that may exist when technology has failures, such as loss of Internet, fostering an understanding of technology and its scope, as well as its correct use. To the extent possible, the organization must have digital devices with the use of the Internet in optimal conditions, updated, vaccinated and with a leadership in the manipulation of resources and their maximization.

In university institutions, as well as in organizations, the promotion of the acquisition of technology with financial support, courses on the use of artificial intelligence that promote community inclusion among peers, whether collaboratively between teacher and student or workers and supervisors depending on the field and the position held, as well as virtual attendance at events where human personnel are motivated to learn how to use new technological tools aimed not only at the work part but also at the part of knowledge, research, resolution of personal conflicts and interaction with the technological environment are some strategies that will combat digital lag in a targeted manner and can promote digital inclusion.

Likewise, the promotion of inclusion for people who do not have knowledge of how technological strategies are used, collaboration between institutions and digital spaces intended for these areas that have a high impact of motivation for the use of technology or promotion incentives in organizations based on digital preparation or use of technological tools will be of great support for this process of promoting technological inclusion.

The motivation to learn to use digitalization can be guided in different stages and moments, which will largely depend on the progress that each of the components of human capital can develop. Remembering that digitalization is a fundamental tool for achieving objectives linked to management and leadership, thus achieving an innovative, successful and competitive organization for the future and the present through data precision, creation of new teaching, business, and learning models through organizational leadership guided by digitalization as a fundamental axis for the entire organization without leaving aside the objective of digital inclusion.

It should be noted that the impact of digitalization and inclusion itself is also immersed in the most widely used social networks worldwide, the These networks also provide all kinds of information and digital tools for humans. These networks promote inclusion by eliminating barriers with visual and auditory content, which also manage to primarily impact the human capital immersed in an organization. These same communication networks applied to specific objectives and the knowledge of their use are also essential for the fulfillment of organizational objectives.

The use of artificial intelligence with machine learning is a fundamental part of digitalization, in which properly directed human capital facilitates the exchange of information. The development of digital dimensions with leadership actions for human capital is imperative.

Human beings are capable of reaching unimaginable places when they are highly motivated and interested in the objectives. If we are able to motivate people with leadership to train and use the digital tool, we can collaborate to combat the lack of digital inclusion and thus achieve impressive forms of management and leadership in the different areas of the organization.

Maintaining a high level of motivation over time is one of the challenges facing any organization. The initial drive with which new employees begin their work adventure is often affected over time, and monotony and experience begin to take their toll on their emotional state.

When employee morale declines, a stagnant work environment is created, which seriously affects the competitive spirit of the organization. As Human Resources managers or team leaders, we must be prepared and carry out initiatives that prevent the emergence of apathy. According to the European Commission (2023), digital inclusion is: It consists of including, contributing and benefiting all people without exception, all people who belong to that company, school, society or organization within all its technological areas, with clear examples such as those mentioned above or access to new technologies (ICT) guaranteeing structure, quality, prices and ease of use in each of the different areas.

Assistive technologies, which facilitate access to people with disabilities who would otherwise not be able to use them, are: Digital literacy, including ICT training in basic education and in people's continuous learning, Social inclusion, focusing on the most disadvantaged sectors of society with specific programs that help them enter the digital world, The digital divide not only divides people with access to the Internet from those who do not. There are other obstacles that prevent sectors of the population from becoming digital citizens:

Lack of skills due to not having the necessary training to use the Internet and online services.

Lack of confidence, partly due to lack of skills, makes some people afraid to enter the Internet.

Lack of motivation in each of the collaborators since many people do not access the Internet because they are unaware of the opportunities it offers.

Poor designs, because not all digital services and products are accessible and easy to use and The most vulnerable sectors of society are those who suffer the most from the digital divide, although there are variations between countries, it usually affects women, the elderly, racial and ethnic minorities, people with disabilities, rural populations and those with low socioeconomic status to a greater extent.

The Objectives and Benefits Of Digital Inclusion

They are usually immersed in the different actions of each of the areas of the organization and are a reflection of the results of each worker, that is, by using this technology there is greater access to information, digital media, which contributes in an important and exponential way to the enrichment of the social and work life of people in general. Likewise There are important associations or organizations such as:

Unesco (2017), which is concerned about global participation and has initiatives around the world to improve the participation of the digital society. It also participates in actions to achieve this inclusion worldwide. It also organizes the "Mobile Learning Week" to explore the possibilities of digital education.

On the other hand, the European Commission, within the Horizon 2020 program, finances a multitude of digital inclusion projects, especially in the field of accessibility, aimed at people with different types of disabilities. Digital leisure, including audiovisual content and video games, is a very valuable tool to promote access to the digital world, to the point that the Creative Europe program promotes the development of this type of content in EU countries.

International Digital Regulations

Within the parameters of use, regulation and optimization of digital resources, there is international regulation, which is responsible for regulating all activities related to the digitalization and use of ICTs.

According to the World Bank (2021), as a result of the SARS-CoV-2 pandemic or known as Covid 19, "Less than half of Latin Americans have high-quality fiber at home" which generates great inequality and promoted the formulation of public policies for the generation of potential private capital investors to combat this inequality. The World Bank (2021) also mentioned that 14.7% of the population of Latin America and the Caribbean had some type of disability, including old-age disorders, an increasingly growing segment. In this report, the formulation of progressive policies that would motivate inclusion through paradigm shift, educational inclusion, labor inclusion, and the application of universal design, among other measures, was proposed. This is an alarming problem in the use of technologies and technological tools used, since this inequality can be a bit problematic for the motivation of the use of technologies. However, it is extremely important to know this regulation in order to be aware that in Latin America there is this digital gap and thus somehow generate strategies to combat this gap, since technology advances very quickly and at the same time the problems of digital lag continue to attract them in a very synergistic way.

According to the list of the University of Alicate, some countries and their current situation regarding this very interesting subject can be observed:

Argentina: Law No. 26,653 on Web Accessibility establishes the standards for the accessibility of public and private sector websites that disseminate public information.

Brazil: Decree No. 5,296/2004 establishes the accessibility standards for people with disabilities on public and private sector websites, and also establishes the obligation of accessibility in the development of computer programs and applications.

Chile: Law No. 20,422 on equal opportunities and social inclusion of people with disabilities establishes the standards for the accessibility of public sector websites.

Colombia: Law 1712 of 2014, also known as the Law on Transparency and Access to Public Information, establishes the standards for the accessibility of public sector websites.

Costa Rica: Guideline No. 051-MTSS-MICITT of 2019 establishes the obligation to apply the WCAG 2.1 standard "Accessibility Guidelines for Web Content" and its subsequent versions, on the pages of its official websites.

Ecuador: The Organic Law on Disabilities establishes the standards for the accessibility of public sector websites.

Panama: Law No. 15 of May 18, 2017 establishes the standards for the accessibility of public sector websites. Peru: Law No. 29973, General Law for Persons with Disabilities, establishes the standards for accessibility of public and private sector websites.

Puerto Rico: Law 229 of 2003, Law to Guarantee Access to Information for Persons with Disabilities, aims to ensure the right to equal access of all citizens to the electronic pages of State entities.

Dominican Republic: NORTIC B2:2017 Standard on web accessibility of the Dominican State establishes the requirements that government agency portals must meet so that they can be used by all citizens, including people with disabilities.

Uruguay: Decree No. 406, of December 22, 2022, defines digital accessibility and implements actions to guarantee it based on the standards, requirements and technical demands stipulated by the Electronic Government and Information and Knowledge Society Agency.

Venezuela: Resolution 026 of 2011 establishes the accessibility "guidelines" (directives or guidelines) that must be applied by the Bodies and Entities of the National Public Administration in the development, implementation and production of Internet Portals.

And finally, Mexico: the General Law for the Inclusion of People with Disabilities establishes the standards for the accessibility of public and private sector websites.

Despite the efforts made, the technological digital gap has not been reduced in these countries, however, collaboration continues to achieve digital inclusion.

Global digital inclusion refers to ensuring that all people, regardless of their geographic location, socioeconomic status or abilities, have equal access to digital technologies and can use them effectively. This implies not only having access to the Internet and devices, but also having the digital skills necessary to fully participate in the information society.

Why is digital inclusion important?

Bridging the digital divide: The digital divide separates those who have access to technologies from those who do not. Digital inclusion seeks to close this gap and create opportunities for all.

Empowerment: Access to information and digital tools empowers people, allowing them to improve their quality of life, access education and employment, and participate in decision-making.

Economic development: Digital inclusion drives economic development by fostering innovation, entrepreneurship and the creation of new businesses.

Democratization of knowledge: By making information accessible to all, digital inclusion promotes the democratization of knowledge and fosters a more informed and participatory society.

Challenges of Global Digital Inclusion:

Internet access: Millions of people around the world still do not have access to the internet, especially in rural and low-income areas.

Devices: The lack of devices such as computers and smartphones limits access to digital technologies.

Digital skills: Many people lack the digital skills needed to use technologies effectively.

Cost: The cost of devices and internet access can be prohibitive for many people.

How to Achieve Global Digital Inclusion?

Infrastructure investment: Expand internet infrastructure and improve connectivity in remote areas.

Digital literacy programs: Offer training programs to develop people's digital skills.

Cost reduction: Promote policies that reduce the cost of devices and internet access.

International cooperation: Foster cooperation between governments, international organizations, and the private sector to address the challenges of digital inclusion.

Some examples of digital inclusion initiatives are:

Computer donation programs: Non-profit organizations and companies donate computers to low-income schools and communities.

Public spaces with internet access: Cities and communities create public spaces with free internet access, such as libraries and community centers.

Educational mobile applications: Development of mobile applications that offer quality education at low cost or for free.

In short, global digital inclusion is a fundamental objective to build a more equitable and sustainable future. By ensuring that all people have access to digital technologies and can use them effectively, we can empower communities, drive economic development and create a more fair and inclusive society.

The role of companies in digital inclusion is based on the fact that companies have a crucial role in promoting digital inclusion. By leveraging their resources and knowledge, they can help close the digital divide and create a more equitable and connected world.

Companies play a fundamental role in promoting digital inclusion worldwide. As drivers of innovation and technological development, they have the ability to significantly impact the lives of millions of people.

It is relevant to know how companies contribute to digital inclusion:

Development of accessible technologies: Many technology companies focus on creating products and services that are accessible to everyone, regardless of their capabilities. This includes developing intuitive user interfaces, customization options, and assistive technologies.

Investment in infrastructure: Telecom and technology companies invest in expanding networks and building digital infrastructure, facilitating internet access in remote and underdeveloped areas.

Education and training programs: Many companies offer digital education and training programs to help people develop the skills needed to use technologies effectively.

Collaboration with governments and nonprofits: Companies work together with governments and nonprofits to develop digital inclusion programs and address the needs of the most vulnerable communities.

Responsible business practices: Companies can promote digital inclusion through their business practices, such as offering products and services at affordable prices and ensuring the privacy and security of users' data.

Benefits of business involvement in digital inclusion:

Improved brand reputation: Companies that commit to digital inclusion are perceived as more responsible and socially conscious.

Access to new markets: Digital inclusion allows businesses to reach new customers and markets, which can lead to increased revenue and growth opportunities.

Innovation: Commitment to digital inclusion fosters innovation and the development of new technological solutions to address social challenges and Strengthening communities: Digital inclusion contributes to strengthening communities by providing access to information, education and economic opportunities.

Concrete examples of business initiatives:

Google: Has developed tools and programs to make the internet more accessible, such as Project Loon to provide connectivity to remote areas and the Digital Skills for Africa program.

Microsoft: Offers digital training programs and software donations to schools and non-profit organizations around the world.

Facebook: Has invested in internet infrastructure in developing countries and has launched initiatives to promote digital literacy.

Promoting digital inclusion is a complex challenge that requires a long-term vision, close collaboration between different actors and constant adaptation to a constantly evolving technological environment. However, the benefits of this initiative are undeniable, both for companies and for society in general.

Promoting digital inclusion is a laudable goal, but companies face a number of challenges that hinder its full implementation. Below are some of the most common ones:

Pre-existing digital divide:

Unequal access: Many communities, especially in rural or low-income areas, lack basic infrastructure such as electricity or internet connectivity.

Devices: Lack of devices such as computers or smartphones limits access to digital services.

Digital literacy: A large part of the population does not have the digital skills necessary to use technologies effectively

Costs and resources:

Initial investment: Implementing digital inclusion programs requires significant investment in infrastructure, technology, and training.

Maintenance: Maintaining these programs over the long term involves ongoing operating and updating costs.

Return on investment: It is not always easy to measure the return on investment in financial terms, making it difficult to justify these expenses to shareholders.

Cultural and linguistic adaptation:

Localized content: Developing digital content that is relevant and accessible to different cultures and languages can be a complex and costly challenge.

Usability: Adapting user interfaces to the needs and preferences of different cultural groups may require additional effort

Collaboration with multiple actors:

Government: It is essential to have the support of governments to create public policies that foster digital inclusion and facilitate collaboration between the public and private sectors.

Civil society organizations: Working with non-profit organizations and local communities is essential to identify specific needs and design appropriate solutions.

Technology provider companies: Collaboration with technology companies is necessary to gain access to the latest technologies and develop innovative solutions.

Impact measurement: Some of the indicators are: Defining clear and measurable indicators to assess the impact of digital inclusion programs can be complex. Long-term: The results of these programs are often long-term, making it difficult to immediately assess their effectiveness.

Changes in the technological environment:

Constant evolution: Technology evolves rapidly, requiring companies to constantly adapt and update their digital inclusion programs.

New technologies: The emergence of new technologies such as artificial intelligence and the Internet of Things poses new challenges and opportunities for digital inclusion.

National Digital Inclusion Regulations

The digital inclusion regulations in Mexico establish a solid framework to guarantee equal access to ICTs and reduce the digital divide. However, it is necessary to continue working to overcome existing challenges and take advantage of the opportunities offered by the digital age. Digital inclusion in Mexico is a highly relevant issue that has driven the creation of a solid regulatory framework to guarantee equal access to information and communication technologies (ICT) for all citizens. This legal framework seeks to reduce the digital divide and promote the social and economic development of the country.

Legal and Political Framework

Although there is no specific law that comprehensively covers digital inclusion in Mexico, various legal systems and public policies are articulated to promote this objective. Some of the main regulatory instruments are:

National Development Plan: This document establishes the government's strategic lines in terms of social and economic development, including digital inclusion as a cross-cutting axis.

Federal Telecommunications and Broadcasting Law: This law regulates the telecommunications sector and establishes obligations for service concessionaires, such as the obligation to guarantee the coverage and quality of services throughout the national territory.

Internet for All Program: This government initiative seeks to expand internet coverage in rural and marginalized areas, facilitating access to ICT for millions of Mexicans.

National Digital Strategy: This strategy defines public policies to promote the country's digital development, promoting innovation, open data and citizen participation.

Key Aspects of the Regulations

The regulations on digital inclusion in Mexico focus on the following aspects:

Access to ICTs: The goal is to ensure that all Mexicans have access to the Internet and digital devices at affordable prices.

Digital literacy: Training programs are promoted to develop the digital skills of the population, especially in vulnerable groups.

Digital content: The creation of digital content in indigenous languages and for people with disabilities is encouraged.

Infrastructure: Investment is made in the expansion of telecommunications infrastructure to improve connectivity throughout the national territory.

Digital governance: Transparency and citizen participation in decision-making related to digital policies are promoted.

Challenges and Opportunities

Despite the progress made, there are still important challenges in terms of digital inclusion in Mexico, such as the persistence of the digital divide in rural and marginalized areas, the lack of access to digital devices, and limited digital literacy in certain sectors of the population.

However, digital inclusion also represents a great opportunity to boost the country's economic and social development, promoting job creation, innovation, and the improvement of public services.

It is important to inform society about the actions that can be carried out together to contribute to these service improvements, such as the following activities described below.

Get informed: Learn about the digital inclusion programs and public policies that exist in your area.

Get trained: Develop your digital skills through online courses and workshops.

Participation: Collaborate in community initiatives that promote access to ICTs.

Dissemination: Share information about the importance of digital inclusion with your family and friends.

The digital inclusion regulations in Mexico establish a solid framework to guarantee equal access to ICTs and reduce the digital divide. However, it is necessary to continue working to overcome existing challenges and take advantage of the opportunities offered by the digital age.

Detailing this regulation a little more, the government actions carried out to combat the digital divide are located below.

Electronic government, or e-government, seeks to modernize public administration through the use of information and communication technologies (ICTs). In Mexico, various initiatives have been implemented with the aim of improving the efficiency, transparency and accessibility of public services.

Main Electronic Government Initiatives in Mexico:

Digital platforms in which the following stand out:

Digital Government: A unified platform that integrates various government procedures and services, allowing citizens to carry out online procedures in a simpler and faster way.

RENIEC: National Registry of Population and Identification, which facilitates obtaining official documents and carrying out procedures related to identity.

SAT: Tax Administration Service, with a wide range of online services for taxpayers, such as filing returns and paying taxes.

Online services:

Online procedures: The possibility of carrying out procedures such as driver's licenses, passports, civil registries, among others, without having to go to government offices.

Online consultations: Access to public information, such as laws, regulations and open data, through government portals.

Electronic signature: Adoption of electronic signature to speed up procedures and guarantee the authenticity of documents.

Open data:

Open data platforms: Making government data available for reuse by citizens, companies and organizations, promoting transparency and innovation.

Citizen participation:

Participatory budgets: Mechanisms that allow citizens to participate in the definition of the public budget.

Public consultations: Platforms for citizens to express their opinions on issues of public interest.

Modernization of public management:

Implementation of electronic document management systems: To improve efficiency and security in the management of information.

Use of collaborative tools: To facilitate teamwork and communication between public servants.

Benefits of these initiatives:

Greater efficiency: Reduction of time and costs in carrying out procedures.

Greater transparency: Access to public information and citizen participation in decision-making.

Greater accessibility: Government services are available to a greater number of people, regardless of their geographic location.

Better quality of services: Errors are reduced and citizen service is improved.

Regarding the Challenges and Opportunities, the following are relevant:

Digital divide: It is necessary to guarantee access to information technologies for all citizens. These tools mentioned are some that help to eliminate the digital gap, that is, what sometimes turns out to be not being done in the best way is the promotion of their use.

Information security: Protecting citizens' personal and sensitive data.

Training: Public servants require training to use new technological tools.

Interoperability: Government information systems must be interoperable to facilitate data exchange.

Work Identity

To promote the realization of personal motivation, it is necessary to know what work identity is with respect to the collaborators immersed in an organization. Work identity is defined as a concept that refers to how people define themselves in relation to their work. That is, it is the way we see and feel ourselves in the work context, and how this influences our self-esteem, motivation and behavior at work.

Work identity is not static and can change over time and as our work experiences evolve. It is influenced by factors such as:

The type of work we do: Our role, responsibilities, and the skills we use.

The company we work for: The company's organizational culture, values, and mission.

Our work relationships: Coworkers, bosses, and clients.

Our career aspirations: Our long-term goals and how work aligns with them. But what defines work identity more broadly is explained below.

Work identity is a relatively new concept and has been studied by a variety of psychologists, sociologists, and human resources experts. There is no single person credited with its original definition, as it is a theoretical construct that has evolved from multiple investigations. Some notable authors who have contributed to the understanding of work identity include:

Dubar: One of the first to explore this concept, defining work identity as the way workers define themselves and are defined by others in the work context.

Walsh and Gordon: These authors emphasized that work identity is a combination of organizational, occupational, and other identities that shape a person's roles at work.

Andrade: According to this author, work identity refers to the relationship people have with their work and how it links to their sense of self.

Importance of work identity

Understanding work identity is essential to:

Improving employee well-being: A strong work identity can increase job satisfaction, engagement, and motivation.

Fostering a better work environment: Employees with a clear and positive work identity tend to be more collaborative and productive.

Reducing absenteeism and staff turnover: When employees feel identified with their work, they are less likely to leave the company.

Increasing organizational effectiveness: A workforce with a strong work identity can contribute to the achievement of company goals.

Work identity is a key aspect of a person's work experience. Understanding how it is formed and how it influences our behavior at work can help us build more satisfying and successful careers.

In this way, in a more organized way, the main areas of intervention of work identity can be identified.

Higher Education

Educational inclusion at the higher level is a process that seeks to ensure that all students participate, learn and achieve, especially those who are at risk of being marginalized or excluded. Educational inclusion is based on the idea that all people have the right to education and that individual differences are opportunities to enrich learning.

Some benefits of educational inclusion are:

It guarantees equal opportunities for all students

It promotes a more equitable, empathetic and diverse society

It helps students develop better academic skills

It helps students to be less absent

It helps students to be more likely to get a job and continue studying

It benefits the peers of students with special educational needs

Educational inclusion also helps to strengthen the educational system

CONCLUSION

The lack of motivation for digital inclusion is a multifactorial problem that requires a comprehensive approach to be addressed. It is essential to design strategies that address both individual and organizational and social factors. Some possible solutions include:

Continuous training: Offer training programs tailored to each employee's needs.

Mentoring: Assign mentors to employees who need additional support.

Incentives: Recognize and reward employees' efforts to develop their digital skills.

Effective communication: Communicate clearly and transparently the benefits of digital inclusion.

Cultural change: Foster an organizational culture that values innovation and adaptation to change.

Summary

Digital inclusion refers to the efforts and strategies aimed at ensuring that all individuals and communities have equal access to information and communication technologies (ICTs). It encompasses not just the availability of these technologies but also the ability to effectively use them to participate in the digital society. Digital inclusion is increasingly vital in our modern world, where technology plays a critical role in education, employment, health care, and civic engagement.

In recent years, the digital divide—the gap between those who have access to technology and those who do not—has become a pressing issue. This divide exists on multiple levels, including economic, geographical, and social dimensions. Economically disadvantaged communities often lack reliable internet access and devices, which limits their ability to access educational resources, apply for jobs, or engage in online services that many take for granted. Rural areas may also face significant challenges due to a lack of infrastructure, leaving residents disconnected from the opportunities that urban areas enjoy.

Additionally, digital literacy is a crucial component of digital inclusion. It is not enough to have access to technology; individuals must also possess the skills to use it effectively. Digital literacy encompasses a range of competencies, including the ability to navigate the internet, use software applications, and critically evaluate online information. Unfortunately, many people, particularly older adults or those with fewer educational opportunities, may struggle with these skills. Thus, digital inclusion initiatives often incorporate training programs to bolster digital literacy and empower individuals to fully utilize technology.

A critical aspect of digital inclusion is the role of government and policy. Many countries recognize the importance of bridging the digital divide and have implemented policies aimed at increasing internet access and promoting digital skills development. Governments may invest in broadband infrastructure, subsidize internet costs for low-income families, or initiate public-private partnerships to expand access to ICTs. Moreover, international organizations and NGOs play an essential role in advocating for digital inclusion globally, often addressing the needs of marginalized communities in developing countries.

Education is another area where digital inclusion is crucial. The COVID-19 pandemic highlighted the disparities in access to digital resources, as many students were forced to shift to remote learning. Those without reliable internet or devices faced significant challenges, while those with access were often able to continue their education with fewer disruptions. This situation has spurred discussions about the necessity of equitable access to technology in the education sector, leading to increased investments in digital resources for schools and training for educators to effectively engage students in a digital learning environment.

Moreover, digital inclusion has significant implications for workforce development. As more jobs require technological proficiency, individuals lacking access to digital tools may find themselves at a disadvantage in the job market. Programs aimed at enhancing digital skills can help prepare underserved populations for the workforce, fostering economic growth and stability. Initiatives such as job training programs, community workshops, and partnerships with local employers can facilitate this transition by equipping individuals with the necessary skills to succeed in a digital economy.

In addition to economic and educational implications, digital inclusion also impacts civic engagement. The ability to participate in democratic processes increasingly depends on access to technology. Individuals without internet access may miss out on important information regarding elections, local government initiatives, and community events. Furthermore, social isolation can be exacerbated for those who cannot connect with others online, highlighting the need for inclusive digital policies that consider mental health and community well-being.

In conclusion, digital inclusion is a multifaceted issue that intersects with various aspects of society, from education and employment to civic engagement and public health. Bridging the digital divide requires a collaborative effort involving governments, educators, businesses, and community organizations. By ensuring equitable access to technology and promoting digital literacy, we can empower individuals and communities to thrive in the digital age. As technology continues to advance and shape our world, prioritizing digital inclusion will be essential to creating a society where everyone has the opportunity to participate and succeed.

Without concerted action towards digital inclusion, we risk perpetuating existing inequalities and leaving vulnerable populations further behind.

Digital motivation for workers involves utilizing technology to enhance engagement and productivity.

Employers can leverage tools such as gamification, virtual rewards, and online recognition platforms to create a positive work environment.

This approach helps to foster connection among remote teams, encourages continuous learning, and enhances overall job satisfaction. By integrating digital motivation strategies, organizations can improve performance and retain talent in today's competitive landscape

REFERENCES

Abarca, S. (2001). Psicología de la motivación. San José, Costa Rica: EUNED. Ajcllo, A. M. (2003). La motivación para aprender. En C. Pontecorvo (Coord.), Manual de psicología de la educación (pp. 251-271). España: Popular. Alonso, J. (1992). ¿Qué es lo mejor para motivar a mis alumnos? Madrid: Universidad Autónoma/Instituto de Ciencias de la Educación

Ajello, A. M. (2003). La motivación para aprender. En C. Pontecorvo (Coord.), Manual de psicología de la educación (pp. 251-271). España: Popular. Alonso, J. (1992). ¿Qué es lo mejor para motivar a mis alumnos? Madrid: Universidad Autónoma/Instituto de Ciencias de la Educación

Alonso, J. (1992). *Qué es lo mejor para motivar a mis alumnos?* Universidad Autónoma/Instituto de Ciencias de la Educación.

Bandura, A. (1997). *Self-efficacy: The exercise of control* [Auto-eficacia: El ejercicio de control]. W. H. Freeman Scoot.

Bisquerra, R. (2000). *Educación emocional y bienestar.* CISSPRAXIS.

Cerezo, M. T., & Casanova, P. F. (2004). Diferencias de género en la motivación académica de los alumnos de educación secundaria obligatoria. Revista Electrónica de Investigación Psicoeducativa, 2(1), 97-112. Departamento de Psicología, Universidad de Jaén, España. Consultado el 24 de enero de 2008, de: http://www.investig acionpsicopedagogica.org/revista/ articulos/3/espannol/Art_3_31.pdf

Herrán Gascón, A. (1999). Didáctica de la motivación. Suplemento Pedagógico Acade, (25), 10-13, y (26), 6-9. Madrid, España. Consultado el 8 de agosto de 2008, de: http:// www.pangea.org/peremarques/dioe/ DIDÁCTICA%20DE%20LA%20 MOTIVACIÓN.pdf García A. E. (2008). Motivación individual. Consultado el 7 de junio del 2008, de: http://grupos. emagister.com/documento/ administracion_motivacion_y_ organizacion_/1048-38669 Hampton, D., Summer, C., y Webber, R. (1989). Manual de desarrollo de recursos humanos. México: Trillas.

Herrera, F., Ramírez, M. I., Roa, J. M., & Herrera, I. (2004). Tratamiento de las creencias motivacionales en contextos educativos pluriculturales. Revista Iberoamericana de Educación, Sección de Investigación, N° 37/2. España.

Iberdrola (2024) ¿Qué es la inclusión Digital y como llevarla a cabo? Recuperado de: https://www.iberdrola.com/compromiso-social/inclusion-digital#:~:text=Seg %C3%BAn%20la%20Comisi%C3%B3n%20Europea%2C%20la,y%20tambi%C3 %A9n%20facilidad%20de%20uso

Naranjo, M. L. (2004). Enfoques conductistas, cognitivos y racional emotivos. San José, C. R.: Universidad de Costa Rica. Universidad de Sevilla. (2005).

Programa Golden5: Una intervención psicoeducativa. Consultado el 14 de abril de 2007, de: http://www.golden5.org/ golden5/ Rice, F. P. (2000). Adolescencia. Desarrollo, relaciones y cultura. Madrid: Prentice Hall.

Chapter 7
Managing Organizational Change in Education for Sustainable Development:
Sustainable Education in the Era of Digital Transformation

Erick Daniel Nava Meléndez
https://orcid.org/0009-0005-7244-2590
Instituto Politécnico Nacional, Mexico

ABSTRACT

The main objective of this research is to analyze institutional management in the context of educational organizations, with the aim of facilitating a significant change in their organizational environment. Special emphasis is placed on the relationship between education and sustainable development, recognizing the need for educational institutions to align themselves with principles that promote a sustainable future. Therefore, the use of learning ecologies is proposed as a tool to promote quality education that is linked to the demands of sustainable development, in addition to creating students who become agents of change for their communities, thus promoting sustainable and conscious development.

DOI: 10.4018/979-8-3693-7086-5.ch007

INTRODUCTION

The versatility that is present in the environment of educational centers as well as the changes that have been generated mainly during the COVID-19 pandemic, shows the need to implement new tools to carry out a management that meets the requirements that society demands to move towards sustainable development.

That is, organizations must create management strategies that are oriented towards the sustainability of the institute, said change requires the commitment of each member of the school, since these transformations demand behaviors and attitudes that allow their adaptation to the environment that is lived today. And as Martínez-Bustos et al., (2018) mention, historically, organizations incorporate new methods and new technologies that make work easier, producing changes in organizational culture and job performance. Globalization and new technologies invite organizations to generate constant change processes with the aim of facing constant transformations in the environment. In the case of educational organizations, change processes in their management enable the sustainability of educational processes in certain communities.

For this reason, it is vital to have comprehensive and coordinated strategies to permeate sustainability to teachers and students of HEIs, to minimize the impact caused to the environment and thus have a balance between the protection of rights, the environment and the important and necessary economic growth (UNICEF, 2021).

Currently, the problem that implies the environmental crisis we are facing is intricate, since it involves substantial damage to the environmental, social and economic environment, which are the interdependent and synergistic pillars of sustainable development, known as the Triple Bottom Line. This crisis has its origins in the era of industrialization during the 18th century, when new technologies drove different types of production and consumption, which implied an overexploitation of non-renewable resources, mainly in underdeveloped countries, who were given the role of producers of raw materials (Sachs, 2015).

Thus, learning ecologies are a useful tool that will help move towards sustainability, since they include informal learning, social networks, and lifelong education. However, there are additional challenges for the educational system and its institutions. These challenges include the need to raise awareness about the different sources of information, the focus on practical skills in addition to theoretical knowledge, and the transition to a teaching-learning process that does not focus solely on the teacher as the only source of knowledge. Therefore, seen from a curricular perspective, learning ecologies are characterized by the importance of lifelong learning, the value of the individual learning trajectory, the acquisition of transversal competences to learn in diverse environments and moments, and the increase in the demand for personalized learning.

In summary, it is essential that HEIs understand and adapt to the new learning ecologies, to offer responses tailored to the needs of students in a changing context such as the current one. Therefore, structural modifications are required to promote a sustainable, interconnected and distributed educational model, thus avoiding the disconnection between the education.

Therefore, the objective of this research is to describe some key factors for the transition towards a sustainable model in the management of educational organizations, through a theoretical-documentary review and in which topics such as institutional management, organizational change in educational institutions as well as the development of education for sustainable development and the use of learning ecologies as a tool for the transition towards sustainable development in education are addressed.

Institutional Management

Institutional Management (IM) is defined as the set of integrated actions to achieve a goal within a certain period, being this an intermediate link between planning and the objectives that are intended to be achieved (Villareal, 2015). For his part, Alvarado (1999) states that it is understood as the application of different techniques, instruments and procedures in the management of resources and development of activities within the institution.

For his part, Sovero (2007) mentions IM as a set of operations and activities for conducting administrative functions that serve as support for management. He also mentioned the main management actions which are the following: planning, organization, communication, control and participation.

Furthermore, Sovero (2007) maintains that institutional management must be based on the following tools:

- Leadership: considered as the ability to get people who are part of the organization to mobilize, with the purpose of achieving institutional objectives (Sovero, 2007).
- Reengineering: understood as modernizing, reorienting or redesigning educational operations or processes to improve the quality of education. Reengineering is also considered as innovation (Sovero, 2007).
- Creative management: aspect that implies that the director and the governing body must be creative in the development of educational management (Sovero, 2007).

According to Villarreal (2015), GI is a process that helps to properly manage projects involving a set of interrelated actions undertaken by the management team of a school to promote and enable the achievement of pedagogical intentionality in, with and for educational opportunity, which is linked to government and direction towards, that is, with the safeguarding and implementation of the necessary mechanisms to achieve the stated objectives and that in this framework, doing is related to thinking, redesigning and evaluating (Villareal, 2015). From this point of view, it lies in the execution of the project; therefore, evaluation and design are included.

On the other hand, the Ibero-American Journal of Education (2017) mentions that the GI should not only be effective, but also adequate, this is because it must put into practice the different elements of the organization, therefore it is required to organize the cooperative actions which lead to the achievement of the shared objectives, which must have been foreseen and evaluated to obtain the necessary feedback, which allows an adequate decision making.

Thus, for the RIE (2017) achieving an effective and adequate institutional management, constitutes one of the transcendental and complex challenges that higher education institutions must face in today's society, understanding the GI as a strategic tool to grow in effectiveness, that is, in the systematization of the actions directed to the achievement of the objectives in addition to being also a tool to advance with greater precision towards the educational ends, which will not be given by budgets. (RIE, 2017).

Academic and administrative management refer to the processes arising from institutional management. For their part, Iniciarte, Marcano and Reyes (2009) make the following distinction between academic and administrative management: the first is "the set of processes through which the different curricular components and subcomponents that support pedagogical practice are administered in the continuum that allows the construction and modeling of the desirable profile of the student", while the second is understood as "an open and flexible system that is made up of processes and principles that guide, balance and make possible the development of the curriculum through actions, under norms, values and procedures that make the processes viable so that they are fulfilled as established by the legal, philosophical and theoretical framework of the institutions" (Iniciarte, Marcano and Reyes, 2009).

The management process is oriented towards achieving the educational objectives of the institution. They take the principles of the academic model and operationalize them for their application to the activities and processes that determine the adequate delivery of the educational programs. Process innovation requires adequate institutional management to meet the needs of users and institutions.

From the above it can be inferred that GI is of utmost importance since the strengths that are developed generate a strategic role in comparison to traditional management. Establishing a comparison between these models, there is congruence with numerous researchers who mention that the traditional model has presented passive, non-participative and indifferent students in the environment in which they develop, this where the main actor is the teacher who maintains an authoritarian position, the above does not promote positive relationships between the actors involved. In contrast to the above, modern GI is oriented towards the formation of active students, who experiment, investigate and build their learning in a particular way, identify with their environment and have a more critical vision of the world around them. For his part, the teacher develops innovative and enthusiastic learning processes based on active methodologies, which promotes work teams since the different curricular programs are adapted and nourished by means of diversification, this in relation to the objectivity of the context.

For Farro (2001), institutional management is the capacity of the entity to implement its strategic plan, through the institutional budgets that it covers, considerably disaggregating the results of the latter, through the annual operating plans, where he highlights the importance of the strategic that must be reflected in the management instruments.

On the other hand, Farro (2001) mentions that some of the very important characteristics in the management of an organization are the adequate institutional climate in which the innovative projects of teachers are recognized, supported and encouraged, as well as the proposals of students and parents, successfully constituting the teams and projects of productive development.

In this context, Buitrón (2006) states that the determining factors in the quality of an educational center fall on the available material resources, the management, the human resources, the management of the center, the academic management, the growth of pedagogical terms such as: the objectives, the contents, the evaluation and the way in which the didactic methodologies are carried out. Therefore, by improving institutional management in an educational center, they will sustain an improvement in its educational quality.

Thus, institutional management refers to the management of human resources that make up an educational institution, towards the achievement of certain objectives and goals, and constitutes an aspect of great importance for the training of new generations of students in the country or a given society.

Organizational Change in Education

Organizational change in education refers to the processes and transformations that educational institutions undergo to adapt to the new demands of society, technological advances and educational policies. In other words, it is the way in which educational centers evolve and renew themselves to improve the quality of the education they offer, as shown in "Figure 1."

Figure 1. Change management

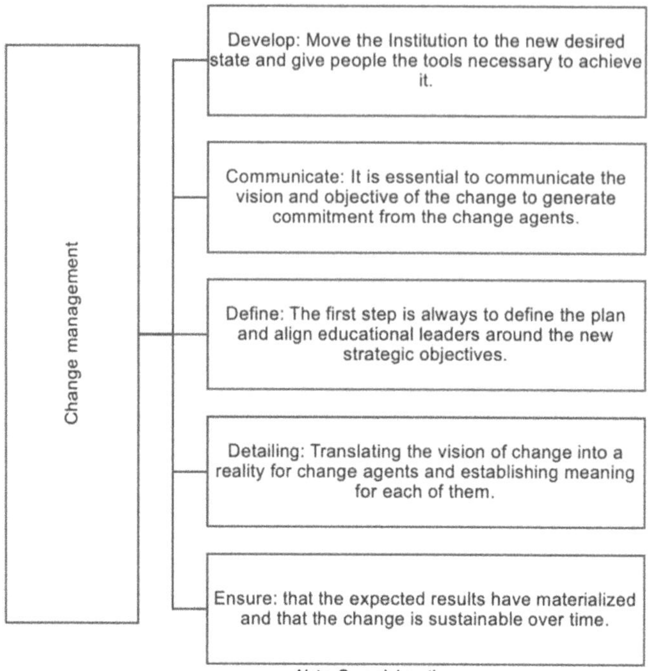

Note: Own elaboration

Furthermore, organizational change is important in educational institutions as it will allow:

- Adaptation to a constantly changing world: societies evolve rapidly, so educational organizations must adapt to these changes to form competent citizens prepared for the future.
- Improvement of educational quality: through organizational change, new teaching methodologies, educational technologies and evaluation strategies can be implemented that allow for improved student results.
- Greater social relevance: Educational organizations need to respond to the needs of society and contribute to the development of communities.
- Greater efficiency: Organizational change will help optimize the resources and internal processes of educational organizations.

However, some of the main organizational changes in education are:

- Structural changes: These are changes in the organization, such as the creation of new areas or departments, the restructuring of schedules or the modification of the relationships between the different educational actors.
- Cultural changes: These involve the transformation of the values, beliefs and norms that guide the behavior of the members of the educational community.
- Technological changes: These are related to the incorporation of new technologies in the teaching and learning processes, such as the use of digital platforms, collaborative tools and mobile devices.
- Pedagogical changes: These focus on innovation in teaching practices, the adoption of new methodologies and the personalization of learning.

Some of the factors that influence the success of organizational change in education are:

- Leadership: Strong and visionary is essential to sustain the change
- Participation: Active participation of all members of the educational institution to achieve the change
- Communication: Clear and transparent to motivate members of the educational community.
- Training: For the development of competencies to implement the change.
- Evaluation: Identify strengths and weaknesses to make the necessary adjustments and implement a successful change.

Therefore, organizational change in education is a complex and challenging process, but it is fundamental to guarantee the relevance and quality of education in a constantly evolving world.

Education for Sustainable Development

Future professionals in all areas must have the relevant training with an ESD perspective, a fundamental requirement to prepare technically competent citizens who contribute to solving problems related to sustainability. However, this task has faced significant difficulties, largely due to the conservative structure of universities (Bravo, 2012), when trying to implement curricular changes in a fluid manner (González and Garza, 2013). Various authors have proposed this change using different terms, such as education for sustainable development (Arbuthnott, 2009).

Thus, these principles guide the development of environmental study plans and programs in all areas of knowledge, in line with the framework for comprehensive student training. However, implementing these principles can be challenging for teachers due to the variety of interpretations they entail. Therefore, it is important to provide a theoretical discussion on the notions related to sustainability (sustainable development (Arbuthnott, 2009), environmental education (González and Arias, 2015), with the purpose of identifying common points and discrepancies that can support managers and decision makers in university policies, when integrating these terms into the curricula of educational institutions as shown in "Figure 2."

Figure 2. Education for sustainable development

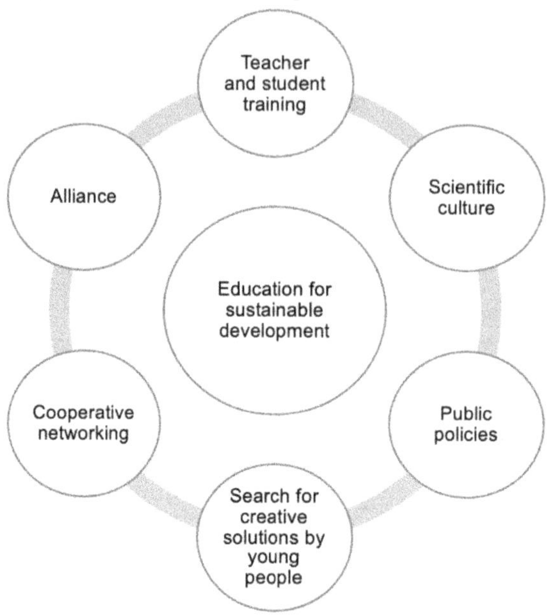

Note: Own elaboration

As a result of this, the term sustainable development arose from the World Commission established in 1987, where the concerns of governments were expressed about the need to conceive new ideas regarding the environment and its deterioration, the result of a development model that exerts pressure on the biosphere and worsens social disparities. In this context, the proposed approach focused on promoting a change that they called sustainable development, a concept that encompasses two closely linked terms: environment and development.

Now, according to the Brundtland report, sustainable development encompasses the social, economic and environmental dimensions, which are intrinsically related, and none can prevail over the others (Curiel, Peniche, Reyes, Alvaradoy and Hernández, 2005; Lescano, Vegas, Collazo, Valdés and Belaúnde, 2008). Through this alternative perspective of development, it is possible to raise the quality of life of people, reduce inequality and environmental degradation, in addition to promoting economic growth in countries.

According to the Institute for Educational Technology Research (INITE) in 2004, sustainable development is defined as that which covers current needs without compromising the opportunities of future generations to meet their own needs.

However, Gutiérrez and González (2010) point out that this concept is holistic and encompasses at least five dimensions: economic, political, cultural, social and environmental. This perspective arises from the need to promote a global development model that is compatible with both environmental conservation and social equity.

According to García, Ramírez and Sánchez (2014), the different approaches to this concept vary between two opposing ideas: some argue that they can use natural resources in an unlimited way, while others maintain that sustainable development implies the protection and conservation of said resources. Therefore, they conclude that it is a diffuse concept, difficult to delimit and define in an absolute way.

Coinciding with what was described by Alba, Benayas and Sánchez (2002), who maintain that with the appearance of the concept of sustainable development, it has deviated from the original objective of the environmental education (EE) approach. These authors argue that EE was conceived to connect people with nature and promote its conservation. However, they also maintain that EE can serve as a mechanism to drive change towards sustainable development models.

However, Aceves-Ávila (2013) point out that there is no consensus on this term and that only the Brundlant Report has been accepted, an argument supported by Bermejo (2014). For their part, Gutiérrez and González (2010) agree that this term is a holistic conceptual proposal with difficulties in the way it is used.

In summary, the debate around the concept of sustainable development is mainly focused on the word development, which implies connotations of extreme visions: on the one hand, a criticism of the unlimited use of natural resources (sustainable development), and on the other, a focus on their rational and lasting use (sustainable development).

Currently, ESD represents an alternative approach to the previously described visions, which is based on the principles that characterize sustainable development. This approach constitutes an innovative educational model, which is compatible with knowledge societies (UNESCO, 2008) and is contrary to the traditional model based on disciplinary training, which at the time satisfied an industrialized society, which was characterized by the specialization of work and the exploitation of natural resources in an excessive manner.

Thus, UNESCO (2017) points out that in the educational field, the role of the International Conferences on Education organized by UNESCO is noteworthy, which adopt a global perspective of education. During these conferences, it has been emphasized that social responsibility is closely linked to the joint participation of educational organizations and the promotion of inclusive policies that address not only the learning needs of marginalized and vulnerable youth and adults, but also the principles and strategies of research and teaching. In this order, it is necessary to promote values and ethical attitudes among students to strengthen their responsibility towards society and their understanding of local, national and global realities (UNESCO, 2008).

In this sense, UNESCO (2017) conceptualizes sustainable development throughout life to acquire values, knowledge and skills that help children, youth and adults find new solutions to the social, economic and environmental problems that affect them (UNESCO, 2017). Thus, the importance of promoting greater collaboration in social responsibility, as well as the clear need for this responsibility to permeate the structures of educational organizations, not only in social, economic and environmental commitments, is clearly reflected in UNESCO documents. The medium-term strategy proposed by UNESCO between 2008 and 2013 highlighted that economic development and progress require countries to educate their citizens and provide continuous learning. In this way, societies committed to innovation will prepare their population to face and adapt to changes, allowing them to control and influence them over time. This education therefore promotes culture, facilitating mutual understanding with the aim of maintaining peaceful societies. UNESCO has defined education as one of the main human rights and as a fundamental element for the integral development of human potential.

According to Ruiz et al. (2010), in the knowledge society, new and diverse forms of economic, social, cultural and political organization emerge, where knowledge becomes the distinctive element that defines social reality. According to this position, educational institutions would have to adapt and provide solutions to the constant changes that disrupt their work, such as globalization, knowledge societies themselves and the knowledge economy (Ruiz et al., 2010).

Likewise, since the publication of the United Nations Decade of Education for Sustainable Development, promulgated in December 2002, various interpretations and applications of this concept have emerged. For example, Bravo (2008) mentions that in various regions an amalgamation has been generated between the orientations of education for sustainable development (EDS) and the approach of environmental education, which allows these to be the main approaches in which the strategies implemented by the country's public universities are oriented.

The concept of sustainability not only encompasses the preservation of the environment, but also includes equity and social justice in educational processes. In this sense, the United Nations (2018) has promoted important programs on social responsibility and sustainable development in education. One of the most important was the United Nations Decade of Education for Sustainable Development, which was established in 2002 for the period 2005-2015 by the United Nations General

Assembly through resolution 57/254. In this decade, the UN highlighted priorities such as poverty reduction, gender equality, health, environmental protection, among various objectives. According to UNESCO (2017), sustainability is defined as a highly complex category that encompasses economic, cultural, social and environmental aspects of human development, which must be considered in educational processes. In this sense, Aznar and Ull (2009) this allows the use of interdisciplinary methodologies and the understanding of complexity as well as the formation of a responsible society.

Thus, the main purpose of the Decade was to engage society in caring for the environment, while also addressing social issues such as poverty and gender equity, to foster a more inclusive and less divided society. According to Gil Osorio (2012), education plays a fundamental role in transforming individual behavior and in modifying the development paradigm of a society. Furthermore, Gil Osorio (2012) mentions that this program clearly emphasized that education and training play a crucial role in the path towards a more sustainable international community. Specifically, governments were urged to consider the possibility of incorporating the Decade into their respective educational systems and strategies.

Furthermore, it was highlighted that the objective of the Decade was to integrate the values, activities and principles of sustainable development in all forms of education and learning, and to promote changes in attitudes, behaviors and values necessary to build a more sustainable future in economic, social and environmental terms (Gil Osorio, 2012). These challenges were thus addressed by promoting cooperation between stakeholders and society.

In turn, UNESCO (2017) assumed the responsibility of managing the "Decade of Education for Sustainable Development", playing a crucial role in this field. The World Declaration on Higher Education in the 21st Century, issued in 1998 and promoted by UNESCO, highlighted the need to further strengthen and promote the fundamental missions and values in higher education, in particular, the objective of contributing to sustainable development and to the improvement of society (UNESCO, 2017).

Furthermore, UNESCO (2017) indicates that education for sustainable development must generate change through critical reflection on the modus vivendi, involving people in decision-making with the aim of actively participating in all sectors of society to build a more sustainable world. In contrast, Heidt and Lambertón (2011) point out that education for sustainable development (ESD) covers 5 fundamental aspects:

1. Projection into the future
2. critical and reflective analysis
3. active participation in decision making

4. collaborative work
5. understanding of systems

Therefore, their choice to use sustainability education is based on Australian legislation which is a pioneer in this practice.

Likewise, Biasutti et al., (2018) point out the relevance of promoting sustainable skills and sustainable development (SD) principles in teachers and students lies in their capacity to transform attitudes and address contemporary challenges. The principles of sustainability encompass:

a) an integrated perspective
b) the integration of disciplines
c) an approach focused on learning
d) experimentation and meaningful learning
e) the application of the Multiple Method
f) the promotion of values and ethics
g) participation in decision-making
h) the connection between the local and the global
i) the application of culturally relevant and contextually appropriate criteria (Bisutti et al. 2016).

Therefore, Bisutti et al., (2016) mention that ESD prioritizes interdisciplinary teaching and a student-centered approach, which makes it transversal to all study programs. These programs must incorporate in their learning outcomes not only the specific knowledge of each discipline, but also the skills linked to sustainable development (Bisutti, 2016). Thus, the fundamental reason why this approach questions other perspectives lies in the understanding that the challenges of sustainable development cannot be successfully addressed from a single discipline.

According to Svanstrom et al., (2008) a curriculum that covers sustainability is not limited only to teaching about ecosystems and the human condition, it also seeks to ensure that students acquire interpersonal and intrapersonal skills, along with the promotion of systemic thinking. On the other hand; Biasutti et al., (2016) point out that the teaching of sustainability can be improved by applying various educational strategies, such as lectures, group discussions, simulations, individual tasks, among other types of activities.

In the United Kingdom, the Quality Assurance Agency for Higher Education (QAA) recognizes that education for sustainable development involves the adoption of teaching and learning approaches that encompass an interdisciplinary perspective, experience-based learning and interaction, critical reflection, meaningful learning focused on real-life problems and situations, as well as participatory learning among peers (Higher Education Academy, 2014).

Furthermore, the adoption of this approach implies a transformation of traditional educational models that prioritize disciplinary teaching with little flexibility. Instead, we promote models focused on the development of competencies that, in addition to the knowledge specific to a discipline, train future professionals to contribute to economic, environmental and social progress.

According to Gradilla (2017), an education that fosters sustainable competencies allows students to acquire the knowledge, skills and values necessary to face the challenges of sustainability in their personal and professional lives. Integrating the ESD approach into the curriculum, then, involves a process that involves tensions regarding how it is understood and applied by teachers in their academic work. In short, this alternative educational approach calls for a set of principles, ideas and methods that can be used to assist students, teachers and administrators in understanding sustainable development.

Learning Ecologies as a Tool to Move Towards Sustainable Development

To begin with, the school learning process is experiencing continuous innovation with the introduction of both tangible and intangible technologies. This is leading to a diversification of learning environments, which in turn allows for the revitalization of face-to-face teaching methods and the opening towards virtual and hybrid learning modalities. This transformation is affecting relationships and learning processes by integrating both gradual and disruptive innovations in the educational field as can be seen in "Figure." 3.

Figure 3. Learning ecology

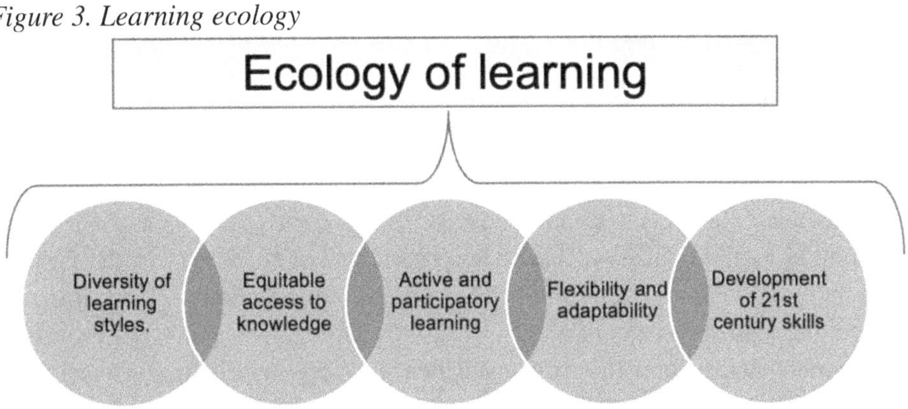

Note: Prepared by Marco Paz (2023) document "Ecology of learning"

Therefore, the disruption in learning processes also encompasses educational objectives, promoting active, participatory and collaborative approaches focused on solving personal, social, cultural and planetary problems and challenges. In this sense, it is urgent to promote sustainable learning, incorporating into education creative and responsible processes in the acquisition, understanding, adaptation and application necessary to address the dilemmas of scientific, humanistic, artistic and technological knowledge, to achieve a sustainable lifestyle in the face of social and environmental challenges.

Thus, contemporary approaches to teaching and learning in education require integration into digital environments that support inclusion in an increasingly globalized world (González-Sanmamed et al., 2020). Learning ecology complements a broader view of the context in which learning takes place, covering both the inside and outside of the classroom in the construction of knowledge (Dado & Bodemer, 2017). In this sense, collaborative virtual learning environments (CSCL) chupi play a fundamental role, since they can more naturally integrate learning ecology, facilitating a personalized approach. Within this paradigm, CSCL have great potential to facilitate deep learning processes. However, it is still necessary to investigate the interactions that occur in these environments to better understand how they affect collaborative learning (Radkowitsch, 2020).

Learning ecologies provide tools for this, by having a lifelong approach, which allows us to understand in what context and with what elements students learn (Arras-Vota et al., 2021). Regarding the results of various investigations, the forum continues to be one of the most used tools in CSCL, since it presents characteristics of interactivity, interaction and negotiation, which proposes that the forum is an adequate tool in this type of process (Chávez et al., 2016). Therefore, the quality of the contributions in most cases is not sufficient to achieve deep learning by the participants (Duque, 2018) Which weighs the forum as a study tool, not only for learning, but to analyze the central aspects of the learning ecology, such as the contexts that the individual uses, such as the place and time of study, among the most relevant.

Likewise, by integrating CSCL models into education, they are naturally accompanied by social approaches to learning (Dado & Bodemer, 2017). Therefore, learning ecology has been the subject of research for several decades, providing complementary elements to collaborative work that enrich the vision of a modern education in higher education (González-Sanmamed et al., 2020). In the field of research, three fundamental aspects of learning ecology stand out. First, it is recognized that learning is a continuous process throughout life and is not limited to specific moments. Second, the growing influence and presence of digital technology in virtually all aspects of daily life has blurred the boundaries between the different physical and institutional environments where learning can take place. Finally, the importance of individual learning trajectories as a means of acquiring knowledge in the information age is emphasized (González-Sanmamed et al., 2020).

Undoubtedly, the implementation of these models is complex. Therefore, it is necessary to investigate the use of the forum as a tool that can facilitate collaborative learning and its capacity to influence certain aspects of the learning ecology. Specifically, a lack of clarity has been identified regarding the factors that affect the characteristics of the messages that students make in their contributions to the forums. In addition, the similarities and differences in the environmental conditions, such as time, space and place in which students experience learning, have not been adequately analyzed. This is relevant, since although these aspects are studied individually, no work has been explored that determines profiles based on how and when learning occurs. Therefore, the important question arises: what are the characteristics of the messages that arise in collaborative forum contexts, considering the type and depth of the contribution? How are these characteristics influenced by the individual effects of the student and their environment? In this context, it is crucial to determine the behavioral profiles of the elements of the learning ecology in students when participating in discussion forums in a collaborative learning environment, considering that learning can occur at any time, place and space.

Furthermore, educational institutions are constantly undergoing transformations which are necessary to integrate their students into today's society, which is increasingly globalized and technological (Jarvela et al., 2019). In this sense, learning ecology emerges as an integrative approach adding a more social perspective to learning, which considers that there is no place or time to learn, since this can happen at any time and place (Jarvela. Et al., 2019), in this way current research shows that collaborative virtual learning environments are increasingly used (Hernández et al., 2019), this is mainly due to the fact that, with the use of technology, collaborative learning strategies can be increased in order to facilitate effective learning processes in education, due to the characteristics of interactivity, interaction, negotiation and self-regulation, which can occur at any time and place (Martínez et al., 2018), the forum being one of the most used tools in collaborative learning.

On the other hand, in the forums, it is important to highlight the need for participants to explicitly and agreed upon strategies or skills of coordination and collaboration, since this effort promotes the development of cognitive and metacognitive skills, which play a crucial role in learning processes (Chávez et al., 2016).

It is observed that, on the one hand, participants often do not take advantage of the communication and collaboration opportunities offered by these tools; and on the other hand, high participation in communicative exchanges between participants does not always lead to the development of collaborative learning or guarantee optimal results (Chávez et al., 2016). In methodological terms, the diversity and heterogeneity of approach are significant, since research on collaborative learning, both in face-to-face interactions and in digital environments, has been divided between qualitative and quantitative approaches (Chávez et al., 2016). In the last decade, this situation has begun to change and studies that employ multi-method methodological strategies are increasingly common (Duque, 2018).

In turn, a stream of research has developed that advocates reconfiguring learning towards learning technologies (Martínez-Rodríguez et al., 2020). These ecologies comprise a variety of processes, contexts, and interactions that provide the student with opportunities and resources to learn, thus facilitating the achievement of established objectives (González-Sanmamed et al., 2020).

This perspective is aligned with the proposal of CSCL (computer-supported collaborative learning) environments and fits the principles of learning ecology. In addition, the ecological metaphor has been used in various fields and fits well with human interactions with their environment, encompassing the processes of doing, learning, and achieving goals, as well as the development of new knowledge in unstructured environments (Martínez-Rodríguez et al., 2020).

A person's learning ecology comprises the process and set of environments, connections, and interactions that provide opportunities and resources for learning, development, and achievement. Personalized learning ecologies are therefore how experiences and learning are woven and integrated into the different contexts and situations that make up a person's life. Learning ecologies therefore have significant conceptual and practical value for the theory and practice of lifelong learning and education.

Also, across represents the traditional, which corresponds to how we connect and integrate our past and current experiences and learning, with a vision towards the future (Peters & Romero, 2019). However, when considering the width, multiple dimensions are encompassed, such as the physical and virtual places and spaces we inhabit; and the meaning we obtain from the contexts and situations that constitute our lives (Peters & Romero, 2019).

Learning ecologies are the fruit of imagination and reason, they serve as a channel for our most creative thoughts and actions. Therefore, they constitute one of the most important environments to foster creativity and give us the opportunity to grow both personally and professionally in all facets of our lives.

In addition to this, the traditional educational model does not easily adapt to this approach, which requires flexibility and a variety of interactions, as well as the integration of technology. The literature points to collaborative online learning environments (COLEs) as a viable option for this purpose (Fatimah et al., 2021), as they incorporate several elements necessary for this type of learning. Furthermore, it focuses on examining how discussion forums continue to be central to collaborative learning, also considering the context in which they are developed.

In relation to the above, the generation of knowledge and the incorporation of new technological devices are promoting a change in the teaching-learning process, thanks to the influence of Information and Communication Technologies (ICT). These technologies offer students a variety of tools and resources that promote the creation of a more interactive and dynamic educational environment, which facilitates more meaningful learning (Fatimah et al., 2021).

Thus, in this modern educational field, digital resources and technological tools are indispensable in the educational process, highlighting their integration using technological devices, which has become characteristic with the arrival and massive use of the Internet (Fatimah et al., 2021).

In turn, the increase and development of learning environments because of the integration of ICTs has promoted the emergence of various forms of educational interaction, generating an interest in the research of learning ecologies and digital educational ecosystems (Ladino et al., 2018).

Therefore, ICTs give students autonomy and the ability to overcome time and space limitations to access knowledge and learning, promoting greater interactivity and control of activities in a collaborative way through communication, which fosters formal, informal and non-formal learning experiences (Ladino et al., 2018).

Thus, this approach is aligned with the concept of learning ecology, which is understood as a dynamic, self-organizing, adaptable and diverse environment that stimulates the learning process (Salinas, 2013). As mentioned above, new learning technologies are closely related to the use of ICT, since they are considered ideal to promote learning in its various modalities, if pedagogical design principles are applied as a reference to guarantee their effectiveness (González-Sanmamed et al., 2020).

In this context, González-Sanmamed et al., (2020) invites us to reflect on how we build our ecologies to learn throughout our lives. Since, learning psychologies are defined as sets of physical or virtual contexts in which structured activities, materials, resources and connected relationships that provide learning opportunities are integrated.

Likewise, González-Sanmamed et al., (2020) argue that learning technologies offer a student-centered experience, allowing them to have, choose and access various educational models that meet unique and specific learning needs.

These ecologies provide students with a wide range of options in topics, activities, exercises, areas of study and projects, where online education (e-learning) plays a fundamental role by providing the resources, tools and virtual spaces that promote student interaction with the elements present in learning ecologies.

Similarly, Haythornwaite & Andrews (2011) when analyzing learning ecologies from the perspective of eLearning, argue that this metaphor is useful to understand online education as a systematic and complex phenomenon. In this context, the predefinition of certain processes is not feasible due to the dynamics and behaviors of individuals and ecosystem components.

Furthermore, in a recent study on a school experience within the framework of the ecological theory of learning using online resources and tools, inspired by Barron (2006), four elements are identified that determine the presence of learning ecology (Caamaño et al., 2018):

a) the plurality of contexts, which refers to the various spaces with their own characteristics, where students go in search of learning resources that cover their interests.
b) The potential consists of the accessibility of the elements that make up a given scenario to develop an educational action and the skills of the person who enters the relationship for its execution.
c) The intercontextual leap is about the application of organized learning activities typical of one scenario to another different one where they are not common.
d) The personal learning environment that highlights the individual uniqueness of the characteristics of technological resources, this means a great diversity of possibilities available to everyone.

In parallel to the learning psychology approach, the concept of networked learning has emerged, which focuses on the study of learning through ICTs in the social educational context. Thus, this perspective is based on the idea that the use of technologies fosters connections between students, teachers, educational actors and digital teaching materials, with the aim of building practical learning communities (Saadatmand & Kumpulaineen, 2012). These connections are usually developed through multimodal and multidirectional communication.

Similarly, the emergence of ICTs has given rise to Personal Learning Environments (PLEs), which contribute to the creation of personalized learning environments using digital applications and tools (Santana et al., 2016). Therefore, these environments provide a unique and personalized space where students are responsible for organizing and adding digital resources to enhance their learning.

This restructuring of the digital educational environment, where hybrid contexts (physical and virtual) of learning environments have gained importance in the academic and educational field, motivating educational organizations to constantly adapt, taking advantage of ICT within an educational framework (Ladino et al., 2016).

On the other hand, young people of the 21st century, also known as Millennials and Generation Z, are identified as the new digital cohorts who have grown up immersed in ICT environments. Therefore, their ways of learning are more linked to social networks than to formal educational environments (Anguita & Ruiz, 2018).

These generations have grown up in a digital era with access to the Internet, mobile devices, applications and social networks (Pizzarro, 2017). In addition, they exhibit a globalized way of thinking, which is characterized by an optimistic and tolerant approach, with a balanced vision between work and personal life, which is broader. In such a way, the use of technology by these young people is not only widespread, but also intensive. Their main device is the mobile phone, which has become an essential element of their identity, their presence and the formation of their opinions, since the use they give it serves in the search for information, entertainment, interaction, communication, construction and redefinition.

Furthermore, it has become a habit rooted in their daily lives, facilitated by the constant recording of their lives. As a result, they represent an interactive and multitasking generation, highly audiovisual, accustomed to searching and accessing information in real time in an easy and accessible way (Anguita & Ruiz, 2018).

According to authors such as Díez, Fernández and Anguita (2011), these generations of Internet users are not only receivers of related content, but also active producers who contribute to the generation of knowledge and the development of a democratizing process through technologies. This has promoted the growth of informal learning using the Internet, as it provides an environment where they can select from various experiences and sources to create personalized learning programs (Hernández-Selles, et al., 2015).

In this context, learning ecologies and expanded education offer a deeper understanding of contemporary educational realities and allow us to identify the experiences that these generations go through, experiences that often go unnoticed. This promotes a comprehensive vision and fosters social justice (Díez & Díaz, 2018).

Furthermore, Díez and Díaz (2018) highlight the potential of expanded learning as a tool that empowers both individuals and groups and social movements. These authors also point out that the integration of this learning approach in the development of soft skills favors autonomy, cooperation, problem solving and the strengthening of civic commitment (Díez & Díaz, 2018).

In recent research, Persico et al., (2019) fully embraced the concept of learning ecology to examine how new knowledge is developed in hybrid and structured environments, where interaction with virtual, physical and social environments gives meaning to the society in which they operate. In turn, Díez & Díaz (2018) consider video games as an integral part of these ecologies, arguing that the relationship between the user and the video game encourages personalized learning modalities and emphasizes that in the creation of these learning ecologies, students and their interests must occupy a central place.

Therefore, more than simply integrating ICT, the real challenge for teachers and educational institutions lies in facilitating students, both individually and as a group, to take advantage of their own learning ecologies (Hernández-Sellés et al., 2015).

Thus, younger generations of students in classrooms are not simply looking for theory; what they crave is confidence, respect, and the opportunity to pursue their passions and interests, making autonomous decisions and feeling in control of their learning. Above all, they desire an education that is rooted (Prensky, 2013). Addressing this challenge requires a reconfiguration in the design of educational programs, moving away from traditional courses and opting for more heterogeneous, diverse, and effective approaches.

This implies considering the intersection between pedagogical, technological, and disciplinary knowledge (Koehler & Mishra, 2009), as well as integrating findings from educational and literary research that inform the development of teaching competencies, especially in virtual environments (Baran, Correira, & Thompson, 2011). In addition, there must be constant adaptation to new emerging technologies, exploring their pedagogical application and their implications in the teaching and learning dynamics (Hernández-Sellés et al., 2015).

Also, in an analysis of the curricular development for the integration of computational thinking in the educational field, motivated by the need to introduce programming in classrooms for the new generations, it is concluded that it is not only necessary to collect experiences on the use of computational thinking in education, but also to apply the findings of educational research and adapt to the new dynamics of learning (Hernández-Sellés et al., 2015). This is because learning environments are changing and constantly innovating (Fernández & Martínez, 2018).

Based on the above, A study on the processes of generation and production of knowledge, as well as the acquisition of knowledge in the "Knowmádica" society, where knowledge is mobile, uncertain and unstable (Fernández & Martínez, 2018), identifies and values four dimensions of learning ecologies that must be considered today:

1) Personal ecologies: referring to the complex, contradictory and discontinuous process of the reconstruction of subjectivity, the mutual transformation of individual and group character, civic socialization by means of ICT, organization of a public stage and the social and political presentation of the self (Rivas-Flores et al., 2018).
2) Community ecologies: observes the community as teaching. In this, dissatisfaction and uncertainty mediate the action, the creations of collaborative development acquire importance, showing the nonconformity before the deficiency of the established structures, seeking the redefinition of the institutional, decision-making and leadership (Rivas-Flores et al., 2018).
3) Resource/means ecologies refer to the increase of resources, the relationships that resources establish with each other (Rivas-Flores et al., 2018).

4) Ecologies of knowledge: it allows to reinterpret, and advance has been another conception of education (Rivas-Flores et al., 2018), where the knowledge of actors and communities, new forms of education and white skills are recognized.

CONCLUSION

Based on the above, educational institutions, as complex entities, face the challenge of integrating sustainability principles into their curricula in line with their commitment to the 2030 Agenda and the sustainable development goals. This implies understanding how these principles are interpreted and applied by the various members of the university community. Furthermore, since sustainability is a multidisciplinary concept, the active participation of all university actors is needed for its effective implementation. Therefore, it is important to recognize that the current structure of educational institutions, which is based on the departmental division of knowledge, contributes to academic fragmentation, which is a problem questioned by ESD. Which advocates the integration of various disciplines to address challenges in a comprehensive manner and develop new theoretical and methodological approaches.

Thus, ESD constitutes an international reference framework that arises from consensus among countries, despite their socioeconomic and environmental differences. Therefore, educational organizations must adapt to changes and decisions at the international level that influence their operation, since HEIs tend to have a bureaucratic structure that makes it difficult to adapt to the changes necessary to address contemporary problems. In addition, it is crucial to foster an educational administration that effectively involves teachers in the integration of sustainability in all study plans. Teachers play a key role in the development of specific and general skills in students, such as systemic thinking and a long-term perspective.

Therefore, institutional leadership is essential to create a learning community where effective practices and educational resources are shared and support and guidance are provided. This not only requires the continuous training of the teaching staff, but also their participation in the development of institutional strategies to promote sustainable development. Since the objective is to train students who will become agents of change to address the challenges of sustainable development.

Therefore, the integration of the perspective of education for sustainable development in educational organizations remains a pending task. Thus, it is necessary to outline crucial aspects that can serve as guidance for managers and policy decision-makers in the process of incorporating sustainability into the curriculum. This implies promoting genuine interdisciplinary training that facilitates dialogue between the different areas of knowledge, since this condition is indispensable to address the challenges of sustainable development. Also, quality education implies the application of methodologies proposed by ESD to guarantee the relevance of education in knowledge societies.

Furthermore, research on the integration of sustainability into curricula in educational organizations is still in a developmental stage, as is the focus of its research. Thus, in this area of study, case analyses and best practices abound, along with theoretical contributions from various authors. Recently, several empirical studies have been conducted to assess the level of sustainability integration in various institutions or education systems. In turn, as an emerging field, the integration of sustainability into curricula offers unexplored opportunities in terms of content and methodology. In addition to the practical interest of the topic, its connection to various areas of research (education, sustainability, organizational changes in educational institutions) makes it a very attractive area for the advancement of scientific knowledge.

On the other hand, the educational system is currently in crisis, due to the transformation brought about by the incorporation of Information and Communication Technologies (ICT) in the classrooms. This has allowed students to access a variety of tools and resources that facilitate the construction of meaningful learning, which is characterized by a more dynamic and interactive environment and the creation of collaborative spaces. However, these changes pose several challenges for the traditional educational system, such as low academic performance, high failure and dropout rates, as well as dissatisfaction and demotivation of both teachers and students.

Thus, learning ecologies, which include informal learning, social networks, and lifelong education, pose additional challenges for the educational system and its institutions. Thus, these challenges include the need to raise awareness about the various sources of information, the constant updating of information, the focus on practical skills in addition to theoretical knowledge, and the transition to a teaching-learning process that does not focus solely on the teacher as the only source of knowledge.

Therefore, seen from a curricular perspective, learning ecologies are characterized by the importance of lifelong learning, the value of the individual learning path, the acquisition of transversal competences to learn in diverse environments and moments, and the increase in the demand for personalized learning.

Therefore, to overcome these challenges, it is necessary to rethink the traditional educational model and adopt an approach that adequately integrates ICTs in collaborative spaces in the teaching-learning process. This implies the creation of dynamic and interactive virtual environments that allow continuous learning, as well as adequate guidance and mediation by educators to encourage critical and collaborative learning.

In short, it is essential that educational institutions understand and adapt to the new learning ecologies to offer responses tailored to the needs of students in a changing context such as the current one. Therefore, structural modifications are required to promote an interconnected and distributed educational model, thus avoiding the disconnection between the educational system and the reality of today's society.

FUTURE DIRECTIONS FOR RESEARCH

It is recommended that future research evaluate through quantitative research to determine dimensions such as the personalization of learning through the adaptation of artificial intelligence and how it can adapt teaching content and methodologies to promote environmental awareness and sustainability skills in students. In addition, it is suggested that qualitative research address some aspects that focus on the perception of the educational community, that is, from their point of view, how they consider different immersive experiences and how different technologies can create more meaningful and memorable learning experiences on sustainable development and the use of face-to-face and online courses that promote sustainability at a pedagogical and technical level.

REFERENCES

Aceves-Ávila, C. (2013). La dimensión transversal de la sostenibilidad en el currículo de instituciones de educación superior: una propuesta innovadora obligada. *Educación superior, gestión, innovación e internacionalización*, 978-84-370-9177-8, 71-92 https://books.google.com.mx/books?id=xBZ2AwAAQBAJypg=PT4&dq=Hern%C3%A1ndez+Casta%C3%B1eda+Rosario&hl=es&sa=X&redir_esc=y#v=onepage&q&f=true

Alvarado, O. (1999). *Gestión Educativa*. Universidad de Lima. Fondo de Desarrollo Editorial.

Anguita, R., & Ruiz, I. (2018). Identidades mediáticas en la sociedad aumentada: las tecno-biografías como estrategia de investigación etnográfica. Madrid: Morata-. *Ecologías de Aprendizaje: Educación Expandida en Contextos Múltiples*, 19, 9–26. DOI: 10.17398/1695-288X.19.1.139

Aranda, G., & Salinas, S. (2013). *Bolívar según Chávez, Ensayo de una tendencia*. RIL Editores.

Arbuthnott, K. (2009). Education for sustainable development beyond attitude change. *International Journal of Sustainability in Higher Education*, 10(2), 152–163. DOI: 10.1108/14676370910945954

Arras-Vota, A., Bordas-Beltrán, J., Porras-Flores, D., & Gómez-Ramírez, J. (2021). Competencias en tecnologías de información y comunicación. Estudios de caso: Universidad Santo Tomas (Colombia) y Universidad Autónoma de Chihuahua (México). *Formación Universitaria*, 14(1), 1. DOI: 10.4067/S0718-50062021000100135

Bermejo, R. (2014). *Del desarrollo sostenible según Brundtland a la sostenibilidad como biomimesis*. Recovered from http://publicaciones.hegoa.ehu.es/publications/315

Biasutti, M., De Baz, T., & Alshawa, H. (2016). Assessing the Infusion of Sustainability Principles into University Curricula. *Journal of Teacher Education for Sustainability*, 18(2), 21–40. https://intapi.sciendo.com/pdf/10.1515/jtes-2016-0012. DOI: 10.1515/jtes-2016-0012

Caamaño, F., Sanmamed, M., & Carril, P. (2018). El desarrollo de las ecologías de aprendizaje a través de las herramientas en línea. *Revista Diálogo Educacional*, 18(56), 128–148. DOI: 10.7213/1981-416X.18.056.DS06

Chávez, J., Montaño, R., & Barrera, R. (2016). Structure and content of messages in an online environment: An approach from participation. *Computers in Human Behavior*, 54(1), 560–568. DOI: 10.1016/j.chb.2015.08.046

Dado, M., & Bodemer, D. (2017). A review of methodological applications of social network analysis in computer-supported collaborative learning. *Educational Research Review*, 22, 159–180. DOI: 10.1016/j.edurev.2017.08.005

Díez, E., & Díaz-Nafría, J. (2018). Ecologías de aprendizaje ubicuo para la ciberciudadanía crítica. *Comunicar*, 54, 49–58. DOI: 10.3916/C54-2018-05

Duque, R. (2018). Affective states in computer-supported collaborative learning: Studying the past to drive the future. *Computers & Education*, 120, 29–50. DOI: 10.1016/j.compedu.2018.01.015

Farro, F. (2001). *Planeamiento Estratégico para Instituciones Educativas de Calidad*. UDEGRAF.

Fatimah, F., Rajiani, S., & Abbas, E. (2021). Cultural and individual characteristics in adopting computer-supported collaborative learning during covid-19 outbreak: Willingness or obligatory to accept technology? *Management Science Letters*, 11(2), 373–378. DOI: 10.5267/j.msl.2020.9.032

González-Sanmamed, M., Sangrà, A., Souto-Seijo, A., & Estévez, I. (2020). Learning ecologies in the digital era: Challenges for higher education. *Publicaciones*, 50(1), 83–102. DOI: 10.30827/publicaciones.v50i1.15671

Gutiérrez, E., & González, E. (2010). *De las teorías del desarrollo, al desarrollo sustentable: Construcción de un enfoque multidisciplinario*. Siglo XXI.

Heidt, T., & Lamberton, G. (2011). Sustainability in the undergraduate and postgraduate business curriculum of a regional university: A critical perspective. *Journal of Management & Organization*, 17(5), 670–690. DOI: 10.5172/jmo.2011.17.5.670

Hernández-Sellés, N., González-Sanmamedy, M., & Muñoz-Carril, P. (2015). El rol docente en las ecologías de aprendizaje: análisis de una experiencia de aprendizaje colaborativo en entornos virtuales. *Profesorado Revista de Currículum y Formación de Profesorado, 19*(2), 147-163. https://revistaseug.ugr.es/index.php/profesorado/article/view/18765

Järvelä, S., Järvenoja, H., & Malmberg, J. (2019). Capturing the dynamic and cyclical nature of regulation: methodological progress in understanding socially shared regulation in learning. *ijcscl, 14*(4), 425-441. DOI: 10.1007/s11412-019-09313-2

Koehler, M., & Mishra, P. (2009). What is technological pedagogical content knowledge? *Contemporary Issues in Technology & Teacher Education*, 9(1), 60–70. https://www.citejournal.org/vol9/iss1/general/article1.cfm

Ladino, D., Bejarano, B., Santana, L., Martínez, O., & Cabrera, D. (2018). Diseño de aprendizaje a partir de las posibilidades de las ecologías de aprendizaje en educación superior. *Revista Virtual Universidad Católica del Norte,* (53), 35-52. https://revistavirtual.ucn.edu.co/index.php/RevistaUCN/article/view/963/1411

Lescano, J., Vegas, E., Collazos, H., Valdez, L., & Belaúnde, M. (2008). *Planteamiento teórico y conceptual del desarrollo sostenible (informe Brundtland) "Nuestro futuro en común.* UniversidadNacional de la Amazona Peruana.

Marcano, S., & Reyes, M. (2009). Administración (12.a edición). México: Pearson https://www.ceut.edu.mx/Biblioteca/books/Administración/Administración-Robbins.pdf

Martínez, O., Steffens, E., Ojeda, D., & Hernández, H. (2018). Estrategias pedagógicas aplicadas a la educación con mediación virtual para la generación del conocimiento global. *Formación Universitaria*, 11(5), 5. DOI: 10.4067/S0718-50062018000500011

Martínez-Rodríguez, R., & Benítez-Corona, L. (2020). The ecology of resilience learning in ubiquitous environments to adverse situations. *Comunicar English ed., 28*(62), 43-52 (2020). DOI: 10.3916/C62-2020-04

Peters, M., & Romero, M. (2019). Lifelong learning ecologies in online higher education: Students' engagement in the continuum between formal and informal learning. *British Journal of Educational Technology*, 50(4), 1729–1743. https://doi.org.ezproxy.usach.cl/10.1111/bjet.12803. DOI: 10.1111/bjet.12803

Radkowitsch, A., Vogel, F., & Fischer, F. (2020). Good for learning, bad for motivation? a meta-analysis on the effects of computer-supported collaboration scripts. *International Journal of Computer-Supported Collaborative Learning*, 15(1), 5–47. DOI: 10.1007/s11412-020-09316-4

Ramírez, D., & Ramírez, J. (2014). *Derecho ambiental y desarrollo sustentable (segunda edición).* Porrúa.

Ruiz, R., Martínez, R., & Valladares, L. (2010). Innovación en la educación superior. Hacia las sociedades del conocimiento. México: *Fondo de Cultura Económica/ UNAM.Sauvé, Enseñanza de las Ciencias, 28*(1), 5–18. https://books.google.com .mx/books/about/Innovación_en_la_educación_superior.html?id=QOcOHijVOosC &redir_esc=y Saadatmand, M., & Kumpulainen, K. (2013). Content Aggregation and Knowledge Sharing in a Personal Learning Environment: Serendipity in Open Online Networks. *International Journal of Emerging Technologies in Learning, 8*(1), 70-78.

Sovero, F. (2007). *Cómo dirigir una Institución Educativa.* AFA, Editores Importadores S.A. Lima.

Unesco. (2017). Recovered from https://www.un.org/sustainabledevelopment/es/ objetivos-de-desarrollo-sostenible/United

ADDITIONAL READING

Baca-Pumarejo, J., Villanueva, V., Gabino, H., & Cantú, D. (2018). Brecha digital en alumnos del sistema de educación primaria en Tamaulipas, México: Un panorama del futuro capital humano del estado. *CienciaUAT*, 13(1), 35–49. DOI: 10.29059/ cienciauat.v13i1.921

Cuantindioy, J., González, L., Muñoz, J., & Díaz, I. (2019). Plataformas virtuales de aprendizaje: Análisis desde su adaptación a estilos de aprendizaje. *Revista Venezolana de Gerencia*, 24(2), 488–501.

Gómez, D., Alvarado, R., Martínez, M., & Díaz-de-León, C. (2018). La brecha digital: Una revisión conceptual y aportaciones metodológicas para su estudio en México. *Entreciencias: Diálogos en la Sociedad del Conocimiento*, 6(16), 49–64. DOI: 10.22201/enesl.20078064e.2018.16.62611

Valles, H., & Parra, H. (2021). La digitalización de la formación universitaria con enfoque socioformativo: un análisis documental. *IE-Revista de Investigación Educativa de la REDIECH, 12,* 1-22. https://doi.org/https://doi.org/10.33010/ie_rie _rediech.v12i0.1199

KEY TERMS AND DEFINITIONS

Curriculum development: Process through which the learning path of each learner is planned, designed and executed, through productive projects that contain Learning Activities, and the application of Active Teaching Techniques that allow the development of their skills with personalized learning rhythms for each one.

Institutional leadership: It involves the establishment and protection of values and institutional character, whose orientation is more focused on self-maintenance and less inclined towards future orientation or change.

Institutional management: Process that helps good management of projects of the set of interrelated actions undertaken by the management team of a school to promote and enable the achievement of pedagogical intentionality in, with and for educational opportunity.

Learning ecologies: They are a product of imagination and reason and are the vehicle of our creative thoughts and actions.

Sustainable development: It involves how we should live today if we want a better future, taking care of present needs without compromising the opportunities of future generations to meet theirs.

Chapter 8
Continuous and Assertive Transformation to Promote Interculturality, Equity, and Social Justice Through Inclusive Leadership in Education

Silvia Daniella Pérez Muñoz
https://orcid.org/0009-0004-8984-0520
Instituto Politécnico Nacional, Mexico

Sandra Viridiana Cortés Ruiz
Instituto Politécnico Nacional, Mexico

ABSTRACT

The situation that concerns Mexico in the educational domain aims to leave behind those barriers that prevent the intercultural growth and development among managers, teachers, students and parents, which for many years was relegated by political, economic and social situations. Likewise, it has been identified that in order to achieve the goals set and obtain as a result a quality, inclusive, equitable, fair, empathetic and resilient education; first of all, it is necessary to recognize that a leader is the key to carry out diverse actions in favor of inclusive and intercultural education; Through his actions, skills and strategies, he tests a management profile that allows to generate within the educational institute under his charge, an optimal, comfortable, inclusive, respectful, free environment, among others; achieving that the staff and school community, have the certainty that they will be guided and

DOI: 10.4018/979-8-3693-7086-5.ch008

accompanied during the academic process being the beginning of a collaborative work and proactive construction with the educational population.

INTRODUCTION

Education begins when the human being is born and experiences a series of factorial experiences that allow him to develop in his environment, through his senses and emotions that cause the beginning of an empirical knowledge; in which, with the course of time, the individual shows a physical, cognitive and emotional development according to his customs and his social environment that allows him to develop in his context.

It is necessary to implement a series of changes in the educational system that will allow the involvement of cultural diversity, through the acceptance and recognition of Mexico's intercultural enrichment, as part of an identity and history that precedes a population with cultural, social, political and economic richness.

In order to work on inclusive leadership, first of all, it is necessary to know the concept and characteristics of an individual who demonstrates leadership and then, how to put this knowledge into practice. Also, having this information, it is considered as a foundation to promote the development of inclusive leadership in education; for this reason, empathy and resilience of educational authorities are needed; who play a primary and relevant role in this role among teachers and managers.

In this sense, interculturality, equity and social justice play a significant and transcendental role for an educational system in the process of transformation and adaptation to the needs that currently affect Mexican society; which allows visualizing new actions and strategies that develop a leadership capable of being inclusive, fair and equitable to meet the basic needs of an educational institution but, most importantly, it is the teaching staff, students and parents, who are a fundamental part of the construction of an inclusive education in Mexico.

I. Leadership and Its Competencies in Education

In the first instance, the concept of leadership is defined as a person who shows to be the guide or orientor of a group of people, who work together for a common goal; where the leader of the group is the one who directs and commands through delegating various functions that allow working in a coordinated and active way.

According to Gómez (2016), cited in Bueno-de la Fuente (2024, p.2) determines that "The conceptualization of leadership is related to its original meaning "laed" which means path, route, course of a ship at sea, journey. In this sense, the leader would be the one who leads in the right direction".

Leadership is a key piece for transformation in education, which allows the development and development of educational projects, which are reflected in the expected results with the goals met, as in the teaching practice, collaborative work with parents and the management of inclusive, comprehensive and humanistic academic with students.

Likewise, Anderson (2024, p. 21) mentions that: "... leadership is a process of transformation in which the leader is encouraged to make a profound change in order to obtain a deeper understanding of himself, the world and his relationship with others". Leadership not only transforms a single subject, in this case the leader, but also the elements (members), who are relevant factors to achieve the goal(s) determined by the leader; achieving a collaborative work.

The leader is the one who promotes a series of transformations to optimize the collaborative work between teachers, students and parents within the educational institution, through the application of a series of strategies that allow the fulfillment of common objectives.

According to Ramón et al. (2024, p.3) states that "exercising a leadership style, or the way of influencing the behavior of employees (Northouse, 2021), from which companies can transfer and implement, in their specific contexts, values such as inclusion, diversity, cooperation, equity, transparency, honesty and freedom" (Choi et al..., 2017; Lopez-Cabrales & Valle-Cabrera, 2020; van Knippenberg & van Ginkel, 2021).

Through leadership, a series of skills are developed that allow transcending through a close link with equity, justice, inclusion, as well as interculturality among the school community that are part of the collaborative work team; managing to develop an empathetic and trusting work environment to freely express their ideas or suggestions, in order to meet the goals set by the teaching and management team.

Figure 1 below shows the competencies that a person must have in order to perform the leadership function in his or her work or educational environment.

Figure 1. Basic competencies for leadership (Own elaboration)

A person is considered a leader when he/she shows his/her collaborators the traits of competence, as a first moment the planning of the activities to be carried out to fulfill a common objective; where the actions to be executed are systematized by means of a strategic communication through the decision making in an assertive and congruent way with what is intended to be accomplished.

In this sense, Juarez (2024, p.9) refers that: "The Plan of Studies for the Bachelor's Degree in Elementary Education (PELEP), derived from both the National Agreement for the Modernization of Basic Education (ANMEB) (DOF, 1992) and the General Law of Education, described and administered the professional being through five dimensions":

- Specific intellectual skills.
- Content mastery.
- Didactic competencies.
- Professional identity and ethics.
- Ability to perceive and respond to the social conditions of the school environment.

Therefore, each dimension refers to traits of *professional competence*, such as knowledge, skills, values and attitudes about teaching practice. To determine the level and relevance of each dimension of the professional leadership profile, the traits covered by each subject are evaluated and the timetable and credits handled within the educational training curriculum are assessed.

Likewise, the existence of different types of leadership shown by the leader when facing a particular situation is shown; starting with two main features according to Ramos Sotos (2022, p. 2), he mentions that "The theories based on the characteristics of the leader are divided into two: those of traits and those of behavioral, the first states that the leader is born not made, has innate characteristics of intelligence, intuition, integrity, ability, foresight; the behavioral theory or behavioral focuses on analyzing the behavior or behavior of the leader..."

The importance of evaluating, determining the skills and abilities of an innate leader in comparison to those who are formed under a scheme of repetition of learning and attitudes that show the tenacity to carry out this function, at the moment is prepared progressively to face various challenges according to their context and the objectives set to meet.

According to Sotos (2022, pp. 2-5) refers that "...organizations require leaders who positively influence the staff for their success, so they become a necessity, and this allows to address the topic of leadership in which other disciplines such as history, psychology, political science and sociology influence..."

Therefore, this leads to the existence of different types of leadership, according to their experiences, knowledge, creativity, tenacity, among other traits. Figure 2 below shows the types of leadership that can be adapted in the family, social, school and work environment.

Figure 2 Types of leadership (Own elaboration)

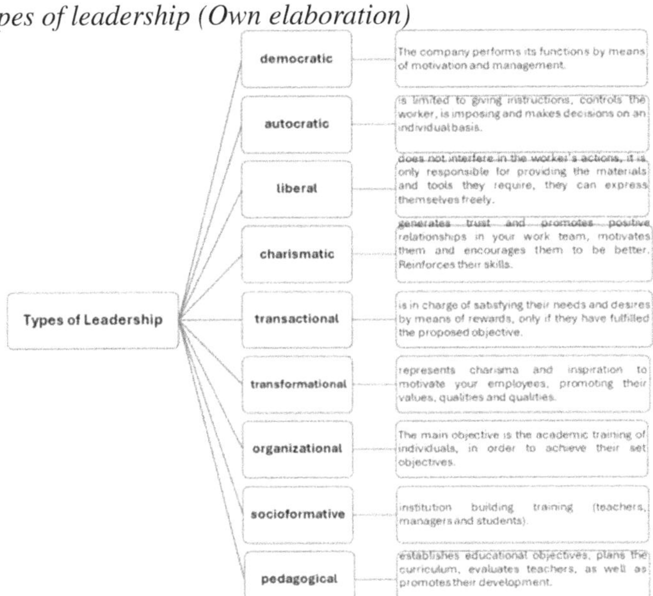

According to Monzoni (2013) cited in Bueno - de la Fuente (2024, p.3) states that "Leadership styles according to different theories and stages represent the principles, techniques and attitudes of their way of leading, putting into practice different skills. In this regard, we find studies related to goal setting, under the paradigm of authentic leadership that have focused on exploring under what conditions employees obtain better results both behaviorally and affectively, coming to affirm that the effectiveness of one leadership style or another (participative, directive) may depend on context variables".

The leadership style will depend on the social and cultural context where the educational institution is located, as well as the direct contact with teachers, students and parents, which will determine the strategies and skills to be used to achieve the established goals, in order to obtain a quality education and excellence.

Accordingly, Panchón & Pautt (2024, para. 14) mention that "The main behaviors associated with transformational leadership include idealized attributed influence - use of charisma, idealized behavioral influence - role modeling, individualized consideration - concern for followers, inspirational motivation - moving followers, and intellectual stimulation - creatively challenging followers".

Transformational leadership is the one who promotes motivation to give continuity to the work of its employees, to achieve the objectives set in time and form, as in the educational field where the manager is responsible for generating an environment of trust, which considers and understands their teachers in various circumstances during their academic work.

According to Flores (2023, p.4) says that "Transactional leadership is usually seen as a kind of exchange (cost-benefit) between the leader and the followers, the challenge for leaders is focused on setting goals and defining the relationship between rewards and punishments".

This leadership differs with the purpose of current education, which seeks to transform from its directive with tools and skills that it possesses to support and guide its school community through assertive communication and collaborative work, although it coincides with the achievement of goals, it requires the support and exchange of teachers, students and parents to achieve what has been established.

In accordance with the above, Montero et al. (2021, p. 4), explains that "positive leadership is recognized as a strategic skill tool to be taken into consideration in the concavity of organizations, because the operational results it emanates have a significant impact on productivity and competitiveness, strengthening in turn, affective bonds between those involved (labor) in the business process".

It is considered that leaders are responsible for maintaining an equitable and organized environment, which allows the growth and use of positive emotions, such as: joy, confidence, security, appreciation and diminishes the negative ones, such as: fear, anger, anxiety, insecurity; it also promotes the development of cognitive abilities that corroborate the strategic elements, considering innovation, creativity and proactivity, which grant individual and collective security in work performance. This attributes to the organizational capacity of the leaders, to face diverse obstacles that arise during the working day.

Positive leadership is composed of several factors, which are shown in Figure 3 below.

Figure 3. Positive leadership factors (Own elaboration)

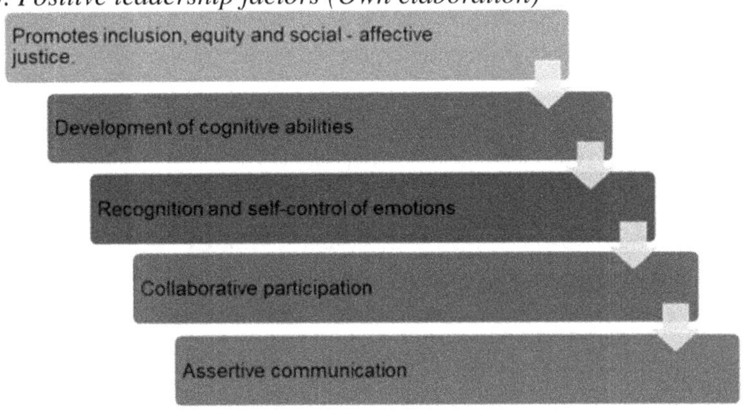

The factors of positive leadership, allows the development of the subjects within their work centers, where they can express their emotions without being labeled, judged, discriminated by the freedom of expression; considering that it promotes competition, inclusion, equity and social - affective justice, obtaining an organized, motivated, enterprising and innovative work environment by trust and assertive accompaniment during the work performed. Equity and social - affective justice, obtaining an organized, motivated, enterprising and innovative work environment through trust and assertive accompaniment during the work performed.

The importance of working and involving the leaders of education is a version of an inclusive leadership; where each of the existing types can be used, in which they can complement each other and generate a pedagogical, transformational, organizational leadership, among others in oneself; developing a leader with a profile capable of facing the challenges that come with the responsibility acquired in the workplace; being that everyone is fulfilling a common goal.

According to Montero et al. (2021, p. 5), he mentions that: "It is through leadership that a group consensus can be achieved, which serves as support to present multiple or alternative scenarios, and to be able to make the right decisions supported by creative behaviors that strengthen the organization"; through the positive leadership profile, relevant and significant changes are achieved with the effective participation of the community, identifying the behaviors and attitudes of those involved in the process of the planned activities.

Likewise, the Museum of Memory and Tolerance, (2024, parr.6), considers that the characteristics of an inclusive society are:

- Determine what are the factors that people experience when they are excluded and thus apply the laws that promote the rights for the attention and care of people who have suffered rejection by society or by a particular group.
- Demonstrate empathy towards people in situations or at risk of exclusion, and attend to the various forms of inclusion, considering the different areas of the social context.
- Freedom in decision making that allows the subject to be part of a society and of a whole; where he/she can cover his/her basic needs, both physical and emotional.
- To improve the living conditions of vulnerable or excluded people, in a continuous and assertive manner; as a constant process where the benefit of the application of the various reforms for an inclusive social path is reflected.
- The development and progress of a country is reflected by an inclusive society that involves minorities to be part of the economic, political, cultural, scientific, educational and technological life. Likewise, these people contribute in different areas, with innovative opinions and alternative proposals to meet the challenges of a society in transformation.

In this sense, Estrada and Ramírez (2021, p. 8) state that: "The exercise of leadership constitutes a pillar for the first steps in the development of new establishments, groups or scientific research units". Therefore, it is understood that leaders play an important role in the definition and direction of a company, in this case an educational institution, consolidating leaders with an exceptional, inclusive, empathetic and resilient academic trajectory for the benefit of the school community.

Reusing the theoretical framework of leadership created by Bolman and Deal (2021), cited in Ayala et al. (2024, p.3) refer that: "in his work to analyze and understand organizations and leadership, he will use the structural, human, political and symbolic frameworks as categories from which to assess how the process of creating the book and the key findings of its chapters can speak directly to some of the most important challenges facing democracy today".

The aforementioned, the leadership role requires first of all attention, awareness and inclusion on the role to be played within an educational institution, which will be responsible for the actions and decision making, for the benefit of the actors of education.

Therefore, it is said that a person has an inclusive leadership by knowing how to balance each one of them during the development of his educational management; which will be addressed in the next point of this chapter.

II. Inclusive Leadership in Education

Inclusive leadership refers to those individuals who exhibit characteristics or skills that possess a commitment to diversity, equity and inclusion. In the educational setting; inclusive leaders show great resilience and empathy towards their teaching staff; as well as towards students, inciting the development of inclusive education with equity and social justice.

According to Améstica - Abarca (2024, para. 1) states that: "The literature shows that leaders must respond to different phenomena of exclusion, such as special educational needs, migration, and the consequences of conflictive socio-political situations. To respond to these phenomena, inclusive school leadership considers three dimensions: a social and ethical dimension, an institutional and educational dimension, and a relational and subjective dimension."

However, inclusive leadership is a fundamental part of the process and development of a group of people in the fulfillment of objectives, with the purpose of motivating, creating, listening, observing and determining, who attribute to the performance of specific activities, being equitable and fair during the designation of tasks.

The European University (2023, parr. 7-13), mentions that the main characteristics of an inclusive leader can be summarized as follows:

Table 1. Characteristics of inclusive leadership

Characteristics of an inclusive leader	
Establish a close relationship with your employees. *(organizational leader)*	**Generate an environment of trust among your employees, letting them know that mistakes are part of a learning process, with the understanding that they will not be penalized for their faults.**
Shows affection ***(charismatic leader)***	It expresses satisfaction and liking for the actions performed by its employees, which generates a feeling of commitment to the fulfillment of the company's activities.
Know and avoid prejudices ***(transformational leader)***	Analyzes and identifies situations of discrimination, from an objective approach to determine the necessary measures that support to avoid these situations.
Empathizes with the experiences of others ***(liberal leader)***	Shows empathy for workers' emotions and promotes the confidence to express themselves freely; being an inclusive leader by valuing and respecting their experiences in the emotional realm.

continued on following page

Table 1. Continued

Characteristics of an inclusive leader	
Establish a close relationship with your employees. *(organizational leader)*	**Generate an environment of trust among your employees, letting them know that mistakes are part of a learning process, with the understanding that they will not be penalized for their faults.**
Encourages feedback and active listening **(*socioformative leader*)**	Active listening to obtain opinions from the work team that provide inclusive proposals; where the leader provides constructive feedback, in which through suggestions and proactive comments workers work together for the fulfillment of a common good.
Prone to collaborator ***(democratic leader)*** ***(educational leader)***	Invites activities that promote collaborative work among workers. Therefore, there is no inclusion without having collaboration; likewise, leaders monitor that it is carried out under the guidelines established by the work team in conjunction with the leader.

Source: Inclusive leadership: why it is important and how to improve it (own creation).

It is observed that there is a synergy between leader and inclusive leadership; where the relevance of working together with the activities and workers is perceived; which is placed as the first instance values, active listening, tolerance and respect for ideas; as well as working in harmony and responsibility in assertive communication and actions; since this will depend on how the relationship between leader - worker, will be the results obtained for or against.

According to the above, if we transfer inclusive leadership to the educational field, an education of excellence and quality would be carried out, because it considers the primary needs of teachers as well as those of students, developing a school community of respect, equity, acceptance and empathy.

Inclusive leadership is one of the main factors to achieve a structural change in the curriculum, allowing to obtain opportunities for equity in intercultural education, where sexual orientation, gender, different abilities and culture are valued and respected in teachers; achieving the promotion of an inclusive education with equity and social justice in students.

Likewise, Padilla and Vargas (2022, p.4) mention that "...it is evident that leadership plays a fundamental role in the principal's management. It is emphasized that educational success depends to a great extent on it..." "...constitutes that representative figure, whose leadership influences, guiding and dictating the rules so that the educational processes are developed in the best way, as well as the administrative processes...".

The role of an inclusive leader is an extremely relevant and transcendental role, since it will depend on him/her that the subjects under his/her charge can carry out the commands or present optimal results that allow growth, in this case of the teachers, having the guarantee and confidence of obtaining a significant process at a personal and work level.

Therefore, in Mexico, commitment is required to share and guide those teachers who require it during their working day, since it depends on the geographical area where the educational institution is located, being a rural or urban school, being a factor that modifies and disrupts a process of inclusive leadership by the shortcomings or needs of the region, where the director is put to the test with the difficulties presented by teachers and students.

However, teachers who have recently graduated from the career require greater commitment and guidance, since they are at an unfavorable level due to the lack of experience in teaching practice. It is for this reason that we intend to establish an evaluation of school directors, as well as educational authorities, where we seek to improve and add inclusive leaders and not mandatory or imposing ones.

In this regard, it is necessary to increase spaces for academic and social learning, where an inclusive community can be built and a sense of collective identity can be developed, promoting cultural diversity, equity and social and emotional justice.

Thus, Hemmer and Elliff (2020), cited in Lazcano and Llorente (2022, p. 3) mention that: "Leadership is different from the more traditional models by emphasizing the educational process in an integral manner, and not exclusively on criteria of effectiveness, in addition to having a strong adaptive component to the demands of the context".

Precisely, leadership integrates a series of characteristics and practices with diverse approaches, such as transformational leadership, instructional (or pedagogical) leadership and distributed leadership, as well as the most current approach, which is leadership for learning or better known as leadership for learning.

Similarly, leadership for learning, or better known as leadership for learning, recognizes the importance of instructional support on the role of leadership; that is, it reinforces the value of importance in teaching and learning; therefore, it is necessary to show some flexibility to the needs and location of the context; to understand that schools are an educational system in the process of transformation. In addition, it is understood that not only principals lead the school organization, since it is a distributed influence in schools; but it includes all educational staff who play a key role in developing an inclusive education.

III. Evaluation of Inclusive Leadership in The Educational Field

The evaluation of an inclusive leadership in the educational field; requires key processes is the individual and collective aspect; which influences organizations to develop the achievement of the basic components; where the innovation process refers to factors such as: planning, development, support, inclusion, communication and follow-up.

Bolívar et al. (2017, paras. 14 and 15) state that "...the six *core components* refer to different dimensions of effective pedagogical leadership focused on learning. They are actions highlighted as influential in improving teacher learning opportunities and teaching practice with students. Therefore, other aspects of leadership such as values and knowledge, which, while important, are not indicated as part of learning-centered leadership behaviors, are not included in the evaluation.

Based on the above, it is possible to determine certain basic components to evaluate the leadership of the person holding this position, which are:

1. Dominant learning objectives: the leader reviews and confirms that the objectives, both individual and collective, are of academic and social quality, focused on learning.
2. Curriculum of excellence: revision of academic content, in favor of comprehensive, reflective, critical and humanistic development for students in different areas or subjects, depending on the academic level.
3. Quality in education: it is essential to have quality teaching, which integrates effective teaching practices, where academic and social learning is achieved in the students.
4. Internalize learning and collaborative work: reinforce the collaborative work environment between directors and teachers, and between teachers and students, with social and academic learning being the main focus.
5. Relationship with the school community: the existence of links with parents and other community institutions is essential to improve social and academic connections through the exchange of experiences and learning.
6. Responsibility for the results obtained: leadership is committed to achieving the objectives established for academic and social learning, both for teachers and students. It also shows the level of commitment on the part of the educational actors.

In the educational field, the people responsible for the directive area need to work in a close, empathetic and resilient relationship with the school community, parents, students and teachers; which encourage them to participate in a collaborative and inclusive way in school activities, achieving a benefit in a particular and collective way; which leads to face new social challenges; however, these tasks will lead to an environment of tolerance and respect for family, cultural and social diversity; reinforcing the commitment with their children and for education in Mexico.

However, Bolivar (2017, para. 43) determines that, "A strategic vision for the school, which learning leaders must have, focuses action on collaboration and engagement with the external community. In addition, effective leadership also ensures that community expectations and interests are part of the school's goals, culture, and decisions."

In such a way that leading an educational institution requires objectives and expectations about the level of academic performance for students; for this reason, it requires a coupling with the external community. Likewise, establishing links with families and other schools in the community, to support the process of academic and social performance.

Therefore, some key skills of an educational leader are shown, which are:

- Building and transforming a community
- Demonstrate and transmit leadership
- Be innovative, visionary and inclusive
- Leading by example
- Creating collaborative and inclusive learning environments
- Conveying trust, security, respect and freedom of expression
- Constant updating on cutting-edge educational topics
- To be reflective and critical about their achievements and mistakes.

Therefore, the evaluation of leadership within the educational environment requires critical and reflective thinking on the part of the individual who is performing this role of academic and administrative management, in which teachers, students and parents should participate, with the aim of improving those areas that are vulnerable and provide quality service with integrity, empathy, resilience and equity.

Lazcano and Llorente (2022, p. 3) state that: "... standardized recipes, widely disseminated in the literature on school leadership, have limitations that are amplified in environments of high sociocultural complexity. The premise is based on the tradition of school leadership research, which has devoted multiple efforts to defining the most effective managerial practices and which denotes an aspiration to characterize and standardize models, as well as a marked emphasis on isolating effects and positioning leadership styles that best explain academic achievement -in particular, pedagogical leadership-".

Based on the above, a leadership does not follow a recipe that shows what or how to decide certain eventualities, nor can the time of acceptance by the community be determined, since this will depend on the actions taken by the leader in favor of equity, inclusion and interculturality of the context in which the educational institution is located. Therefore, the school community is the one who will determine and evaluate the leadership role during its management.

In this sense, Pérez-Castro (2021, p. 4) mentions that: "There is a diversity of ways of understanding inclusion and its implications. Sometimes, the focus has been on pedagogical strategies to respond to the needs of students and the elimination of barriers, while in others the attention has been placed on accessibility and the collaboration of stakeholders. It has also been seen as a balancing process between academic standards and multimodal assessment and, finally, it has been defined as a holistic-comprehensive approach to teaching and learning for different groups of learners".

Leadership is a fundamental axis that will cover the needs of students, teachers and parents, reducing the barriers that limit the link between these actors to develop an inclusive, equitable, comprehensive, reflective and humanistic school community, with the opportunity to grow and contribute proactively to achieve an academic level of quality and excellence.

IV. Education as a Social and Intercultural Right

Education is a social right that allows obtaining multidisciplinary knowledge where individuals demonstrate diverse capacities, skills or strategies in their work, personal, social, political or economic environment.

According to Bermúdez (2021, p. 7), he refers that: "Contemporary society requires social law to establish a specific set of rules through its various branches, which contributes to the achievement of the common good, of social justice. A normative set that allows equal development opportunities to the members of a society, regardless of their economic, cultural or social situation".

Therefore, the social right is part of a normative, which is necessary for the organization and equity of education in a country; in which several factors are involved, such as interculturality, which allows complementing each other for a common and prosperous good for teachers and students.

Likewise, education promotes interculturality, making students recognize the diverse cultures allowing the interaction of experiences through an assertive and equitable communication, as part of a personal development growth in the identification of a cultural identity; therefore, it creates a sensitivity and empathy to revalue social justice in which respect for ideas, customs and language of the population is promoted.

According to the UNIR (2020, parr.2-6), it mentions that: "Intercultural education is a concept based on values such as freedom, equality and dignity of all people, which pursues a peaceful coexistence among members of the classroom and school. It aims to help children develop as social beings and to acquire positive concepts about other cultures and their history, their political and religious differences, allowing them to feel accepted and integrated in the school environment".

However, it is necessary to work from an inclusive leadership that allows the development of intercultural education inside and outside the classroom; having the empathy to promote and respect the customs that concern us as a society and identity; valuing our history, recognizing and reinforcing this knowledge and getting it to be transmitted from generation to generation; achieving the breaking of paradigms and stigmas that for years have caused havoc by the lack of inclusion in education in Mexico.

Therefore, through schooling, it is intended to meet certain objectives such as social change and intercultural education. For this, it is necessary to take into account the following keys according to UNIR (2020):

- Recognize the diversity of cultures.
- Relate with individuals and groups from different cultures.
- Common standards that can be shared.

This allows the promotion of an education with an intercultural perspective, which develops an analysis and reflection on how to carry out an inclusive and equitable education, which allows critical and humanistic thinking for a growth of cultural diversity.

On the other hand, Schmelks (2024, p. 13 - 14), mentions that "...when educational systems emphasize memorization, obedience and discipline and disregard the development of critical and creative thinking. The latter requires the management of pedagogies that stimulate higher cognitive skills such as analysis, synthesis, deduction, induction, inquisitive mentality fostered by the ability to doubt and question, hypothetical thinking and logical thinking."

Likewise, the social and intercultural approach in education in Mexico, intends to give a turn in the pedagogical field, which involves the development of the capacities and abilities of the students from a humanistic and integral perspective; giving cavity to equity and social justice; forming as a complete part of the development of education.

In this sense, the social-normative aspect qualifies and stops the teacher's life by concepts, affections, desires, practices and expectations. In other words, this simple work, becomes how multiple and dispersed of the teaching profession, however, from the perspective of post-metaphysical discursive analysis, which seeks to design various strategies relating to political theory, considering any investment of principles or actions expected in the leader's performance, because the possibilities of the educational institution, is reflected broken by a constitutive fissure. Therefore, this fissure allows the leader to get involved in the participation of a dynamic, which promotes activities that enable the interaction between the actors of education.

V. Educational Equity and Social Justice in Education

According to Oklahoma City Public Schools (2020, para. 1), "Educational equity is defined as making decisions strategically based on equity principles, which includes providing a variety of educational resources, models, programs, and strategies according to student needs that may not be the same for all students or schools with the intent to lead to equity in academic outcomes."

For this reason, it is important that education be based on the principle of equity, allowing students to participate and have the same opportunities for learning and knowledge that will allow them to develop strategies and apply the necessary tools to apply them in their environment.

According to UNESCO (2020, paras. 4 - 10): "Equity, the approach adopted, is based on the need for a vision that goes beyond the concept of formal equality - which makes inequities and differences invisible - as well as perspectives that contemplate equality of opportunities rather than equality of results, recognition and educational consequences".

Likewise, equity in school education is considered as an educational compensation, so that obstructed to generate the opportunity for all students, where only paths or itineraries with little social value are offered, as part of the problem that allows to provide an opportunity to overcome, as well as the historical oblivion of the multicultural richness of our region.

Under these considerations on inclusion and equity, UNESCO (2020), shows a theme that requires considering the different parameters, to make the relevant changes to generate an intercultural and equity education; which are:

Ensure that people of the required age to attend school can receive a quality education from the basic aspects such as infrastructure, teaching staff, pedagogical resources, curriculum map, and school time.

2. Promote the exchange of experiences and learning, regardless of their customs or family traditions or the context in which they live.
3. To promote the understanding of culture, as well as respect for it; without making distinctions in a particular way in certain social groups, to avoid marginalizing and creating specific singularities of the population.
4. Avoid conditioning on students once they have completed their studies, regardless of the level, they have the freedom to continue their education in the faculty of their choice.
5. Guarantee that the State assumes responsibility for access and quality of education, as well as the support to reach educational institutions, having free transit and transportation that facilitates their attendance during the course of study in basic education.

Therefore, the aim is for education to be equitable, where all students have the same opportunities to develop without prejudice or limitations, achieving a quality, multidisciplinary and intercultural education.

According to Sánchez-Corral, Fernández (2021, para. 20) states that: "Social justice involves access to rights and opportunities to ensure full participation of human beings in life in society, particularly for those who have been systematically excluded on the basis of race or ethnicity, gender, age, physical or mental disability, education, sexual orientation, socioeconomic status, religion, educational level, nationality or other background characteristics or group affiliation. Social justice is based on the conviction that all people are entitled to equal treatment, support to defend their human rights and a fair distribution of social resources."

It refers to equity and social justice as part of an intercultural and comprehensive education, from an inclusive approach that allows freedom and respect for students with physical disabilities, race, sex, age, religion, sexual orientation, having the same opportunities to obtain knowledge and recognition of their studies with official validity without prejudice or stereotypes.

However, Alberti and Emmons, (2006), cited in Velandia and Zamora (2024, pp. 8-9) mention that: "Assertive behavior promotes equality in human relationships, enabling them to act in their own interest, to defend themselves without anxiety, to express their personal rights without undermining the rights of others". "In this sense, a hypothesis can be hazarded about the phenomenon of participation and the states or behavioral changes noticed by researchers: the higher the levels of assertiveness, the higher the levels of participation".

Assertive behavior, complements and directs the acquisition of actions based on social justice and equity; which give cause to participation and equal opportunities, allowing the development of new strategies that promote inclusion in education, demonstrating better results in communication between the educational community (principals, teachers, students), ultimately, increases their interest in promoting assertiveness in education.

V.I The Importance of Affective Justice in Education

According to Cruz (2022, p.14 -15), he mentions that: "...to speak of affective justice implies recovering the complexity of the educational act and, above all, pointing out the role of the pertinence and relevance of the contents, so that they can fix meanings in the students. However, this act necessarily refers to a series of affective relationships that unfold in an important way in the learning process".

However, the educational institution requires a series of relationships, dispositions, attitudes and behaviors that are necessary for the permanence of students during their academic formation; developing a series of abilities, skills, attitudes and aptitudes that allow students to develop freely in an affective and meaningful way for their daily lives.

On the other hand, Liberating Learning Canada Universidad Iberoamericana Ciudad de México (2024, p. 4), states that: "... the Department of Education of the Universidad Iberoamericana stresses the urgency of promoting not only academic excellence, but also human formation that drives transformational initiatives. Education must transcend academic boundaries and address multidimensional challenges, from reconciliation and justice, contributing to projects that impact locally, regionally and globally".

Similarly, it is necessary to promote human formation, giving rise to affective justice; where transformation is part of both, being the student as the main actor to develop a series of skills and abilities that leads to an academic formation with affective bases that allows him to transcend in a significant way in his integral and human growth in the face of the adversities of his context.

However, Castro Saucedo, et al. (2022, p. 4) states that: "The responsible application of tutoring will make it possible to know the individual characteristics, personal interests, professional and work expectations, and life projects of young people, and thus establish interpersonal relationships between the teacher-tutor and the student, which will benefit not only both, but also the environment in which they develop...".

In addition to this, the participation and action of a tutor allows the development of a socio-affective relationship that allows both actors (director - teacher) to share personal and work experiences, which leads to the establishment of fair actions for their academic and inclusive leadership training in an educational environment.

With respect to Angulo Rasco (2022, p. 56) refers that: "Affective justice claims a right that is, in a way, part of our own nature. Developing the bond with others, caring for others, possesses an extraordinary affective force" "...we need to rely on honesty, empathy, trust, esteem, cooperation, solidarity and willingness to share, defending affective justice becomes not only a fundamental claim, but the very meaning of public school".

In addition, affective justice shows a series of emotions that provoke the well-being and security of people, when this is carried out in a correct and inclusive way, where affective contexts are manifested, having as a guide, a counselor, who takes them step by step to promote their integral, equitable, democratic development, achieving an empathic accompaniment that allows applying through these actions the power of self-regulation of emotions, to give continuity to the revaluation of equal opportunities in the educational field.

Emotions are recognized as mechanisms of human behavior, through psychophysiological reactions; which allow us to perform various actions through the perception of cognitive programs that influence the way we regulate neuropsychological states; such as gestures, postures and facial expressions.

The lack of social and affective justice is undermined by inequalities that do not allow the growth and social and affective development of students; therefore, the following topic refers to the inequalities that a society presents in education.

V.II Social Inequalities in Education

Social inequality is understood as the conditions under which people have limited or restricted access, due to their social, educational and economic status, to resources, services and positions valued by society, which marks a superior or inferior level for others.

According to Cazarez (2022, p. 7) mentions that: "...social and economic inequalities exist as long as there is equal equality of opportunities, and that such inequalities benefit the less advantaged. In other words, inequalities could be "fair" as long as those who are disadvantaged perceive that they have access to more primary social goods than they could have under conditions of total equality".

Inequalities are also present in the educational field, due to the fact of belonging to a geographical area, to a social and economic group, to the customs and traditions of a population, to the language; which leads to the search for equality between managers, teachers, students and the school community; identifying the basic needs and remedying the shortcomings of a school inequality.

On the other hand, Cazarez (2022, p. 16) refers that: "The human rights approach has been used as a conceptual basis for understanding justice in education and for measuring progress related to the fulfillment of educational objectives".

However, this approach shows that human rights, within a normative framework, has done hard work to develop justice in education. The objective is to provide the regulatory confirmation to assume a commitment among teachers, students and the school community to extend educational opportunities.

In a certain way, this perspective is considered in terms of justice as a measure of human capabilities; which manages opportunities of choice, with the freedom and certainty of dimensioning such capabilities in relation to others, with the vision of obtaining equality in the social, economic and educational fields; with a magnitude in a perspective of equality and justice; considering the introduction of interculturality in education in Mexico.

VI. Interculturality and its Problems in Mexico

Previously to expose the various problems that concern us as a country at intercultural level, it is necessary to leave in the understanding that interculturality in Mexico has been a great controversy that has led to researchers, historians, sociologists, educators, teachers and other actors in education, where currently has had a boom of recognition and respect by the political management of President Andrés Manuel López Obrador, who has staged the relevance of preserving our culture and identity as Mexicans.

Interculturality is defined as that which establishes permanence and respect in the interaction of diverse cultures, in order to achieve equality that allows free expression and sharing of cultural experiences. Therefore, intercultural education promotes the generation of transforming attitudes in the educational institution, such as respect for diversity, collaboration, assertive communication, tolerance and respect.

Likewise, Art. 3°, section II, paragraph g) of the Political Constitution of the United Mexican States establishes that: "It will be intercultural, by promoting harmonious coexistence between people and communities for the respect and recognition of their differences and rights, within a framework of social inclusion". Therefore, through the law, it favors promoting interculturality at all levels of education, in order to improve and generate actions that promote the recognition of cultures and customs, achieving inclusion among the actors of education.

In a way, interculturality differs from the concept of pluriculturality, which characterizes a situation, whereas interculturality describes a relationship between cultures.

Likewise, intercultural education presents several challenges, which are shown in Figure 4.

Figure 4. Challenges in intercultural education (Own elaboration)

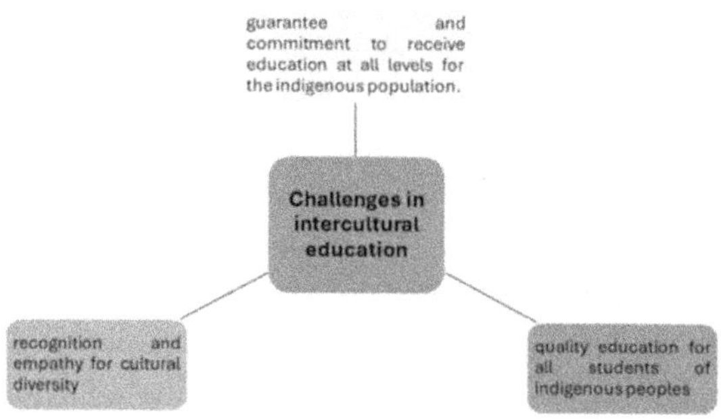

According to the above, it can be mentioned that intercultural education has several challenges to face and overcome; however, it promotes inclusion in the processes of learning, socialization and coexistence in the educational environment, in order to achieve intercultural education and thus combat discrimination and racism.

In this sense, if we talk about the quality of work done by a leader in the educational field, it is perceived by the interest and level of preparation, through various courses, workshops, diploma courses, among others that promote inclusion, interculturality, equity and justice, based on a real context; where it consolidates an integrated and humanistic curriculum, which generates strategies and programs, in order to support the school community; also, linking this approach between some educational institutions that join the proactive transformation, through inclusive leadership.

VI.I Intercultural Issues in The Educational Social Environment

One of the problems in intercultural education in Mexico, according to Valdillo and Fernandez, refers that: "...it represents a policy whose articulating principle is the annihilation of barriers (architectural, attitudinal, curricular, etc.) that prevent any student, regardless of condition, characteristic, belief, quality, capacity, etc., from participating in equal conditions in an education that allows him/her to develop as a person and citizen and thus favor autonomous processes in accordance with the dignity present in every human being".

In accordance with this intercultural social problem, it becomes a starting point to lower those barriers that prevent the improvement of the condition of acceptance and revaluation of interculturality in education, where it seeks to promote equal opportunities and privileges for those groups that are in a state of vulnerability within the same society.

On the other hand, López - Cava (2024, p. 4) states that: "Likewise, for violent environments, it is necessary to educate in a model of coexistence that leads to peace; as for the democratic crisis, school and university would be privileged instances to develop democratic citizenship. With regard to exclusion, education could transform this into inclusive and tolerant spaces; when profitability is pressing, education systems could be oriented towards promoting capacities for human development and justice...".

According to the above, the problem of exclusion is unfortunately one of the factors that affects education regardless of the academic level; however, this has severe repercussions, being an obstacle in the integral and humanistic development in the interculturality of students; where the social environment is considerably diminished for a perspective of an inclusive society.

VI.II Intercultural Issues in The Educational Policy Field

Likewise, these problems have been dragging on with every six-year political term in Mexico; where students, teachers and directors are affected by the lack of follow-up, detection and prompt solution to the needs and deficiencies faced by education in this country, despite the existence of the social program "The School is Ours", where a monetary contribution is received every year for the improvement of public schools.

The New Mexican School (NEM), is the current educational reform in Mexico; which seeks to ensure the education of the Mexican population; with a comprehensive, humanistic, critical and inclusive approach, which recognizes multiculturalism and multilingualism to promote social awareness, justice, solidarity and freedom; which is stated in art. 3°, section II, paragraph e) of the Political Constitution of the United Mexican States, which establishes the following: "In indigenous peoples and communities, plurilingual and intercultural education will be provided based on the respect, promotion and preservation of the historical heritage and culture".

In accordance with the above, interculturality tends to be a fundamental factor for the educational process in Mexico, with a perspective towards inclusion, so that all students have the same learning opportunities, regardless of their geographic location and social group, thus achieving equity and equality for students at the basic and university levels.

However, in order to transform an educational structure, it requires the development of certain conditions, which set the tone of what is expected to be achieved during the work in the planning of plans and programs, curriculum map, teaching materials, among others, with a comprehensive and humanistic approach; however, this model replaces a traditional and doctrinaire educational system, where the teaching practice is involved in an abysmal change *by wanting to do, for the duty to do*; also, an introspection is made on the current educational conversion.

In this sense, Juárez (2024, p. 11) determines that: "Science and technique appeared as nodal points of the modern system of reason, tending to disinvolve the pre-individual affections of teachers in order to constitute them as a "neutral", functional and "de-ideologized" entity, which will function as a transmission belt between scientific knowledge and the learner. However, given that the teaching profession is identified when it puts into action the rules of modernizing agency, it is not possible to identify the modern rural educational agent without analyzing how these rules appear in the narrated practice of directors, teachers and students of the Escuela Normal Rural".

However, the problems in the political sphere refer to the various social programs that have been implemented during this six-year term, giving meaning to the importance and relevance of directing education in an intercultural approach, promoting equal opportunities and the development of a leadership capable of facing political, social and economic challenges in the educational sphere.

In particular, leaders are the key to safeguarding integrity and humanism from fissures and refutations. Likewise, the importance of leadership in the democratic educational arena. Therefore, the need for leaders willing to challenge the status quo and preserve democratic principles is externalized, however, leadership development intrinsically implies the formation and development of inclusive leaders; therefore, schools need democracy, social justice, equity and inclusion; understanding that democracy requires leaders who promote democracy in their academic activities and with the collaborative work of the school community.

According to Rojas et al. (2024, p.20) refers that: "In the context of education, the construction of democratic learning spaces is an arduous task. It requires a change of mentality, a willingness to accept uncertainty and complexity, and a commitment to defend the rights and dignity of all students. Democracy demands an openness to take moral responsibility for working through differences and negotiating between the desire to conclude slowly or quickly. We also found that the development and application of a strong shared framework guides and organizes the application of democratic principles in diverse educational settings."

In addition to the above, it is considered that the context of the educational institution influences the development of democratic academic activities; therefore, leadership plays a relevant role to provide continuity and follow-up during the development and application of strategies that allow being immersed in democratic principles as an aspect for the transformation of a school society.

VI.III Intercultural Problems in the Economic and Educational Sphere

The general director of the LEN (National Education Law) program, Ruíz (2023, para.9), stated that: "the money is delivered directly to the schools, without intermediaries, and it is the school communities that decide how the funds are spent for the benefit of each school.

The social program The School is Ours, promotes the participation of the school community, through the formation of a School Committee for Participatory Administration (CEAP), which is chaired under an assembly to determine the use of resources, in order to improve the conditions of educational spaces and provide quality education for the benefit of students; However, it is very far from achieving this proposal, due to the interests agreed upon by parents, teachers and directors, which unfortunately are affected by the lack of an inclusive leadership organization, which dissolves and unifies the differences between what is agreed and the priority needs in relation to the basic ones.

Therefore, in order to achieve inclusive leadership it is necessary to determine and identify the deficiencies of schools in both rural and urban areas, since this implies that there is a contradiction with what is expected to be obtained with the reality of an educational community that is remedied with government support; however, this is not enough, taking up the infrastructure aspect of a public institution, it is observed deteriorated internally, which does not cover the needs of students with physical disabilities; as well as the design of classrooms, stairs, school yards, etc.

Ruiz (2023, para.11) stated that: "With the support, it is possible to fix from the bathrooms to the purchase of computers, and this is decided by parents and students, because the trust is placed in the people"; however, the reality is that parents are the ones who make the decision to carry out a repair or purchase materials, which during this process the purpose of the process is lost, where only the needs of the students are artificially and momentarily covered, leaving behind the infrastructural part of the school.

In this sense, to promote an educational service, based on intercultural inclusion, it is required to provide quality assistance and excellence that contains the necessary and basic elements to achieve the established purposes, leaving aside the limitations of the barriers of the economic problem that concerns the educational institution, through the link between the school community and the school institution; in this case, the work of inclusive leadership will be reflected.

On the other hand, in a press release from the Government of Mexico, it informed that the program Our School is Ours, 200 thousand pesos were given to Basic Education schools, which have less than 50 students; from 51 to 150 students, they receive 250 thousand pesos; but if the school has more than 150 students, as is the case in most of the schools in the State of Mexico, they receive 600 thousand pesos. Likewise, the Secretary of Public Education, Leticia Ramírez Amaya, asked the 113 thousand beneficiary school communities throughout the country to take ownership of the (The School is Ours) LEN so that public Basic Education institutions are recognized as the center of the community.

In addition to the above, this type of action demonstrates the willingness of the Mexican Government to meet the needs of the population in the educational field so that everyone has the same opportunities to have an education; however, the question is: Why do the economic problems affect each of the public schools? Why is not enough money allocated to support infrastructure improvements in public schools? What actions does the leader of each educational institution carry out to safeguard the interculturality of the school community; as these and other questions are involved in a system that unfortunately still lacks organization and inclusion.

VII. Cultural Discrimination in Education

Discrimination arises when it gives rise to prejudice based on gender, culture and customs, language or language, clothing, sexual orientation, religion, economic situation, among others; which causes an attitude of rejection and consequences that unfortunately cannot be remedied, which generates uncertainty, distrust, fear, insecurity, among others.

In this sense, the Museum of Memory and Tolerance, Quintero (2024, para. 1), determines that: “Discrimination consists of giving unfavorable and unfair treatment to another person or group, generally because of their origin, identity or way of life. As a result of ignorance, fear and intolerance, discrimination sweeps away fundamental rights, denies opportunities and leads to situations of injustice”.

Cultural discrimination occurs when one part of society considers certain traditions, beliefs, customs or habits to be inferior to others. Therefore, individuals or groups that possess or are accustomed to these different characteristics are subjected to mistreatment.

Cultural discrimination is a factor that hinders optimal development in education; therefore, we intend to identify how to apply various strategies that allow us to propose changes in the teaching-learning structure with an intercultural, reflective, equitable and social justice perspective.

Unfortunately, cultural discrimination is still observed in education, whether on the basis of disability, gender, language, currency, ethnicity, religion, migration or displacement.

According to data from the UNESCO Institute for Statistics (2023, para.6), it mentions that: “About 258 million children and youth worldwide are out of school, while 773 million adults, two-thirds of whom are women, are illiterate”.

According to the above, this concerns us as a society, where it is observed in the data provided by UNESCO, that the female gender is the most vulnerable, for reasons of religious beliefs, culture, customs, economic, among others; which is an alarming factor, because it is not generating adequate support for equality, equity and justice for women.

According to Schmelkes (2024, p.3), “Societies have historically experienced injustices and inequalities. The maintenance of the structures that perpetuate and justify these injustices and inequalities has often required the establishment of authoritarian regimes that have oppressed large sectors of the population and kept them in conditions of poverty”.

Therefore, this generates a problem, being discrimination a factor that unfortunately takes over entire populations, where vulnerable people are in constant uncertainty for wanting to generate liking or fit into a group of people who direct or determine what is or is not correct, leaving out the rules or laws that attributes to a society believed to be democratic.

Likewise, the aim is to look for alternatives that will allow to reduce cultural discrimination within the educational environment; achieving a gradual but permanent transformation, where all subjects have the same opportunities in an equitable, inclusive, fair, empathetic and integral manner.

Figure 5 shows the possible alternatives suggested by the decrease in cultural discrimination in education.

Figure 5. Alternatives to decline in educational cultural discrimination (Own elaboration)

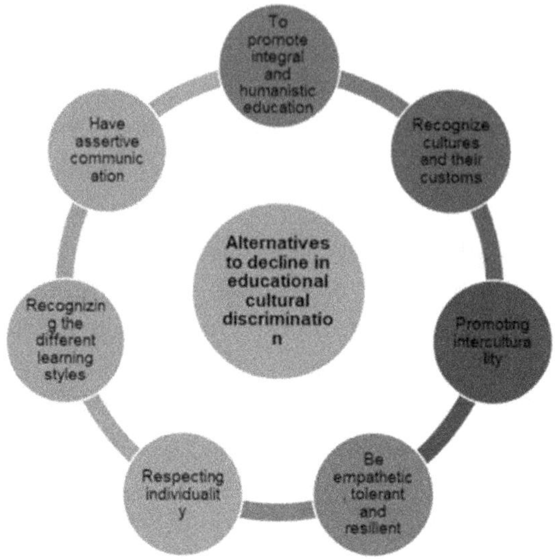

However, the alternatives to reduce cultural discrimination in education are proposals that, if implemented in their entirety in all public and private schools that provide services in the country, education in Mexico would benefit from being one of the countries with the highest number of students enrolled in school; perhaps it is utopia; However, it requires the support of the government and the school community (principals, teachers, students and parents), to position itself as a subject of constant change, where it can learn and share its experience, being able to be transmitted from generation to generation and from context to context, breaking established paradigms, but without forgetting the bases and the history for which it is today.

The leadership function plays a relevant role in promoting a democratic, inclusive, equitable, just and intercultural education; however, the role they play within the educational environment is a great constant challenge that demands time, dedication, commitment, updating, empathy, affective actions, among others, in order to develop a suitable leadership according to the needs of the school context.

Therefore, leading an educational institution, whether public or private, requires leadership with an inclusive profile, which awakens the interest and motivation of its teaching staff; being an echo for students and parents, where they can work collaboratively, with social justice and equity; promoting an environment of safety, trust, free expression and affection; achieving lower standards established to seek a proactive transformation in the development of academic activities.

In short, the importance of building a culture of equity, social justice and interculturality through an inclusive leadership, which becomes established actions among directors, teachers and students. Interculturality is a right that cannot be left forgotten, lagging behind or by an uncertain intention of the school community, but to promote a cross-cutting policy that encompasses the various dimensions of the school system of each educational institution. In this work, the participation of all members of the educational community is required, linking other public and private instances that have worked for the inclusion of interculturality through an empathetic and resilient leadership.

CONCLUSION

Finally, inclusive leadership is one of the pillars to provide the necessary strategies and tools to develop an intercultural education, with equity and social justice, where these factors allow the growth of a reflective, critical, collaborative and humanistic society.

Likewise, positive leadership and its discordances in educational practices, generate a pragmatic change for the benefit of those school entities that allow the unification between the labor and the emotional, having an assertive communication, with specific purposes that produce successful, reliable and beneficial results for the school community (teachers, students and parents), generating an inclusive, fair and equitable link; in which various strategic scenarios can be developed to make the right decisions for the convenience of all those involved in the educational organization.

Therefore, structural changes are required from an intercultural and social point of view, where discrimination and desertion of a vulnerable population can be reduced. In this sense, the integration strategy, by a positive and inclusive leadership, which allows an assertive communication channel, which develops quality and excellence in the development of teachers, students and parents during the process of the work to be done.

Inclusive leadership is a relevant topic in the construction and transcendental transformation that offers the possibility of entering a line of research with a mixed methodology, with qualitative and quantitative results, obtaining the opportunity to innovate and change from society to the educational environment according to its school context; allowing the study of how it diminishes or optimizes the impact of leadership within the educational institution and what it entails during its management.

In conclusion, it is necessary to carry out a social participation management, through an inclusive leadership, represented by the manager of the educational institution, who is committed to promote respect for diversity, be congruent and objective in decision making, work collaboratively, regardless of their religious beliefs, gender, ethnicity, ability, classism, racial, among others; however, training and constant updating of the manager is required to provide assertive and inclusive way to work together with the school community.

"As long as we do not work for equality and justice we will not have an inclusive, democratic and prosperous country."
Quintero (2024).

"The one who promotes interculturality during his leadership, allows to create open thoughts and minds within a complex, but not impossible society."
Pérez Muñoz (2024)

REFERENCES

Améstica – Abarca. José Manuel. (2024). Liderazgo escolar inclusivo: estado del arte sobre un concepto ambiguo. Revista Caribeña de Investigación Educativa. https://revistas.isfodosu.edu.do/index.php/recie/article/view/663#:~:text=La%20literatura%20muestra%20que%20los,fen%C3%B3meno%20en%20el%20contexto%20chileno

Anderson, B. (2024). *Dominar el liderazgo.* Leadership circle. https://leadershipcircle.com/wp-content/uploads/2024/01/Mastering-Leadership_2023-09_LATAM.pdf

Botía, B., & Antonio, C. R. K. García – Garnica, Marina. (2017) 25 (95) 01-24. *Evaluación multidimensional del liderazgo pedagógico: claves para la mejora escolar.*https://www.redalyc.org/journal/3995/399550706009/html/

Bueno-de la Fuente, C., & De la Fuente-Anuncibay, R. (2024). El contexto laboral y género, diferenciadores del estilo de liderazgo [Work context and gender, differentiators of leadership styleWork context and gender, differentiators of leadership style]. *European Public & Social Innovation Review*, 9, 1–17. DOI: 10.31637/epsir-2024-420

Camacho Marín, R. J., Castro González, A. E., Zurita Minango, A. V., Zabala Maya, I. G., Villota Palacios, M., & Villarreal Guerrero, Z. T. (2024). Innovaciones en la administración educativa: Efectos del liderazgo efectivo en el logro de metas educativas y el desarrollo estudiantil. *Emergentes -. Revista Científica (Maracaibo)*, 4(2), 739–753. DOI: 10.60112/erc.v4i2.185

Constitución Política de los Estados Unidos Mexicanos que reforma la de 5 de febrero de 1857. Art. 3°, Fracc. II, incisos e) y g). Ultima reforma, Constitución publicada en el Diario Oficial de la Federación el 5 de febrero de 1917. DOF (2024). Secretaria General. Secretaria de Servicios Parlamentarios. Cámara de Diputados H. Congreso de la Unión. https://www.diputados.gob.mx/LeyesBiblio/pdf/CPEUM.pdf

Cruz Vadillo Rodolfo. (2022) LII(3), 15-40. *Justicia afectiva: micropolítica y construcción de una habitabilidad escolar.* Revista Latinoamericana de Estudios Educativos. https://www.redalyc.org/articulo.oa?id=27071219002

Díaz, P., Eduardo, O., & Vargas, F. J. A. (2022) 6(1). *El liderazgo en la gestión del director. Revista Andina de Educación*https://www.redalyc.org/articulo.oa?id=730076236009

Estrada Mota, I. L., & Ramírez García, R. G. (2021). *Constructores de instituciones científicas. Papel del liderazgo en la creación de la Unidad Mérida* del Cinvestav. *Perfiles Educativos*, XLIII(173), 128–145. DOI: 10.22201/iisue.24486167e.2021.173.59768

Flores, L. M. V., Martínez, I. A. M., & Nava, V. X. (2024). Influencia de estilos de liderazgo transformacional, transaccional y laissez faire en la responsabilidad social corporativa, la imagen y reputación, así como en variables de resultado organizacional. *Contaduría y Administración*, 69(3), 324–347. https://dialnet.unirioja.es/servlet/articulo?codigo=9364206

Juárez Némer, O. C. (2024). La modernización de la formación del maestro rural en México: Expectativas y resignificaciones. *Revista Latinoamericana de Estudios Educativos (México)*, LIV(1), 189–212. DOI: 10.48102/rlee.2024.54.1.620

Lazcano, C., & Llorente, C. (2022). *Liderazgo en escuelas de alta complejidad sociocultural.* Diez miradas. *Perfiles Educativos*, XLIV(175), 194–199. DOI: 10.22201/iisue.24486167e.2022.175.60971

Liberating Learning, Canadá Universidad Iberoamericana Ciudad de México, México. (2024) LIV(1), 7-10. *¿Educar para qué? Los propósitos de la educación para el mundo que viene.* Revista Latinoamericana de Estudios Educativos. https://www.redalyc.org/articulo.oa?id=27075657020

López-Calva Juan Martín. (2024), LIV(1), 11-42. *El sentido de la educación: dos tendencias y una apuesta humanista hacia un Antropoceno positivo.* Revista Latinoamericana de Estudios Educativos https://www.redalyc.org/articulo.oa?id=27075657004

Mendizábal Bermúdez Gabriela. (2021). LIV(162), 167-185. *Hacia la construcción de un derecho social comparado.* Boletín Mexicano de Derecho Comparado. https://www.redalyc.org/articulo.oa?id=42775436008

Mendoza Cazarez Dulce Carolina. (2022) 27 (94), 829-953. *¿Cómo entender y promover justicia social en educación? Implicaciones para las políticas educativas en contextos de emergencia.* Revista Mexicana de Investigación Educativa https://www.redalyc.org/articulo.oa?id=14072628007

Montero, S., Karina, I., Mariño, R., Javier, M., Cajas, C., Viviana, E., & Tanqueño, C. O. P. (2021). *Liderazgo positivo en organizaciones saludables.* Revista Venezolana de Gerencia. https://www.redalyc.org/articulo.oa?id=29069613005

Museo Memoria y Tolerancia. (2024). *Inclusión.* https://www.myt.org.mx/tolerancia_url/inclusion

Oklahoma City Public Schools. (2020). *Equidad. Compromiso con la equidad educacional en OKCPS.* https://www.okcps.org/Page/5738#:~:text=La%20equidad%20educativa%20se%20define,para%20todos%20los%20estudiantes%20o

Oyarzún, J., Parcerisa, L., & Carrasco, A. (2022). Discriminación étnica y cultural en procesos de elección de escuela en minorías socioculturales en Chile. *Psicoperspectivas*, 21(1). Advance online publication. https://www.psicoperspectivas.cl/index.php/psicoperspectivas/article/viewFile/2537/1565. DOI: 10.5027/psicoperspectivas-Vol21-Issue1-fulltext-2537

Pachón-Palacios, M. L., & Pautt-Torres, G. M. (2024). *Liderazgo en el aula y la eficacia docente como variable moderadora en el rendimiento académico.* Revista Colombiana de Educación, (92), 370-396. https://revistas.upn.edu.co/index.php/RCE/article/view/17229

Pérez-Castro, J. (2021). XII(33), 138-157. *Condiciones para la docencia inclusiva: Análisis desde las barreras y los facilitadores.Revista Iberoamericana de Educación Superior.* Advance online publication. DOI: 10.22201/iisue.20072872e.2021.33.862

Pobreza y formación para el trabajo: la necesaria apuesta por la calidad. (2022). Revista Latinoamericana de Estudios Educativos (México), LII(2), 7-16. https://doi.org/DOI: 10.48102/rlee.2022.52.2.503

Quintero, L. (2024*). ¿Qué es la discriminación*? Museo Memoria y Tolerancia. https://www.myt.org.mx/tolerancia_url/discriminacion

Rasco, A., & Felix, J. (2022). *Justicia afectiva: Una necesidad educativa y política inaplazable.* Revista de Estudios Parlamentarios. Hemiciclo. https://www.researchgate.net/publication/378549662_JUSTICIA_AFECTIVA_UNA_NECESIDAD_EDUCATIVA_Y_POLITICA_INAPLAZABLE

Rojas Ayala, G., Nathan, L., & Mendonca, J. (2024). The Study of Democratic Schools and its Contribution to the Reinvigoration of Democracy. *Revista Latinoamericana de Estudios Educativos (México)*, LIV(1), 93–112. DOI: 10.48102/rlee.2024.54.1.610

Rueda López, R., Aja Valle, J., García García, L., & Vázquez García, M. J. (2024). *La influencia del liderazgo inclusivo sobre el bienestar laboral de las personas trabajadoras. 33 (1).* Revista Galega de Economía.

Sánchez-Corral Fernández. Elsa. (2021). *Educar para la justicia social: una apuesta desde el análisis interseccional para estudiantes de grupos privilegiados.* Revista Latinoamericana de Estudios Educativos, vol. LI (3), pp. 97-124. https://www.redalyc.org/journal/270/27066944003/html/

Saucedo, C., Karina, L., Udave, N., Fabiola, L., Cadena, G., Humberto, C., García, T., Jaqueline, E., & Alvarado César Arnulfo de León Alvarado, L. (2022) 13 (14) 1-22. *Validez de la Escala de Confianza en la Tutoría Afectiva y utilidad de la tutoría académica. Diálogos sobre educación. Temas actuales en investigación educativa*https://www.redalyc.org/articulo.oa?id=553474080019

Secretaria de Educación Pública. (2024). La Escuela es Nuestra. Gobierno de México. https://laescuelaesnuestra.sep.gob.mx/

Secretaría del Trabajo y Previsión Social. (2023). *Entrega Gobierno de México medios de pago de la Escuela es Nuestra y Jóvenes construyendo el Futuro en el Estado de México.* Gobierno de México. https://www.gob.mx/stps/prensa/entrega-gobierno-de-mexico-medios-de-pago-de-la-escuela-es-nuestra-y-jovenes-construyendo-el-futuro-en-el-estado-de-mexico#:~:text=Inform%C3%B3%20que%20el%20programa%20entrega,M%C3%A9xico%2C%20reciben%20600%20mil%20pesos

Soto, R., & Luz, A. (2022). Evidencias educativas que mejoran al mundo. *Tipos de liderazgo y su función dentro de las organizaciones.* Universidad Autónoma Benito Juárez de Oaxaca. https://amieedu.org/actascimie21/wp-content/uploads/2022/01/Ana-Luz-Ramos-Soto.pdf

Sylvia, S. (2024). LIV(1), 411-430. *El potencial de la educación para conservar y para transformar.* Revista Latinoamericana de Estudios Educativos (México). https://www.redalyc.org/articulo.oa?id=27075657009

UNESCO. Oficina para América Latina y el Caribe del IIPE UNESCO. (2020). *Inclusión y Equidad.*https://siteal.iiep.unesco.org/eje/inclusion_y_equidad

UNESCO. (2023). *Poner fin a la discriminación en la educación: un instrumento clave para proteger el derecho a la educación.*https://www.unesco.org/es/articles/poner-fin-la-discriminacion-en-la-educacion-un-instrumento-clave-para-proteger-el-derecho-la

UNIR. Universidad en Internet. (2020). *La interculturalidad en la educación: ¿Qué retos plantea en el aula?*https://www.unir.net/educacion/revista/interculturalidad-en-educacion/

Universidad Europea. (2023). *Liderazgo inclusivo: por qué es importante y cómo mejorarlo.* Empresa y Tecnología. https://universidadeuropea.com/blog/liderazgo-inclusivo/

Vadillo, R. C., & Fernández, P. I. (2023) 14 *Educación inclusiva y educación especial en México: dilemas, relaciones y articulaciones*. Inclusive education and special education in Mexico: dilemmas, relationships and joints. IE Revista de Investigación Educativa de la REDIECH. Red de Investigadores Educativos Chihuahua A. C. https://www.redalyc.org/journal/5216/521674411014/

Velandia, H. Wilmer A., Guzmán Zamora Nelson. (2024), LIV(1), 225-254. *La asertividad para el fortalecimiento de las democracias. Niveles de asertividad y participación ciudadana en población universitaria.* Revista Latinoamericana de Estudios Educativos (México) https://www.redalyc.org/articulo.oa?id=27075657010

Chapter 9
Digital Skills in the Formation of Human Capital for Tourism Activity

Rosa María Rivas García
https://orcid.org/0000-0002-8371-6068
Instituto Politécnico Nacional, Mexico

Jésica Alhelí Cortés Ruiz
https://orcid.org/0000-0002-5459-4874
Instituto Politécnico Nacional, Mexico

Marcial Dayan Alonso García
https://orcid.org/0009-0006-8649-4575
Instituto Politécnico Nacional, Mexico

Alma Karina Aguilar Corona
https://orcid.org/0009-0005-9774-4835
Instituto Politécnico Nacional, Mexico

ABSTRACT

The formation of human capital aimed at developing digital skills impacts the competitiveness of the tourism sector. The purpose of this chapter is to outline a proposal for the digital skills necessary for the formation of human capital in the tourism industry based on the educational theory for the development of skills. The chapter addresses issues related to the conceptualization of tourism and the industries that make up the activity, the concepts and classification of digital skills with global parameters, the formation of human capital and the vision of UN Tourism for

DOI: 10.4018/979-8-3693-7086-5.ch009

the digitalization of the sector; with the purpose of specifying, based on the list of tourism industries, the skills aimed at developing digital skills. The result outlines the confluence of digital skills with Knowledge, Know-How, Transversal Competencies and Skills of Being; emphasizing Know-How Competencies and Using specialized software for the tourism industry with the specification of Tourism Industries and commonly used specialized software.

INTRODUCTION

The information from UN Tourism (n.d.a) indicates that as the main international organization in the tourism field, it advocates tourism that contributes to economic growth, inclusive development and environmental sustainability. It also states the organizational priorities, the systematic integration of tourism in the global agenda, the improvement of tourism competitiveness, the promotion of sustainable development, the drive for the contribution of tourism to poverty reduction and development, the promotion of knowledge, teaching and training, as well as partnerships with key actors in favor of tourism activity.

Derived from the previous information, tourism is fundamental in the economic, social and environmental fields, since it promotes the progress of regions by generating income through the creation of jobs in the tourism industries. In the social field, it encourages cultural exchange, understanding between communities, strengthening the sense of identity and belonging. Regarding the environmental approach, properly managed tourism can promote the conservation of ecosystems, as well as the sustainable use of natural resources.

Emphasizing economic data that illustrate the importance of tourism activity, UN Tourism (2024) reported the recovery of the sector in the face of the global health contingency due to COVID-19, reaching 97% of 2019 levels in the first quarter of 2024. In addition, it estimated that 285 million tourists traveled internationally in the first three months of 2024, around 20% more than in the same period in 2023. These results were driven by continued strong demand, the opening of Asian markets, as well as better air connectivity and visa facilitation.

KPMG (2024) states that digitalization in the tourism industry provides opportunities for companies through the personalization of higher value offers for customers. In addition, it increases the productivity of their operational processes. In this constantly evolving ecosystem, data management is a key element that will establish the leadership of organizations in the tourism sector.

Digital innovations, and more recently artificial intelligence (AI), are already part of tourism and these changes are reflected in their capacity to disrupt traditional economic models. In addition, the unprecedented speed with which these innovations are driving the tourism sector globally is changing consumer habits, influencing travelers' decisions and redefining competition in the industry (WEF, 2017).

The relevance of global tourism is reflected in the vision of the Directorate of UN Tourism (n.d.b.), which bases its work on five pillars:

1. Making tourism smarter, by promoting innovation and leading the digital transformation of the sector;
2. Making tourism more competitive at all levels, by promoting investment and entrepreneurship;
3. Creating more and better jobs and offering relevant training;
4. Strengthening resilience and promoting safe and seamless travel; and
5. Harnessing tourism's unique potential to protect cultural and natural heritage and support communities economically and socially.

This chapter aims to bring together pillars 1 and 3 of UN Tourism's work, which consist of "making tourism smarter, by promoting innovation and leading the digital transformation of the sector" and "creating more and better jobs and offering relevant training"; Therefore, in the development of subsequent topics, the digital skills necessary for human capital in the tourism sector are addressed.

Tourism

UN Tourism (n.d.c.) states that tourism is a social, cultural and economic phenomenon that involves the movement of people to countries or places outside their usual environment for personal, professional or business reasons. These people are called travelers (who can be either tourists or excursionists; residents or non-residents) and tourism covers their activities, some of which involve tourist expenditure.

The term tourism has evolved and has been studied from various perspectives. With a research focus, it began to be of interest in the period between the two world wars of the 20th century and since then it has seen changes and adaptations due to its social characteristics. With the purpose of specifying the conceptual evolution in table 1, a brief review.

Table 1. Evolution of the concept of tourism

Quote	Tourism
Fernández (1967)	The first documented instance of the word tour was in England in 1760 (make a tour). The term "tour" is of French origin, which is not surprising considering that the British nobility and upper classes used French as a distinctive language, appropriate to their status.
Bormann (1931)	Trips undertaken for reasons of rest, entertainment, business or professional reasons, often initiated by special events or situations, where the absence from home is temporary and excludes travel to workplaces.
Mathieson y Wall (1982)	Tourism is the temporary movement of people, for periods of less than one year, to destinations outside the place of residence and work, the activities undertaken during the stay and the facilities to satisfy the needs of tourists.
OMT (2000)	Tourism includes "activities carried out by people during their trips and stays in places other than their usual environment, for a consecutive period of less than one year for leisure purposes, for business and other reasons not related to the exercise of a remunerated activity in the place visited."
Dachary y Arnaiz (2006)	The fourth generation of the conception of tourism goes from ecotourism to sustainable tourism, going through very deep focal studies in search of two major goals: to place this activity in the new dynamics of sustainable development and to adjust it to the major changes that the 21st century poses in technology, and demands a combination that will be fundamental to enhance this complex activity.

Note: Resource structured based on the cited authors.

Tourism from an industrial perspective plays a strategic role in the world economy, being an agent of development for sectors linked to the tourism industry by boosting job creation in key sectors, such as visitor accommodation, food and beverage supply companies, transportation systems, etc.; generating positive effects on the value chain that optimize the productivity and competitiveness of suppliers and services in host communities. Likewise, this industry favors investments in infrastructure and technology, which significantly boosts economic growth by contributing to the capture of foreign currency by promoting the consumption of goods and services.

Tourism Industries

The World Tourism Organization (2023) defines the products purchased by visitors and the activities that produce them as "characteristic products of tourism" (those that meet certain criteria) and "characteristic activities of tourism" (those that normally produce characteristic products of tourism). The list of tourism characteristic activities (tourism industries) grouped by main categories according to the International Standard Industrial Classification of All Economic Activities (ISIC), Rev. 4. Statistical Reports (M Series, No. 4/Rev.4) of the United Nations (2009), is referred to in Figure 1. It is worth mentioning that the specification of tourism industries is intended to frame the formation of human capital in the digital skills required by the activity.

Figure 1. List of tourism industries (characteristic activities) and grouping by main categories according to ISIC Rev. 4 (Retrieved from UNWTO, 2023)

Accommodation for visitors	5510	Short term accommodation activities
	5520	Camping grounds, recreational vehicle parks and trailer parks
	5590	Other accommodation
	6810	Real estate activities with own or leased property*
	6820	Real estate activities on a fee or contract basis*
Food and beverage serving activities	5610	Restaurants and mobile food service activities
	5629	Other food service activities
	5630	Beverage serving activities
Railway passenger transport	4911	Passenger rail transport, interurban
Road passenger transport	4922	Other passenger land transport
Water passenger transport	5011	Sea and coastal passenger water transport
	5021	Inland passenger water transport
Air passenger transport	5110	Passenger air transport
Transport equipment rental	7710	Renting and leasing of motor vehicles
Travel agencies and other reservation service activities	7911	Travel agency activities
	7912	Tour operator activities
	7990	Other reservation service and related activities
Cultural activities	9000	Creative, arts and entertainment activities
	9102	Museums activities and operation of historical sites and buildinç
	9103	Botanical and zoological gardens and nature reserves activities
Sports and Recreational activities	7721	Renting and leasing of recreational and sports goods
	9200	Gambling and betting activities
	9311	Operation of sports facilities
	9319	Other sports activities
	9321	Activities of amusement parks and theme parks
	9329	Other amusement and recreation activities n.e.c.
Retail trade of country-specific tourism characteristic goods		Duty free shops**
		Specialized retail trade of souvernirs**
		Specialized retail trade of handicrafts**
		Other specialized retail trade of tourism characteristic goods**
Other country-specific tourism characteristic activities		

The topic of digital skills is addressed below with the purpose of contextualizing the concepts and classifications and then focusing their application on the training of human capital that collaborates in the tourism industries specified previously.

Digital Skills: Concepts and Classification

The contribution of the General Directorate of Computing and Information and Communication Technologies (DGTIC) of the National Autonomous University of Mexico (2014) mentions that digital skills are the set of knowledge (know-how and knowledge about doing) related to the use of communication tools, access, processing and production of information.

Van Deursen and van Dijk (2014) propose a conceptual as well as operational definition of digital skills, in four domains with a sequential relationship: operational, formal, information and strategic. By operational skills they understand the actions that allow the use of digital media tools, such as navigation bars, buttons or links, ways of entering information in fields or pages, possibilities of downloading or saving files, and the like. As for formal skills, they refer to navigation and orientation in structures specific to digital media (essentially hypertextual), such as knowing if one is on one site or another, identifying the way of navigating the sites, orienting oneself or getting lost while performing a task. Information skills are related to knowing how to search, select and evaluate information from the Internet in its different forms (text, image, video). Lastly, strategic skills have to do with using the information obtained to achieve a personal or professional goal. The first two skills are related to the medium, while the last two are categorized as related to the content.

Regarding Lemus Pool (2017), he indicates that digital skills are made up of different dimensions for a better understanding and synthesizes them into instrumental, cognitive, communicative, ethical and didactic. He also provides a brief definition:

- Instrumental: referring to knowledge, technical mastery and use of technologies;
- Cognitive: ability to develop search, analysis and processing processes of different sources of information;
- Communicative: skills to generate feedback, exchange and manage didactic interaction in virtual environments;
- Ethics: respect for sources of information; and, finally,
- Didactic: it is associated with teaching learning strategies supported by ICTs.

The United Nations Educational, Scientific and Cultural Organization (UNESCO) (2021) states that digital skills are the sum of knowledge, capabilities, attitudes and strategies required for the use of technologies and the Internet. These skills are divided into two broad categories: fundamental digital skills and instrumental digital skills.

Fundamental digital skills involve strengthening critical and creative thinking to understand how the digital environment works and identify the major dilemmas and challenges generated using the Internet (p. 6).

Instrumental digital skills refer to aptitudes and skills linked to the use of the tool. Because they are focused on the instrument, they are called instrumental digital skills; they allow technology to be used to respond to instructions or specific needs. They propose a practical approach to devices. And they teach how to use tools for specific functions and actions (p. 7).

Table 2. Digital Skills by UNESCO (2021)

Fundamental digital skills	Instrumental digital skills
Explore the meaning of privacy, identity and digital footprint Analyze, evaluate and select the information circulating on the Internet, to recognize its reliability and relevance. Understand how algorithms work and how they affect daily life Communicate in the online universe, connect and collaborate with others, interact in virtual communities and networks. Create content making efficient and empathetic use of digital language Use the Internet for participation and problem solving	The generation and use of email The use of spreadsheets and spreadsheets The creation of digital presentations The downloading and installation of applications The creation of videos and digital content The use of social networks to share texts and images

Note: Retrieved from UNESCO (2021).

Instrumental digital skills will not be able to promote good management of technology if critical thinking and understanding of how the digital environment works are not strengthened.

The influence of educational policies and government support in the development of digital skills is vital for people to acquire, from basic education, skills that enable connectivity, communication, application and interaction in local, national and even global digital environments. Below is a brief review of some educational policies for the development of digital skills in various educational contexts.

UNESCO (2023) has issued the Guidelines for the formulation of ICT policies and master plans in education; and presents the main challenges; 1) Avoid technological solutionism, 2) Protect the well-being of teachers and students, 3) Reduce and neutralize the digital carbon footprint, 4) Consider humanistic principles in digital inclusion, 5) Include different voices and cultures, 6) Guarantee data privacy and cybersecurity.

Vera and Rivas (2023) describe the monitoring of digital education policies (DEP) in Latin America and the Caribbean, through four analytical axes: digital inclusion policies; digital policies to enhance the quality of learning; policies linked to learning digital skills for students; and policies focused on digital teacher competences. Based on the analysis, Vera and Rivas (2023) state that the permanent evolution of technology requires efforts to develop indicators and collaborate in the construction of more precise diagnoses, to develop better policies and periodically monitor the progress of digital education policies.

The European Commission (2020) designed the Digital Education Action Plan (2021-2027), which is a renewed political initiative of the European Union (EU), establishes a common vision of high-quality, inclusive and accessible digital education in Europe, and aims to support the adaptation of the education and training systems of the Member States to the digital age.

Regarding Africa, the "ICT Transforming Education in Africa" project was launched in 2015 with the aim of promoting human and social development in African countries using information and communication technology (ICT) for education (UNESCO, 2024).

According to Feijoo et al (2021), a series of important national economic initiatives have been launched in China since 2014 that refer to AI and its areas of development. The expected effect of these initiatives will make China a world leader in technology-based industries in the coming decades, such as AI, 5G, robotics or the Internet of Things. At the international level, online education is part of what is known as the Digital Silk Road, launched in 2015, which includes new technologies and aims to build a community with cyberspace as a common destination.

In Mexico, the Ministry of Public Education (SEP) has implemented programs to integrate the use of information and communication technologies (ICT) from basic education, using educational spaces and technological means to create processes that allow students to develop digital skills. Therefore, in the Mexican educational agenda there have been educational programs such as the telesecundaria supported by the Edusat Network (Satellite Education Network) and the telebachilleratos, along with the programs Enciclomedia, Digital Skills for All (HDT), Mi Compu.mx, the Digital Inclusion and Literacy Program, and the National Digital Agenda (Navarrete, 2023).

Human Capital Training

Human capital development is vital from a strategic perspective because it facilitates the development of "skills" to achieve objectives. It is based on ensuring that people's knowledge, skills and attitudes are aligned with the needs of the organization, both in the present and in the long term.

Human capital training is essential for all industrial activities, since they are inserted in a socioeconomic environment that faces constant changes derived from a global scope and technological advances that facilitate communication, promote trade openness between countries and increase business relations that lead to social interactions; this requires that companies have competent personnel and continuous learning. The training of human capital from the educational field is vital because in the future, it will be integrated into economic activities and will contribute to growth and competitiveness, so it is essential to establish collaborative relationships so that future professionals develop skills from academic training. Below is a brief review of the educational competencies that promote the generation of professional competencies.

A competence, according to the Organization for Economic Cooperation and Development (2013), goes beyond simple knowledge and skills. It implies the ability to respond to complex demands using and mobilizing psychosocial resources, which include skills and attitudes, in a particular context. The approach to professional competences is focused on the knowledge and abilities that a person develops through their university education. Arévalo and Juanes (2022) indicate that competences currently constitute a conceptualization and a way of operating in the management of human resources that allows for greater articulation between management, work and education.

Regarding digital competences, Llamas and Macías (2016) refer that it is the ability to develop and generate knowledge in the face of the different possibilities associated with technologies and the different challenges that arise in a society where it is increasingly necessary to participate in a meaningful and active way.

Regarding George (2021), he indicates that digital competencies encompass a set of interrelated skills and attitudes that cover technical, informational, content creation, media, communication, problem-solving aspects, as well as strategic and ethical decision-making.

Digitalization in the Tourism Sector

UN Tourism (n.d.) reports that Tourism was one of the first sectors to digitalize business processes on a global scale, bringing flight and hotel booking online to become a digital pioneer. As information and communications technology (ICT) became a global phenomenon, tourism was a consistent early adopter of new technologies and platforms.

Digitalization has significantly changed the tourism industry; by 2024, planning, purchasing and making a trip is feasible with a few clicks. Digital platforms have significantly reduced the costs involved in the production of various tourism services (Schwab, 2017). According to the Orange Foundation (2016), digitalization in the tourism sector is based on four key technologies: the cloud, social networks, mobile devices and information and communication technologies; these tools allow the creation of closer relationships with customers of companies in the hospitality and tourism sector, which facilitates access to new business opportunities.

According to UN Tourism (n.d.), the use of technologies including the 'Internet of Things', location-based services, artificial intelligence, augmented and virtual reality, and blockchain technology has resulted in a tourism offer that is more attractive, efficient, inclusive, and economically, socially and environmentally sustainable than its predecessor.

In addition to the above, Pedreño and Moreno (2019) indicate the disruptive digital technologies that are driving changes in tourism business activity; AI (artificial intelligence), big data, Internet of Things (IoT), blockchain, robotics or virtual reality.

The competences of the tourism professional based on the educational theory according to Rivas et al (2024) are referred to as the competences of Knowledge (Cognitive, Disciplinary, Conceptual), competences of Knowing How (Proceeding, Instrumental), competences of Being (Attitudinal, Values) and includes the Generic-Transversal competences. In relation to the digitalization of the tourism sector, the competences of Knowing How imply the use of communication and information technologies and the use of specialized software in tourism (Reservation Systems (GDS), Hotel Management Systems) and information and communication technologies. Likewise, the relevant transversal competences are the information management skills

In the following section, a proposal of the key digital competences for the performance of human capital in the tourist activity is stated

Based on the confluence of digital skills, the competences of the tourism professional based on educational theory, information, and communication technologies (ICT) and technologies related to the digitalization of tourism, the following summary proposal of digital competences for the formation of human capital in the tourist activity is presented

Figure 2. Proposal for key digital skills in tourism activity

Knowledge Competencies

Knowledge of the tourism sector to identify the hardware and software used for the competitiveness of the tourism industry for the performance of digital skills.

Know How Competencies

Basic digital skills	Procedural digital skills
• Access to information for analysis, estimation and selection by searching for information on the web through various browsers. • Online communication, collaboration and interaction through digital communication tools (e.g. email, blog, social networks, shared files, instant messaging, videoconferences, etc.). • Information security and privacy for identity protection through passwords and biometric information. Knowledge of the existence of computer viruses and use of antivirus to generate secure downloads. • Knowledge and use of computing devices (hardware) and mobile devices, storage units.	• Processing, managing and storing information using word processors, spreadsheets, digital presentations, databases, cloud storage. • Creating digital content in various formats (image, video, audio, applications, webinars, etc.), making efficient and empathetic use of digital language. • Media management (social networks, email, blogs, web pages). • Using specialized software for the tourism industry*.

* Tourism Industries and commonly used specialized software

Accommodation for visitors

- Examples of PMS (Property Management System): Opera PMS, Cloudbeds, Oracle Hospitality, HotelManager, Little Hotelier, InnQuest, Shiji Group, WebRezPro, Am Hotel, ThinkReservations, Hotelgest, Acihotel, Preno, Mews, TCA Hospitaildad, Site Minder.
- Examples of CRM for accommodation for visitors: Bing by Zoho CRM, Octopus24, Dailypoint, Wolkvox, Hotelogix, WoowUp, Pipedrive, Profitroom.
- Examples of RMS (Revenue Management System): WebRezPro, Atomize, Smoobu, Diamo, Guesty, Hotelitix, PriceLabs, OwnerRez, RateGenie, Wheelhouse, RDPWin, Shiji Enterprise Platform.
- GDS

Food and beverage serving activities

- Point of sale software vendor examples: Soft Restaurant, Anova, Lightspeed, NCR Aloha, Wansoft, ManagementPro, PosTouch, Square
- Restaurant management software vendor examples: HMSHost International, Restroworks, Market Man, Lavu, Wansoft, KI-REST, Givex, Infocaja

Railway passenger transport: ERP, CRM and GDS
Road passenger transport: ERP, CRM and GDS
Water passenger transport: ERP, CRM and GDS
Air passenger transport: ERP, CRM and GDS

Transport equipment rental: ERP, CRM and GDS

Travel agencies and other reservation service activities: ERP, CRM and GDS

Cultural activities: ERP and CRM

Sport and recreational activities: ERP and CRM
Retail trade of country – specific tourism characteristic goods: In some cases, ERP and CRM
Other country – specific tourism characteristic activities: In some cases, ERP and CRM

Examples of leading ERP, CRM and GDS

- ERP (Enterprise Resource Planning) vendors: SAP, ORACLE, Microsoft Dynamics 365, SAGE, SYSPRO, UNIT4 ERP, RAMCO, DELTEK MACONOMY, QAD, EPICOR, Workday Enterprise.
- CRM (Customer Relationship Management): HubSpot, Salesforce, Oracle CRM, Pipedrive, SugarCRM, ZohoCRM, Salesnet, AllProWebTools, Microsoft Dynamics CRM.
- GDS (Global Distribution System): Amadeus, Travelport – Galileo, Saber Holdings, TravelSky

Skills of Being

- Have a marked orientation towards customer service using CRM software.
- Collaboration, interaction, communication and ability to work in multidisciplinary and interdisciplinary teams through digital communication tools.
- Ability to work in an international context using digital skills.

Transversal competencies

Critical thinking and understanding of the functioning and impact of the digital environment to promote good practices through attitudes and strategies in the management and proper handling of technologies and information.

FUTURE RESEARCH DIRECTIONS

Given the breadth and diversification of the industries and activities characteristic of tourism, research on digital skills in the formation of human capital is also extensive. Although the above proposal describes digital skills based on the educational competency scheme, the Know-How competencies (specifically, the use of specialized software in the tourism industry) are oriented toward the marketing and provision of tourism services. Therefore, it is necessary to continue studying digital skills aimed at sustainability, planning of the tourist space and design of tourist products (to mention some priority topics in the tourism field), with the purpose of the human capital of the sector developing greater competence in its professional activity.

Another line for future research is related to the challenges faced by digitalization in tourism, such as the digital divide, unequal access to technology and resistance to change, among others. Since micro, small and medium-sized enterprises in the tourism sector face inequality in access, use and appropriation of information and communication technologies, this causes a lack of competitiveness that further jeopardizes their permanence in the market.

CONCLUSION

The competitiveness of the tourism sector in the international context must be strengthened through the generation, promotion and exchange of knowledge for the teaching and training of human capital inserted in the tourism activity. The development of digital skills must be constant since the digital environment is changing as well as the way in which businesses operate and the preferences of tourists. The training of tourism professionals oriented to digital skills optimizes operational efficiency, promotes adaptation to new technologies, improves the customer experience by creating technological solutions in favor of interactions, develops comprehensive marketing communication through digital environments, in addition to motivating innovation in the offer of tourist services.

REFERENCES

Adobe. (2024). *¿Qué es la realidad virtual? Explicación de la realidad virtual.* https://www.adobe.com/mx/products/substance3d/discover/what-is-vr.html

Arévalo, J., & Juanes, B. (2022). La formación de competencias desde el contexto latinoamericano. *Revista Universidad y Sociedad,* 14(1), 517-523. http://scielo.sld.cu/scielo.php?script=sci_arttext&pid=S2218-36202022000100517&lng=es&tlng=es

Bormann, A. (1931). *Der Deustche im Fremdenverkehr des Europaischen Auslands.* Citado en 5, Sociología del Turismo (Hans Joachin Knebel) Hispano Europea.

Cloud, G. (2024). *What is Artificial Intelligence (AI)?*https://cloud.google.com/learn/what-is-artificial-intelligence?hl=en

Dachary, A. C., Burne, A., & Maris, S. (2006). El estudio del turismo: ¿Un paradigma en formación? *Estudios y Perspectivas en Turismo*, 15(2), 179–192. https://www.scielo.org.ar/scielo.php?script=sci_arttext&pid=S1851-17322006000200004&lng=es&tlng=es

DGTIC. UNAM. (2014). *Matriz de habilidades digitales.* http://www.educatic.unam.mx

Europea, C. (2020). *Plan de Acción de Educación Digital (2021-2027).*https://education.ec.europa.eu/es/focus-topics/digital-education/action-plan

Feijóo, C., Fernández, J., Arenal, A., Armuña, C., & Ramos, S. (2021), Educational technologies in China, Cabrera Giraldez, M., Maghiros, I., Punie, Y. and Vuorikari, R. editor(s), Publications Office of the European Union, Luxembourg, 2021, ISBN 978-92-76-32626-7, , JRC124648.DOI: 10.2760/604641

Fernández, L. (1967). *Teoría y Técnica del Turismo*. Editora Nacional.

George, C. (2021). Competencias digitales básicas para garantizar la continuidad académica provocada por el Covid-19. *Apertura (Guadalajara, Jal.)*, 13(1), 36–51. http://www.udgvirtual.udg.mx/apertura/index.php/apertura/article/view/1942

IBM. (2024). *¿Qué es el Internet de las cosas (IoT)?*https://www.ibm.com/mx-es/topics/internet-of-things

IBM. (2024a). *¿Qué es blockchain?*https://www.ibm.com/mx-es/topics/blockchain

KPMG. (2024). El *futuro del sector turístico: hacia la máxima digitalización y personalización de los servicios al cliente.*https://www.tendencias.kpmg.es/2024/07/futuro-sector-turistico-digitalizacion-personalizacion/

Llamas, F., & Macías, E. (2016). Formación inicial de docentes en educación básica para la generación de conocimiento con las Tecnologías de la Información y la Comunicación. *Revista Complutense de Educación*, 29(2), 577–593. DOI: 10.5209/RCED.53520

Mathieson, A., & Wall, G. (1982). *Tourism: economic, physical, and social impacts.* 2° Ed. Canada: Longman.

Navarrete, Z. (2023). Políticas educativas para la integración de las TIC en el sistema educativo nacional mexicano. *Apertura (Guadalajara, Jal.)*, 15(2), 134–151. DOI: 10.32870/Ap.v15n2.2419

OCI. (2024). *What Is Big Data?*https://www.oracle.com/big-data/what-is-big-data/

ORACLE. (2024). *What is ERP?*https://www.oracle.com/erp/what-is-erp/

Orange, F. (2016). *España: La transformación digital en el sector turístico.*https://www.fundacionorange.es/wp

Organización de las Naciones Unidas para la Educación, la Ciencia y la Cultura [UNESCO] (2021). *Competencias y habilidades digitales.*https://unesdoc.unesco.org/ark:/48223/pf0000380113.locale=en

Organización de las Naciones Unidas para la Educación, la Ciencia y la Cultura [UNESCO] (2023). Directrices para la formulación de políticas y planes maestros de TIC en educación. https://unesdoc.unesco.org/ark:/48223/pf0000385091

Organización de las Naciones Unidas para la Educación, la Ciencia y la Cultura [UNESCO] (2024). *Transformar la educación en África mediante las TIC.*https://www.unesco.org/es/digital-education/kfit-africa

Organización Mundial del Turismo. (2000). *Recomendaciones sobre estadísticas de turismo.*https://unstats.un.org/unsd/statcom/doc00/m83-s.pdf

Organización Mundial del Turismo. (2023). *Notas metodológicas de la base de datos de estadísticas de turismo, Edición 2023.* OMT., DOI: 10.18111/9789284424160

Organización para la Cooperación y el Desarrollo Económico (OCDE). (2013). *Panorama de la educación 2013 Indicadores de la OCDE.* Santillana.

Pedreño-Muñoz, A., & Ramón-Rodríguez, A. B. (2019): *«Por qué el turismo necesita imperiosamente la Inteligencia Artificial (y mucha tecnología digital».* Instituto tecnológico hotelero. https://www.ithotelero. com/blog/por-que-el-turismo-necesita-imperiosamente-la-inteligencia-artificial-y-muchatecnologia-digital/

Pool, L., & Consuelo, M. (2017). *El desarrollo de habilidades digitales en profesores universitarios, el caso mexicano de Habitat Puma en la UNAM*. Editorial Académica Española.

Rivas García, R. M., Cardoso Espinosa, E. O., & Roldan Castellanos, M. L. (2024). Planteamiento de las Competencias Profesionales en Turismo desde la perspectiva de los egresados en México. *RIDE Revista Iberoamericana para la Investigación y el Desarrollo Educativo*, 15(29). Advance online publication. DOI: 10.23913/ride.v15i29.2094

Sabre. (2024). *What is GDS in travel?*https://www.sabre.com/transforming-global-distribution-system/

Schwab, K. (2017). *The fourth industrial revolution*. New York: Currency. UN Tourism. (s.f.). *Digital Transformation*. https://www.unwto.org/digital-transformation

Turismo, O. N. U. (2024). *Últimos datos sobre turismo*.https://www.unwto.org/es/barometro-del-turismo-mundial-de-onu-turismo

Turismo, O. N. U. (n.d.a.). *Turismo responsable, sostenible y accesible*.https://www.unwto.org/es/acerca-de-onu-turismo#:~:text=ONU%20Turismo%2C%20como%20principal%20organizaci%C3%B3n,sus%20conocimientos%20y%20pol%C3%ADticas%20tur%C3%ADsticas

Turismo, O. N. U. (n.d.b.). *Acerca de ONU Turismo*.https://www.unwto.org/es/acerca-de-la-organizacion-mundial-turismo

Turismo, O. N. U. (n.d.c.). *Glosario de términos de turismo*.https://www.unwto.org/es/glosario-terminos-turisticos

Unidas, N. (2009). *Clasificación Industrial Internacional Uniforme de todas las actividades Económicas (CIIU) Revisión 4*.https://unstats.un.org/unsd/publication/SeriesM/seriesm_4rev4s.pdf

Van Deursen, A., & Van Dijk, M. (2014). *Modeling traditional literacy, Internet skills and Internet usage: An empirical study. Interacting with Computers*. Advance., DOI: 10.1093/iwc/iwu027

Vera, A., & Rivas, A. (2023). *El monitoreo de políticas educativas digitales en América Latina y el Caribe*. Oficina para América Latina y el Caribe del IIPE UNESCO.

WEF. (2017). The travel & tourism competitiveness report 2017. Paving the way for a more sustainable and inclusive future. Geneva, Switzerland.

KEY TERMS AND DEFINITIONS

Artificial intelligence (AI): is a set of technologies that enable computers to perform a variety of advanced functions, including the ability to see, understand and translate spoken and written language, analyze data, make recommendations, and more. (Google Cloud, 2024).

Big data: refers to extremely large and complex data sets that cannot be easily managed or analyzed with traditional data processing tools, particularly spreadsheets. Big data includes structured data, like an inventory database or list of financial transactions; unstructured data, such as social posts or videos; and mixed data sets, like those used to train large language models for AI (OCI, 2024).

Blockchain: is a shared, immutable ledger that facilitates the process of recording transactions and tracking assets across a business network (IBM, 2024a).

Enterprise resource planning (ERP): systems are complete, integrated platforms, either on-premises or in the cloud, managing all aspects of a production-based or distribution business. Furthermore, ERP systems support all aspects of financial management, human resources, supply chain management, and manufacturing with your core accounting function. (ORACLE, 2024).

Global Distribution System: (GDS) is a computerized network system that facilitates transactions between travel service providers such as airlines, hotels, car rental companies and travel agencies. The GDS software offers a centralized platform for distributing travel-related content and plays a vital role in streamlining the travel booking process, connecting travel agencies with a diverse range of service providers, and ensuring a smooth flow of information and transactions within the travel ecosystem (Sabre, 2024).

Internet: of Things (IoT) a network of physical devices, vehicles, and other physical objects that are embedded with built-in sensors, software, and network connectivity, allowing them to collect and share data (IBM, 2024).

Virtual Reality and Augmented Reality: A virtual reality experience involves entering a computer-generated simulation, with equipment playing a key role. VR headsets provide visual and audible information about the world the participant is exploring, while a vast array of sensors and technologies translate the person's movements into the virtual world. Augmented reality (AR), on the other hand, does not offer users the ability to explore an entirely digital reality, but rather overlays layers of additional content on top of the real world before them. With augmented reality apps, you can point your phone's camera at the scene in front of you and those apps will complement the existing scene in front of you (Adobe, 2024).

Chapter 10
Matrix for Assessing Key Competences

María Elena Zepeda Hurtado
https://orcid.org/0000-0001-9764-5013
Instituto Politécnico Nacional, Mexico

Claudia Mirla Padilla Cruz
https://orcid.org/0009-0009-2406-9292
Instituto Politécnico Nacional, Mexico

María Trinidad Cerecedo Mercado
Instituto Politécnico Nacional, Mexico

ABSTRACT

Competency-based teaching establishes the possibility of organizing learning content into units of complete meaning, solving one problem at a time, with strong interrelations between its components. Therefore, competency-based assessment within its multiple components has advantages, allowing the assessment of competencies through criteria, indicators and performance levels using different assessment instruments. The problem identified is that there are no instruments to measure achievements in key competencies, generic competencies or soft skills. Once the key competencies have been identified according to the graduate profile, criteria, indicators and performance levels are developed that will be the origin of the proposal for a competency matrix or rubric.

DOI: 10.4018/979-8-3693-7086-5.ch010

MATRIX FOR TEACHERS TO EVALUATE KEY COMPETENCIES IN STUDENTS.

Since the implementation of competency-based education at any educational level, several challenges have arisen: teacher training, updating of study plans and programs, equipment and materials needed in classrooms, and among the most important, the evaluation system that will not only assess knowledge in the traditional way, but will also assess the competencies and skills developed or strengthened in the classroom with appropriate performance instruments, hence the concern of choosing a viable instrument to assess key competencies, soft skills . skills in students.

The proposal put forward in this chapter is that of a competency matrix for the specific assessment of key competencies. This assessment instrument is based on international references, is consistent and coherent with the competency-based approach, that is, it qualitatively assesses the performance and level of mastery of these competencies.

INTRODUCTION

In the world and at all times, the school has been given one of the most important roles to play in helping to solve various challenges: economic, environmental, social, technological, etc. For this, student training is required, at any educational level from basic to higher education, which encourages problem solving in real contexts. It is, above all, in relation to the development of key competencies where we find the main contributions to contextualized and coherent learning regarding the needs of today's society (Jiménez et al., 2019).

One of the main responses to these challenges has been to change the focus of education from focusing only on knowledge to focusing on the development of skills to face the challenges of personal, academic and professional life, which according to UNESCO defines skills as:

...specific attributes that individuals need for action and autonomy in different contexts and complex situations. They include cognitive, affective, volitional and motivational elements. Therefore, they are an interaction between knowledge, capacities and skills, interests and affective dispositions. Competencies cannot be taught, but must be developed by the students themselves. They are acquired during action, based on experience and reflection. (p. 10).

On the other hand, according to García Acosta & García González (2022), education and the challenges it has for the 21st century imply the redefinition of what a competence is, that is, knowing how to be (the attitudinal - affective), knowing how to do (the procedural, the practical), knowing how to undertake, develop new challenges, adapt to changes and one of the most important, teach how to learn to live together, to share, to be supportive and with a social conscience defined ethically and responsibly, so as far as can be seen, emphasis is placed on the development of non-cognitive skills mainly to face challenges of social coexistence. Competence, therefore, can be defined from a holistic perspective of these components, as the ability of a person to show: 1) A particular behavior in 2) A particular context and with 3) A particular characteristic. (García & Ledesma, 2024)

Competencies are therefore the skills that allow us to perform roles effectively, complete complex tasks or achieve specific objectives, such as: critical thinking, responsible decision-making, collaborative ability. (Cabrero, 2018), which allows a person to adapt to tasks and demands that may arise in various environments.

Competency-based teaching establishes the possibility of organizing learning content into units of complete meaning, solving one problem at a time, with strong interrelations between its components. (Morgan, 2023) . Competencies are an integral part of the development and growth of an individual, where he or she brings into play his or her arbitrary skills and knowledge, which allow him or her to enrich himself or herself through the interaction between his or her community and family; which implies a meaningful and comprehensive learning methodology for his or her continuous personal, school and social development. As García & Ledesma (2024) point out, students choose from a wide range of learning experiences in the face-to-face environment, online, and in their community. Teachers work with diverse partners and students to promote learning changes at the individual level that adapt to students' interests and learning styles.

BACKGROUND

Competency-Based Educational Models.

Competency-based educational models have gained popularity in recent decades as an alternative to the traditional model characterized by rote learning of content. On the contrary, the competency-based approach seeks to have students use knowledge applied to solve problems.

The competency model must focus on proposing responses to the problems and needs we face in the new conditions in which we live, which is why it is necessary to mobilize all the accumulated experience, the knowledge of the different domains of knowledge, the capacities for action, interaction, to generate a model that integrates knowledge, actions, social interaction and self-knowledge, a comprehensive, holistic, dynamic perspective (García, 2011), so that, despite the time, the validity of the approach continues to recognize that the transfer of knowledge into skills and abilities in solving proposals or solving problems in existing situations.

Hence the origin of the term competencies, which was initially coined in the workplace, but was transferred and is still current in the school environment due to its potential to transform and make student development more efficient.

The competency-based educational model emerged as a response to the need to align education with the changing demands of society and the labour market. Although its roots can be traced back to the educational theories of the mid-20th century, such as those proposed by Dewey Bruner and Ausubel, it was in the last decades of the 20th century when its theoretical and practical foundations were consolidated.

In essence, the competency-based model proposes that the main objective of education should not be limited to the acquisition of theoretical knowledge, but should focus on the development of practical skills and specific competencies that allow students to solve problems, make decisions and adapt to new and complex situations.

The relevance of continuing under the competency-based approach is varied: Academic training has clear and shared goals expressed in common profiles by academic level that have a common profile to function in the 21st century established in Common Curricular Frameworks (MCC). The goal of this learning is to provide students with the environment, activities, and support to develop information search, analysis, and synthesis skills, as well as problem solving, dialogue, and expression skills (García-Bullé, 2021).

In the Common Curriculum Frameworks (MCC) it is based on the development of student graduation profiles that coincide between the subsystems, in terminal performances that will promote and develop personal and social capacities, to continue higher studies or to access the labor market, where the challenges are identified to overcome them and levels to make it concrete; there is a special interest in teaching, this is conceived in a different way to the traditional one and that promotes the development of generic, disciplinary and professional competences in students and improves academic performance to achieve the graduation profile.

For its part, The Future of Jobs Report 2020 (World Economic Forum, 2020) sets out which skills will be most in demand by employers by 2025: 1. Analytical thinking and innovation; 2. Active learning and learning strategies; 3. Complex problem solving; 4. Critical thinking and analysis; 5. Creativity, originality and initiative; 6. Leadership and social influence; 7. Use, control and monitoring of technology; 8. Design and programming of technology; 9. Resilience, stress tolerance and flexibility and, 10. Reasoning, problem solving and generation of ideas (ideation), now identified or known as soft skills.

So the question is, what is the purpose of formal education? For Rincón (2024) the purposes of education for the world to come are four: to support the development of people so that they know themselves; learn and think for themselves; take care of themselves, others and the planet, and improve the world. Cámara (2024) affirms that the multiple learnings with which they come to school, experience the power to transform things to achieve what they want and learn to live in dialogue with their peers. The essence of learning is to open yourself to the surrounding reality and find in it the particular unity that explains in a situational way what we are, need and want.

For comprehensive training, emotional life and the development of socio-emotional skills are present as elements that are integrated into formal education; their insertion implies the strengthening of values and attitudes in favor of a better society, a better world.

Soft Skills, Key or Solf Skills

Soft skills have their origin in the change in the concept of intelligence in the 1980s, from the field of psychology to the educational field. It was Garner who originated the term interpersonal and intrapersonal intelligence, in the field of formal education they are susceptible to being developed. According to Barrera et al. (2022), emotional intelligence implies considering that emotions regulate our thoughts and that these, in turn, our actions. The presence or lack of this type of intelligence has repercussions in the personal educational and social interaction field.

Soft skills or also known as Soft Skills are considered as the abilities or capacities that a person performs related to inter and intrapersonal characteristics, such as motivation, creativity, communication, leadership, mainly.

Furthermore, they are just as important as specific knowledge of an area or discipline, which is why they are already required in employers' entry profiles. Since their importance lies in their transversal nature, they transcend disciplines and, therefore, are not related to disciplinary situations or specific tasks (UNESCO, 2016).

In this sense, soft skills are the competencies, attitudes, knowledge and values that allow a person to solve problems or provide a relevant response to a new or specific situation, mainly in the workplace. They also include work habits and basic socio-emotional skills relevant to on-the-job training (Mexico, 2019). Thus, these skills have to do with putting into practice – in an integrated way – attitudes, personality traits, knowledge and values (Cordero, Córdova, & Moreira, 2020).

On the other hand, it is suggested that generic skills are known by different names. Vera, Tejada & Morales, (2022) propose a diversity: key skills, basic skills, essential skills, work skills, life skills, socio-emotional skills, key skills, professional skills, necessary skills, transferable skills, applied skills, skills for employment and employability skills. In the industry, the use of terms such as employability skills or soft skills is more common, unlike in educational institutions where they are called generic or key skills.

The truth is that, despite the different denominations, various definitions or a certain lack of clarity, each of these denominations is based on different theoretical perspectives or comes from different disciplines or areas of study such as psychology, economics or public health (Arias, Hincapié & Paredes, 2020). Given the diversification and in order to propose an instrument for its evaluation, it requires reference frameworks in the educational field.

Below is presented in Table 1. Taxonomy of emotional skills from different references (UNESCO, 2021) with the internationally used reference frameworks such as UNESCO, OECD, UNICEF, in the contributions one can observe the tendency towards the development of social, cognitive and emotional skills that allow human beings to adapt and contribute to a world, a present and a future, in addition to being uncertain, complex. The table graphically relates the approaches, these diverge both theoretically and in the categorization, dimensions and skills that should be promoted, the synthesis and integration of the approaches can also be observed.

Table 1. Taxonomy of emotional skills from different references

FRAME OF REFERENCE	INSTITUTION/ ORGANIZATION	CONCEPTUALIZATION	DIMENSION	SKILLS
SKILLS FOR THE 21ST CENTURY	National Research Council (United States) 2012	Important skills for coping with the unexpected, managing to respond to multiple demands, controlling impulses and working effectively with others. (OECD, 2016)	Cognitive	Critical thinking, problem solving, decision making, creativity, innovation
				Openness, adaptability, personal and social responsibility, curiosity, perseverance, citizenship, emotional stability, self-regulation
			Interpersonal	Collaboration, teamwork, empathy, conflict resolution, extroversion, leadership
			Intrapersonal	Identification of emotions, self-confidence, self-efficacy, specific self-perception

continued on following page

Table 1. Continued

FRAME OF REFERENCE	INSTITUTION/ ORGANIZATION	CONCEPTUALIZATION	DIMENSION	SKILLS
SOCIAL-EMOTIONAL LEARNING	CASEL (Collaborative for Academic, social and emotional learning) 2013	Learning and practicing knowledge, attitudes and skills to: Understand and manage emotions, set and achieve goals, feel and show empathy, establish and maintain positive relationships, and make responsible decisions. (CASEL, 2017)	Responsible decision making	Impulse control, stress management, achievement focus, self-motivation Problem identification, evaluation, ethical responsibility.
			Social awareness	Problem identification, evaluation, ethical responsibility
			Relationship skills	Perspective taking, empathy, appreciation for diversity, respect for others Communication, social commitment, cooperation, conflict resolution, teamwork
			Self conscious	Recognize your emotions and thoughts and their influence. Assess strengths and challenges, confidence and optimism
			Self-control	Regulate emotions, thoughts and behaviors in different situations

continued on following page

Table 1. Continued

FRAME OF REFERENCE	INSTITUTION/ ORGANIZATION	CONCEPTUALIZATION	DIMENSION	SKILLS
Big Five Personality Factors	OECD (Organization for Economic Cooperation and Development)	It marks a pattern used for the study of personality, based on the 5 traits or dimensions	Extraversion	Sociability, assertiveness, energy
			Pleasantness	Empathy, trust, collaboration
			Meticulousness	Achievement orientation, responsibility, self-control and persistence
			Emotional stability	Stress resistance, optimism, emotional control
			Opening	Curiosity, tolerance and creativity
Education for peace, global citizenship and socio-emotional learning	Institute of Education for Peace and Sustainable Development Mahatma Gandhi, UNESCO	Global citizenship is based on the fact that we are connected to a global community, so that by contributing positively to it, we can influence regional, national and local change. Building peace through education, reminding humanity of our common bonds (UNESCO, 2016)	Global Citizenship Sustainability dad	Empathy Compassion Mindfulness Critical thinking

continued on following page

Table 1. Continued

FRAME OF REFERENCE	INSTITUTION/ ORGANIZATION	CONCEPTUALIZATION	DIMENSION	SKILLS
Life skills	UNICEF (United Nations Children's Fund)	Or psychosocial competencies, are the ability of a person to successfully cope with the demands and challenges of daily life. They are acquired through direct experience, through training intentional, through modeling or imitation (UNICEF, 2017)	Making decisions and maintaining critical thinking	Evaluate situations Determine problems and their causes Reflection and analysis
			Self-management and coping with problems	Confidence, self-esteem, goal setting, self-evaluation and self-awareness Responsibility for one's own feelings Stress management
			Interpersonal communication	Negotiation, handling rejection, empathy, cooperation and teamwork, persuasion, establishing and maintaining contact networks

Source: Adapted from UNESCO 2021, p. 11 and 12

Once the information was carefully reviewed, the authors undertook the following activity, which consisted of reviewing the coincidences between the information, which gave rise to a new reorganization of the dimensions or performances, indicators and descriptors of the key competencies.

Table 2. Taxonomy of emotional skills, groups the skills that coincide in the different dimensions, providing a clear view of the similarities in the information of the references presented in Table 1. Taxonomy of key competencies from different references.

Table 2. Taxonomy of key competencies

Performances Dimensions	Indicators	Descriptors
Cognitive	Mental processes	Critical thinking, identification of causes and problem solving, reflection and analysis, creativity, innovation
Interpersonal	Teamwork Socialization Relationship skills Communication	Collaboration, empathy, leadership, perseverance Sociability, assertiveness, energy, confidence Achievement orientation, responsibility, self-control and persistence Negotiation, persuasion, establishing and maintaining contact networks
Intrapersonal	Self-awareness Emotional stability Self-management	Identification of emotions, confidence, self-efficacy, self-perception, motivation, self-regulation Resistance and stress management, optimism, emotional control, tolerance Self-assessment, goal setting, self-evaluation
Global Citizenship	Social awareness	Sustainability, evaluation, ethical responsibility, appreciation for diversity, respect for others, personal and social responsibility, citizenship, social commitment, empathy, cooperation, openness, adaptability

Source: Own elaboration

As can be seen, the development of competencies and skills in the student allows them personal development, comprehensive training to face challenges and opportunities for ethical, real and innovative solutions to challenges and problems in an immediate, local and global environment. Schmelkes (2024) states that there is knowledge capable of transforming reality, it is knowledge that every person must have and that is obtained gradually; among the fundamental skills are: those that allow learning socially and in communication with others, critical thinking, continuing to learn throughout life, learning to learn.

Problem

As mentioned at the beginning, in the implementation of competency-based education, several challenges were presented: teacher training, updating of study plans and programs, equipment and materials needed in classrooms, and among the most important, the evaluation system that will not only assess knowledge in the traditional way, but will also assess key competencies and skills, with appropriate instruments on performance, hence the concern of choosing a viable instrument to assess key competencies in the student.

Here, a proposal is made for a competency matrix that is congruent and consistent with the competency-based approach that is on the performance or assessment of competencies and the level of mastery, in such a way that the development and strengthening of competencies is monitored during the training process and the graduate has them according to what society demands.

Competence Assesment

In any activity, process, procedure, evaluation is an important phase to establish performance, achievements, deficiencies in a given period and context. It is carried out with the purpose of making decisions, making changes in the necessary areas or aspects and expanding or strengthening those that generate better results.

Under the competency-based orientation in the educational field, evaluation is the central approach to provide feedback on the learning integration process in terms of achievements and not knowledge; said achievements have minimum performance standards in a given context and under certain operating conditions. Considering Hincapié & Clemenza (2022), learning assessment implies that each student should focus on their comprehensive training, appropriating the competencies that allow them to understand the world, developing attitudes, thinking skills, learning to face conflicts, making assertive decisions that lead to mediation, making use of values, and assuming a responsible critical stance that promotes harmonious interaction based on actions of solidarity towards others.

In the field of competencies for Morales, Hershberger & Acosta (2020), evaluation involves the management of qualitative and quantitative information that allows judging the progress, achievements or deficiencies of the study plans, in general, and of the teaching-learning process, in particular, in order to base decision-making to redirect and improve the process itself. Evaluation is a process in which information is obtained and interpreted to build a value judgment to guide or reorient the curricular design, teacher training and development, improve educational practices and promote educational innovation. As Tobón (2018) points out, it is the methodological work carried out by teachers, understanding it as "the set of theoretical and practical activities aimed at improving teaching and learning."

This type of competency-based assessment, among its many advantages, allows for the assessment of skills through criteria, indicators and performance levels using different assessment instruments. In addition to other benefits, for example, the management of various types of assessment; the use of assessment by actors (hetero-assessment, co-assessment and self-assessment) and, likewise, assessment is required according to its timing (diagnostic, procedural and final) and its functionality (formative). (Berlanga & Juárez-Hernández, 2020).

In the evaluation, different methods and instruments are used to determine at what level a competency has been mastered and, depending on the scope of the learning to be measured, the intention and the population to be evaluated (sample or census), they are developed at a global, national and regional level, in a particular classroom, and are developed by organizations specialized in the design or by the teacher himself.

The challenge of competency-based assessment is to determine the level of achievement in problem solving by relating a series of indicators with mastery level descriptors (Neil & Zemborain, 2022), which implies that the teacher develops instruments so that the student shows with evidence (executions) that he/she performs the tasks involved in a competency: what he/she should know, what he/she should know how to do and how he/she should know how to be and act. The central objective of the evaluation should be based on four stages, starting with the diagnostic, formative, motivating (summative) and as a generator of change; without having to be carried out separately, with a holistic approach to these stages. (Aquino, 2022).

In this regard, Domínguez (2022) specifies what the types of evaluation consist of at the time and purpose for which it is applied: 1) The diagnostic, predictive or initial evaluation can be defined as that where it is desired to obtain precise information that allows identifying the degree of adequacy of the general and specific cognitive capacities of the students, in relation to the pedagogical program to which they are going to join. 2) In the formative or continuous evaluation there is an interest in emphasizing and valuing the successes or achievements that students are achieving in the construction process. 3) And the summative or final evaluation It is the assessment carried out at the end of an instructional process or educational cycle. One of the main purposes is to verify the degree to which the educational intentions have been achieved, to know if the learning stipulated in the intentions were fulfilled according to the criteria and conditions expressed in them. A general balance of the results achieved at the end of a teaching-learning process is established.

According to the actors involved or the evaluating agents in the evaluation process, the following classification is considered: 1) Self-evaluation is carried out by the person being evaluated with the intention of reflecting on the results obtained, thus recognizing their strengths and weaknesses and making decisions on how to self-regulate learning. 2) Co-evaluation is the evaluation carried out by several people (in this case students and teachers) of a given activity with the objective of establishing a discussion on the significant aspects of said activity. 3) Hetero-evaluation, in which the teacher controls the student's activity. It is quantitative and qualitative.

Competency-based assessment involves integrating and combining the moments, purposes and evaluating agents, which is why it is different from the traditional assessment, in the understanding that competencies are inferred through evidence, in its different forms, whether through knowledge, product, performance or attitudes. Competency-based assessment then makes it easier for students to generate meaningful learning environments that bring their academic experiences closer to the professional world, allowing the development of integrated and action-oriented skills, with the aim of being able to solve practical problems in the context. (García Acosta & García González, 2022).

The learning assessment process has been modified to aim to promote levels of mastery of a competency or skill, link them to learning activities, and provide feedback. Hincapié & Clemenza de (2022) define competency-based assessment as an active and constructive process that seeks to gather evidence on student achievements and the development of proposed knowledge and delimited in the learning objectives or performances of a subject.

Like any assessment process, it requires systematically collecting information about how skills and competencies are being developed. To do this, it is necessary to locate each of the elements of the competency, the performance criteria, knowledge and evidence required.

Similarly, it requires planning assessment techniques and instruments according to the components of each competency element, which will be useful for defining the assessment or performance criteria for designing the instruments.

Various assessment instruments are used in competency-based assessment processes: observation guides, written tests, practical or performance tests, evidence portfolios, checklists, estimation scales and rubrics.

Once it is identified what to evaluate, in this case, the key competencies according to the graduation profile, the criteria, indicators and performance levels that will be the origin of the proposal of a competence matrix or rubric will have to be developed. It is defined as an evaluation tool that enables the assessment of performance in solving real problems in the environment, relating a series of indicators with descriptors of levels of mastery (Hernández-Mosqueda et al., 2016).

In general, the competencies that make up the graduation profile of any educational level: basic, high school, professional and postgraduate, are integrated by the segregation or breakdown of levels of mastery that range from simple to complex or from initial to advanced levels, these give rise to the evaluation criteria and scores defined in scales, through an assessment matrix.

The proposal for this chapter will be an assessment matrix that includes: performances (level of suitability of the students' competence) indicators (specific performance parameters), descriptors (achievement of the indicators) and the weighting (score given to each of them) or rating scale. Finally, it is important to note that they are expressed in an integral way on a quantitative and a qualitative scale.

These assessment scales are not isolated; they respond to the demands of the curriculum, the importance of training within the profile of graduates from educational institutions and within an international reference framework.

In summary, evaluation is conceived as a process to assess whether a performance or evidence complies with pre-established attributes or parameters, through evidence and instruments that provide information for decision-making. An instrument must necessarily be practical and flexible for the student, in order to obtain a favorable response to what was requested in the evaluation, minimizing the risk of confusing the student and representing an obstacle when showing their knowledge (Aquino, 2022)

Another component inherent to the evaluation of competencies is that these must be expressed in indicators or behaviors that can be observed in some way. A possible alternative to this is to use a double-entry table, also called a rubric (Pantoja, 2012).

A rubric is an instrument that lists criteria and weights them. It is an instrument that defines specific tasks, activities or behaviors that are to be assessed, as well as the performance levels associated with each of these. Milán & Austrich (2021) state that rubrics provide a broad overview of what is intended to be achieved from students, based on clear objectives or goals, with specific performance levels and taking into account the learning processes. According to Neil, Battaglia & Zemborain (2022), rubrics allow to evaluate and systematize the degree of mastery of the competencies and to assess complex, imprecise and subjective aspects. The rubric establishes a relationship between a qualitative object (text) and a quantitative object (units), in which the student's performance is determined, ranging from the least acceptable to exemplary performance, passing through various intermediate levels (Morales, et al., 2020).

For grading rubrics, they are rules used to frame the quality of a student's performance, within levels that usually range from excellence, considered the highest level, to inadequate, as the lowest. Otálvaro, Giraldo & Granada (2018) rubrics are matrices that are basically composed of categories and grading scales. The categories refer to the competence or elements to be evaluated, which are evidenced by indicators that represent the achievement of an objective or the development of a competence. The grading scales, on the other hand, define to what degree the objectives are achieved.

A rubric is, as indicated, an evaluative record that has certain criteria or dimensions to be evaluated and does so following certain levels or gradations of quality and typifying them.

There are two types of rubric: holistic, which provides a single score based on the comprehensive assessment of student performance, and analytical, which provides a different score for each component of the rubric. (UNAM, 2020).

The rubric presents three key characteristics, considering Gatica & Uribarren (2013) as a reference: 1) Evaluation criteria. These are the factors that will determine the quality of a student's work. They are also known as indicators or guides. They reflect the processes and contents that are judged important. 2) Definitions of quality. They provide a detailed explanation of what the student must do to demonstrate their levels of efficiency, to reach a certain level of objectives. These definitions must provide feedback to students. 3) Scoring strategies that can be through descriptors or numbers, such as: Bad, regular, good, very good; or by levels: 1,2,3,4 and 5, other options are: initial, intermediate, advanced; insufficient, sufficient, notable and outstanding.

Generally, the structure of the rubric is presented in the form of a matrix that includes rows and columns, in which descriptors (characteristics, tasks or behaviors) and performance levels are presented. Rubrics are structured with evaluation criteria, which have a percentage, and also include five levels of performance (qualitative and quantitative). Likewise, for each level and evaluation criterion, a point rating is included to make it easier to add up the criteria and obtain the total score.

The proposal of Nova and Tobón (2017) is that the levels of execution should determine the level of achievement or performance in problem solving through criteria, indicators and descriptors that are graduated according to the achievement of the competence or skill.

The proposal made in this chapter is a rubric to evaluate key competencies. It is an analytical rubric, since it incorporates the skills to be evaluated, which we have called dimensions defined as the general categories that make up the key competencies according to the analysis carried out previously. In addition, a quantitatively and qualitatively defined assessment scale is included.

It is easy to identify the rating scale as it contains a space to record a numerical rating for each of the dimensions and categories: excellent (5), very good (4), good (3), average (2) and does not comply (1). At the end, an additional column has been included to perform the total rating by dimension or category.

It is possible and advisable to include the last column of observations, which has a double function: for students to integrate comments and doubts, or for the teacher to include notes on details that need to be improved.

Below is the rubric developed to assessment key competencies in any field, whether work, professional or academic at its different educational levels in the Table 3.

Table 3(a). Rubric for assessing key competencies

DIMENSIONS	EXCELLENT (4)	VERY GOOD (3)	GOOD (2)
COGNITIVE	**Demonstrates a command of knowledge and applies it critically and creatively in different contexts to solve a problem.**	**Understand and apply knowledge accurately, showing critical analysis in a given problem**	**Understand the basic concepts and apply them correctly to a given problem**
INTERPERSONAL	Collaborates and communicates effectively in a team, showing leadership, empathy and negotiating to resolve conflicts.	Actively participates in teamwork and respects the opinions of others, although with limited leadership and empathy skills for conflict resolution.	Contributes to teamwork, although participation is inconsistent in conflict resolution.
INTRAPERSONAL	Demonstrates strong self-management, tolerance, resilience and capacity for self-reflection and continuous improvement.	Manages time, activities and resources appropriately, with the ability to reflect on mistakes.	Demonstrates some self-management, but with difficulties in reflecting and improving his actions.
GLOBAL CITIZENSHIP	He deeply understands global problems, acting with ethical conscience and social responsibility.	Knows and acts according to ethical principles in global situations, although with a less critical vision.	Shows interest in global issues, but with a limited understanding of their ethical implications.

Source: Own elaboration

Table 3(b). Rubric for assessing key competencies

REGULAR (1)	DOES NOT COMPLY (0)	TOTAL	OBSERVATIONS
Has limited understanding, with errors in the application of concepts in the proposed solution to a problem	**Does not demonstrate understanding or adequate application of knowledge of a problem posed**		
Participates minimally in the team, with difficulties respecting other people's opinions.	Does not collaborate or show willingness to work as a team and		
Requires constant support to manage time and activities and shows no reflection on mistakes.	Shows no control over time or willingness to improve.		
Has a basic understanding of global issues and little initiative to get involved.	He is unaware of or ignores global problems and shows no ethical responsibility.		

Source: Own elaboration

This rubric is a proposal that may be subject to modifications in terms of the quantitative and qualitative descriptors that compose it, as well as in the dimensions or levels of execution of the key competencies.

Competency-based assessment addresses contextual problems that, through criteria and evidence, show their levels of performance and continuous development. Therefore, rubrics are a valuable assessment instrument that provides this information and enables the identification of student needs, predicts the consequences of performance and allows for timely correction (Nova & Tobón, 2017).

So rubrics do not provide a number but information about performance levels that allow for immediate feedback.

Assessing by competencies is assessing performances. Performances are graded according to the process of mastery achieved in a period, for which performance tests are used. On the one hand, a student is asked to carry out a key process, task, activity or solution to a problem that will be evaluated in the demonstration of a correct execution in which the following are put into play in an integral manner: knowledge, procedures and attitudes.

For this reason, in companies, industry and educational institutions, importance is given to the development and training of key competences, generic competences, soft skills or sof skills .

CONCLUSION

Since key competencies are not determined by arbitrary decisions but by and for the proper functioning of society, they are determined by demands made by society, such as: rapid and continuous changes in technology, the renewal and transformation of society and the interdependence of countries economically, politically, culturally and technologically.

Given the above consideration, it is advisable to continually review the modifications that the key competencies undergo: conceptualization, inclusion, updating, etc. to ensure their validity in terms of the references and taxonomy used in this work, and consequently, the validity and relevance of the proposed rubric as an assessment instrument.

It will be necessary to carry out the methodological treatment to review the validation of the relevance, clarity and organization of the instrument (performance levels), once applied, receive feedback from the students themselves, academic peers and experts, given that key competencies tend to be complex in themselves.

It is also necessary to adapt the competency matrix to the characteristics and nature of the learning unit in which it will be included, as well as the moment (diagnostic, formative or summative) of the actors involved and the specific profiles of each educational level. However, for now a proposal is made based on universal references that unify performances, indicators and descriptors.

The truth is that the development and strengthening of key competencies, as we have called it in this chapter, is essential at this time and for the near future, through the design of learning processes it supposes an enrichment in the experiences of the students, strengthening and developing key competencies that allow them to transfer knowledge to any situation (Marcos et al., 2020). Job performance is based on the occupational competencies of human talent, but, above all, on personal competencies, which together play an important role in organizational performance. (Galarza et al.,2020).

REFERENCES

Acosta, G., Guillermo, J., & González, G. Máryuri. (2022). Evaluation by competencies in the training process. Cuban Journal of Higher Education, 41(2). Epub May 10, 2022.http://scielo.sld.cu/scielo.php?script=sci_arttext&pid=S025743142022000200022&lng=es&tlng=es

Cabrero, BG (2018). Socio-emotional, non-cognitive or "soft" skills: approaches to their assessment. Digital university journal, 19(6).

Cabrero, G., & Benilde, L. R. Anisai. (2024). The evaluation of competencies in higher education: traditional approaches and innovative strategies. https://cuaed.unam.mx/publicaciones/libro-evaluacion/pdf/Capitulo-37- EVALUATION-OF-COMPETENCES-IN-HIGHER-EDUCATION.pdf

Camacho, A. M. P., & Ceja, M. S. (2022). The importance of emotional intelligence in primary education. *Strategic Training*, 6(02), 60–75.

Cano, E. (2015). Teacher Training. *Journal of Curriculum and Teacher Training*, 19(2), 265–280.

CASEL. (2017). SEL Discussion Series for Parents and Caregivers. Supporting Parents and Caregivers with Social and Emotional Learning. http://www.casel.org/wpcontent/uploads/2017/11/CASELCaregiverGuide_English.pdf

Cordero, A., Córdova, N., & Moreira, C. (2020). Soft skills, a factor of competitiveness in the profile of the public servant. Knowledge Pole, 41-63.

Domínguez-Rodríguez, Y. (2022). Instruments and types of evaluation. *Con-Ciencia Serrana Scientific Bulletin of the Ixtlahuaco Preparatory School*, 4(7), 37–39.

Galarza Cachiguango, IS, Aguinaga, C., López Egas, PX, Molina, R., & Rosero Ortega, G. (2020). Labor Competences in the restaurant sector: a framework of key competencies for its management (Labor Competences in the restaurant sector). Restoration Sector: A Framework of Key Competences for Its Management). *Tourism and society, 27* .

García-Bulle, S. (2021). Observatory. Institute for the Future of Education. https://observatorio.tec.mx/edu-news/aprendizaje-activo

García Retana, J. Á. (2011). Competence-based educational model: Importance and necessity. Electronic Journal. *Current Research in Education*, 11(3), 1–24.

Gatica-Lara, F., & Uribarren -Berrueta, TDNJ. (2013). How to develop a rubric? *Research in Medical Education*, 2(5), 61–65.

Hernández-Mosqueda, J. S., Tobón-Tobón, S., & Guerrero-Rosas, G. (2016). Towards a comprehensive performance evaluation: Socio-formative rubrics. *Ra Ximhai*, 12(6), 359–376. https://www.redalyc.org/pdf/461/46148194025.pdf

Hincapié Parejo, N. F., & Clemenza de Araujo, C. (2022). Assessment of learning by competencies: A theoretical look from the Colombian context. *Journal of Social Sciences*, XXVIII(1), 106–122.

Jiménez, AB, Hinojosa, VC, Ramos, JC, Sánchez, RM, Blasco, VJQ, & Mendoza, CA (2019). Challenge-based learning as a proposal for the development of key competencies. Parents and Teachers/ Journal of Parents and Teachers, (380), 50-55.

Life skills. Tools for good treatment and prevention of violence. https://www.unicef .org/venezuela/media/431/file/Habilidades

López, Morales, Sara, Hershberger del Arenal, Rebeca, & Acosta Arreguín, Eduardo. (2020). Competency-based assessment: How is it done? *Journal of the Faculty of Medicine (Mexico)*, 63(3), 46–56. DOI: 10.22201/fm.24484865e.2019.63.3.08

Marcos Salas, B., Alarcón Martínez, V., Serrano Amarilla, N., Cuetos Revuelta, MJ, & Manzanal Martínez, AI (2020). Application of learning styles according to the Felder and Silverman model for the development of key competencies in teaching practice. *Pedagogical trends* .

Milan, JAP, & Austrich, YL (2021). The Rubric: an assessment matrix as an educational resource in higher education in Cuba, a strong evaluative tool.

National Autonomous University of Mexico (2020). Assessment of and for Learning: Instruments and Strategies

Neil, C., Battaglia, N., & Zemborain, MEDV (2022). Methodological framework for the design of analytical rubrics. Edutec, Electronic Journal of Educational Technology, (80).

Nova, JAD, & Tobón, ST (2017). Assessment instruments: socio-formative rubrics. Research praxis ReDIE: electronic journal of the Durango Network of Educational Researchers, 9(17), 79-86.

OECD. (2016). *Skills beyond school: Synthesis*. OECD Publishing., DOI: 10.1787/9789264230804-

OECD. (2016). Skills for social progress: The power of social and emotional skills. UNESCO Institute for Statistics, Paris. https://www.oecdilibrary.org/docserver/9789264253292es.pdf?expires=1588082606&id=id&accname=guest&checksum=95527013AD0B0EDD8F71CF6C0B88357C

Otálvaro, SMC, Giraldo, JVB, Giraldo, IAR, & Granada, DPV (2018). Design of a rubric for the evaluation of learning based on a game in industrial engineering.

Pantoja, M. L. (2012) Assessment in competencies? Pedagogical Studies XXXVIII, No. 1: 353-366, 2012. https://scielo.conicyt.cl/pdf/estped/v38n1/art22.pdf

Berlanga Ramírez, Ma. de la Luz, & Juárez-Hernández, Luis Gibran. (2020). Evaluation paradigms: from traditional to socio-formative. Dialogues on education. Current topics in educational research, 11(21), 00017. Epub March 03, 2021.DOI: 10.32870/dse.v0i21.646

Ramírez, Mario H, Méndez-Sánchez, Arturo F, Pérez-Trejo, Leonor, & Olvera-Aldana, Miguel. (2013). Hierarchy of specific competencies in the physics program of the Higher School of Physics and Mathematics of the IPN-Mexico using the Morganov -Heredia matrix. *University training, 6* (5), 21-28. Unesco, Conceptual framework for the evaluation of competenciesDOI: 10.4067/S0718-50062013000500004

Rincón- Gallardo, S. (. (2024). Educating for what? The purposes of education in and beyond the collapse. *Latin American Journal of Educational Studies (Mexico)*, LIV(1), 71–92. DOI: 10.48102/rlee.2024.54.1.608

Schmelkes, S. (2024). The potential of education to conserve and transform. https://www.redalyc.org/journal/270/27075657009/

Tobón, S., & Posada, R. E. Q. (2008). Competence-based assessment. In *First International Congress "Competencies in 21st Century Education."*

UNESCO. (2016) Conceptual framework for the assessment of competencies. https://unesdoc.unesco.org/ark:/48223/pf0000245195_eng

UNESCO. (2017). Education for the Sustainable Development Goals. Learning objectives. https://unesdoc.unesco.org/ark:/48223/ pf0000247444

UNESCO. (2023) The future of higher education: skills for tomorrow's world. https://www.iesalc.unesco.org/2023/08/11/the-future-of-higher-education-skills-for-tomorrows-world/

UNESCO MGIEP. (2017). Rethinking schooling for the 21st century. New Delhi: Mahatma Gandhi Institute of Education for Peace and Sustainable Development (MGIEP), UNESCO.

Vera, F., Tejada, E., & Morales, M. (2022). Development of generic competencies in students of the Bachelor's Degree in Hispanic American Language and Literature. Transformar, 3(1), 14–25. Retrieved from https://www.revistatransformar.cl/index.php/transformar/article/view/49

Walko, Aquino, Ludmilla. (. (2022). Characteristics of the most efficient instrument design in the assessment of learning. *Academo (Asuncion)*, 9(1), 1–10. DOI: 10.30545/academo.2022.ene-jun.1

World Economic Forum. (October 20, 2020). The future of job report 2020. https://www.weforum.org/reports/the-future-of-jobs-report-2020/in-full/infographics-e4e69e4de7

Chapter 11
Programmer Profile in Terms of Job Vacancies Compared to University Vocational Training

Maria Fernanda Trejo Carrillo
Instituto Politécnico Nacional, Mexico

Esteban Martínez Díaz
Instituto Politécnico Nacional, Mexico

Dulce María Monroy Becerril
Instituto Politécnico Nacional, Mexico

ABSTRACT

As part of the problem of the study, it was found that programmers are not clear about what are the skills and digital knowledge they need to acquire to enter the labor field, therefore, the objective of this study was to channel the requirements requested by IT consultancies when hiring a programmer, in order to obtain a technical profile for a software developer in the year 2024. The methodology used was a comparative evaluation of the web platforms where companies publish the vacancies they request, filters were used to determine only those that corresponded to software developer positions in Mexico City. Likewise, a matrix was made by platform to compare the academic degree, years of experience and technical knowledge requested by the IT consulting firms. As part of the results, it was found that companies are looking for programmers with specific technical knowledge in programming languages, web programming, databases, interfaces, software architecture, web and mobile applications as well as some soft skills: communication, teamwork and proactivity.

DOI: 10.4018/979-8-3693-7086-5.ch011

INTRODUCTION

The world of software is visualized in all electronic devices that are used every day, it is part of the essential functioning of each artifact that the activities of the human being are easier to perform. The process for the realization of this software involves a set of tasks that take their due time, which not only works one person, but with the collaboration of a team with specialized technical skills around programming, in addition to having the technological knowledge and recognize the needs of today's society.

Software development is not exclusive to amusement and entertainment devices, but "Programming, in today's digital age, occupies a central place in numerous sectors of industry and the economy." (Beltrán Torres et al., 2023). That is, it is used by everyone in any job, for example: in the stock market by having specialized programs that calculate probabilities in stock changes, in the health sector by having specific machinery to perform scans to the whole body or in education by having specific platforms for teaching subjects and support the teaching-learning process.

Since technology is not a constant entity, it becomes a necessity to have specialists in the area who recognize the technological change and are suitable to continue giving life to all those elements that make human life easier.

Thus, "Software development, by itself, is not a trivial task; it is recognized by experts as an activity whose complexity may exceed human capabilities to handle it." (Ventura Roque Hernández et al., 2015, p. 154). In this way, a professional in software development is in the obligation to be constantly trained to continue driving technological development, even though he/she is a recent graduate.

In Mexico there are three schools that have the objective of training computer engineers or system engineers who are capable of proposing solutions in the world of technology. Within the schools, students carry out activities and work in the fields of web programming, computer algorithms, systems design, requirements engineering, databases, computer security, to name a few.

Software development involves more than just coding in the various programming languages that currently exist, you go beyond just making an electronic device work, as mentioned by Colomo-Palacios "Software design is, in fact, the natural professional activity of a computer engineer because it requires competencies that are unique to his profile." (2010 as cited in Ferré et al., 2019, p. 23).

But, given the technological advances, recently graduated programmers are struggling to keep on training, since the knowledge they have is not enough to enter the labor field so easily, which leads to another problem due to the dizzying change of technology.

Every day companies are looking for highly trained professionals in software development, so their employees are obliged to comply with the requirements established by the organization at the time of their contract. And they are looking for the best way to advertise those job vacancies to reach a better trained population. It is at this time when a new tool is used to advertise the requested places through the web, thus having new platforms for job vacancies, "the generation of employment through this technological tool has become an effective way to get a job" (Melo Campos, 2019, p. 1). The problem is that they describe in detail the specifications of each job that on many occasions programmers do not meet those requirements.

In addition, as time goes by, requirements are increasing, making vacancies more and more demanding.

The Importance of Software Development

It is already known that technology is changing over time, just as new needs are appearing or even inventing some totally innovative ones, "what is certain is that every sector is being strongly impacted by digitization, automation and artificial intelligence." (2019, p. 133), as mentioned by Scasserra.

Such is the example that, for fun, augmented reality glasses were created to increase the player's experience with some first-person video games, but these new artifacts need two important elements: hardware and software.

Hardware is defined as any physical element that contributes to the operation of an electronic device, from the wiring and circuitry to the motion sensors and keys on a laptop.

On the other hand, the software is limited to the programmable logic operation of each hardware element contained in the electronic device, which is moldable and made by software developers.

Scientific and technological advances are not only for entertainment, but also for different areas, such as education, medicine, security, home, professional. At every moment the needs of society are growing and with it the technology, as mentioned by Contieri "As technology advances, low-level programmers will no longer be required in the same way that no one is looking for librarians today" (2021, p. 59).

Another example are the new technologies that are born to facilitate the tasks caused by the pandemic, such as: digital temperature thermometers, home delivery applications, *pick up* systems in supermarkets, online shopping websites or videoconferencing applications.

At the beginning, few software development professionals were trained in these new technologies, but the global need led companies to hire or train their programmers to provide maintenance or increase user capacity due to the need of the population at that time, so the consultancies sought "that these professionals have a set of characteristics, skills and abilities that allow them to meet the demands of the labor market and contribute effectively to the companies" (Beltrán Torres et al., 2023, p. 27).

These communication requirements not only occurred in the education or business sectors, but also had to modify the ways of life of a family at home, thus taking a significant importance for new programmers who were solving the problems presented, since software development is not dedicated to coding to make a problem work, it involves other activities that happen in less than a minute to a dilemma presented.

Another example of the importance of software development was an event that occurred in the middle of the year 2024 where the BBVA bank platform had problems for the login of its users. (Campuzano, 2024). This collapsed the company's database and prevented customers from accessing their monetary funds for at least a week. This problem occurred when the mobile application was updated, causing the system to stop working and users were unable to make any type of banking transactions.

It was extremely serious that customers did not have access to their money, causing great inconvenience to the population and seeking solutions directly at the teller window to make cash withdrawals from bank accounts. Given the circumstances, the programmers in charge of the BBVA mobile application made the necessary modifications to return to a previous point where everything worked correctly and thus prevent users from continuing to fill the physical branches and make their movements via cell phones.

These are situations where software developers demonstrate the ability to solve problems and how they use technical knowledge to solve a scenario in a short period of time and that without software development would not easily perform financial transactions, even more safely than going to a branch office.

On the other hand, software development has also proven to be essential in scientific research in the creation of information management applications that help researchers in the organization of articles, books and chapters for later use, such as: Zootero, Mendeley or Google Scholar.

The first two were developed with the purpose of creating a personal database in the preparation of articles, thus facilitating the set of references used by the authors and integrating them according to the format chosen by the researcher (APA, IEEE, Vancouver, etc.).

The third helps to create a profile for each researcher by linking published articles, books, papers and chapters. It generates the citation and reference, as well as specifies how many times the researcher has been referenced in other publications.

It sounds nice when you consider in theory that software development has done so much for today's society, but it is not only about creating applications that are pleasing to the eye and that work the first time, it is also about giving them maintenance, expanding the information, updating them to new devices that are coming out, translating them to other languages or retrieving information if necessary.

Software development is an activity that incorporates complexity from several areas. An application must not only implement all functional requirements, but also non-functional requirements such as robustness, responsiveness, maintainability, verifiability, scalability, security, support, monitoring and disaster recovery in order to meet not only the immediate needs of organizations. (Ventura Roque Hernández et al., 2015, p. 154).

In conclusion, software is of utmost relevance for both electronic devices and digital applications. No device would be able to function if it does not have its internal programming, therefore, it gives an important weight to the programmers, since they have the technical knowledge to make them work. Likewise, no mobile application is static, on the contrary, it adjusts to the needs of the devices that are also changing day by day.

It is a double-edged sword, it is known that the human being is becoming addicted to the use of web applications, but clearly it is no longer seen performing tasks as it was done in previous years and to have that comfort that technology gives, software development is one of the careers that will not disappear over time.

Importance of a Skilled Programmer

As already mentioned, the hardware is advancing with new devices, so the software has the requirement to make those physical elements work, thus being the programmer the only professional in identifying those hardware needs and adapt them through coding, therefore, "One of the most demanded IT profiles by the labor market is the software designer and developer." (Adecco, 2016, as cited in Ferré et al., 2019, p. 23), including one of the best paid jobs worldwide.

In the labor market, and especially in the technological area, the programmer who is better prepared is the one who wins over those who are just entering the companies, "The current market is looking for programmers to stack bricks using their fashionable languages [...] Such professionals are trained in specific tools that have very short life cycles and then become obsolete." (Contieri, 2021, p. 57). Unfortunately, on some occasions, they only obtain an internship position in the hope of having a growth within the organization. This is because they do not have the complete profile that the company needs, and they look for some internal or external training to forge the programmer according to internal requirements.

Another important point is that being a career of the future, training will be constant for programmers, as mentioned by Ventura et al. "One of the biggest problems of our high-tech society is to train new and complex technical skills such as programming, with the aim of educating our present and future workforce in this discipline." (2015, p. 154). It would be necessary to analyze how the training of current students is being given to be the next generation that will follow with innovations in information and communication technologies.

The updating of curricula will depend on the educational authorities of each country "higher education institutions should improve SD certification programs and implement training courses for those who need or wish to reinforce the knowledge acquired" (Torres-Castillo et al., 2022, p. 504).

In the case of Mexico, it depends on the Ministry of Public Education for universities belonging to the governmental system and in the case of UNAM, being autonomous, they will have the obligation to update their curricula.

The training of a programmer takes place in the university classrooms in computer science degrees or engineering, depending on the house of studies will be the technical knowledge with which he will have at the time of graduation. This situation is explained by Domínguez and Mexicano:

Finally, the training of engineers should be one of the main occupations of a Higher Education Institution and therefore it should implement actions that allow it to know throughout the process, the degree of progress in the achievement of the graduation competencies that it establishes in its study programs, since this contributes to the progress of the economy society and in general of our country. (Domínguez Martínez & Mexicano Reyes, 2018, p. 9)

In the case of Mexico City, there are three important academic units where a graduate can work as a programmer upon completion of his or her degree (Figure 1).

As can be seen, there are similarities in the three careers despite being from different houses of study, the graduate profile of the Universidad Autónoma de México (UAM), El Instituto Politécnico Nacional (IPN) and la Universidad Nacional Autónoma de México (UNAM) was compared. One of the most important similarities is the preparation of students in the management of projects based on computer systems with the help of interdisciplinarity, through methodologies where the student does the design, coding and testing of a software system.

The study plans and programs respond to the needs of the labor market, so they are created from the various studies in the most important economic sectors to integrate the subjects and the appropriate knowledge of programmers. With the passage of time, plans and programs are modified and especially in the technological area "Learning to program is an important goal in our society and understanding how to acquire this knowledge has a huge educational impact." (Ventura Roque Hernández et al., 2015, p. 153). That is, learning to program is no longer only a requirement of large companies such as Google or Amazon, but even in small and medium enterprises that are dedicated to making websites, small databases for grocery stores or accounting programs that support small entrepreneurs.

It is then when the preparation of the programmer takes an important point since, in companies, "One of the strengths of human capital comes from the professional preparation in the areas of science and engineering. To develop high quality software, you need highly skilled developers." (Prathan and Ow, 2020 as cited in Torres-Castillo et al., 2022, p. 500). The better trained the staff is, the more likely they will be to increase productivity and the customers they work for.

One of the advantages in the world of software development is that projects are not always done from scratch, sometimes the modules are already described and only modifications are made. In the case of those who want a customized module, the consulting firms already have code bases to add the elements that the client needs "In today's software industry it is very unlikely to encounter the need to do a development from scratch, with a completely blank page. The shelf life of a specific programmer ages along with the language in vogue."(Contieri, 2021, p. 58).

If anything, the only detail is in the temporality and validity of programming languages. As time goes by, new codes are also created looking for the ease and comfort of the programmers for the coding of modules, which means that recent graduates urgently seek training in programming models and languages that are fashionable, as well as those who are working, they will need an update or else they will be replaced by software developers who do have the knowledge.

For this reason, the following are the most popular digital platforms in Mexico where employers post their vacancies, in addition to the requirements described by companies to 2024 to identify the ideal profile of a programmer that meets the needs of the labor world.

Results Obtained from the Main Job Vacancy Platforms

In Mexico, there are several web platforms that are famous among Mexican workers. Here the companies specify the vacancies and the requirements of each one so that the users have the possibility to participate. Depending on the platform, the user has the possibility to create his/her academic and professional profile, in this way, the companies make a first filter and choose the best option for the vacancy they are looking for.

Previously, one way of dissemination used by organizations was through newspapers or special job magazines where users would go to the nearest newsstand and buy the day's edition to look for a job that matches the skills.

As time went by, companies began to use other types of advertising, sticking notices in stores and light poles, thus attracting the attention of those interested in participating in a vacancy. It was also very common that vacancies were passed on by the voice of one of the internal collaborators, mentioning to their acquaintances about the existence of a space to enter the workplace.

Information and communication technologies changed the course on the internal organization of companies "it is through this type of technologies that many companies and traders in their role as employers manage to carry out different mercantile operations in which they are necessarily forced to use human personnel, personnel that largely serves their economic objectives" (Melo Campos, 2019, p. 2).

Likewise, the publication of job vacancies was also affected by ICTs, giving them an opportunity to reach more people with better preparation.

The most famous platforms for posting vacancies are:

- Linkedin
- Computrabajo
- Indeed
- OCCMundial

All of them are generally recognized as a social network that allows users to enter a personalized profile, in which they describe their skills, schooling, extra courses, languages and professional experience so that companies can save time in verifying if they meet the requirements for the vacancy.

On the other hand, companies create their own profile with the necessary information to give veracity to the publication and create confidence in those who are applying for a vacancy. Depending on the web platform, they are given a verification dove or star indicating that the company exists, and the vacancies are real, giving more security to the user about where they want to apply.

In the case of the publication of vacancies, companies comply with a specific format that describes the position, duration of employment, salary, benefits, necessary experience, technical requirements, place and way of work. Thus, users looking for jobs, with the help of filters, will easily find the option that interests them. Subsequently, with a click on the computer, users apply to the vacancy, thus, the company receives a list of applicants who are interested in working with them.

The selection process will depend on the company, but in some platforms, it is possible to perform an internal analysis and show Human Resources which are the profiles that best fit the requested vacancy, providing them with the user's contact numbers and e-mails.

In this way, the posting and recruitment process becomes faster, more efficient and effective, but it is still possible to find flaws in relying on a machine - after all, machines are not perfect.

Below are some vacancies that were found on the platforms towards the programming area, published in August and September 2024.

As mentioned above, the need for skilled programmers is no longer an option, it is an obligation. That is why every day companies are becoming more specific about the requirements they need for vacancies even though there is still some uncertainty about it:

Despite the abundance of information on the subject, there is still a lack of clarity about what are the most critical skills and competencies that programmers must possess to be successful in the workplace. This lack of clarity can hinder the job placement of recent graduates and the professional development of practicing programmers. (Beltrán Torres et al., 2023, p. 28).

According to the vacancies offered in the previously mentioned platforms, a comparison was made on what are the soft and hard skills that programmers need in their professional profile, so that it is easier for graduates to seek specialized training (distance, classroom or hybrid), and thus, to participate for a position with better economic possibilities.

It should be noted that the requirements for joining a company are as follows

LA UNIR Mexico (2022) makes a description of the general skills of a skilled programmer for 2022, among them are:

- Design of programs and/or applications.
- Investigation of customer needs.
- Definition of the technical specifications of the project.
- Use of programming languages.
- Maintenance and updating of the code
- Testing and testing of the program performed.
- Monitor and carry out program improvements and enhancements.
- Monitor software operation.
- Perform constant updates.

On the other hand, Beltrán Torres et al. (2023) made a comparison of different companies in Mexico and the competencies they need especially to enter the IT area (Table 1).

Table 1. Skills and competencies in companies in Mexico

ITEM / COMPANY	SyA Mexico	Alert Group	Corporate Valladolid Educational System	Bizopps Group
Skills and technical characteristics	We are looking for self-sufficient and self-taught candidates with networking skills	Skills in developmental logic problem solving, self-learnin	Systems analysis and design good programming practices programming logic	Skills in specific technologies implementation of solutions, use of tools such as Git, Jira, Docker
Programming languages	C++, Java, JavaScript, among others	Variety of languages, C++, Java, JavaScript, among others. including Visual FoxPro, MySQL, HTML, PHP, JavaScript, React, Laravel, among others.	PHP, JavaScript, C#, Delphi, among others	JavaScript, PHP, Python, React-Native, Laravel, Angular, Django, among others
Soft skills	Self-sufficiency and problem solving on their own.	Teamwork, communication, humility and effective problem-solving skills	Teamwork , communication, humility and the ability to recognize weaknesses and turn them into opportunities.	Teamwork , communication, humility and ability to resolve conflicts effectively.

continued on following page

Table 1. Continued

ITEM / COMPANY	SyA Mexico	Alert Group	Corporate Valladolid Educational System	Bizopps Group
Important attitudes and values	Enthusiasm to work and be self-sufficient.	Honesty, collaboration, commitment, empathy, respect towards colleagues	Honesty, collaboration, commitment, empathy, respect towards colleagues	A passion for learning, self-learning, humility and good communication skills
Programmer profile	Know how to deal with problems, where to look for information, preferably have knowledge in mobile application development and databases	Self-starter, proactive, honest, collaborative, committed and with communication skills	Self-starter, proactive, with analytical and documentation skills	Fullstack, capable of independently implementing solutions

Note: (Beltrán Torres et al., 2023).

In general, companies are looking for candidates who are problem solvers, self-taught, use technological tools and have programming experience. Depending on the organization and the activities performed, the programming skills required for each vacancy will depend on the organization. Some ask for languages used to create web pages (JavaScript, PHP, Python, HTML, among others).

They also ask that future workers have soft skills such as teamwork, communication, humility, effective problem solving, as well as people with values and respect for their colleagues. In one of the companies, programmers are required to be *full-stack* programmers, which means that they must have diverse skills in the creation of software in all its modalities: databases, user interface, code logic, testing and testing, improvement and updating of the programs.

Table 2. Description of vacancies published in CompuTrabajo

Location	Global Mexicana de Infraestructura SAPI de CV	IDS Comercial S.A. de C.V.	DIGIS01 Digital solutions	KODE IT
Job position	Web developer	Fullstack Developer	Junior Developer	JAVA Developer
Academic background	Bachelor's degree in computer systems, information technology, ICT	Bachelor's degree / engineering in computer or systems	Bachelor's degree or engineering degree in computer science	Bachelor's degree in computer science
Experience	3 years in web development	3-5 years	Students / recent graduates	3 years
Skills / knowledge	- Handling of HTML, - CSS - JavaScript - frameworks such as Bootstrap, react - adobe, figma, Photoshop, Illustrator. - Development and structuring of aesthetically pleasing and practical landing pages and websites - Responsive design, user experience UX and interface UI - SEM and SEO Optimization Google Analitycs SQL	- C - ADO .NET - CORE.NET - Microservices - Python angularjs 8, 12 - JavaScript - Bootstrap - Typescript - NPM - SQL Server - Oracle - Connection - RDBMS - Injection of dapper dependencies - Cloud Azure or GCP - CICD - Jenkins - Infrastructure with IAC code - Docker - Kubernetes	- Application development with Microsoft .NET, Java SE, Android or iOS technologies. - Web application development	- Advanced proficiency in Java 8 or higher. - Management of Spring Boot, Spring MVC and/or Spring - Framework. - Knowledge in web services, API's and/or microservices. - FrontEnd Development (HTML, CSS, JavaScript, Angular). - Knowledge in relational and non-relational databases. - Knowledge in AWS (S3, ECS, ECR, CloudWatch). - Knowledge in Docker.

Note. (Computrabajo Group, 2024)

In the case of CompuTrabajo's job offers, we compared four IT consulting firms and the skills they are looking for in programmers for Mexico City in face-to-face or remote vacancies (Table 2).

The main difference is the number of years of experience that companies in Mexico are looking for, approximately 3-5 years. In addition, they mention the mandatory schooling for workers being a degree or engineering in computer science, software development or systems, as well as the name of the position where they are going to get web developer, fullstack or junior.

The technical skills that programmers are looking for are based on knowledge of computer tools, different programming languages, software infrastructure, software methodologies and databases. Some companies that offer a considerable amount in salary require the use of languages and programs too specific for the development of applications, it is no longer enough just to know how to program.

It is necessary for programmers to use diverse software development architecture systems to carry out multi-disciplinary projects, and, if necessary, to be able to adapt to any step of the project. That is to say that the programmer must master the methodologies in software development. However, be able to create mobile applications and web applications. This is one of the most demanding platforms even though they only ask for 3 years of experience as a minimum.

In another comparison of companies that published on LinkedIn (Table 3), there was a company that gives the opportunity to professionals with less years of experience (one to two years). Similarly, they ask for a bachelor's or engineering degree as a minimum in academic training and related to software development.

As well as a list of technical requirements in programming languages, software development methodologies, specific programming languages, system architecture, databases and cloud storage tools. Specifically in the company IDOM asks for intermediate to advanced English language because of the possible requirement meetings they have with foreign customers and because of the code manuals with which the programmer will work in English, only in some cases they ask that the applicant has an intermediate level around reading comprehension since some programs are exclusive in that language.

Table 3. Description of vacancies posted on LinkedIn

Location	Booth 8 technology services	NEORIS	Gentera	IDOM Consulting, Engineering, Architecture
Job position	JAVA Developer	JAVA Developer	Sr. BackEnd JAVA Developer	Sr Web Developer
Academic background	Bachelor's degree or engineering degree in computer science	Bachelor's degree or engineering degree in computer science	Bachelor's degree or engineering degree in computer science	Bachelor's degree or engineering degree in computer science
Experience	3 years	2 years of experience	4 years	1 year
Skills / knowledge	- Knowledge in Agile Methodologies. - Experience in Cloud environments (Azure, AWS or GCP). - Advanced knowledge of Java 17 and Springboot. - Proficiency in Microservices / restful API. - Familiarity with Secure Code. - Experience using Git/Gitflow. - Knowledge of AKS (Azure managed Kubernetes Service). - Experience with integrator tools such as Axway and Azure API Management.	- Knowledge of Python, Java Script, SQL. - Ability to design and develop AI conversations with responses from external APIs. - Collaborate with BackEnd application integration teams to understand the mechanisms through which the Chatbot solution will be used. - Consuming the Chatbot service through different platforms.	- Java Backend Development, (Spring Boot, Spring Data) - Essential experience with modern devops development tools - In-depth knowledge of API 4 development principles. - Experience with SQL and NoSQL database systems - Ability to perform effective unit tests - Experience in cloud development - Experience in event-oriented architecture	- Web development - BackEnd and FrontEnd - Angular / react - Net Framework JAVA - HTML + CSSPHP - Python - C# - JavaScript - Typescript - JQuery - SQL - PostgreSQL - Ms-SQL - Postgis - Internet Information Service - Flask - Azure devops - Git - OneDrive - Intermediate to advanced English - Knowledge in development of GIS solutions with ESRI technology Knowledge in tasks of analysis, design and development of Business Intelligence solutions (powerbi, Tableau, Qlik, Pentaho) Knowledge in solutions for process automation (BPMS, RPA)

Note. (LinkedIn Group, 2024)

From another perspective, the companies that published vacancies on Indeed (Table 4) are looking for personnel who are recent graduates from educational institutions or have at least one year of experience. What they are looking for is to train new professionals in the knowledge they need and, in this way, avoid looking for personnel who are offering a higher salary for the knowledge they have invested in for years.

The technical skills they request are almost the same as the other companies previously mentioned, only the type of language and certificates in the use of software architecture change.

Table 4. Description of vacancies posted on Indeed

Location	INTERCAM Bank	RIMAC Agente de Seguros SA de CV	Inmega	Terra Energy
Job position	Full Stack Jr.	Full Stack Developer	Programmer	Full Stack Web Programmer
Academic background	Bachelor's degree or engineering in computer science or related field.	Bachelor's degree in computer science, programmer or related career.	Bachelors or Engineering degrees in Computer Science, Computer Systems, Information Technology, Technology, and related fields.	Bachelor's degree or engineering in computer science or related field.
Experience	3 years	1 year	Recent graduate	1 year
Skills / knowledge	- Experience with angularjs and JavaScript - Handling of HTML5 and CSS. - Management of Oracle relational database managers. - Desirable to use openshift. - GitHub experience.	- Node - React - HTML5. - CSS3 (Bootstrap 4). - MYSQL relational databases - Generate web services - Git version management - Self-employed. - Proactive. - Organized. - Reliable. - Fast learning. - English: basic-intermediate. - Easy to talk to. - Teamwork. - react and/ or node.js technology	- Knowledge in: PHP, HTML, SQL Server Database Management Java Script, Stored Procedures, framework (Laravel, Angular, etc.), Python. - Analysis, design and development of software applications based on scripting (survey programming), client or end-user applications, Web applications with large volumes of information, according to the requirements of each study. - Problem support to our internal customers for the VOXCO platform	- Native PHP, use of various libraries. - MySQL with management of store procedures - JavaScript, use of various libraries. - Integration of several Apis with third party services - Laravel- VUE JS- Docker- Composer - Python- GIT version control - Management of AWS services for infrastructure: EC2 servers, balancers, certificate manager, as well as site configuration. - RDS Database - Cognito Administration and Configuration - S3 File Manager - Route 53 Domains - VPN and virtual hosts configuration - SNS - English (Intermediate reading level) - SCRUM Methodology

Note. (Indeed Group, 2024)

Finally, a comparison was made of four more companies on the OCC Mundial platform (Table 5). Here it was found that in the same way they give opportunity to those with few years of experience, therefore, the technical requirements are lower than the other platforms. Among the programming languages are SQL for databases, .NET for the creation of applications, JAVA and HTML for the development of web pages, as well as the use of web application design and presentation tools.

Table 5. Description of vacancies published in OCCMundial

Location	**SIGMUN Pharmaceutical Group**	**Indra**	**Salinas Tlalpan Group**	**Marketing Ideas and Technologies SA de CV**
Job position	Sr Programmer	JAVA Jr. Developer	.net developer	C and C# Developer
Academic background	Bachelor's degree or Systems Engineering or equivalent	Bachelor's degree or Systems Engineering or equivalent	Bachelor's degree or Systems Engineering or equivalent	Engineering and/or Computer Science Degrees
Experience	2 years	1 year	1-3 years	3 years
Skills / knowledge	- .NET, SQL Server, ASP .Net, MVC, JavaScript, Angular JS software management - Software development in .NET - Programming of interfaces for communication between systems (web and winservices). - Modeling techniques - Development of programming for mobile devices - Use of web application design and presentation tools	- Java 8 Development - Solid knowledge in POO - Spring Batch. - Linux - Spring Framework. - Database (Oracle, SQL). - MVC, Eclipse, Maven. - DevOps Tools Management (Git, Bitbucket, Sonar, Jenkins) - Non-relational database (Mongo DB) - Apache Spark framework - ETHER SOFTWARE DEVELOPMENT PLATFORM tools (console, ecs-cli, stacker)	- Net - SQL - ASP .NET - WCF - MVC - Database - Web development - Develop applications and/or software programs that provide technological solutions, guaranteeing their quality and correct operation.	- C# - C - JAVA 11 OR HIGHER - REACT, HTML - Development of new functionality in the systems - Systems maintenance, Creation of user manuals - Support in the integration and implementation of the developed systems.

Note. (OCCMundial Group, 2024)

As part of the discussion of this book chapter, it was noted that depending on the platform are the vacancies being posted.

In the case of LinkedIn, being a formal social network between companies and workers, the vacancies contain more specific requirements with more experience and extensive knowledge in software architecture, unlike the platforms that allow recent graduates to start working to grow in the working world.

Although the platforms ask the employers to add all the details of the vacancy, not all of them add the salary to be paid, but on average for an expert programmer with 3 years of experience they get a salary of up to $35 000 MXN, for programmers with 1-2 years of experience they charge an approximate of $22 000 MXN and recent graduates an average fee of $12 000 MXN.

Finally, from the data obtained from the comparison of vacancies on Internet employment platforms, the following table with categories and subcategories is presented as a reference for further studies (Table 6).

Table 6. Technical profile of a programmer in 2024

Job position	**Programmer or Web Developer**
Academic background	Bachelor's degree or Systems Engineering or equivalent
Average experience	3 years
Skills / knowledge	- .NET, ASP .Net, MVC, JavaScript, Angular JS - C, C# - Python - SQL, SQL Server, Oracle, MySQL - HTML, PHP, HTML5, CSS - Software development in .NET - ADO .NET - CORE.NET - Programming of interfaces for communication between systems (web and winservices). - Modeling techniques - Agile Methodologies - Cloud storage tools - Development of programming for mobile devices - Use of design and presentation tools for web applications. - Software architecture - BackEnd and FrontEnd Development - English language (intermediate-advanced) - UX and UI user experience - Self-taught, responsible, committed, honest, honest - Troubleshooting - Proactive - Communication and teamwork skills

Note: Own elaboration

Among the requirements for the profile of a programmer in 2024 in IT consulting firms in Mexico, it was found that the technical skills are varied and depend a lot on the position to which they will apply. In general, knowledge of common programming languages in mobile applications and systems, databases, languages for websites, software architecture and some soft skills in communication, teamwork and languages are required.

CONCLUSION

It is not surprising that technology changes to meet the needs of human beings and to maintain it requires professionals trained in the use and management of programming.

As noted above, programmers need a wide range of digital skills to integrate into the world of work, regardless of whether it is a trained expert with years of experience or an intern who is just starting to train in the labor field.

According to the companies analyzed in the literature, programmers are required to have not only one, but several specializations in the management of coding languages, databases, software architecture and data analysis. It is important to clarify that in these job offers only appear the digital skills but not the skills in the management of hardware for the case of Mexico City in the year 2024.

In addition, a highly trained programmer will have the skills to compete in the best IT consulting firms in the area where he/she is located, with a competitive salary, legal benefits and a better position. To reach this point, the software professional will seek to increase his or her skills through training and with the results obtained from the theoretical analysis will be a guide for graduates seeking to enter the working world, as well as for software development professionals who have not yet found a stable job or do not pass the first technical interview.

Although there are many technical requirements that companies look for to join an IT consulting firm, soft skills are necessary, although not all vacancies describe them. These requirements are usually explained in interviews with Human Resources, the job web platforms are only a support for both companies and workers in the search for vacancies.

In this way, the hiring process is simplified, and it is easier for companies to choose the right resume and avoid staff turnover in the future.

Also, benefits and salaries are higher when it comes to a highly experienced programmer, but the requirements for admission to the consultancy become specific in conjunction with other software development skills. This means that if a recent graduate is looking to integrate quickly as a software developer, he/she will have to look for courses or training during the degree or, failing that, integrate as an intern with a low salary for a period to acquire knowledge in a specific area.

Therefore, being a review of the literature and the vacancies that are presented on the web by the major labor market offering websites, it is concluded that companies use this type of platforms to save time in finding candidates for vacant positions, similarly, the specifications of each vacancy will depend on the employer requesting it with the possibility of leaving lack of information and causing doubts to applicants, or, strictly establishing the requirements causing candidates not to apply for not fulfilling them to the letter.

This research serves as a theoretical basis for students who are studying a career in software development and give them an idea of what are the elements that companies are looking for today, thus, training in areas of opportunity that they consider necessary to facilitate finding a job with excellent benefits.

Finally, the conclusions and theory of this study can be used as a foundation for the development of a data collection instrument to compare the digital knowledge and skills with which students graduate in programming and analyze whether they satisfy the requirements of the labor market, which would be tested in different contexts to visualize the changes in the skills of a programmer in different cities in the Mexican Republic.

REFERENCES

Beltrán Torres, J. A., Corral Trujillo, E., & Cristerna González, R. D. (2023). Características, aptitudes y habilidades que un programador debe tener al ingresar en el campo laboral. *Revista Digital de Tecnologías Informáticas y Sistemas*, 7(1), 27–34. DOI: 10.61530/redtis.vol7.n1.2023.156.27-34

Campuzano, J. (2024, June 28). ¡Se cae app de BBVA en viernes de quincena! Usuarios reportan fallas. *El Excelsior*. https://www.excelsior.com.mx/nacional/fallas-bbva-app-hoy-28-junio-2024/1659938

Contieri, M. (2021). Formando programadores para el futuro. *DOSSIER, 13*.

Domínguez Martínez, A., & Mexicano Reyes, Y. (2018). Evaluación de competencias de programación. *Revista Electrónica ANFEI Digital, 4*(8). www.anfei.org.mx/revista

Ferré, M., García-Barroso, C., García-Famoso, M., Sánchez, D., & Valls, A. (2019). Mejora de la formación en el diseño y desarrollo de software a partir de la coordinación de distintas asignaturas. *Actas de Las Jenui, 4*.

Grupo Computrabajo. (2024). *Empleos*. Computrabajo. https://mx.computrabajo.com/trabajo-de-programadores

Grupo Indeed. (2024). *Empleos*. Indeed. https://mx.indeed.com/jobs?q=programador&l=&from=searchOnHP

Grupo LinkedIn. (2024). *Empleos*. LinkedIn. https://www.linkedin.com/jobs/search?trk=guest_homepage-basic_guest_nav_menu_jobs&original_referer=https%3A%2F%2Fwww.linkedin.com%2Fhome&position=1&pageNum=0

Grupo OCCMundial. (2024). *Empleos*. OCCMundial. https://www.occ.com.mx/empleos/de-programador/en-ciudad-de-mexico/

Melo Campos, A. (2019). *Regulación de las nuevas formas de empleo que surgen por medio de las plataformas digitales*. Universidad Católica de Colombia. Facultad de Derecho.

México, U. N. I. R. (2022, September 21). *¿Qué hace un programador? Funciones, requisitos y situación laboral en México*. La Universidad En Internet. https://mexico.unir.net/noticias/ingenieria/que-hace-programador/

Scasserra, S. (2019). El despotismo de los algoritmos. Cómo regular el empleo en las plataformas. *Nueva Sociedad, 279*.

Torres-Castillo, F., Cantú-Mata, J., & Cantú-Mata, M. (2022). Competencias y habilidades de estudiantes en el área de desarrollo de software y la percepción de la adaptación a la formación a distancia. *Interciencia*, 47(11).

Ventura Roque Hernández, R., Salinas Escandón, J. M., & López Mendoza, A. (2015). La complejidad de entender y enfrentar la formación de futuros desarrolladores de software. *Ciencia Ergo Sum*, 22(2), 153–159.

Chapter 12
Challenges in the Formation of Human Capital at the Postgraduate Level in the Digital Era

Edgar Oliver Cardoso Espinosa
https://orcid.org/0000-0001-7588-9439
Instituto Politécnico Nacional, Mexico

ABSTRACT

The objective of the chapter is to analyze the main challenges of the formation of human capital at the postgraduate level in the digital era in order to determine the main competencies to be developed by students. The postgraduate degree is the educational level oriented towards the development of professional skills of human capital that allows them to be autonomous professionals prepared to perform effectively and efficiently in a digital world. The challenges that the Fourth Industrial Revolution has established for the educational system: Incorporation of technological impact in academic training; formulation of proposals to innovate in training processes; generation of knowledge based on social innovation. Students who access the postgraduate level need to acquire skills that allow them to adapt to a work environment in constant technological evolution, in addition to acquiring both technical knowledge and relevant social skills. Digital leadership has become a strategic factor for organizational success in the era of technological transformation

DOI: 10.4018/979-8-3693-7086-5.ch012

INTRODUCTION[1]

Higher education has evolved over the centuries both in its organizational structure and in the educational models it uses to train students (Neave, 2021). However, the speed of change in the world is faster than the updating of educational plans and content (Altbach et al., 2019).

The main objective of higher education is to provide a set of skills oriented towards a transformative relationship with knowledge that allows them a holistic understanding of who they are and what changes are required to improve the environment in which they live and no longer focus solely on training for working life (Ashwin, 2020).

Thus, higher education faces challenges such as new teaching and learning processes; new approaches based on the production of knowledge and its dissemination; the types of leadership that are necessary to manage organizational development; the impact of digital technologies and their incorporation into training processes and the creation of new graduate profiles that are congruent with the world (Anand and Chellamani, 2021; Cohen, 2021).

Thus, the digital transformation of higher education is necessary in four categories: innovation in teaching and learning processes; transformation based on knowledge; transformation in the organization and values; and transformation to impact the person and their development (Gallifa and Sangrà, 2021).

Likewise, these authors identified tensions regarding digital transformation, which are:

- Full confidence in digitalization
- Adaptation of training to the needs of the labor sector
- Expectations about the effects of the COVID-19 pandemic
- Promotion of critical thinking
- Developing skills in a changing world of work
- Co-creation of knowledge with the environment
- Promoting communication and marketing of the contributions of higher education to the world
- Each university focuses on achieving its mission
- Each university is oriented to research as a primary function
- Educating for a humanistic education that fosters dialogue and pluralism

Based on the above, the term digitalization refers to processes and strategies aimed at continuously incorporating and implementing technological tools in any field, system or organization (Espinosa, 2022).

Thus, the impact of advanced digital technologies that are considered relevant for higher education that allow innovation are shown in Table 1.

Table 1. Advanced digital technologies

New reality	Computing	Data	Connectivity	Tools
• Mixed / extended reality • Augmented reality • Virtual worlds	• Robotics • Computational thinking • Artificial intelligence	• Learning analytics • Natural language processing • Blockchain (data chains) • Big data	• Internet of things • 5G • Cloud computing • Connected industry • Home automation	• Platforms • Apps • Robots • Human-machine communication devices • Videogames

Source: Prendes-Espinosa and Cerdán (2021)

Based on Table 1, it is identified that to promote digital transformation it is necessary to foster interest in its use in people, which requires organizational changes motivated by leadership to modify the organizational culture.

Based on the above, postgraduate studies are the educational level oriented towards the professionalization of human capital with the aim of assimilating a set of capabilities aimed at intervening effectively in the organizations in which they work. Likewise, postgraduate studies are relevant for comprehensive training that includes the various competencies related not only to the area of specialization but also to others with the aim of providing students with a holistic vision.

The purpose of training at the postgraduate level is to provide human capital that influences organizational processes such as the achievement of organizational objectives, job performance, organizational productivity, positioning, creativity and innovation, job satisfaction, positive image, affective commitment, normative and continuity, as well as individual well-being.

In this sense, the most important resource in an organization immersed in a given context is qualified and educated people (Drucker, 1992). That is, the interrelation of the human capital capabilities that make up the organization allows the achievement of goals and positioning. Likewise, this author mentions that technology is culture and its foundation is knowledge, so its systematic acquisition by human capital through academic training is a necessary condition to evolve both as people and as organizations and even for countries.

The rapid evolution of digital technologies has had a significant impact on the educational field because they have expanded the possibilities of communication as well as transforming the student's academic training processes (Chiu, 2021; Dana et al., 2022).

In this way, educational institutions have a fundamental role in the development of professional skills of human capital that allows them to continuously incorporate the various technological tools that allow them to be autonomous professionals prepared to perform effectively and efficiently in a digital world in constant evolution (Peña et al., 2020; Espino-Díaz et al., 2020).

For its part, the abrupt appearance of the COVID-19 pandemic generated a sudden shift towards online learning, which has generated important transformations in professional practices of human capital (Pinargote-Macías et al., 2022).

Thus, the contemporary educational landscape presents as a fundamental challenge the need to create and integrate digital ecosystems that allow the socio-academic development of students (Moreira-Choez et al., 2024).

Based on the above, the chapter aims to: Analyze the main challenges of training human capital at the postgraduate level in the digital age in order to determine the main skills to be developed by students.

BACKGROUND

During the 20th century, countries, organizations and individuals identified that changes are continuous and that the main characteristics of the context are uncertainty and competitiveness. According to Ynzunza et al. (2017), this panorama implies a high investment in technology, and by extension also the development of human capital skills because workers need to acquire a new set of capabilities related to data management and analysis, computer-assisted production, online simulation, programming and predictive maintenance.

For the 21st century, it has been recognized at the international level that education is a strategic and priority factor for the human, social and economic development of countries, so to achieve it it is no longer only necessary to comply with the coverage and quality that allow promote the competitiveness of organizations but now it is necessary to include digital literacy in citizens. According to Torres and Prieto (2014), the postgraduate program is a relevant space whose orientation is to generate training processes aimed at solving organizational needs with the respective transfer of knowledge.

For their part, Araujo and Balduzzi (2010) emphasize that a redefinition of organizations is required towards the establishment of a new technological-productive model based on a reorganization of space and time, as well as new ways of managing and implementing new forms of work based on the use of technologies. This implies a modification of the rigid control system towards a free type that refers to the fact that it is no longer necessary for the employee to be permanently in the organization due to the insertion of ICTs that now allow a discipline and rigor based on the use of knowledge.

Since the World Economic Forum (WEF, 2017), the phenomenon of the Fourth Industrial Revolution has been identified based on the various disruptive technological changes that are transforming social relationships between humans and objects. In this way, the widespread use of the Internet, the absolute use of mobile devices at both a personal and organizational level, the population census through big data, tax collection through blockchain, as well as incorporating artificial intelligence in management meetings have been incorporated.

Subsequently, the World Economic Forum (WEF, 2018): the relevant competencies to develop in people for the 21st century from basic to higher education are complex problem solving, critical thinking, creativity, collaboration and literacy. digital, which are essential to allow people to remain flexible and adaptable to the changing needs of society. Particularly, the WEF made recommendations regarding the development of work skills for the Fourth Industrial Revolution and they are the following: 1) Creativity; 2) People management ; 3) Coordination with others; 4) Emotional intelligence; 5) Judgment and decision making; 6) Service orientation; 7) Negotiation and 8) Cognitive flexibility.

The Fourth Industrial Revolution is characterized by the use of new exponential technologies such as advanced robotics, autonomous transportation, artificial intelligence, data collection sensors, the Internet of Things, 3D printing manufacturing, nanotechnology or quantum computing (Coleman, 2016).

Thus, the Fourth Industrial Revolution has generated a social, cultural and economic transformation based on the generalization of the use of artificial intelligence and its application in robotics, which is why it is influencing not only industrialization processes but also the economy. society and politics, therefore it implies a change in human and organizational relationships (Velásquez, 2019).

Therefore, the Fourth Industrial Revolution has established new skills to be developed associated with specialized processes for the formation of human capital, among which the following stand out (Scott, 2015):

- Knowledge of digital technologies: Skills for managing computer systems focused on the analysis of large amounts of data, programming and interconnectivity of machinery, selection of algorithms and expert systems, analysis of trends generated by artificial intelligence and data science and even computer security systems;
- Collaboration in work teams in multicultural environments: Integration of global production chains with the participation of members of different cultures in order to facilitate interaction both in person and virtually;

- Critical and creative thinking: In the era of hyperconnectivity, the availability of information is immediate, so the analysis of information is required as part of its validation to determine both its validity and importance for decision making.
- Communication skills: Oral and written communication skills in various languages;
- Ethical awareness: The relationships of human beings with technology imply challenges regarding its regulations for the access and use of information.
- Sustainability awareness: The incorporation of digital technologies implies the conservation of natural ecosystems by reducing the use of non-renewable resources.

Given this scenario, a transformation of the map of professions is established to respond to the work dynamics called Smart Factory or Industry 4.0.

Industry 4.0 emerged in Germany in 2011 and is characterized by automation, the digitalization of processes and the use of technologies in manufacturing. In addition, it considers the customization of production, the provision of services and the creation of added value, which implies a combination and exchange of information between people and machines.

It is called this way because it is made up of four pillars:

1) The use of data is related to the connectivity of systems and the collection of large amounts of information, which requires the use of technologies such as the Internet of Things, big data or cloud technology.
2) Artificial intelligence that focuses on the use of systems capable of analyzing information and making improvement decisions.
3) The human-machine link where the work activities carried out by people are automated by incorporating elements of virtual reality or augmented reality, and
4) The transformation from digital to physical refers to 3D printing for prototypes and final parts after having simulated their behavior by a computer. Likewise, it includes the integration of robots to carry out repetitive tasks that have little added value.

In this sense, Industry 4.0 implies a complete communication network that will exist between companies, social organizations, suppliers, government and clients with the purpose of optimizing scarce resources, as well as real time depending on the demands and state of the associated sections in the network, which will lead to a reduction in costs and pollution, raw materials and $CO_{2\ \mathrm{emissions}}$. Thus, Industry 4.0 represents an approach to the innovation of new products and processes, through intelligent processes integrated into work networks throughout the value chain, which gives rise to new forms of collaboration.

In this way, the integration of technologies allows the manufacturing industry to be potentiated with fully integrated, automated and optimized production processes, giving significant results in improving operational efficiency and organizational performance. This situation has generated an impact that is affecting the various areas of the company, from production and organization to research and development, coupled with inventory control, management and customer service.

In this sense, Ynzunza et al. (2017) establish that the implications of Industry 4.0 in business and employment are:

In business it will generate changes in the type of products from physical to digital; higher levels of integration of the organization and the environment; establishment of work networks that create value; shared cloud infrastructure and services; intelligent and global supply chains, as well as business models based on cloud services, logistics and distribution.

As for employment, it will allow the creation of new collaboration schemes and social infrastructures; other forms of human-machine interaction; highly specialized job profiles; more complex work processes; assisted and technology-dependent work environments combined with requirements for the management of digital technologies, robots, programming and data interpretation as transversal skills.

Consequently, Industry 4.0 is generating various transformations oriented towards the digitalization of information and production systems for management activities; automation systems for data acquisition of machinery and production lines; with the exchange of information for the monitoring and control of processes and decision making in real time, which implies that the members of the organization also adapt to these fundamental changes.

Thus, in the contextual framework of the Fourth Industrial Revolution, a world of continuous alterations is glimpsed, where science and technology are at the base of the economic competitiveness of countries, where innovation plays a strategic role in competition., so they are forced to meet a series of requirements to compete successfully in an increasingly globalized economy, including high investments in both education and research. With respect to organizations and individuals, the acquisition of new qualities is required to adapt to the rapid changes in the context, which implies continuous or permanent training. As long as countries, organizations or individuals fail to meet these requirements, they run the risk of being excluded from the knowledge society and, with it, from globalized economic competition.

Therefore, the incorporation, influence and positioning of digital technologies at the levels of the educational system is unquestionable, so HEIs have to reinvent themselves, evolve and innovate towards the construction of flexible learning experiences in the student body in relation to what, the where, when and how. Furthermore, they will be relevant because they will allow the elimination of barriers because they will enable access to education without boundaries of time or space, therefore they will increase collaboration between people regardless of their geographical location, thus generating information exchange networks (Castaño et al., 2014).

Consequently, the challenges that the Fourth Industrial Revolution has established for the countries' educational system are (Frey and Osborne, 2017):

Firstly, the incorporation of the technological impact in the training path of the professionals required for this new context, which requires the incorporation of new curricular designs and relevant training programs that respond to these new economic, social and cultural needs. .

Secondly, it is necessary to analyze the impact of this transformation on the academic management of organizations in order to formulate proposals that allow innovation in both teaching and learning methodologies and in the professional performance of graduates.

And thirdly, promote the generation of new knowledge in a framework of social innovation in order to exercise a prospective vision of this transformation based on both positive and negative results that arise.

Based on the above, the postgraduate program faces the need to generate and implement educational programs that impact the social and economic development of countries, and that in turn meet the criteria of relevance, innovation, quality, inclusion and equity. .

In this way, the postgraduate program continues to play a fundamental role in the training of professionals, high-level specialists, scientists and researchers that the country demands. In this context, a priority is to ensure that they are functioning at the forefront of intellectual and scientific development (Mercado et al. 2016; Reyes, 2018).

Based on the above, the fundamental challenge for any country is to ensure that all its citizens have the appropriate skills for an increasingly digitalized and globalized world that allows both promoting inclusive labor markets and stimulating innovation, productivity and growth. Particularly, skills are needed: technical and professional skills, use of ICT for workers who manage digital infrastructures and the functioning of the digital ecosystem; soft skills such as leadership, communication and teamwork, required for the growing number of opportunities for collaborative work mediated by ICT (OECD, 2015; OECD, 2016a; Grundke et al., 2017).

To achieve this, educational systems are required to focus on anticipating changing skills needs to adapt the programs they offer to guide students toward options that lead to good results. Thus, it is not enough for workers to have skills necessary for the digital economy but employers must fully use these skills to deliver its benefits in terms of higher productivity and greater competitiveness (OECD, 2016b).

Also, it is necessary to promote the use of high-performance work practices such as teamwork, work autonomy, flexible training that allows promoting better organization and management of work within companies and throughout the economy, as well as promoting the necessary skills. to consolidate the organization (OECD, 2016c).

It has been recognized that the various social, economic, political and educational effects of the COVID-19 pandemic at the international and national level have influenced the environment of uncertainty, as well as altered the dynamics of organizations and people (Cabrera, 2020). .

In this sense, the COVID-19 pandemic has been classified as a phenomenon that has to be addressed, in addition to a crisis, also as an opportunity, which is why it is important to train human talent capable of living in a world of uncertainty to promote transformation. of the rigid and centralized operating strategies of institutions, which requires new methodological approaches for the development of fundamental competencies that allow sustainable organizational development in the new normal (Chehaibar, 2020).

Derived from the above, in the post-COVID era, one of the main objectives of organizations is to develop the learning capacity that ensures excellence. In the same way, in the digital era, characterized by technological advances, the importance of both technical and soft skills that allow both adapting, innovating and collaborating in the current work environment has increased (Loáiciga-Gutiérrez and Chanto-Espinoza, 2024).

Likewise, it implies the generation of organizational changes to integrate the digitalization of its processes, so to achieve this, a necessary condition to be implemented successfully is the formation of human capital. In this sense, Lokuge et al. (2019) indicate that it is necessary for the organization to identify the technological tools that can be adopted, developed and implemented effectively in its various processes. Thus, change depends on leadership to adapt to new requirements and technologies, which implies generating commitment among the members of the organization (Kurniawati et al., 2024; Haffar et al., 2023).

Therefore, the postgraduate level currently faces another fundamental challenge, which is the acquisition of technical and soft skills in an era dominated by technology where processes are being automated in different organizations.

Previously, UNESCO (2005) established that in the 21st century, competent people who understand their sociocultural and technological environment are required to be able to integrate creativity and innovation into their jobs in order to solve the various problems that arise in the organizations. Therefore, a new perspective on training for employment has been generated, focusing on the management of professional skills in relation to their development, linkage with the labor sector and decision making, so human talent is the fundamental element that allows generate innovative strategies in companies that allow them to respond to changing conditions in the markets, as well as promote not only economic but also comprehensive growth in organizations (UNESCO, 2010).

As anticipated by the OECD (2017) with respect to the formation of human capital that in the 21st century, skills are the key factor to achieve individual well-being and organizational success and the development of society, so without an investment In human talent, technological progress is not generated and therefore there is no economic and social growth, which is why countries do not develop.

In this way, students who access the postgraduate level need to acquire skills that allow them to adapt to a work environment in constant technological evolution, in addition to acquiring technical knowledge related to their discipline, as well as promoting relevant capabilities such as creativity, thinking. criticality and adaptability. However, it is important to recognize that a challenge to face is that society has become digitalized in such a way that it has caused personal interaction to be minimized in such a way that it is necessary to include others such as empathy, self-regulation and assertive communication .

As Arias (2020) mentions, the formation of soft skills in society is an important factor because they create awareness in people to promote empathy, collaboration and communication at an individual and organizational level. Their relevance in the digital era is because they impact the improvement of interpersonal relationships, which in the short and long term, impacts work productivity and the results obtained by the organization, which generates satisfaction in various areas.

Therefore, the challenge is to prepare professionals who know how to adapt to a digital society that demands both soft and technical skills, since this will enable human capital to have an optimal relationship with others, clients, competitors and suppliers, and with an attitude of service and adaptation to changes in both the environment and the organisation. It also implies that at the end of training at the postgraduate level, each graduate will have to face a work environment in which they will put into practice both their technical or specialised knowledge and their soft skills such as teamwork, emotional management, assertive communication, decision-making, conflict resolution, creativity and leadership.

As Araya-Fernández and Garita-González (2019) establish: It is imperative to continually update the education provided at the postgraduate level to the modern requirements and professional profile of each area of specialization to face the challenges of the digital economy. Thus, it is necessary that the postgraduate level promotes social competencies that strengthen leadership training that allows them to assume not only strategic positions in organizations but also foster an organizational climate ideal for the positioning of the organization and the well-being of its members (Herrera and Torres, 2020).

Thus, learning organizations are an integrated system in which members learn and can be implemented in action, which results in the generation of a culture oriented toward learning (Garvin et al., 2008). To achieve this, leadership that supports learning is required (Khan and Isameil, 2017). An organization that has a learning culture implies that it will be able to create, acquire, transfer knowledge and change its behavior to reflect new knowledge (Joo and Shim, 2010).

To achieve this, the health emergency caused disruptive changes in school organizations such as the use of digital tools to continue the academic training of students, as well as the implementation of digital teaching resources that supported the role of teachers combined with the design of emerging practices. that supported administrative processes through technological platforms. Thus, leadership competencies such as time management, synchronous and asynchronous communication, negotiation, inter and intrapersonal relationships, conflict resolution, emotional intelligence and ethical management have emerged.

The previous panorama implies the recognition of a new type of leadership called digital, which refers to the ability of a person to influence and direct others towards the achievement of common goals or objectives; motivate members of the organization to inspire the formation of innovative, creative and productive teams, which consequently improves the quality of the products and services offered by the organization (Arias et al., 2023).

In this way, the challenges of leading an organization are complex, so achieving success depends on the capabilities and leadership style developed by the manager, which are oriented toward the formation of work teams, problem solving, and establishing goals. inter- and intra-group relationships in an environment of cordiality, communication and integration of the various members of the organization (Sepúlveda and Aparicio, 2017).

Therefore, Harms et al. (2017); Ahn et al. (2018) confirm that leadership is a strategic factor that affects the successful achievement of organizational performance indicators, effectiveness in organizational processes and the achievement of results. It should be noted that leadership is not a generic element but is associated with the particular context in which it occurs (Zaccaro et al., 2018).

DISCUSSION

In the digital environment, organizations face a large amount of data that needs to be organized and analyzed to be used for making strategic decisions that allow not only profitability and growth but also positioning. In this sense, digital leadership is relevant due to its significance in information management and the promotion of a data-based culture (Arias et al., 2023).

According to Araujo et al. (2021), a digital leader has the ability to navigate and organize data in order to identify specific patterns and trends to make informed decisions.

For their part, He et al. (2019) establish that a digital leader has the ability to create a collaborative work environment characterized by diversity of thought to promote creativity and innovation through experimentation and implementation of technologies.

In this way, digital leadership is conceptualized as the ability to lead and manage both the skills and knowledge related to the effective management of digital technologies and tools to guide the organization and take Vdigital in constant change (Kahai et al., 2017) .

In this sense, digital leadership has become a strategic factor for organizational success in the era of technological transformation. Thus, a digital leader plays a fundamental role in facilitating the change and adoption of digital technologies in order to promote a data-driven culture, encourage collaboration, innovation and make informed decisions in a complex environment. In addition, it promotes motivation and belonging to the organization because members feel valued when working in an environment that is at the forefront of digital transformation (Davenport and Westerman, 2018).

The main characteristics of digital leadership are:

- Adaptation to change: Ability to recognize the constantly evolving environment and anticipate the consequences of technological changes for the organization.
- Technology management: Knowledge of the technological tools and platforms available to be applied in the organization in order to generate online collaborative work and asynchronous and synchronous communication.
- Remote Leadership: Ability to lead and manage teams remotely using technological tools to achieve the collaboration and efficiency necessary for organizational achievement.
- Strategic vision: Ability to formulate and implement a vision for the organization in a digital environment, anticipating opportunities and challenges for making informed decisions based on the identification and analysis of data.
- Digital competencies: Set of skills related to the management of tools such as cybersecurity, data analysis, blockchain, artificial intelligence to effectively manage the achievement of organizational goals in a digital environment.
- Innovation and learning: Capacity aimed at promoting a culture of innovation, collaboration and continuous learning in the organization based on the

technological tools available to improve not only productivity but permanence in the organization.

The above implies that digital leadership requires comprehensive training based on specific competencies such as adaptive capacity, emotional intelligence, strategic thinking and digital literacy. In this sense, the postgraduate course is the recommended training space to address the development of these skills.

To achieve digital leadership training at the postgraduate level, it is necessary to consider the concept of digital leadership literacies in higher education (DELLHE) by Arnold and Sangrà (2018). These authors establish that digital education is the mobilization of technology to support teaching and learning in the digital age. They also consider leadership as the process of social influence that aims to achieve common goals.

Particularly, the DELLHE has a set of dimensions that allow higher education leaders to address complex problems related to the integration of digital tools and which are shown in Figure 1.

Figure 1. Dimensions of the DELLHE framework (Based on Arnold and Sangr, 2018)

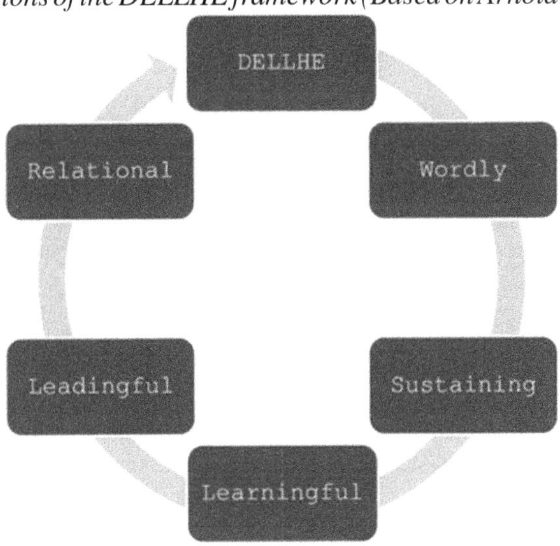

From Figure 1, five dimensions of the DELLHE framework are presented, the content of which is:

- Wordly: Values and culture; vision, policy and strategy; pedagogy and technology

- Sustaining: Human, environmental and financial impact of the choice of technologies
- Learningful: Leadership development and organizational learning
- Leadingful: Leadership behaviors, mindsets and attitudes that support digital transformation
- Relational: Interpersonal relationships and organizational dynamics

Therefore, leadership is multidimensional because it is a hybrid model that is made up of elements of authentic, transactional and transformational leadership (Prince, 2018). Likewise, Eberl and Drews (2021) establish that an integrated scale is necessary to investigate digital leadership practices. In this sense, Abbu et al. (2022) determined the main dimensions of digital leadership as those shown in Figure 2.

Figure 2. Dimensions of digital leadership (Based on Abbu et al., 2022)

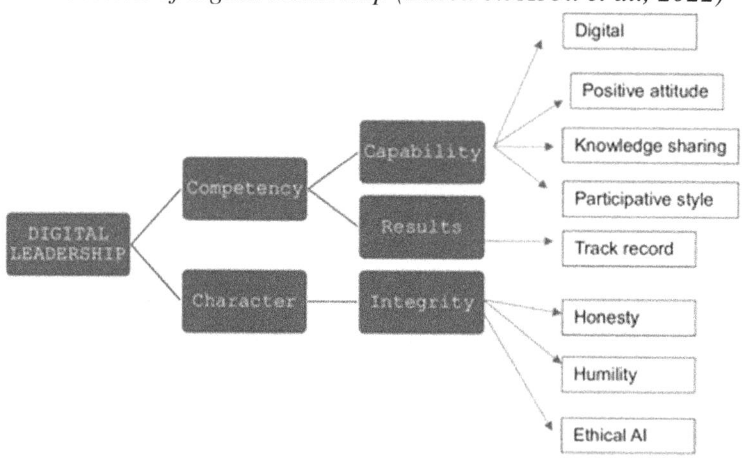

CONCLUSION

Since the era of globalization, organizations are focused on the professional skills of the human capital they have to face the workplace. Thus, it implies an accumulation not only of knowledge but also of attitudes in a state of constant updating, taking into account scientific and technological advances linked to the professional field.

For its part, the contemporary environment promotes the generation of knowledge through the incorporation and constant use of digital technologies, so graduates need to consider these challenges to include them in their academic training so that their graduates have a more fluid transition to the world. labor field by being equipped with the skills required to perform successfully. In addition, it will contribute to this human capital having the skills of critical thinking, collaborative work, creativity and problem solving that will allow them to position themselves in the workplace.

Digital leadership is a relevant component in the era of digital transformation due to technological evolution and the incorporation of digital tools in both personal and organizational life. Thus, its importance is that it allows both the success and sustainability of organizations in the 21st century.

In the context of the postgraduate level, the training of digital leaders is preponderant to achieve professionals trained to face the challenges of a digitalized and competitive environment.

The above is important because organizations have to be at the forefront, which implies the digitalization of their processes, which has generated advantages in terms of sustainability, time reduction and energy savings that have allowed them to achieve their strategic objectives.

ACKNOWLEDGMENT

This research was supported by the Instituto Politécnico Nacional, México [SIP number 20240865].

REFERENCES

Abbu, H., Mugge, P., Gudergan, G., Hoeborn, G., & Kwiatkowski, A. (2022). Measuring the Human Dimensions of Digital Leadership for Successful Digital Transformation. *Research Technology Management*, 65(3), 39–49. https://doi-org.bibliotecaipn.idm.oclc.org/10.1080/08956308.2022.2048588. DOI: 10.1080/08956308.2022.2048588

Ahn, J., Lee, S., & Yun, S. (2018). Leaders' core self-evaluation, ethical leadership, and employees' job performance: The moderating role of employees' exchange ideology. *Journal of Business Ethics*, 148(2), 457–470. DOI: 10.1007/s10551-016-3030-0

Anand, K., & Chellamani, K. (2021). Pedagogical challenges and neurocognition in education for the 21st Century. In Thomas, K. A., Kureethara, J. V., & Bhattacharyya, S. (Eds.), *Neuro-Systemic applications in learning* (pp. 179–201). Springer., DOI: 10.1007/978-3-030-72400-9_9

Araujo, S., & Balduzzi, M. (2010). Transformaciones culturales, organización del trabajo y posgraduación en las dinámicas laborales universitarias y extrauniversitarias. *Revista Argentina de Educación Superior*, 2, 134–151.

Araya-Fernández, E., & Garita-González, G. (2020). Habilidades blandas: Elementos para una visión holística en la formación de profesionales en informática. Trilogía. Ciencia. *Tecnología y Sociedad*, 12(23), 11–36. DOI: 10.22430/21457778.1614

Arias, J., & Rossetti, S. (2023). Evaluación del liderazgo digital en estudiantes universitarios. *Revista Vértice Universitario*, 25(94), 77–86. DOI: 10.36792/rvu.v25i94.77

Arias, L. A. (2020). *Desarrollo de habilidades blandas para la atención virtual de la Universidad El Bosque*. http://hdl.handle.net/10654/36787

Arnold, D., & Sangrà, A. (2018). Developing a framework of e-Leadership literacies for technologyEnhanced learning in higher education: A Delphi Study. In Duart, J. M., & Szucs, A. (Eds.), *Towards personalized guidance and support for learning. Proceedings of the 10th European distance and E-Learning network research workshop* (pp. 161–169). European Distance and E-learning Network., http://www.eden-online.org/wp-content/uploads/2018/11/RW10_2018_ Barcelona_Proceedings.pdf#page=169

Ashwin, P. (2020). *Transforming University education: A manifesto*. Bloomsbury Academic. DOI: 10.5040/9781350157279

Cabrera, L. (2020). Efectos del coronavirus en el Sistema educativo: Aumenta la desigualdad de oportunidades educativas en España. *Journal of Sociology of Education*, 13(2), 114–139. DOI: 10.7203/RASE.13.2.17125

Castaño, J., Redecker, C., Vuorikari, R., & Punie, Y. (2014). Open Education 2030: Planning the future of adult learning in Europe. *Open Learning*, 28(3), 171–186. DOI: 10.1080/02680513.2013.871199

Chehaibar, L. (2020). Flexibilidad curricular. Tensiones en tiempos de pandemia. En H. Casanova (Coord.), *Educación y pandemia. Una visión académica* (pp. 83-91). UNAM.

Chiu, W.-K. (2021). Pedagogy of Emerging Technologies in Chemical Education during the Era of Digitalization and Artificial Intelligence: A Systematic Review. *Education Sciences*, 11(11), 709. DOI: 10.3390/educsci11110709

Cohen, E. (2021). *The University and its boundaries*. Routledge. DOI: 10.4324/9781003102953

Coleman, G. (2016). *The next industry revolution will not be televised*. World Economic Forum. Retrieved from www.weforum.org/agenda/2016/01/the-next-industry-revolution-will-not-be-televised/

Dana, L.-P., Salamzadeh, A., Mortazavi, S., & Hadizadeh, M. (2022). Investigating the Impact of International Markets and New Digital Technologies on Business Innovation in Emerging Markets. *Sustainability (Basel)*, 14(2), 983. DOI: 10.3390/su14020983

Davenport, T. H., & Westerman, G. (2018). Why So Many High-Profile Digital Transformations Fail Harvard Business Review. https://hbr.org/2018/03/why-so-many-high-profile-digital-transformations-fail

de Araujo, L. M., Priadana, S., Paramarta, V., & Sunarsi, D. (2021). Digital leadership in business organizations: An overview. *International Journal of Educational Administration, Management, and Leadership*, 2(1), 45–56. DOI: 10.51629/ijeamal.v2i1.18

Drucker, P. (1992). *Post-capitalist Society*. Butterworth-Heinemann.

Eberl, J., & Drews, P. (2021). *Digital leadership–Mountain or molehill? A Literature Review*. 16th International Conference on WirtschaftsinformatikAt: Duisburg & Essen, Germany. DOI: 10.1007/978-3-030-86800-0_17

Espino-Díaz, L., Fernandez-Caminero, G., Hernandez-Lloret, C.-M., Gonzalez-Gonzalez, H., & Alvarez-Castillo, J.-L. (2020). Analyzing the Impact of COVID-19 on Education Professionals. Toward a Paradigm Shift: ICT and Neuroeducation as a Binomial of Action. *Sustainability (Basel)*, 12(14), 5646. DOI: 10.3390/su12145646

Espinosa, M. (2022). Hacia la e-Universidad del siglo XXI: el impacto de la digitalización en la formación superior. Revista RUEDA, 7. https://cedu.es/revista-rued/

Frey, C., & Osborne, M. (2017). The future of employment: How susceptible are Jobs to computerization? *Technological Forecasting and Social Change*, 114, 254–280. DOI: 10.1016/j.techfore.2016.08.019

Gallifa, J., & Sangrà, A. (2021). Transformar la Universidad. Desafíos, oportunidades y propuestas desde una mirada global. Barcelona: Editorial UOC. http://hdl.handle.net/10609134926

Grundke, R., Squicciarini, M., Jamet, S., & Kalamova, M. (2017). *Having the right mix: the role of skill bundles for comparative advantage and industry performance in GVCs*. OECD Publishing., DOI: 10.1787/518151965

Haffar, M., Al-Hyari, K., Djebarni, R., Alnsour, J. A., Oster, F., Al-Shamali, A., & Alaya, A. (2023). The mediating effect of affective commitment to change in the readiness for change–TQM relationship. *Total Quality Management & Business Excellence*, 34(3–4), 326–344. DOI: 10.1080/14783363.2022.2054695

Harms, P. D., Cred, M., Tynan, M., Leon, M., & Jeung, W. (2017). Leadership and stress: A meta-analytic review. *The Leadership Quarterly*, 28(1), 178–194. DOI: 10.1016/j.leaqua.2016.10.006

He, W., Yu, S., Yu, T., & Wang, C. (2019). The effect of digital leadership on knowledge sharing and creativity: The mediating roles of innovative self-efficacy and intrinsic motivation. *Information & Management*, 56(8), 103175.

Herrera, C. A. H., & Torres, J. C. N. (2020). Las habilidades blandas en estudiantes de ingeniería de tres instituciones públicas de educación superior. *RIDE Revista Iberoamericana para la Investigación y el Desarrollo Educativo*, 10(20), 20. Advance online publication. DOI: 10.23913/ride.v10i20.678

Kahai, S., Avolio, B. J., & Sosik, J. J. (2017). E-Leadership. In Hertel, G., Stone, D. L., Johnson, R. D., & Passmore, J. (Eds.), *The Wiley Blackwell Handbook of the Psychology of the Internet at Work*., DOI: 10.1002/9781119256151.ch14

Kurniawati, D. T., Fernando, Y., & Dzil Ikhram, W. (2024). Financial technology readiness for Shariah-compliant banking services: Post–merger perspectives. *Journal of Islamic Marketing*, 15(6), 1651–1671. DOI: 10.1108/JIMA-08-2023-0236

Loáiciga-Gutiérrez, J., & Chanto-Espinoza, C. (2024). Desarrollo de habilidades blandas en la formación universitaria en la era digital. *Revista Multidisciplinaria Perspectivas Investigativas*, 4(3), 2–11. DOI: 10.62574/rmpi.v4i3.150

Lokuge, S., Sedera, D., Grover, V., & Dongming, X. (2019). Organizational readiness for digital innovation: Development and empirical calibration of a construct. *Information & Management*, 56(3), 445–461. DOI: 10.1016/j.im.2018.09.001

Mercado, Cernas y Nava (2016): Mercado, P. Cernas, D. y Nava, R. La Interdisciplinariedad Económico-Administrativa en la Conformación de una Comunidad Científica y la Formación de Investigadores. *Revista de la Educación Superior*, XLV (177), 43 – 65.

Moreira-Choez, J. S., Lamus de Rodríguez, T. M., Olmedo-Cañarte, P. A., & Macías-Macías, J. D. (2024). Valorando el futuro de la educación: Competencias Digitales y Tecnologías de Información y Comunicación en Universidades. *Revista Venezolana de Gerencia*, 29(105), 271–288. DOI: 10.52080/rvgluz.29.105.18

OCDE. (2015). *OECD Science, Technology and Industry Scoreboard 2015*. OECD., DOI: 10.1787/sti_scoreboard-2015-

OCDE. (2016a). *Skills for a Digital World: 2016 Ministerial Meeting on the Digital Economy Background Report*. OECD., DOI: 10.1787/5jlwz83z3wnw-

OECD. (2016b). *Getting Skills Right: Anticipating and Responding to Changing Skill Needs*. OECD Publishing., DOI: 10.1787/9789264252073-

OECD. (2016c). *New Markets and New Jobs*. OECD Publishing., DOI: 10.1787/5jlwt496h37l-

OECD. (2017). *Diagnóstico de la OCDE sobre la Estrategia de Competencias, Destrezas y Habilidades de México*. Resumen Ejecutivo. México: OECD. Recuperado de https://www.oecd.org/mexico/Diagnostico-de-la-OCDE-sobre-la-Estrategia-de-Competencias-Destrezas-y-Habilidades-de-Mexico-Resumen-Ejecutivo.pdf

Organización de las Naciones Unidas para la Educación, la Ciencia y la Cultura (UNESCO, 2005). *Educación para todos: el imperativo de la calidad. Informe de Seguimiento de Educación para Todos en el Mundo*. París: UNESCO.

Organización de las Naciones Unidas para la Educación, la Ciencia y la Cultura (UNESCO, 2010). *Desafíos de la educación*. Buenos Aires: IIPE-UNESCO. https://bit.ly/2W7k2wY

Peña Miguel, N., Corral Lage, J., & Mata Galindez, A. (2020). Assessment of the Development of Professional Skills in University Students: Sustainability and Serious Games. *Sustainability (Basel)*, 12(3), 1014. DOI: 10.3390/su12031014

Pinargote-Macías, E. I., Vega Intriago, J. O., Moreira Choez, J. S., & Díaz Macías, T. M. (2022). Competencias del docente universitario en tiempos de pandemia. *Revista Venezolana de Gerencia, 27*(Edición Especial 7), 347–359. https://doi.org/ DOI: 10.52080/rvgluz.27.7.23

Prendes-Espinosa, M. P., & Cerdán Cartagena, F. (2021). Tecnologías avanzadas para afrontar el reto de la innovación educativa. *RIED Revista Iberoamericana de Educación a Distancia*, 24(1), 35–53. DOI: 10.5944/ried.24.1.28415

Prince, K. A. (2018). *Digital Leadership: Transitioning into the Digital Age*. James Cook University.

Reyes, G. (2018). Análisis comparativo de programas de Maestría en Tecnología Educativa, tendencias actuales en la formación de futuros profesionistas. *International Journal of Information Systems and Software Engineering for Big Companies*, 5(2), 29–40.

Scott, C. (2015). El futuro del aprendizaje2 ¿Qué tipo de aprendizaje se necesita en el siglo XXI? Investigación y Prospectiva en Educación, 14, 1-19. https://unesdoc.unesco.org/ark:/48223/pf0000242996_spa

Sepúlveda, F., & Aparicio, C. (2017). El desafío de los directores de escuelas chilenas: Liderando a partir de un enfoque instruccional hacia un enfoque distribuido. Revista Gestión de la Educación, 7(2), 1-19. https://revistas.ucr.ac.cr/index.php/gestedu

Torres, D., & Prieto, J. (2014). Posgrados: Visión y percepción en la Universidad Pedagógica y Tecnológica de Colombia. *Revista Historia de la Educación Latinoamericana*, 16(22), 249–273. DOI: 10.19053/01227238.2720

Velásquez, O. (2019). La 4RI. Como parte de la reflexión universitaria. *Pensamiento Universitario,* 29, 2. https://ascun.org.co/uploads/default/publications/5aeee20947a9b5676665ca2a7d4f286d.pdf

World Economic Forum. [WEF]. (2017). *Project Plan Overview: 21st Century Curriculum Project.* Sydney, Australia: World Economic Forum.

World Economic Forum. (WEF, 2018). *Temas claves de la agenda global.* https://toplink.weforum.org/knowledge/insight/a1Gb0000000LPFfEAO/explore/summary

Ynzunza, C., Izar, J., Bocarando, J., Aguilar, F., & Larios, M. (2017). El Entorno de la Industria 4.0: Implicaciones y Perspectivas Futuras. *Conciencia Tecnológica*, 54, 86-98. Retrieved from https://www.redalyc.org/jatsRepo/944/94454631006/94454631006.pdf

ADDITIONAL READING

Anwar, J., & Abadi, F. (2023). Transformational leadership, knowledge sharing, and innovation capability: Improving the performance of MSME organizations in East Nusa Tenggara province. [IIJSE]. *Indonesian Interdisciplinary Journal of Sharia Economics*, 6(3), 1894–1920. DOI: 10.31538/iijse.v6i3.3423

Arafah, B., & Hasyim, M. (2023). Digital literacy: The right solution to overcome the various problems of meaning and communication on social media. *Studies in Media and Communication*, 11(4), 19–30. DOI: 10.11114/smc.v11i4.6003

Canossa-Montes de Oca and Peraza-Villareal, N. (2024). Human talent management in the era of artificial intelligence: challenges and opportunities in the work environment. Digital Publisher CEIT, 9(1), 302-319. https://doi.org/DOI: 10.33386/593dp.2024.1.2170

Jacociunas, T., Renato, J., & Marlon, J. (2024). Digital transformation of higher education institutions: A framework for strategic decision making. *International Journal of Higher Education*, 10, 1–26.

Kurniasari, F., Lestari, E. D., & Tannady, H. (2023). Pursuing long-term business performance: Investigating the effects of financial and technological factors on digital adoption to leverage SME performance and business sustainability-evidence from Indonesian SMEs in the traditional market. *Sustainability (Basel)*, 15(16), 1–20. DOI: 10.3390/su151612668

Masyhuri, S., Sudiro, A., Palupi Prabandari, S., & Tri Kurniawati, D. (2024). The effect of human capital on organizational performance in the service industry 4.0: Mediation analysis from Indonesia. *Problems and Perspectives in Management*, 22(1), 418–431. DOI: 10.21511/ppm.22(1).2024.34

Mumtaz, S., Selvarajah, C., & Meyer, D. (2024). How does human relations climate and organizational support affect readiness to change? The mediating role of employee participation and leadership excellence. *Global Business and Organizational Excellence*, 43(2), 79–91. DOI: 10.1002/joe.22223

Ojobo, C. A., Orga, C. C., & Okechukwu, E. U. (2023). Impact of digital literacy on the performance of Small-scale business in Enugu State. Advance Journal of Business and Entrepreneurship Development, 7(1), 57–78. https://aspjournals.org/ajbed/index.php/ajbed

Pertiwi, W., Setyawati, S. M., & Anggraeni, A. I. (2023). Transformational Leadership, Digital Literacy, Propensity to Trust, and Creativity of MSMEs: Mediating Effects of Knowledge Sharing. *The Journal of Behavioral Science*, 18(3), 83–100. https://so06.tci-thaijo.org/index.php/IJBS/article/view/266619

Turanin, V., & Posokhova, Y. (2024). The impact of digital transformation on society and the right to education. Interaction and Perspective. *Journal of Social Work : JSW*, 14(1), 211–220.

KEY TERMS AND DEFINITIONS

Artificial intelligence: Simulation of cognitive processes that are usually associated with human intelligence, corresponding to computer systems designed to interact with the world through functionalities (such as visual perception and voice recognition) and intelligent behaviors that we conceive as essentially human (for example, evaluate the available information and act in the most sensible way to achieve a certain objective).

Augmented reality: Use of technology that complements the perception and interaction with the real world and allows the student to superimpose a layer of information on reality, thus providing richer and more immersive learning experiences.

Competence: Ability that the person has in being, knowing and knowing how to do in real situations, before a new task, to solve problems, make decisions and develop projects, from an entrepreneurial and managerial vision.

Fourth Industrial Revolution: it is identified as the digital interconnection of people, machines and objects that offers immense possibilities of increasing production efficiency to individuals, companies and nations.

Internet of things: Interconnection of everyday objects with the Internet so it uses objects equipped with embedded processors or sensors that are capable of transmitting information through the network. These connections allow remote administration, status monitoring, tracking and alerts.

Endnote

1 This research was supported by the Instituto Politécnico Nacional, México [SIP number 20240865].

Compilation of References

Abarca, S. (2001). Psicología de la motivación. San José, Costa Rica: EUNED. Ajello, A. M. (2003). La motivación para aprender. En C. Pontecorvo (Coord.), Manual de psicología de la educación (pp. 251-271). España: Popular. Alonso, J. (1992). ¿Qué es lo mejor para motivar a mis alumnos? Madrid: Universidad Autónoma/Instituto de Ciencias de la Educación

Abbu, H., Mugge, P., Gudergan, G., Hoeborn, G., & Kwiatkowski, A. (2022). Measuring the Human Dimensions of Digital Leadership for Successful Digital Transformation. *Research Technology Management*, 65(3), 39–49. https://doi-org.bibliotecaipn.idm.oclc.org/10.1080/08956308.2022.2048588. DOI: 10.1080/08956308.2022.2048588

Aceves-Ávila, C. (2013). La dimensión transversal de la sostenibilidad en el currículo de instituciones de educación superior: una propuesta innovadora obligada. *Educación superior, gestión, innovación e internacionalización*, 978-84-370-9177-8, 71-92 https://books.google.com.mx/books?id=xBZ2AwAAQBAJypg=PT4&dq=Hern%C3%A1ndez+Casta%C3%B1eda+Rosario&hl=es&sa=X&redir_esc=y#v=onepage&q&f=true

Acosta, G., Guillermo, J., & González, G. Máryuri. (2022). Evaluation by competencies in the training process. Cuban Journal of Higher Education, 41(2). Epub May 10, 2022.http://scielo.sld.cu/scielo.php?script=sci_arttext&pid=S025743142022000200022&lng=es&tlng=es

Acosta, A. (2020). *El Buen Vivir: Sumak Kawsay una oportunidad para imaginar otros mundos*. Icaria.

Adobe. (2024). *¿Qué es la realidad virtual? Explicación de la realidad virtual.* https://www.adobe.com/mx/products/substance3d/discover/what-is-vr.html

Ahmad, S., & Wahid, N. A. (2019). Digital leadership, social media competence, and decision-making quality among school leaders in Malaysia. *International Journal of Leadership in Education*, 22(3), 333–348. DOI: 10.1080/13603124.2018.1450998

Ahn, J., Lee, S., & Yun, S. (2018). Leaders' core self-evaluation, ethical leadership, and employees' job performance: The moderating role of employees' exchange ideology. *Journal of Business Ethics*, 148(2), 457–470. DOI: 10.1007/s10551-016-3030-0

Ainscow, M. (2020). Promoting inclusion and equity in education: Lessons from international experiences. *Prospects*, 49, 9–21. DOI: 10.1007/s11125-020-09495-8

Ajello, A. M. (2003). La motivación para aprender. En C. Pontecorvo (Coord.), Manual de psicología de la educación (pp. 251-271). España: Popular. Alonso, J. (1992). ¿Qué es lo mejor para motivar a mis alumnos? Madrid: Universidad Autónoma/Instituto de Ciencias de la Educación

Ajunwa, I., Crawford, K., & Schultz, J. (2017). Limitless worker surveillance. *California Law Review*, 105, 735.

Aleven, V.. (2024). *AI-adaptive tutoring in educational diversity*. Carnegie Mellon University.

Aleven, V., McLaughlin, E., Glenn, R. M., & Koedinger, K. R. (2016). Intelligent tutoring systems. *International Journal of Artificial Intelligence in Education*, 26(1), 150–166.

Alonso, J. (1992). *Qué es lo mejor para motivar a mis alumnos?* Universidad Autónoma/Instituto de Ciencias de la Educación.

Altbach, P. G., & Peterson, P. M. (2023). *Global Perspectives on Higher Education*. Routledge.

Alvarado, O. (1999). *Gestión Educativa*. Universidad de Lima. Fondo de Desarrollo Editorial.

Amador, M., Torres, G., & Lagunes, D. (2023). Problem-based learning for the development of competencies in students. *Revisión sistemática de literatura.RECEIN*, 15(59), 131–166. DOI: 10.26457/recein.v15i59.3491

Amankwah-Amoah, J., Khan, Z., Wood, G., & Knight, G. (2021). COVID-19 and digitalization: The great acceleration. *Journal of Business Research*, 136, 602–611. DOI: 10.1016/j.jbusres.2021.08.011 PMID: 34538980

Améstica – Abarca. José Manuel. (2024). Liderazgo escolar inclusivo: estado del arte sobre un concepto ambiguo. Revista Caribeña de Investigación Educativa. https://revistas.isfodosu.edu.do/index.php/recie/article/view/663#:~:text=La%20literatura%20muestra%20que%20los,fen%C3%B3meno%20en%20el%20contexto%20chileno

Anand, K., & Chellamani, K. (2021). Pedagogical challenges and neurocognition in education for the 21st Century. In Thomas, K. A., Kureethara, J. V., & Bhattacharyya, S. (Eds.), *Neuro-Systemic applications in learning* (pp. 179–201). Springer., DOI: 10.1007/978-3-030-72400-9_9

Anderson, B. (2024). *Dominar el liderazgo.* Leadership circle. https://leadershipcircle.com/wp-content/uploads/2024/01/Mastering-Leadership_2023-09_LATAM.pdf

Anguita, R., & Ruiz, I. (2018). Identidades mediáticas en la sociedad aumentada: las tecno-biografías como estrategia de investigación etnográfica. Madrid: Morata-. *Ecologías de Aprendizaje: Educación Expandida en Contextos Múltiples*, 19, 9–26. DOI: 10.17398/1695-288X.19.1.139

Aranda, G., & Salinas, S. (2013). *Bolívar según Chávez, Ensayo de una tendencia.* RIL Editores.

Araujo, S., & Balduzzi, M. (2010). Transformaciones culturales, organización del trabajo y posgraduación en las dinámicas laborales universitarias y extrauniversitarias. *Revista Argentina de Educación Superior*, 2, 134–151.

Araya-Fernández, E., & Garita-González, G. (2020). Habilidades blandas: Elementos para una visión holística en la formación de profesionales en informática. Trilogía. Ciencia. *Tecnología y Sociedad*, 12(23), 11–36. DOI: 10.22430/21457778.1614

Arbuthnott, K. (2009). Education for sustainable development beyond attitude change. *International Journal of Sustainability in Higher Education*, 10(2), 152–163. DOI: 10.1108/14676370910945954

Arévalo, J., & Juanes, B. (2022). La formación de competencias desde el contexto latinoamericano. *Revista Universidad y Sociedad,* 14(1), 517-523. http://scielo.sld.cu/scielo.php?script=sci_arttext&pid=S2218-36202022000100517&lng=es&tlng=es

Arias, L. A. (2020). *Desarrollo de habilidades blandas para la atención virtual de la Universidad El Bosque*. http://hdl.handle.net/10654/36787

Arias, J., & Rossetti, S. (2023). Evaluación del liderazgo digital en estudiantes universitarios. *Revista Vértice Universitario*, 25(94), 77–86. DOI: 10.36792/rvu.v25i94.77

Aristóteles. (1999). *Ética a Nicómaco (Trans. de A. Zozaya)*. Ediciones Akal.

Arnold, D., & Sangrà, A. (2018). Developing a framework of e-Leadership literacies for technologyEnhanced learning in higher education: A Delphi Study. In Duart, J. M., & Szucs, A. (Eds.), *Towards personalized guidance and support for learning. Proceedings of the 10th European distance and E-Learning network research workshop* (pp. 161–169). European Distance and E-learning Network., http://www.eden-online.org/wp-content/uploads/2018/11/RW10_2018_ Barcelona_Proceedings.pdf#page=169

Arras-Vota, A., Bordas-Beltrán, J., Porras-Flores, D., & Gómez-Ramírez, J. (2021). Competencias en tecnologías de información y comunicación. Estudios de caso: Universidad Santo Tomas (Colombia) y Universidad Autónoma de Chihuahua (México). *Formación Universitaria*, 14(1), 1. DOI: 10.4067/S0718-50062021000100135

Ashwin, P. (2020). *Transforming University education: A manifesto*. Bloombsbury Academic. DOI: 10.5040/9781350157279

Audisio, M., Rueda, M., & Rodríguez, R. (2021). Uso de aplicaciones de gestión de proyectos como herramientas de apoyo, en espacios académicos de las instituciones de educación superior. *Revista Difusiones*, 21(2), 148–162.

Avalos, C. (2016). *How does communication work?* Vivir Es Aprender.

Avolio, B. J., & Yammarino, F. J. (Eds.). (2013). Introduction to, and overview of, transformational and charismatic leadership. In *Transformational and charismatic leadership: The road ahead 10th anniversary edition* (pp. xxvii-xxxiii). Emerald Group Publishing Limited.Daft, R. L. (2021). *The Leadership Experience* (8a ed.). Cengage Learning. DOI: 10.1108/S1479-357120130000005005

Avolio, B. J., & Gardner, W. L. (2005). Authentic leadership development: Getting to the root of positive forms of leadership. *The Leadership Quarterly*, 16(3), 315–338. DOI: 10.1016/j.leaqua.2005.03.001

Avolio, B. J., & Gibbons, T. C. (2020). Developing authentic leaders for the digital era. In Antonakis, J., & Day, D. V. (Eds.), *The Nature of Leadership* (3rd ed., pp. 474–494). SAGE Publications.

Avolio, B. J., & Kahai, S. (2003). Adding the "e" to e-leadership: How it may impact your leadership. *Organizational Dynamics*, 31(4), 325–338. DOI: 10.1016/S0090-2616(02)00133-X

Avolio, B. J., Sosik, J. J., Kahai, S., & Baker, B. (2014). E-leadership: Re-examining transformations in leadership source and transmission. *The Leadership Quarterly*, 25(1), 105–131. DOI: 10.1016/j.leaqua.2013.11.003

Azienda Comunale Elettricità e Acque. (2018). Human capital development and communications. *Human Capital Development and Communications.*http://sostenibilita2018.gruppo.acea.it/en/relation-whit-stakeholders/personnel/human-capital-development-and-communications

Bailenson, J. (2018). *Experience on Demand: What Virtual Reality Is, How It Works, and What It Can Do*. W. W. Norton & Company.

Bailenson, J. (2023). Virtual reality in education: Promises and pitfalls. *Harvard Educational Review*, 93(2), 145–170.

Ballesteros, L. (2021). Implementación y práctica de scrum en la asignatura de formulación y evaluación de proyectos en la facultad de ciencias económicas y administrativas de la Universidad El Bosque. *Panorama*, 15(29), 7. DOI: 10.15765/pnrm.v15i29.2538

Bandura, A. (1997). *Self-efficacy: The exercise of control* [Auto-eficacia: El ejercicio de control]. W. H. Freeman Scoot.

Banks, J. A. (2007). *Educating Citizens in a Multicultural Society*. Teachers College Press.

Banks, J. A. (2023). *Diversity, Equity, and Inclusion in Digital Education*. Teachers College Press.

Barrientos, C., Silva, P. & Antúnez, S. (2016). El papel directivo y la promoción de la participación de las familias y la comunidad en las escuelas básicas. El caso de la Comuna de Panguipulli-Chile. REICE. *Revista Iberoamericana sobre Calidad. Eficacia y Cambio en Educación*,

Bass, B. M., & Riggio, R. E. (2006). *Transformational leadership*. Psychology Press. DOI: 10.4324/9781410617095

Bass, B. M., & Stogdill, R. M. (1990). *Bass & Stogdill's Handbook of Leadership: Theory, Research, and Managerial Applications*. Free Press.

Bellamy, F. X. (2021). Transmission crisis and innovation fever. *Teoría de la Educación.Revista Interuniversitaria*, 33(2), 1–10. DOI: 10.14201/teri.25407

Beltrán Torres, J. A., Corral Trujillo, E., & Cristerna González, R. D. (2023). Características, aptitudes y habilidades que un programador debe tener al ingresar en el campo laboral. *Revista Digital de Tecnologías Informáticas y Sistemas*, 7(1), 27–34. DOI: 10.61530/redtis.vol7.n1.2023.156.27-34

Benkler, Y. (2021). *The Wealth of Networks: How Social Production Transforms Markets and Freedom* (2nd ed.). Yale University Press.

Bergmann, J., & Sams, A. (2024). *Flipped Learning: Gateway to Student Engagement* (3rd ed.). International Society for Technology in Education.

Berlanga Ramírez, Ma. de la Luz, & Juárez-Hernández, Luis Gibran. (2020). Evaluation paradigms: from traditional to socio-formative. Dialogues on education. Current topics in educational research, 11(21), 00017. Epub March 03, 2021.DOI: 10.32870/dse.v0i21.646

Bermejo, R. (2014). *Del desarrollo sostenible según Brundtland a la sostenibilidad como biomimesis*. Recovered from http://publicaciones.hegoa.ehu.es/publications/315

Biasutti, M., De Baz, T., & Alshawa, H. (2016). Assessing the Infusion of Sustainability Principles into University Curricula. *Journal of Teacher Education for Sustainability*, 18(2), 21–40. https://intapi.sciendo.com/pdf/10.1515/jtes-2016-0012. DOI: 10.1515/jtes-2016-0012

Biesta, G. (2022). *World-Centered Education: A View for the Present*. Routledge.

Biesta, G. (2023). *The Beautiful Risk of Education* (2nd ed.). Routledge.

Bisquerra, R. (2000). *Educación emocional y bienestar*. CISSPRAXIS.

Blas-Rivera, M. J., Cardoso-Espinosa, E. O., & Nava-Meléndez, E. D. (2023). School leadership models during the pandemic to face the post-covid era. *Revista Iberoamericana para la Investigación y el Desarrollo Educativo RIDE*, 14(27), e571. DOI: 10.23913/ride.v14i27.1713

Bolman, L., & Terrence, E. (1995). *Leadership perspectives considered by Bolman and Deal.* Recuperado de https://www.redalyc.org/pdf/993/99326637004.pdf

Bonnet, D., & Westerman, G. (2021). The New Elements of Digital Transformation. *MIT Sloan Management Review*, 62(2), 82–89.

Booth, T., & Ainscow, M. (2011). Index for inclusion: Developing learning and participation in schools. Bristol: Centre for Studies on Inclusive Education (CSIE).

Booth, T., & Ainscow, M. (2005). *Index for inclusion*. Centre for Studies on Inclusive Education.

Bormann, A. (1931). *Der Deustche im Fremdenverkehr des Europaischen Auslands.* Citado en 5, Sociología del Turismo (Hans Joachin Knebel) Hispano Europea.

Bosco, F. A., Aguinis, H., Singh, K., Field, J. G., & Pierce, C. A. (2015). Correlational effect size benchmarks. *The Journal of Applied Psychology*, 100(2), 431–449. DOI: 10.1037/a0038047 PMID: 25314367

Botía, B., & Antonio, C. R. K. García – Garnica, Marina. (2017) 25 (95) 01-24. *Evaluación multidimensional del liderazgo pedagógico: claves para la mejora escolar.*https://www.redalyc.org/journal/3995/399550706009/html/

Brynjolfsson, E., & McAfee, A. (2014). *The Second Machine Age: Work, Progress, and Prosperity in a Time of Brilliant Technologies.* W. W. Norton & Company.

Bueno-de la Fuente, C., & De la Fuente-Anuncibay, R. (2024). El contexto laboral y género, diferenciadores del estilo de liderazgo [Work context and gender, differentiators of leadership styleWork context and gender, differentiators of leadership style]. *European Public & Social Innovation Review*, 9, 1–17. DOI: 10.31637/epsir-2024-420

Caamaño, F., Sanmamed, M., & Carril, P. (2018). El desarrollo de las ecologías de aprendizaje a través de las herramientas en línea. *Revista Diálogo Educacional*, 18(56), 128–148. DOI: 10.7213/1981-416X.18.056.DS06

Cabrera, L. (2020). Efectos del coronavirus en el Sistema educativo: Aumenta la desigualdad de oportunidades educativas en España. *Journal of Sociology of Education*, 13(2), 114–139. DOI: 10.7203/RASE.13.2.17125

Cabrero, BG (2018). Socio-emotional, non-cognitive or "soft" skills: approaches to their assessment. Digital university journal, 19(6).

Cabrero, G., & Benilde, L. R. Anisai. (2024). The evaluation of competencies in higher education: traditional approaches and innovative strategies. https://cuaed.unam.mx/publicaciones/libro-evaluacion/pdf/Capitulo-37- EVALUATION-OF-COMPETENCES-IN-HIGHER-EDUCATION.pdf

Camacho Marín, R. J., Castro González, A. E., Zurita Minango, A. V., Zabala Maya, I. G., Villota Palacios, M., & Villarreal Guerrero, Z. T. (2024). Innovaciones en la administración educativa: Efectos del liderazgo efectivo en el logro de metas educativas y el desarrollo estudiantil. *Emergentes -. Revista Científica (Maracaibo)*, 4(2), 739–753. DOI: 10.60112/erc.v4i2.185

Camacho, A. M. P., & Ceja, M. S. (2022). The importance of emotional intelligence in primary education. *Strategic Training*, 6(02), 60–75.

Campuzano, J. (2024, June 28). ¡Se cae app de BBVA en viernes de quincena! Usuarios reportan fallas. *El Excelsior*. https://www.excelsior.com.mx/nacional/fallas-bbva-app-hoy-28-junio-2024/1659938

Candi, M., Melia, M., & Colurcio, M. (2020). Two birds with one stone: The quest for addressing both business goals and social needs with innovation. *Journal of Business Ethics*, 160(4), 1019–1033. DOI: 10.1007/s10551-018-3853-y

Cano, E. (2015). Teacher Training. *Journal of Curriculum and Teacher Training*, 19(2), 265–280.

Carrazana, V. (2002). The concept of mental health in humanistic-existential psychology. *AJAYU Órgano de Difusión Del Departamento de Psicología*, 1, 19.

CASEL. (2017). SEL Discussion Series for Parents and Caregivers. Supporting Parents and Caregivers with Social and Emotional Learning. http://www.casel.org/wpcontent/uploads/2017/11/CASELCaregiverGuide_English.pdf

Castaño, J., Redecker, C., Vuorikari, R., & Punie, Y. (2014). Open Education 2030: Planning the future of adult learning in Europe. *Open Learning*, 28(3), 171–186. DOI: 10.1080/02680513.2013.871199

Castells, M. (2021). *The Rise of the Network Society* (3rd ed.). Wiley-Blackwell.

Castells, M. (2022). Digital education networks: A case study of Barcelona's "Schools in Network" project. *Journal of Education Policy*, 37(3), 321–340.

Cegos (2023). *Liderazgo digital, clave para el éxito en la era digital.* Recovered from https://www.cegoslatam.com/actualidades/liderazgo-digital

Cerezo, M. T., & Casanova, P. F. (2004). Diferencias de género en la motivación académica de los alumnos de educación secundaria obligatoria. Revista Electrónica de Investigación Psicoeducativa, 2(1), 97-112. Departamento de Psicología, Universidad de Jaén, España. Consultado el 24 de enero de 2008, de: http://www.investigacionpsicopedagogica.org/revista/ articulos/3/espannol/Art_3_31.pdf

Chávez, N. (2022). Education for Digital Transformation. Recovered from https://www.ift.org.mx/transformacion-digital/blog/educacion-para-la-transformacion-digital

Chávez, J., Montaño, R., & Barrera, R. (2016). Structure and content of messages in an online environment: An approach from participation. *Computers in Human Behavior*, 54(1), 560–568. DOI: 10.1016/j.chb.2015.08.046

Chávez-Márquez, I., Ordóñez, A., & Flores, C. (2023). Digital skills in university students through educational innovations: A review of current literature. *Apertura (Guadalajara, Jal.)*, 15(2), 74–87. DOI: 10.32870/Ap.v15n2.2398

Chehaibar, L. (2020). Flexibilidad curricular. Tensiones en tiempos de pandemia. En H. Casanova (Coord.), *Educación y pandemia. Una visión académica* (pp. 83-91). UNAM.

Chen, L., Johnson, D. J., & Smith, S. (2023). *Educational Technology in Higher Education: Current Trends and Future Directions.* Springer.

Chiu, W.-K. (2021). Pedagogy of Emerging Technologies in Chemical Education during the Era of Digitalization and Artificial Intelligence: A Systematic Review. *Education Sciences*, 11(11), 709. DOI: 10.3390/educsci11110709

Christensen, C. M., Horn, M. B., & Johnson, C. W. (2016). *Disrupting Class: How Disruptive Innovation Will Change the Way the World Learns*. McGraw-Hill Education.

Cifuentes-Medina, E., González-Pulido, W., & González-Pulido, A. (2020). Effects of school leadership on learning. *Revista Panorama*, 14(26), 78–93. DOI: 10.15765/pnrm.v14i26.1482

Cloud, G. (2024). *What is Artificial Intelligence (AI)?*https://cloud.google.com/learn/what-is-artificial-intelligence?hl=en

Cobeñas, P., & Grimaldi, V. (2021). Discusiones sobre inclusión educativa: una perspectiva desde la educación inclusiva. In Cobeñas, P., Grimaldi, V., Broitman, C., Sancha, I., & Escobar, M. (Eds.), *La enseñanza de las matemáticas a alumnos con discapacidad* (pp. 104–162). UDULP.

Cohen, E. (2021). *The University and its boundaries*. Routledge. DOI: 10.4324/9781003102953

Colbert, A., Yee, N., & George, G. (2016). The digital workforce and the workplace of the future: Implications for organizational behavior. *The Academy of Management Perspectives*, 30(3), 1–17. DOI: 10.5465/amp.2015.0072

Coleman, G. (2016). *The next industry revolution will not be televised*. World Economic Forum. Retrieved from www.weforum.org/agenda/2016/01/the-next-industry-revolution-will-not-be-televised/

Collet-Sabe, J. (2020). Las relaciones entre la escuela y las familias desde una perspectiva democrática: Ejes de análisis y propuestas para la equidad. *Educar*, 56(1), 241–258. DOI: 10.5565/rev/educar.1012

Constitución Política de los Estados Unidos Mexicanos que reforma la de 5 de febrero de 1857. Art. 3°, Fracc. II, incisos e) y g). Ultima reforma, Constitución publicada en el Diario Oficial de la Federación el 5 de febrero de 1917. DOF (2024). Secretaria General. Secretaria de Servicios Parlamentarios. Cámara de Diputados H. Congreso de la Unión. https://www.diputados.gob.mx/LeyesBiblio/pdf/CPEUM.pdf

Contieri, M. (2021). Formando programadores para el futuro. *DOSSIER, 13*.

Cope, B., & Kalantzis, M. (2024). *e-Learning Ecologies: Principles for New Learning and Assessment*. Routledge.

Cordero, A., Córdova, N., & Moreira, C. (2020). Soft skills, a factor of competitiveness in the profile of the public servant. Knowledge Pole, 41-63.

Cortellazzo, L., Bruni, E., & Zampieri, R. (2019). The role of leadership in a digitalized world: A review. *Frontiers in Psychology*, 10, 1938. DOI: 10.3389/fpsyg.2019.01938 PMID: 31507494

Couldry, N.. (2024). Digital storytelling as a tool for intercultural understanding: Lessons from the UNESCO Intercultural Digital Narratives Project. *International Journal of Cultural Studies*, 27(2), 178–195.

Crisol, E., Romero, M.A., Burgos, A., & Sánchez, Y. (2022). Liderazgo inclusivo desde la perspectiva familiar en la Educación Obligatoria. *Revista de nuevos enfoques en investigación educativa*, 11 (2), 226-245. DOI: 10.7821/naer.2022.7.937

Cruz Vadillo Rodolfo. (2022) LII(3), 15-40. *Justicia afectiva: micropolítica y construcción de una habitabilidad escolar.* Revista Latinoamericana de Estudios Educativos. https://www.redalyc.org/articulo.oa?id=27071219002

Cuevas, J. (2023). *Evaluación de un programa de formación docente hacia universitarios con discapacidad* [Tesis para obtener el grado de maestría]. Universidad de Sonora.

Cuevas, J., Hoyos, G., Quintana, O., Norzagaray, C., & Figueroa, C. (2022). Percepción de las funciones básicas de los estudiantes universitarios con discapacidad. *RIDE Revista Iberoamericana para la Investigación y el Desarrollo Educativo*, 13(25). Advance online publication. DOI: 10.23913/ride.v13i25.1369

Cuevas, J., Quintana, M., Figueroa, C., & Hoyos, G. (2022). Perfil de ingreso de estudiantes con discapacidad en la Universidad de Sonora. In Norzagaray, C., & Fraijo, J. (Eds.), *Inclusión educative de estudiantes con discapacidad en las instituciones de educación superior*. Fontamara.

Czerniewicz, L. (2022). *Open Education in the Global South: Stories from the Field.* MIT Press.

Dachary, A. C., Burne, A., & Maris, S. (2006). El estudio del turismo: ¿Un paradigma en formación? *Estudios y Perspectivas en Turismo*, 15(2), 179–192. https://www.scielo.org.ar/scielo.php?script=sci_arttext&pid=S1851-17322006000200004&lng=es&tlng=es

Dado, M., & Bodemer, D. (2017). A review of methodological applications of social network analysis in computer-supported collaborative learning. *Educational Research Review*, 22, 159–180. DOI: 10.1016/j.edurev.2017.08.005

Dana, L.-P., Salamzadeh, A., Mortazavi, S., & Hadizadeh, M. (2022). Investigating the Impact of International Markets and New Digital Technologies on Business Innovation in Emerging Markets. *Sustainability (Basel)*, 14(2), 983. DOI: 10.3390/su14020983

Darling-Hammond, L. (2023). *Powerful Teacher Education: Lessons from Exemplary Programs* (2nd ed.). Jossey-Bass.

Darling-Hammond, L.. (2020). *Restarting and Reinventing School: Learning in the Time of COVID and Beyond*. Learning Policy Institute.

Davenport, T. H., & Westerman, G. (2018). Why So Many High-Profile Digital Transformations Fail Harvard Business Review. https://hbr.org/2018/03/why-so-many-high-profile-digital-transformations-fail

Dávila-Cervantes, A. (2014). Simulation in medical education. *Investigación en Educación Médica*, 3(10), 100–105. DOI: 10.1016/S2007-5057(14)72733-4

de Araujo, L. M., Priadana, S., Paramarta, V., & Sunarsi, D. (2021). Digital leadership in business organizations: An overview. *International Journal of Educational Administration, Management, and Leadership*, 2(1), 45–56. DOI: 10.51629/ijeamal.v2i1.18

Deimann, M., & Farrow, R. (2021). Democratising education with open educational resources: A critical look at MOOCs and open education. *Distance Education*, 42(2), 235–251.

Deterding, S.. (2024). Gamification in education: What, how, why bother? *Educational Researcher*, 53(3), 178–189.

Dewey, J. (1995). *Democracia y educación: una introducción a la filosofía de la educación*. Ediciones Morata.

DGTIC. UNAM. (2014). *Matriz de habilidades digitales*. http://www.educatic.unam.mx

Díaz, P., Eduardo, O., & Vargas, F. J. A. (2022) 6(1). *El liderazgo en la gestión del director. Revista Andina de Educación*https://www.redalyc.org/articulo.oa?id=730076236009

Díaz, J., Ledesma, M., Tito, J., & Díaz, L. (2021). Leadership skills in a context of health emergency, COVID-19 in Peru. *Revista Venezolana de Gerencia*, 26(5), 505–519.

Díez, E., & Díaz-Nafría, J. (2018). Ecologías de aprendizaje ubicuo para la ciberciudadanía crítica. *Comunicar*, 54, 49–58. DOI: 10.3916/C54-2018-05

Dignum, V. (2018). Ethics in artificial intelligence: Introduction to the special issue. *Ethics and Information Technology*, 20(1), 1–3. DOI: 10.1007/s10676-018-9450-z

Domínguez Martínez, A., & Mexicano Reyes, Y. (2018). Evaluación de competencias de programación. *Revista Electrónica ANFEI Digital, 4*(8). www.anfei.org.mx/revista

Domínguez-Rodríguez, Y. (2022). Instruments and types of evaluation. *Con-Ciencia Serrana Scientific Bulletin of the Ixtlahuaco Preparatory School*, 4(7), 37–39.

Drucker, P. (1992). *Post-capitalist Society*. Butterworth-Heinemann.

Dugatkin, L. A. (2019). *The Prince of Evolution: Peter Kropotkin's Adventures in Science and Politics*. University of Chicago Press.

Duque, R. (2018). Affective states in computer-supported collaborative learning: Studying the past to drive the future. *Computers & Education*, 120, 29–50. DOI: 10.1016/j.compedu.2018.01.015

Dweck, C., & Yeager, D. S. (2023). *Mindset: The New Psychology of Success* (Updated edition). Random House.

Earl, L., & Fullan, M. (2023). *Using Data for School Improvement* (3rd ed.). Corwin.

Eberl, J., & Drews, P. (2021). *Digital leadership–Mountain or molehill? A Literature Review.* 16th International Conference on WirtschaftsinformatikAt: Duisburg & Essen, Germany. DOI: 10.1007/978-3-030-86800-0_17

Echeverría, F., León, M., Musso, L., & Pozo, E. (2021). SCRUMM como método ágil al aprendizaje dentro de cursos de estudiantes de maestría. *Revista Ibérica de Sistemas y Tecnologías de Información*, 47(1), 1–12.

El Sawy, O. A., Kræmmergaard, P., Amsinck, H., & Vinther, A. L. (2016). How LEGO Built the Foundations and Enterprise Capabilities for Digital Leadership. *MIS Quarterly Executive*, 15(2).

ElSayary, A. (2024). Integrating Generative AI in Active Learning Environments: Enhancing Metacognition and Technological Skills. *Journal of Systemics, Cybernetics and Informatics*, 22(3), 34–37. DOI: 10.54808/JSCI.22.03.34

Escuela Europea de Excelencia. (2024). *Liderazgo digital: adaptándose a la era de la tecnología.* Recovered from https://www.escuelaeuropeaexcelencia.com/2024/07/liderazgo-digital-adaptandose-a-la-era-de-la-tecnologia/

Espino-Díaz, L., Fernandez-Caminero, G., Hernandez-Lloret, C.-M., Gonzalez-Gonzalez, H., & Alvarez-Castillo, J.-L. (2020). Analyzing the Impact of COVID-19 on Education Professionals. Toward a Paradigm Shift: ICT and Neuroeducation as a Binomial of Action. *Sustainability (Basel)*, 12(14), 5646. DOI: 10.3390/su12145646

Espinosa, M. (2022). Hacia la e-Universidad del siglo XXI: el impacto de la digitalización en la formación superior. Revista RUEDA, 7. https://cedu.es/revista-rued/

Estrada Mota, I. L., & Ramírez García, R. G. (2021). *Constructores de instituciones científicas. Papel del liderazgo en la creación de la Unidad Mérida* del Cinvestav. *Perfiles Educativos*, XLIII(173), 128–145. DOI: 10.22201/iisue.24486167e.2021.173.59768

Europea, C. (2020). *Plan de Acción de Educación Digital (2021-2027).*https://education.ec.europa.eu/es/focus-topics/digital-education/action-plan

European Agency for Special Needs and Inclusive Education. (2019). *Inclusive School Leadership: Exploring Policies Across Europe. Retrieved from*https://www.european-agency.org/resources/publications/inclusive-school-leadership-synthesis

Eva, N., Robin, M., Sendjaya, S., van Dierendonck, D., & Liden, R. C. (2019). Servant leadership: A systematic review and call for future research. *The Leadership Quarterly*, 30(1), 111–132. DOI: 10.1016/j.leaqua.2018.07.004

Farro, F. (2001). *Planeamiento Estratégico para Instituciones Educativas de Calidad*. UDEGRAF.

Fatimah, F., Rajiani, S., & Abbas, E. (2021). Cultural and individual characteristics in adopting computer-supported collaborative learning during covid-19 outbreak: Willingness or obligatory to accept technology? *Management Science Letters*, 11(2), 373–378. DOI: 10.5267/j.msl.2020.9.032

Feijóo, C., Fernández, J., Arenal, A., Armuña, C., & Ramos, S. (2021), Educational technologies in China, Cabrera Giraldez, M., Maghiros, I., Punie, Y. and Vuorikari, R. editor(s), Publications Office of the European Union, Luxembourg, 2021, ISBN 978-92-76-32626-7, , JRC124648.DOI: 10.2760/604641

Fernández, E., & Shaw, G. P. (2020). Academic leadership in a time of crisis: The coronavirus and COVID-19. *Journal of Leadership Studies*, 14(1), 39–45. DOI: 10.1002/jls.21684

Fernández, K. (2018). Programa de inclusion y equidad educative: Perspectiva docente. *Academia Journals*, 10(2), 608–612.

Fernández, L. (1967). *Teoría y Técnica del Turismo*. Editora Nacional.

Ferré, M., García-Barroso, C., García-Famoso, M., Sánchez, D., & Valls, A. (2019). Mejora de la formación en el diseño y desarrollo de software a partir de la coordinación de distintas asignaturas. *Actas de Las Jenui, 4.*

Fitzgerald, M., Kruschwitz, N., Bonnet, D., & Welch, M. (2014). Embracing digital technology: A new strategic imperative. *MIT Sloan Management Review*, 55(2), 1.

Flores, L. M. V., Martínez, I. A. M., & Nava, V. X. (2024). Influencia de estilos de liderazgo transformacional, transaccional y laissez faire en la responsabilidad social corporativa, la imagen y reputación, así como en variables de resultado organizacional. *Contaduría y Administración*, 69(3), 324–347. https://dialnet.unirioja.es/servlet/articulo?codigo=9364206

Florian, L., & Black-Hawkins, K. (2011). Exploring inclusive pedagogy. *British Educational Research Journal*, 37(5), 813–828. DOI: 10.1080/01411926.2010.501096

Floridi, L. (2018). Soft ethics and the governance of the digital. *Philosophy & Technology*, 31(1), 1–8. DOI: 10.1007/s13347-018-0303-9 PMID: 30322997

Floridi, L. (2022). *The Ethics of Digital Ethics.* Oxford University Press.

Floridi, L. (2023). *The Philosophy of Information* (2nd ed.). Oxford University Press.

Foucault, M. (1994). *The Order of Things: An Archaeology of the Human Sciences.* Vintage.

Frey, C., & Osborne, M. (2017). The future of employment: How susceptible are Jobs to computerization? *Technological Forecasting and Social Change*, 114, 254–280. DOI: 10.1016/j.techfore.2016.08.019

Fullan, M. (2020). *Leading in a Culture of Change* (2nd ed.). Jossey-Bass.

Fullan, M., & Quinn, J. (2016). *Coherence: The Right Drivers in Action for Schools, Districts, and Systems.* Corwin Press.

Galarza Cachiguango, IS, Aguinaga, C., López Egas, PX, Molina, R., & Rosero Ortega, G. (2020). Labor Competences in the restaurant sector: a framework of key competencies for its management (Labor Competences in the restaurant sector). Restoration Sector: A Framework of Key Competences for Its Management). *Tourism and society, 27* .

Gallego, E. M. (2023). Formación Docente Para La Educación Inclusiva en Instituciones Públicas Del Quindío. *Siglo Cero*, 54(4), 11–27. DOI: 10.14201/scero.31473

Gallifa, J., & Sangrà, A. (2021). Transformar la Universidad. Desafíos, oportunidades y propuestas desde una mirada global. Barcelona: Editorial UOC. http://hdl.handle.net/10609134926

Gandomani, T. J., Zulzalil, H., Ghani, A. A. A., & Sultan, A. B. M. (2013). Towards comprehensive and disciplined change management strategy in agile transformation process. *Research Journal of Applied Sciences, Engineering and Technology*, 6(13), 2345–2351. DOI: 10.19026/rjaset.6.3706

García Retana, J. Á. (2011). Competence-based educational model: Importance and necessity. Electronic Journal. *Current Research in Education*, 11(3), 1–24.

García-Bulle, S. (2021). Observatory. Institute for the Future of Education. https://observatorio.tec.mx/edu-news/aprendizaje-activo

Garcia-Carbonell, N., Martin-Alcazar, F., & Sanchez-Gardey, G. (2014). Understanding the HRM-performance link: A literature review on the HRM strategy formulation process. *International Journal of Business Administration*, 5(2), 71. DOI: 10.5430/ijba.v5n2p71

García-Peñalvo, F. J. (2024). Digital transformation in education: Challenges and opportunities. *International Journal of Educational Technology in Higher Education*, 21(1), 1–18.

Gatica-Lara, F., & Uribarren -Berrueta, TDNJ. (2013). How to develop a rubric? *Research in Medical Education*, 2(5), 61–65.

George, C. (2021). Competencias digitales básicas para garantizar la continuidad académica provocada por el Covid-19. *Apertura (Guadalajara, Jal.)*, 13(1), 36–51. http://www.udgvirtual.udg.mx/apertura/index.php/apertura/article/view/1942

Giroux, H. A. (2023). *Critical Digital Pedagogy: A Reader*. Bloomsbury Academic.

Gobble, M. (2018). Digital strategy and digital transformation. *Research Technology Management*, 61(5), 66–71. DOI: 10.1080/08956308.2018.1495969

Godoy, M., & Hidalgo, M. (2020). *Guía de accesibilidad digital para la docencia online*. Ediciones UVM.

Goleman, D. (2000). Leadership That Gets Results. *Harvard Business Review*, 78(2), 78–90.

González-Sanmamed, M., Sangrà, A., Souto-Seijo, A., & Estévez, I. (2020). Learning ecologies in the digital era: Challenges for higher education. *Publicaciones*, 50(1), 83–102. DOI: 10.30827/publicaciones.v50i1.15671

Grundke, R., Squicciarini, M., Jamet, S., & Kalamova, M. (2017). *Having the right mix: the role of skill bundles for comparative advantage and industry performance in GVCs.* OECD Publishing., DOI: 10.1787/518151965

Grupo Computrabajo. (2024). *Empleos.* Computrabajo. https://mx.computrabajo.com/trabajo-de-programadores

Grupo Indeed. (2024). *Empleos.* Indeed. https://mx.indeed.com/jobs?q=programador&l=&from=searchOnHP

Grupo LinkedIn. (2024). *Empleos.* LinkedIn. https://www.linkedin.com/jobs/search?trk=guest_homepage-basic_guest_nav_menu_jobs&original_referer=https%3A%2F%2Fwww.linkedin.com%2Fhome&position=1&pageNum=0

Grupo OCCMundial. (2024). *Empleos.* OCCMundial. https://www.occ.com.mx/empleos/de-programador/en-ciudad-de-mexico/

Gümüş, S., & Beyhan, Ö. (2023). School principals as digital leaders: Challenges and opportunities. *International Journal of Educational Leadership and Management*, 11(2), 156–174. DOI: 10.17583/ijelm.2023.12345

Gutiérrez, E., & González, E. (2010). *De las teorías del desarrollo, al desarrollo sustentable: Construcción de un enfoque multidisciplinario.* Siglo XXI.

Gutiérrez, M., Hernández, R., & Jenaro, C. (2019). Escala de evaluación de la inclusión (EEI) para centros y servicios para personas con discapacidad: Validación preliminar. *Revista Nacional e Internacional de Educación Inclusiva*, 12(1), 97–118.

Haffar, M., Al-Hyari, K., Djebarni, R., Alnsour, J. A., Oster, F., Al-Shamali, A., & Alaya, A. (2023). The mediating effect of affective commitment to change in the readiness for change–TQM relationship. *Total Quality Management & Business Excellence*, 34(3–4), 326–344. DOI: 10.1080/14783363.2022.2054695

Halverson, E. R., & Sheridan, K. (2023). The maker movement in education. *Harvard Educational Review*, 93(4), 495–528. DOI: 10.17763/haer.84.4.34j1g68140382063

Harari, Y. N. (2018). *21 Lessons for the 21st Century.* Spiegel & Grau.

Hargreaves, A. (2023). *Digital Leadership for Human-Centered Education.* Teachers College Press.

Hargreaves, A., & Fullan, M. (2020). *Professional Capital: Transforming Teaching in Every School* (2nd ed.). Teachers College Press.

Hargreaves, A., & O'Connor, M. T. (2018). *Collaborative Professionalism: When Teaching Together Means Learning for All.* Corwin.

Hargreaves, A., & O'Connor, M. T. (2022). *Leading Collaborative Professionalism*. Corwin.

Harms, P. D., Cred, M., Tynan, M., Leon, M., & Jeung, W. (2017). Leadership and stress: A meta-analytic review. *The Leadership Quarterly*, 28(1), 178–194. DOI: 10.1016/j.leaqua.2016.10.006

Harris, A., & Jones, M. (2023). *Distributed Leadership in Digital Contexts*. Routledge.

Hartl, E., & Hess, T. (2017). The role of cultural values for digital transformation: Insights from a Delphi study. *Twenty-third Americas Conference on Information Systems*, Boston.

Hasan, A. jafa, Fraij, J., & Várallyai, L. (2021). The Role of Agile Management in HRM Environment Change. Journal of Agricultural Informatics / Agrárinformatika Folyóirat, 12(2), 37–45. DOI: 10.17700/jai.2021.12.2.606

Heidt, T., & Lamberton, G. (2011). Sustainability in the undergraduate and postgraduate business curriculum of a regional university: A critical perspective. *Journal of Management & Organization*, 17(5), 670–690. DOI: 10.5172/jmo.2011.17.5.670

Heifetz, R.. (2024). *The Practice of Adaptive Leadership: Tools and Tactics for Changing Your Organization and the World* (2nd ed.). Harvard Business Review Press.

Hernandez, C., Fernández, M., Carrión, J., & Avilés, B. (2018). La inclusión educative en la Universidad de Minho. Percepciones y actitudes sobre el alumnado con discapacidad. *Revista Complutense de Educación.*, 30(4), 1097–1112. DOI: 10.5209/rced.60106

Hernández-Mosqueda, J. S., Tobón-Tobón, S., & Guerrero-Rosas, G. (2016). Towards a comprehensive performance evaluation: Socio-formative rubrics. *Ra Ximhai*, 12(6), 359–376. https://www.redalyc.org/pdf/461/46148194025.pdf

Hernández-Sellés, N., González-Sanmamedy, M., & Muñoz-Carril, P. (2015). El rol docente en las ecologías de aprendizaje: análisis de una experiencia de aprendizaje colaborativo en entornos virtuales. *Profesorado Revista de Currículum y Formación de Profesorado, 19*(2), 147-163. https://revistaseug.ugr.es/index.php/profesorado/article/view/18765

Herrán Gascón, A. (1999). Didáctica de la motivación. Suplemento Pedagógico Acade, (25), 10-13, y (26), 6-9. Madrid, España. Consultado el 8 de agosto de 2008, de: http:// www.pangea.org/peremarques/dioe/ DIDÁCTICA%20DE%20LA%20 MOTIVACIÓN.pdf García A. E. (2008). Motivación individual. Consultado el 7 de junio del 2008, de: http://grupos. emagister.com/documento/ administracion_motivacion_y_ organizacion_/1048-38669 Hampton, D., Summer, C., y Webber, R. (1989). Manual de desarrollo de recursos humanos. México: Trillas.

Herrera, F., Ramírez, M. I., Roa, J. M., & Herrera, I. (2004). Tratamiento de las creencias motivacionales en contextos educativos pluriculturales. Revista Iberoamericana de Educación, Sección de Investigación, N° 37/2. España.

Herrera, C. A. H., & Torres, J. C. N. (2020). Las habilidades blandas en estudiantes de ingeniería de tres instituciones públicas de educación superior. *RIDE Revista Iberoamericana para la Investigación y el Desarrollo Educativo*, 10(20), 20. Advance online publication. DOI: 10.23913/ride.v10i20.678

Heskett, J. (2022). *Win from Within: Build Organizational Culture for Competitive Advantage*. Columbia University Press. DOI: 10.7312/hesk20300

He, W., Yu, S., Yu, T., & Wang, C. (2019). The effect of digital leadership on knowledge sharing and creativity: The mediating roles of innovative self-efficacy and intrinsic motivation. *Information & Management*, 56(8), 103175.

Hicks, T., Miller, M., & Young, R. (2024). *Mental Health and Wellbeing in Higher Education*. Palgrave Macmillan.

Hincapié Parejo, N. F., & Clemenza de Araujo, C. (2022). Assessment of learning by competencies: A theoretical look from the Colombian context. *Journal of Social Sciences*, XXVIII(1), 106–122.

Hinings, B., Gegenhuber, T., & Greenwood, R. (2018). Digital innovation and transformation: An institutional perspective. *Information and Organization*, 28(1), 52–56. DOI: 10.1016/j.infoandorg.2018.02.004

Holbeche, L. (2018). *The agile organization: How to build an innovative, sustainable and resilient business*. Kogan Page Publishers.

Hoyos, G., Salas, A., & Cuevas, J. (2021). *Percepción de universitarios sobre sus compañeros con discapacidad*. Editorial Académica Española.

Iberdrola (2024) ¿Qué es la inclusión Digital y como llevarla a cabo? Recuperado de: https://www.iberdrola.com/compromiso-social/inclusion-digital#:~:text=Seg%C3%BAn%20la%20Comisi%C3%B3n%20Europea%2C%20la,y%20tambi%C3%A9n%20facilidad%20de%20uso

IBM. (2024). *¿Qué es el Internet de las cosas (IoT)?*https://www.ibm.com/mx-es/topics/internet-of-things

IBM. (2024a). *¿Qué es blockchain?*https://www.ibm.com/mx-es/topics/blockchain

INEGI. (2023). *Students enrolled, graduates and holders of higher education degrees at the bachelor's level of normal, university and technological education of the school modality by territorial demarcation and field of academic training. Retrievedfrom*https://www.inegi.org.mx/app/cuadroentidad/CDMX/2018/06/6_18

Islas, C., & Carranza, M. (2017). Digital ecosystems and their manifestation in learning: Literature analysis. *RED*, (55), 1–13. DOI: 10.6018/red/55/9

Itati, S., Cardozo, G., & Alfonzo, P. (2021). Agilidad en el aprendizaje active: Propuesta en la asignatura modelos y simulación. Mendive. *Review of Education*, 19(2), 542–554.

Ito, M.. (2024). *Connected Learning: An Agenda for Research and Design*. Digital Media and Learning Research Hub.

Järvelä, S., Järvenoja, H., & Malmberg, J. (2019). Capturing the dynamic and cyclical nature of regulation: methodological progress in understanding socially shared regulation in learning. *ijcscl, 14*(4), 425-441. DOI: 10.1007/s11412-019-09313-2

Jeffrey, H. L., Beswick, E., & Meade, J. (2015). Learning and unlearning sexism in the workplace: Two important barriers prevent a more inclusive environment. *Human Resource Management International Digest*, 23(5), 18–20. DOI: 10.1108/HRMID-05-2015-0086

Jenkins, H.. (2024). *Participatory Culture in a Networked Era* (2nd ed.). Polity.

Jiménez, AB, Hinojosa, VC, Ramos, JC, Sánchez, RM, Blasco, VJQ, & Mendoza, CA (2019). Challenge-based learning as a proposal for the development of key competencies. Parents and Teachers/ Journal of Parents and Teachers, (380), 50-55.

Jiménez, D. L., Dittmar, E. C., & Portillo, J. P. V. (2021). Cooperation and relationship in the triple helix model of innovation. *International Journal of Knowledge and Learning*, 14(1), 1–9. DOI: 10.1504/IJKL.2021.115025

Johnson, L.. (2024). *NMC Horizon Report: Higher Education Edition*. The New Media Consortium.

Juárez Némer, O. C. (2024). La modernización de la formación del maestro rural en México: Expectativas y resignificaciones. *Revista Latinoamericana de Estudios Educativos (México)*, LIV(1), 189–212. DOI: 10.48102/rlee.2024.54.1.620

Kahai, S., Avolio, B. J., & Sosik, J. J. (2017). E-Leadership. In Hertel, G., Stone, D. L., Johnson, R. D., & Passmore, J. (Eds.), *The Wiley Blackwell Handbook of the Psychology of the Internet at Work.*, DOI: 10.1002/9781119256151.ch14

Kane, G. C., Phillips, A. N., Copulsky, J. R., & Andrus, G. R. (2019). *The technology fallacy: How people are the real key to digital transformation.* MIT Press. DOI: 10.7551/mitpress/11661.001.0001

Kapp, K. M. (2012). *The gamification of learning and instruction: Game-based methods and strategies for training and education.* John Wiley & Sons. Recovered from https://www.wiley.com/enushe+Gamification+of+Learning+and+Instruction %3A+Game+based+Methods+and+Strategies+for+Training+and+Education-p -9781118191989

Kärkkäinen, K., & Vincent-Lancrin, S. (2023). *Trustworthy artificial intelligence (AI) in education: Promises and challenges.* OECD Publishing.

Kelemen, M. L., & Rumens, N. (2008). *An introduction to critical management research.* Sage. DOI: 10.4135/9780857024336

Koehler, M., & Mishra, P. (2009). What is technological pedagogical content knowledge? *Contemporary Issues in Technology & Teacher Education*, 9(1), 60–70. https://www.citejournal.org/vol9/iss1/general/article1.cfm

Kotter, J. P. (2023). *Leading Change* (2nd ed.). Harvard Business Review Press.

Kouzes, J. M., & Posner, B. Z. (2017). *The Leadership Challenge: How to Make Extraordinary Things Happen in Organizations.* Wiley.

Kozma, R. B. (2019). *Transforming Education: The Power of ICT Policies.* UNESCO.

KPMG. (2024). El *futuro del sector turístico: hacia la máxima digitalización y personalización de los servicios al cliente.*https://www.tendencias.kpmg.es/2024/07/futuro-sector-turistico-digitalizacion-personalizacion/

Kuh, G. D. (2024). *Financing Higher Education: Challenges and Solutions.* Jossey-Bass.

Kurniawati, D. T., Fernando, Y., & Dzil Ikhram, W. (2024). Financial technology readiness for Shariah-compliant banking services: Post–merger perspectives. *Journal of Islamic Marketing*, 15(6), 1651–1671. DOI: 10.1108/JIMA-08-2023-0236

Ladino, D., Bejarano, B., Santana, L., Martínez, O., & Cabrera, D. (2018). Diseño de aprendizaje a partir de las posibilidades de las ecologías de aprendizaje en educación superior. *Revista Virtual Universidad Católica del Norte,* (53), 35-52. https://revistavirtual.ucn.edu.co/index.php/RevistaUCN/article/view/963/1411

Lapicki, R. S., & Terlato, A. N. (2021). Empresas ágiles - Claves para sobrevivir a la complejidad del ambiente. *Documentos de Trabajo*, 777, 1–30.

Larjovuori, R. L.. (2023). Digital leadership: Leveraging digital technologies for organizational value creation. *Journal of Management Development*, 42(4), 256–270.

Larmer, J.. (2024). *Project-Based Learning: Your Field Guide to Real-World Projects in the Digital Age* (3rd ed.). Buck Institute for Education.

Lazcano, C., & Llorente, C. (2022). *Liderazgo en escuelas de alta complejidad sociocultural.* Diez miradas. *Perfiles Educativos*, XLIV(175), 194–199. DOI: 10.22201/iisue.24486167e.2022.175.60971

Le Grand, T., & Deneckere, R. (2019). COOC: an agile change management method. In 2019 IEEE 21st Conference on Business Informatics (CBI) 2, pp. 28-37. IEEE. Doi: DOI: 10.1109/CBI.2019.10093

Lee, L., & Guth, S. (2024). Virtual exchange as a tool for developing intercultural competence: A case study of the Global Virtual Exchange Program. *Language Learning & Technology*, 28(2), 10–30.

Lescano, J., Vegas, E., Collazos, H., Valdez, L., & Belaúnde, M. (2008). *Planteamiento teórico y conceptual del desarrollo sostenible (informe Brundtland) "Nuestro futuro en común.* UniversidadNacional de la Amazona Peruana.

Liberating Learning, Canadá Universidad Iberoamericana Ciudad de México, México. (2024) LIV(1), 7-10. *¿Educar para qué? Los propósitos de la educación para el mundo que viene.* Revista Latinoamericana de Estudios Educativos. https://www.redalyc.org/articulo.oa?id=27075657020

Li, C. (2010). *Open Leadership: How Social Technology Can Transform the Way You Lead.* Jossey-Bass.

Li, C., & Solis, B. (2013). *The Seven Success Factors of Social Business Strategy.* Jossey-Bass.

Life skills. Tools for good treatment and prevention of violence. https://www.unicef.org/venezuela/media/431/file/Habilidades

Livari, N.. (2020). Digital transformation of everyday life: How COVID-19 pandemic transformed the basic education of the young generation and why information management research should care? *International Journal of Information Management*, 55, 102183. DOI: 10.1016/j.ijinfomgt.2020.102183 PMID: 32836640

Llamas, F., & Macías, E. (2016). Formación inicial de docentes en educación básica para la generación de conocimiento con las Tecnologías de la Información y la Comunicación. *Revista Complutense de Educación*, 29(2), 577–593. DOI: 10.5209/RCED.53520

Loáiciga-Gutiérrez, J., & Chanto-Espinoza, C. (2024). Desarrollo de habilidades blandas en la formación universitaria en la era digital. *Revista Multidisciplinaria Perspectivas Investigativas*, 4(3), 2–11. DOI: 10.62574/rmpi.v4i3.150

Lokuge, S., Sedera, D., Grover, V., & Dongming, X. (2019). Organizational readiness for digital innovation: Development and empirical calibration of a construct. *Information & Management*, 56(3), 445–461. DOI: 10.1016/j.im.2018.09.001

Looi, C. K., & Wong, L. H. (2023). *Seamless Learning in the Age of Connectivity* (2nd ed.). Springer.

López Jiménez, D., Dittmar, E. C., & Vargas Portillo, J. P. (2021). New directions in corporate social responsibility and ethics: Codes of conduct in the digital environment. *Journal of Business Ethics*, •••, 1–11. DOI: 10.1007/s10551-021-04753-z

López-Calva Juan Martín. (2024), LIV(1), 11-42. *El sentido de la educación: dos tendencias y una apuesta humanista hacia un Antropoceno positivo.* Revista Latinoamericana de Estudios Educativos https://www.redalyc.org/articulo.oa?id=27075657004

López, Morales, Sara, Hershberger del Arenal, Rebeca, & Acosta Arreguín, Eduardo. (2020). Competency-based assessment: How is it done? *Journal of the Faculty of Medicine (Mexico)*, 63(3), 46–56. DOI: 10.22201/fm.24484865e.2019.63.3.08

Luckin, R.. (2023). *Intelligence Unleashed: An Argument for AI in Education* (2nd ed.). Pearson.

Luckin, R.. (2024). *Enhancing Learning and Teaching with Technology: What the Research Says* (2nd ed.). UCL IOE Press.

Maldonado, M. (2007). Collaborative work in the university classroom. *Laurus Revista de Educación*, 13, 263–278.

Marcano, S., & Reyes, M. (2009). Administración (12.a edición). México: Pearson https://www.ceut.edu.mx/Biblioteca/books/Administración/Administración-Robbins.pdf

Marcos Salas, B., Alarcón Martínez, V., Serrano Amarilla, N., Cuetos Revuelta, MJ, & Manzanal Martínez, AI (2020). Application of learning styles according to the Felder and Silverman model for the development of key competencies in teaching practice. *Pedagogical trends* .

Marginson, S. (2024). *Higher Education and the Knowledge Economy*. Cambridge University Press.

Marín, V. I.. (2022). Emergency remote teaching in higher education: Mapping the first global online semester. *International Journal of Educational Technology in Higher Education*, 19(1), 1–24. PMID: 35013716

Márquez, , Sandoval, M., Sánchez, S., Simón, C., Moriña, A., Morgado, B., Moreno-Medina, I., García, J. A., Díaz-Gandasegui, V., & Elizalde-San Miguel, B. (2020). Evaluación de la inclusión en educación superior mediante indicadores. *REICE. Revista Electrónica Iberoamericana sobre Calidad, Eficacia y Cambio en Educación*, 19(3), 39–59. DOI: 10.15366/reice2021.19.3.003

Martínez, O., Steffens, E., Ojeda, D., & Hernández, H. (2018). Estrategias pedagógicas aplicadas a la educación con mediación virtual para la generación del conocimiento global. *Formación Universitaria*, 11(5), 5. DOI: 10.4067/S0718-50062018000500011

Martínez-Rodríguez, R., & Benítez-Corona, L. (2020). The ecology of resilience learning in ubiquitous environments to adverse situations. *Comunicar English ed., 28*(62), 43-52 (2020). DOI: 10.3916/C62-2020-04

Mathieson, A., & Wall, G. (1982). *Tourism: economic, physical, and social impacts*. 2° Ed. Canada: Longman.

McAfee, A., & Brynjolfsson, E. (2012). Big data: The management revolution. *Harvard Business Review*, 90(10), 60–68. PMID: 23074865

McCarthy, A., Maor, D., McConney, A., & Cavanaugh, C. (2023). Digital transformation in education: Critical components for leaders of system change. *Social Sciences & Humanities Open*, 8(1), 100479. DOI: 10.1016/j.ssaho.2023.100479

McKinsey & Company. (2018). McKinsey, Company Unlocking success in digital transformations. Recovered from https://www.mckinsey.com/capabilities/people-and-organizational-performance/our-insights/unlocking-success-in-digital-transformations

McLeod, S. (2020). Rising to the challenge and looking ahead: School leadership during the pandemic. *Journal UCEA*, 61(2), 17–19.

McLeod, S., & Dulsky, S. (2021). Resilience, Reorientation, and Reinvention: School Leadership During the Early Months of the COVID-19 Pandemic. *Frontiers in Education*, 6, 637075. DOI: 10.3389/feduc.2021.637075

Mejía, P., & Ullauri, J. (2022). Actitudes de estudiates sobre el proceso inclusive de una persona Sorda en un contexto áulico Universitario, una experiencia inicial en la Universidad Nacional de Educación. *Revisma MAMAKUNA*, 19, 104–115.

Melo Campos, A. (2019). *Regulación de las nuevas formas de empleo que surgen por medio de las plataformas digitales*. Universidad Católica de Colombia. Facultad de Derecho.

Mendizábal Bermúdez Gabriela. (2021). LIV(162), 167-185. *Hacia la construcción de un derecho social comparado*. Boletín Mexicano de Derecho Comparado. https://www.redalyc.org/articulo.oa?id=42775436008

Mendoza Cazarez Dulce Carolina. (2022) 27 (94), 829-953. *¿Cómo entender y promover justicia social en educación? Implicaciones para las políticas educativas en contextos de emergencia*. Revista Mexicana de Investigación Educativa https://www.redalyc.org/articulo.oa?id=14072628007

Mercado, Cernas y Nava (2016): Mercado, P. Cernas, D. y Nava, R. La Interdisciplinariedad Económico-Administrativa en la Conformación de una Comunidad Científica y la Formación de Investigadores. *Revista de la Educación Superior*, XLV (177), 43 – 65.

México, U. N. I. R. (2022, September 21). *¿Qué hace un programador? Funciones, requisitos y situación laboral en México*. La Universidad En Internet. https://mexico.unir.net/noticias/ingenieria/que-hace-programador/

Milan, JAP, & Austrich, YL (2021). The Rubric: an assessment matrix as an educational resource in higher education in Cuba, a strong evaluative tool.

Mingote, C., & Núñez, C. (2011). Importance of mental health in labour health management: A shared liability. *Medicina y Seguridad del Trabajo*, 57, 24.

Ministerio de Educación de Chile [MINEDUC]. (2019). Guía de Herramientas para el desarrollo de recursos personales en equipos directivos. Herramienta 2. *Liderazgo escolar: reconociendo tipos de liderazgo. División de Educación General, 2*(9.1), 196. https://hdl.handle.net/20.500.12365/14511

Mishra, P., & Koehler, M. J. (2023). *Technological Pedagogical Content Knowledge: A Framework for Teacher Knowledge in a Digital Age* (2nd ed.). Teachers College Press.

Molina, M., Lian, R., Garcés, R., Rojas, Y., Dulzaides, M., & Selín, M. (2015). The Communication Process Mediated by Information Technologies. Advantages and Disadvantages in Various Spheres of Social Life. *University of Medical Sciences*, 13. http://scielo.sld.cu/pdf/ms/v13n4/ms04413.pdf. http://scielo.sld.cu/pdf/ms/v13n4/ms04413.pdf

Montero, S., Karina, I., Mariño, R., Javier, M., Cajas, C., Viviana, E., & Tanqueño, C. O. P. (2021). *Liderazgo positivo en organizaciones saludables*. Revista Venezolana de Gerencia. https://www.redalyc.org/articulo.oa?id=29069613005

Moreira-Choez, J. S., Lamus de Rodríguez, T. M., Olmedo-Cañarte, P. A., & Macías-Macías, J. D. (2024). Valorando el futuro de la educación: Competencias Digitales y Tecnologías de Información y Comunicación en Universidades. *Revista Venezolana de Gerencia*, 29(105), 271–288. DOI: 10.52080/rvgluz.29.105.18

Morin, E. (2020). *Seven Complex Lessons in Education for the Future*. UNESCO.

Murillo, F. J. (2006). Una dirección escolar para el cambio: Del liderazgo transformacional al liderazgo distribuido. REICE. *Revista Electrónica Iberoamericana sobre Calidad, Eficacia y Cambio en Educación*, 4(4), 11–24. https://www.redalyc.org/articulo.oa?id=55140403

Museo Memoria y Tolerancia. (2024). *Inclusión*.https://www.myt.org.mx/tolerancia_url/inclusion

Naranjo, M. & Carrasco, A. (2022). Participación estudiantil e inclusión digital en la Universidad. Un studio en contextos iberoamericanos. Foro de educación, 20(1), 10-38.

Naranjo, M. L. (2004). Enfoques conductistas, cognitivos y racional emotivos. San José, C. R.: Universidad de Costa Rica. Universidad de Sevilla. (2005).

National Autonomous University of Mexico (2020). Assessment of and for Learning: Instruments and Strategies

Navarrete, Z. (2023). Políticas educativas para la integración de las TIC en el sistema educativo nacional mexicano. *Apertura (Guadalajara, Jal.)*, 15(2), 134–151. DOI: 10.32870/Ap.v15n2.2419

Neil, C., Battaglia, N., & Zemborain, MEDV (2022). Methodological framework for the design of analytical rubrics. Edutec, Electronic Journal of Educational Technology, (80).

Nietzsche, F. (2003). *Beyond Good and Evil: Prelude to a Philosophy of the Future*. Penguin Classics. (Original work published 1886)

Noddings, N. (2024). *Philosophy of Education* (5th ed.). Routledge.

Northouse, P. G. (2021). *Leadership: Theory and Practice* (9a ed.). SAGE Publications.

Northouse, P. G. (2018). *Leadership: Theory and Practice*. Sage Publications.

Nova, JAD, & Tobón, ST (2017). Assessment instruments: socio-formative rubrics. Research praxis ReDIE: electronic journal of the Durango Network of Educational Researchers, 9(17), 79-86.

Nussbaum, M. C. (2024). *Creating Capabilities: The Human Development Approach* (2nd ed.). Belknap Press.

OCDE. (2015). *OECD Science, Technology and Industry Scoreboard 2015*. OECD., DOI: 10.1787/sti_scoreboard-2015-

OCDE. (2016a). *Skills for a Digital World: 2016 Ministerial Meeting on the Digital Economy Background Report*. OECD., DOI: 10.1787/5jlwz83z3wnw-

OCDE. (2023). *OECD Skills Outlook 2023: The State of Global Education*. OECD Publishing.

OCDE. (2024). *Education at a Glance 2024: OECD Indicators*. OECD Publishing.

OCI. (2024). *What Is Big Data?*https://www.oracle.com/big-data/what-is-big-data/

OECD. (2016). *Skills beyond school: Synthesis*. OECD Publishing., DOI: 10.1787/9789264230804-

OECD. (2016). Skills for social progress: The power of social and emotional skills. UNESCO Institute for Statistics, Paris. https://www.oecdilibrary.org/docserver/9789264253292es.pdf?expires=1588082606&id=id&accname=guest&checksum=95527013AD0B0EDD8F71CF6C0B88357C

OECD. (2016b). *Getting Skills Right: Anticipating and Responding to Changing Skill Needs*. OECD Publishing., DOI: 10.1787/9789264252073-

OECD. (2016c). *New Markets and New Jobs*. OECD Publishing., DOI: 10.1787/5jlwt496h37l-

OECD. (2017). *Diagnóstico de la OCDE sobre la Estrategia de Competencias, Destrezas y Habilidades de México*. Resumen Ejecutivo. México: OECD. Recuperado de https://www.oecd.org/mexico/Diagnostico-de-la-OCDE-sobre-la-Estrategia-de-Competencias-Destrezas-y-Habilidades-de-Mexico-Resumen-Ejecutivo.pdf

OECD. (2019). *Future of education and skills 2030.* https://www.oecd.org/education/2030-project/

OECD. (2019). *Going digital: Shaping policies, improving lives.* OECD Publishing., DOI: 10.1787/9789264312012-

Oklahoma City Public Schools. (2020). *Equidad. Compromiso con la equidad educacional en OKCPS.*https://www.okcps.org/Page/5738#:~:text=La%20equidad%20educativa%20se%20define,para%20todos%20los%20estudiantes%20o

Okoko, J. M. (2019). Towards school leadership development: The essence of working with culturally and linguistically diverse newcomer families in Saskatchewan. *Research in Educational Administration & Leadership*, 4(2), 195–229. DOI: 10.30828/real/2019.2.1

O'Neil, C. (2022). *Weapons of Math Destruction: How Big Data Increases Inequality and Threatens Democracy* (Updated edition). Crown.

ORACLE. (2024). *What is ERP?*https://www.oracle.com/erp/what-is-erp/

Orange, F. (2016). *España: La transformación digital en el sector turístico.*https://www.fundacionorange.es/wp

Ordoñez, H., Escobar, A., Velandia, D., & Cobos, C. (2015). Business Processes as a Strategy to Improve Re-quirements Elicitation in Extreme Programming (XP). In *Memorias del VII Congreso de Telematica CITA*.

Ore, O., & Sposato, M. (2022). Opportunities and risks of artificial intelligence in recruitment and selection. *The International Journal of Organizational Analysis*, 30(6), 1771–1782. DOI: 10.1108/IJOA-07-2020-2291

Organización de las Naciones Unidas para la Educación, la Ciencia y la Cultura (UNESCO, 2005). *Educación para todos: el imperativo de la calidad. Informe de Seguimiento de Educación para Todos en el Mundo*. París: UNESCO.

Organización de las Naciones Unidas para la Educación, la Ciencia y la Cultura (UNESCO, 2010). *Desafíos de la educación*. Buenos Aires: IIPE-UNESCO. https://bit.ly/2W7k2wY

Organización de las Naciones Unidas para la Educación, la Ciencia y la Cultura [UNESCO] (2021). *Competencias y habilidades digitales.*https://unesdoc.unesco.org/ark:/48223/pf0000380113.locale=en

Organización de las Naciones Unidas para la Educación, la Ciencia y la Cultura [UNESCO] (2023). Directrices para la formulación de políticas y planes maestros de TIC en educación. https://unesdoc.unesco.org/ark:/48223/pf0000385091

Organización de las Naciones Unidas para la Educación, la Ciencia y la Cultura [UNESCO] (2024). *Transformar la educación en África mediante las TIC.*https://www.unesco.org/es/digital-education/kfit-africa

Organización Mundial del Turismo. (2000). *Recomendaciones sobre estadísticas de turismo.*https://unstats.un.org/unsd/statcom/doc00/m83-s.pdf

Organización Mundial del Turismo. (2023). *Notas metodológicas de la base de datos de estadísticas de turismo, Edición 2023.* OMT., DOI: 10.18111/9789284424160

Organización para la Cooperación y el Desarrollo Económico (OCDE). (2013). *Panorama de la educación 2013 Indicadores de la OCDE.* Santillana.

Orozco, J., Nuñes, P., & Orozco, M. (2019). The challenges of Mexico's higher education in the 21st century. *InterSedes*, 20, 11. https://www.scielo.sa.cr/scielo.php?script=sci_arttext&pid=S2215-24582019000100076

Ossa, C., Castro, F., Castañeda, M., & Castro, J. (2014). Cultura y liderazgo escolar: Factores claves para el desarrollo de la inclusión educativa. *Revista Electrónica. Actualidades Investigativas en Educación*, 14(3). Advance online publication. DOI: 10.15517/aie.v14i3.16157

Otálvaro, SMC, Giraldo, JVB, Giraldo, IAR, & Granada, DPV (2018). Design of a rubric for the evaluation of learning based on a game in industrial engineering.

Oyarzún, J., Parcerisa, L., & Carrasco, A. (2022). Discriminación étnica y cultural en procesos de elección de escuela en minorías socioculturales en Chile. *Psicoperspectivas*, 21(1). Advance online publication. https://www.psicoperspectivas.cl/index.php/psicoperspectivas/article/viewFile/2537/1565. DOI: 10.5027/psicoperspectivas-Vol21-Issue1-fulltext-2537

Pachón-Palacios, M. L., & Pautt-Torres, G. M. (2024). *Liderazgo en el aula y la eficacia docente como variable moderadora en el rendimiento académico.* Revista Colombiana de Educación, (92), 370-396. https://revistas.upn.edu.co/index.php/RCE/article/view/17229

Paľová, D., & Vejačka, M. (2023). Transformative Education with Agile Project Management and Project-Based Learning. *Ad Alta: Journal of Interdisciplinary Research*, 13(2), 197–206. DOI: 10.33543/j.1302.197206

Pantoja, M. L. (2012) Assessment in competencies? Pedagogical Studies XXXVIII, No. 1: 353-366, 2012. https://scielo.conicyt.cl/pdf/estped/v38n1/art22.pdf

Papeles de Economía Española. (2024). Desafíos y oportunidades para el futuro de la educación superior. Resúmenes ejecutivos (N.° 180). ISSN: 0210-9107

Pazmay-Pazmay, D. (2023). Plataformas virtuales y fomento del aprendizaje con sentido en la educación superior. *Revista Científica FIPCAEC*, 8(1), 411–425. DOI: 10.23857/fipcaec.v8i1

Pedreño-Muñoz, A., & Ramón-Rodríguez, A. B. (2019): *«Por qué el turismo necesita imperiosamente la Inteligencia Artificial (y mucha tecnología digital»*. Instituto tecnológico hotelero. https://www.ithotelero. com/blog/por-que-el-turismo-necesita-imperiosamente-la-inteligencia-artificial-y-muchatecnologia-digital/

Peña Miguel, N., Corral Lage, J., & Mata Galindez, A. (2020). Assessment of the Development of Professional Skills in University Students: Sustainability and Serious Games. *Sustainability (Basel)*, 12(3), 1014. DOI: 10.3390/su12031014

Pérez-Castro, J. (2021). XII(33), 138-157. *Condiciones para la docencia inclusiva: Análisis desde las barreras y los facilitadores.Revista Iberoamericana de Educación Superior*. Advance online publication. DOI: 10.22201/iisue.20072872e.2021.33.862

Peters, M., & Romero, M. (2019). Lifelong learning ecologies in online higher education: Students' engagement in the continuum between formal and informal learning. *British Journal of Educational Technology*, 50(4), 1729–1743. https://doi .org.ezproxy.usach.cl/10.1111/bjet.12803. DOI: 10.1111/bjet.12803

Petrucci, T., & Rivera, M. (2018). Leading growth through the digital leader. *Journal of Leadership Studies*, 12(3), 53–56. DOI: 10.1002/jls.21595

Piderit, S. K. (2023). *Rethinking Resistance and Recognizing Ambivalence: A Multidimensional View of Attitudes Toward an Organizational Change* (2nd ed.). Academy of Management Review.

Pinargote-Macías, E. I., Vega Intriago, J. O., Moreira Choez, J. S., & Díaz Macías, T. M. (2022). Competencias del docente universitario en tiempos de pandemia. *Revista Venezolana de Gerencia, 27*(Edición Especial 7), 347–359. https://doi.org/ DOI: 10.52080/rvgluz.27.7.23

Pobreza y formación para el trabajo: la necesaria apuesta por la calidad. (2022). Revista Latinoamericana de Estudios Educativos (México), LII(2), 7-16. https://doi .org/DOI: 10.48102/rlee.2022.52.2.503

Pool, L., & Consuelo, M. (2017). *El desarrollo de habilidades digitales en profesores universitarios, el caso mexicano de Habitat Puma en la UNAM*. Editorial Académica Española.

Popenici, S. A., & Kerr, S. (2017). Exploring the impact of artificial intelligence on teaching and learning in higher education. *Research and Practice in Technology Enhanced Learning*, 12(1), 22. DOI: 10.1186/s41039-017-0062-8 PMID: 30595727

Prendes-Espinosa, M. P., & Cerdán Cartagena, F. (2021). Tecnologías avanzadas para afrontar el reto de la innovación educativa. *RIED Revista Iberoamericana de Educación a Distancia*, 24(1), 35–53. DOI: 10.5944/ried.24.1.28415

Prince, K. A. (2018). *Digital Leadership: Transitioning into the Digital Age*. James Cook University.

Prinsloo, P. (2023). Student privacy self-management: Implications for learning analytics. *LAK '23: Proceedings of the 13th International Conference on Learning Analytics and Knowledge*.

Prinsloo, P., & Slade, S. (2024). *Student Privacy in Learning Analytics: An Ethical Perspective*. Routledge.

Programa Golden5: Una intervención psicoeducativa. Consultado el 14 de abril de 2007, de: http://www.golden5.org/ golden5/ Rice, F. P. (2000). Adolescencia. Desarrollo, relaciones y cultura. Madrid: Prentice Hall.

Quijada, K. (2021). Acciones afirmativas para la inclusion universitaria de estudiantes afrodescendientes e indígenas en Brasil, Colombia y México. *Ciencia y Cultura*, 46, 135–162.

Quintero, L. (2024). *¿Qué es la discriminación*? Museo Memoria y Tolerancia. https://www.myt.org.mx/tolerancia_url/discriminacion

Radkowitsch, A., Vogel, F., & Fischer, F. (2020). Good for learning, bad for motivation? a meta-analysis on the effects of computer-supported collaboration scripts. *International Journal of Computer-Supported Collaborative Learning*, 15(1), 5–47. DOI: 10.1007/s11412-020-09316-4

RAE. (2014). *Liderazgo*. Recuperado de https://dirae.es/palabras/liderazgo

Ramírez, Mario H, Méndez-Sánchez, Arturo F, Pérez-Trejo, Leonor, & Olvera-Aldana, Miguel. (2013). Hierarchy of specific competencies in the physics program of the Higher School of Physics and Mathematics of the IPN-Mexico using the Morganov -Heredia matrix. *University training, 6* (5), 21-28. Unesco, Conceptual framework for the evaluation of competenciesDOI: 10.4067/S0718-50062013000500004

Ramírez, D., & Ramírez, J. (2014). *Derecho ambiental y desarrollo sustentable (segunda edición)*. Porrúa.

Rapanta, C., Botturi, L., Goodyear, P., Guàrdia, L., & Koole, M. (2020). Online university teaching during and after the Covid-19 crisis: Refocusing teacher presence and learning activity. *Postdigital Science and Education*, 2(3), 923–945. DOI: 10.1007/s42438-020-00155-y

Rasco, A., & Felix, J. (2022). *Justicia afectiva: Una necesidad educativa y política inaplazable.* Revista de Estudios Parlamentarios. Hemiciclo. https://www.researchgate.net/publication/378549662_JUSTICIA_AFECTIVA_UNA_NECESIDAD_EDUCATIVA_Y_POLITICA_INAPLAZABLE

Raza, S. A.. (2021). Factors affecting the adoption of online teaching in higher education institutions: The perspective of faculty members. *International Journal of Educational Management*, 35(5), 1050–1067.

Reich, J. (2023). *Failure to Disrupt: Why Technology Alone Can't Transform Education.* Harvard University Press.

Reyes, G. (2018). Análisis comparativo de programas de Maestría en Tecnología Educativa, tendencias actuales en la formación de futuros profesionistas. *International Journal of Information Systems and Software Engineering for Big Companies*, 5(2), 29–40.

Rigby, J., Forman, S., Foster, L., Kazemi, E., & Clancey, S. (2020). *Promising District Leadership Practices for Transformative Change in the Context of COVID-19.* https://education.uw.edu/sites/default/files/pdf/Promising-Leadership-Practices-Brief.pdf

Rincón- Gallardo, S. (. (2024). Educating for what? The purposes of education in and beyond the collapse. *Latin American Journal of Educational Studies (Mexico)*, LIV(1), 71–92. DOI: 10.48102/rlee.2024.54.1.608

Riofrio, E. (2018). Communication in institutional development. *Universidad Técnica Particular de Loja*, 1.

Rivas García, R. M., Cardoso Espinosa, E. O., & Roldan Castellanos, M. L. (2024). Planteamiento de las Competencias Profesionales en Turismo desde la perspectiva de los egresados en México. *RIDE Revista Iberoamericana para la Investigación y el Desarrollo Educativo*, 15(29). Advance online publication. DOI: 10.23913/ride.v15i29.2094

Robles, V., Contreras, F., Barbosa-Ramírez, D., & Juárez, F. (2013). Liderazgo en directivos colombianos vs. mexicanos. Un estudio comparativo. *Revista Investigación y Desarrollo, 21*(2), 395-418. https://www.redalyc.org/articulo.oa?id=26828939004

Rodríguez, D. (2019). *Metodología ágil en la gestión de proyectos de medios educativos basados en las tecnologías de información para el SENA* [Tesis para obtener grado de maestría]. Universidad EAN.

Rodríguez-Molina, G. (2021). Digital leadership in schools: Exploring the relationship between digital competence and leadership. *Computers & Education*, 167, 104221.

Rodríguez, R., Rabassa, G., Salas, R., & Pardo, A. (2017). *Protocolo de identificación y evaluación del alumnado de altas capacidades en centros escolares.* Univesitat Santillana.

Rofcanin, Y., & Anand, S. (2020). Human Relations virtual special issue: Virtual working. *Human Relations*, 73(7), 1036–1041. DOI: 10.1177/0018726720926457

Rojas Ayala, G., Nathan, L., & Mendonca, J. (2024). The Study of Democratic Schools and its Contribution to the Reinvigoration of Democracy. *Revista Latinoamericana de Estudios Educativos (México)*, LIV(1), 93–112. DOI: 10.48102/rlee.2024.54.1.610

Rojas, R. A. (2023). La educación superior para el 2050. Desafíos y oportunidades para un futuro no tan lejano . Revista Educación Superior Y Sociedad (ESS), 35(1), 152-178. DOI: 10.54674/ess.v35i1.751

Rose, D. H., & Meyer, A. (2023). *Universal Design for Learning: Theory and Practice* (2nd ed.). CAST Professional Publishing.

Rueda López, R., Aja Valle, J., García García, L., & Vázquez García, M. J. (2024). *La influencia del liderazgo inclusivo sobre el bienestar laboral de las personas trabajadoras. 33 (1).* Revista Galega de Economía.

Ruiz, R., Martínez, R., & Valladares, L. (2010). Innovación en la educación superior. Hacia las sociedades del conocimiento. México: *Fondo de Cultura Económica/ UNAM.Sauvé, Enseñanza de las Ciencias, 28*(1), 5–18. https://books.google.com.mx/books/about/Innovación_en_la_educación_superior.html?id=QOcOHijVOosC&redir_esc=y Saadatmand, M., & Kumpulainen, K. (2013). Content Aggregation and Knowledge Sharing in a Personal Learning Environment: Serendipity in Open Online Networks. *International Journal of Emerging Technologies in Learning, 8*(1), 70-78.

Sabre. (2024). *What is GDS in travel?*https://www.sabre.com/transforming-global-distribution-system/

Salmon, G. (2021). *E-Moderating: The Key to Online Teaching and Learning* (4th ed.). Routledge.

Sá, M. J., & Serpa, S. (2020). The COVID-19 pandemic as an opportunity to foster the sustainable development of teaching in higher education. *Sustainability (Basel)*, 12(20), 8525. DOI: 10.3390/su12208525

Sánchez-Corral Fernández. Elsa. (2021). *Educar para la justicia social: una apuesta desde el análisis interseccional para estudiantes de grupos privilegiados.* Revista Latinoamericana de Estudios Educativos, vol. LI (3), pp. 97-124. https://www.redalyc.org/journal/270/27066944003/html/

Sánchez-Cruzado, C.. (2021). Digital competence in higher education faculty: Systematic literature review. *International Journal of Educational Technology in Higher Education*, 18(1), 1–21.

Sánchez-Monedero, J., Dencik, L., & Edwards, L. (2020). What does it mean to 'solve' the problem of discrimination in hiring? Social, technical and legal perspectives from the UK on automated hiring systems. In *Proceedings of the 2020 Conference on Fairness, Accountability, and Transparency* (pp. 458-468). DOI: 10.1145/3351095.3372849

Saucedo, C., Karina, L., Udave, N., Fabiola, L., Cadena, G., Humberto, C., García, T., Jaqueline, E., & Alvarado César Arnulfo de León Alvarado, L. (2022) 13 (14) 1-22. *Validez de la Escala de Confianza en la Tutoría Afectiva y utilidad de la tutoría académica. Diálogos sobre educación. Temas actuales en investigación educativa*https://www.redalyc.org/articulo.oa?id=553474080019

Scasserra, S. (2019). El despotismo de los algoritmos. Cómo regular el empleo en las plataformas. *Nueva Sociedad, 279.*

Schein, E. H. (2024). *Organizational Culture and Leadership* (6th ed.). Jossey-Bass.

Schmelkes, S. (2024). The potential of education to conserve and transform. https://www.redalyc.org/journal/270/27075657009/

Schrum, L., & Levin, B. B. (2021). *Leading 21st-Century Schools: Harnessing Technology for Engagement and Achievement* (3rd ed.). Corwin.

Schwab, K. (2017). *The fourth industrial revolution.* New York: Currency. UN Tourism. (s.f.). *Digital Transformation.* https://www.unwto.org/digital-transformation

Schwarzmüller, T., Brosi, P., Duman, D., & Welpe, I. M. (2018). How does the digital transformation affect organizations? Key themes of change in work design and leadership. *Management Review*, 29(2), 114–138.

Scott, C. (2015). El futuro del aprendizaje2 ¿Qué tipo de aprendizaje se necesita en el siglo XXI? Investigación y Prospectiva en Educación, 14, 1-19. https://unesdoc.unesco.org/ark:/48223/pf0000242996_spa

Secretaria de Educación Pública. (2024). La Escuela es Nuestra. Gobierno de México. https://laescuelaesnuestra.sep.gob.mx/

Secretaría del Trabajo y Previsión Social. (2023). *Entrega Gobierno de México medios de pago de la Escuela es Nuestra y Jóvenes construyendo el Futuro en el Estado de México*. Gobierno de México. https://www.gob.mx/stps/prensa/entrega-gobierno-de-mexico-medios-de-pago-de-la-escuela-es-nuestra-y-jovenes-construyendo-el-futuro-en-el-estado-de-mexico#:~:text=Inform%C3%B3%20que%20el%20programa%20entrega,M%C3%A9xico%2C%20reciben%20600%20mil%20pesos

Selwyn, N. (2021). *Digital technology and the futures of education: Towards 'non-stupid' optimism*. UNESCO.

Selwyn, N. (2023). Should Robots Replace Teachers? AI and the Future of Education. *Polity*.

Selwyn, N. (2024). *Education and Technology: Key Issues and Debates* (4th ed.). Bloomsbury Academic.

Selwyn, N., & Facer, K. (2024). *The Ethics of Educational Technology*. Routledge.

Senge, P. M. (2020). *The Fifth Discipline: The Art and Practice of the Learning Organization* (Revised and updated ed.). Currency.

Senge, P., ... (2024). *Schools That Learn: A Fifth Discipline Fieldbook for Educators, Parents, and Everyone Who Cares About Education* (Updated and revised ed.). Crown Business.

Senge, P. M., & Schein, E. H. (2023). *Organizational Learning and Leadership for the Digital Age*. MIT Press.

Sepúlveda, F., & Aparicio, C. (2017). El desafío de los directores de escuelas chilenas: Liderando a partir de un enfoque instruccional hacia un enfoque distribuido. Revista Gestión de la Educación, 7(2), 1-19. https://revistas.ucr.ac.cr/index.php/gestedu

Sevilla, D., Martín, M., & Jenaro, C. (2018). Actitud del docente hacia la educación inclusiva y hacia los estudiantes con necesidades educativas especiales. *Innovación Educativa (México, D.F.)*, 18(78), 115–142.

Siemens, G. (2021). Learning analytics and educational data mining: Towards communication and collaboration. *LAK '21: Proceedings of the 11th International Conference on Learning Analytics and Knowledge*.

Siemens, G., & Baker, R. S. (2023). *Learning Analytics Handbook*. Society for Learning Analytics Research.

Siemens, G., & Downes, S. (2023). *Connectivism: A Learning Theory for the Digital Age* (2nd ed.). Athabasca University Press.

Siemens, G., & Long, P. (2024). Penetrating the fog: Analytics in learning and education. *EDUCAUSE Review*.

Sordo, I. (2023). *8 signs of poor communication in your company and how to reverse them*. Hubspot.

Soto, R., & Luz, A. (2022). Evidencias educativas que mejoran al mundo. *Tipos de liderazgo y su función dentro de las organizaciones*. Universidad Autónoma Benito Juárez de Oaxaca. https://amieedu.org/actascimie21/wp-content/uploads/2022/01/Ana-Luz-Ramos-Soto.pdf

Sotomayor, P., Muñoz, J., Martínez, P., & Araya, A. (2020). Liderazgo, cultura y prácticas inclusivas desde la mirada de equipos directivos de establecimientos educativos. *Revista de Investigación en Comunicación y Desarrollo*, 11(1), 5–15. DOI: 10.33595/2226-1478.11.1.375

Sovero, F. (2007). *Cómo dirigir una Institución Educativa*. AFA, Editores Importadores S.A. Lima.

Spillane, J. P., & Diamond, J. B. (2023). *Distributed Leadership in Practice* (2nd ed.). Teachers College Press.

Sposato, M. (2019). Understanding paternalistic leadership: How to work with Chinese leaders. *Development and Learning in Organizations*, 33(6), 19–21. DOI: 10.1108/DLO-12-2018-0169

Sposato, M. (2021). A critical perspective on gender and paternalistic leadership in China. *International Journal of Business Innovation and Research*, 24(3), 417–428. DOI: 10.1504/IJBIR.2021.113513

Sposato, M. (2024). Leadership training and development in the age of artificial intelligence. *Development and Learning in Organizations*, 38(4), 4–7. DOI: 10.1108/DLO-12-2023-0256

Sylvia, S. (2024). LIV(1), 411-430. *El potencial de la educación para conservar y para transformar.* Revista Latinoamericana de Estudios Educativos (México). https://www.redalyc.org/articulo.oa?id=27075657009

Tapia, W. (n.d.). Media and humanism. *Universidad La República*, 1. https://periodismo.uchile.cl/asepecs/ponencias/3pwturep.htm

The Chronicle of Higher Education. (2023). *Post-pandemic higher education: Challenges and opportunities*. The Chronicle of Higher Education. https://www.chronicle.com/article/post-pandemic-higher-education-challenges-and-opportunities

Tiwana, A. (2014). *Platform ecosystems: Aligning architecture, governance, and strategy*. Newnes. DOI: 10.1016/B978-0-12-408066-9.00001-1

Tobón, S., & Posada, R. E. Q. (2008). Competence-based assessment. In *First International Congress "Competencies in 21st Century Education."*

Torres, A., Pérez, L., López, A., & Toro, J. (2021). Política educativa implementada a partir de la emergencia sanitaria por COVID-19 en el nivel de educación superior. *Revista Docencia Politécnica, 2*(6), 25-39. https://www.ipn.mx/assets/files/innovacion/docs/docencia-politecnica/docencia-politecnica-6/Politica-educativa-implementada-a-partir-de-la-emergencia-sanitaria-por-COVID-19-en-el-nivel-de-educacion-superior%20.pdf

Torres-Castillo, F., Cantú-Mata, J., & Cantú-Mata, M. (2022). Competencias y habilidades de estudiantes en el área de desarrollo de software y la percepción de la adaptación a la formación a distancia. *Interciencia*, 47(11).

Torres, D., & Prieto, J. (2014). Posgrados: Visión y percepción en la Universidad Pedagógica y Tecnológica de Colombia. *Revista Historia de la Educación Latinoamericana*, 16(22), 249–273. DOI: 10.19053/01227238.2720

Treviño, L. K., den Nieuwenboer, N. A., & Kish-Gephart, J. J. (2014). (Un)ethical behavior in organizations. *Annual Review of Psychology*, 65(1), 635–660. DOI: 10.1146/annurev-psych-113011-143745 PMID: 23834354

Turismo, O. N. U. (2024). *Últimos datos sobre turismo.*https://www.unwto.org/es/barometro-del-turismo-mundial-de-onu-turismo

Turismo, O. N. U. (n.d.a.). *Turismo responsable, sostenible y accesible.*https://www.unwto.org/es/acerca-de-onu-turismo#:~:text=ONU%20Turismo%2C%20como%20principal%20organizaci%C3%B3n,sus%20conocimientos%20y%20pol%C3%ADticas%20tur%C3%ADsticas

Turismo, O. N. U. (n.d.b.). *Acerca de ONU Turismo.*https://www.unwto.org/es/acerca-de-la-organizacion-mundial-turismo

Turismo, O. N. U. (n.d.c.). *Glosario de términos de turismo.*https://www.unwto.org/es/glosario-terminos-turisticos

Turkle, S. (2023). *Reclaiming Conversation: The Power of Talk in a Digital Age* (2nd ed.). Penguin Books.

UNESCO MGIEP. (2017). Rethinking schooling for the 21st century. New Delhi: Mahatma Gandhi Institute of Education for Peace and Sustainable Development (MGIEP), UNESCO.

UNESCO. (2016) Conceptual framework for the assessment of competencies. https://unesdoc.unesco.org/ark:/48223/pf0000245195_eng

UNESCO. (2017). Education for the Sustainable Development Goals. Learning objectives. https://unesdoc.unesco.org/ark:/48223/ pf0000247444

Unesco. (2017). Recovered from https://www.un.org/sustainabledevelopment/es/objetivos-de-desarrollo-sostenible/United

UNESCO. (2023) The future of higher education: skills for tomorrow's world. https://www.iesalc.unesco.org/2023/08/11/the-future-of-higher-education-skills-for-tomorrows-world/

UNESCO. (2023). *Global Education Monitoring Report 2023*. UNESCO.

UNESCO. (2023). *Poner fin a la discriminación en la educación: un instrumento clave para proteger el derecho a la educación.*https://www.unesco.org/es/articles/poner-fin-la-discriminacion-en-la-educacion-un-instrumento-clave-para-proteger-el-derecho-la

UNESCO. (2024). *Global Report on Digital Skills Gap*. UNESCO.

UNESCO. Oficina para América Latina y el Caribe del IIPE UNESCO. (2020). *Inclusión y Equidad.*https://siteal.iiep.unesco.org/eje/inclusion_y_equidad

Unidas, N. (2009). *Clasificación Industrial Internacional Uniforme de todas las actividades Económicas (CIIU) Revisión 4.*https://unstats.un.org/unsd/publication/SeriesM/seriesm_4rev4s.pdf

UNIR. Universidad en Internet. (2020). *La interculturalidad en la educación: ¿Qué retos plantea en el aula?*https://www.unir.net/educacion/revista/interculturalidad-en-educacion/

Universidad Europea. (2023). *Liderazgo inclusivo: por qué es importante y cómo mejorarlo.* Empresa y Tecnología. https://universidadeuropea.com/blog/liderazgo-inclusivo/

Vadillo, R. C., & Fernández, P. I. (2023) 14 *Educación inclusiva y educación especial en México: dilemas, relaciones y articulaciones.* Inclusive education and special education in Mexico: dilemmas, relationships and joints. IE Revista de Investigación Educativa de la REDIECH. Red de Investigadores Educativos Chihuahua A. C. https://www.redalyc.org/journal/5216/521674411014/

Valdés, R., & Gómez-Hurtado, I. (2019). Competencias y prácticas de liderazgo escolar para la inclusión y la justicia social. *Perspectiva educativa.Formación de Profesores*, 58(2), 47–68. DOI: 10.4151/07189729

Van Deursen, A., & Van Dijk, M. (2014). *Modeling traditional literacy, Internet skills and Internet usage: An empirical study. Interacting with Computers*. Advance., DOI: 10.1093/iwc/iwu027

Van Dijk, J. A. (2023). *The Digital Divide* (2nd ed.). Polity.

Van Dijk, J. A. (2024). *The Network Society* (5th ed.).

Velandia, H. Wilmer A., Guzmán Zamora Nelson. (2024), LIV(1), 225-254. *La asertividad para el fortalecimiento de las democracias. Niveles de asertividad y participación ciudadana en población universitaria.* Revista Latinoamericana de Estudios Educativos (México) https://www.redalyc.org/articulo.oa?id=27075657010

Velásquez, O. (2019). La 4RI. Como parte de la reflexión universitaria. *Pensamiento Universitario,* 29, 2. https://ascun.org.co/uploads/default/publications/5aeee20947a9b5676665ca2a7d4f286d.pdf

Ventura Roque Hernández, R., Salinas Escandón, J. M., & López Mendoza, A. (2015). La complejidad de entender y enfrentar la formación de futuros desarrolladores de software. *Ciencia Ergo Sum*, 22(2), 153–159.

Vera, F., Tejada, E., & Morales, M. (2022). Development of generic competencies in students of the Bachelor's Degree in Hispanic American Language and Literature. Transformar, 3(1), 14–25. Retrieved from https://www.revistatransformar.cl/index.php/transformar/article/view/49

Vera, A., & Rivas, A. (2023). *El monitoreo de políticas educativas digitales en América Latina y el Caribe*. Oficina para América Latina y el Caribe del IIPE UNESCO.

Vial, G. (2019). Understanding digital transformation: A review and a research agenda. *The Journal of Strategic Information Systems*, 28(2), 118–144. DOI: 10.1016/j.jsis.2019.01.003

Voogt, J., & Knezek, G. (2022). *International Handbook of Information Technology in Primary and Secondary Education* (2nd ed.). Springer.

Vuorikari, R.. (2020). eTwinning in the time of COVID-19: Agents of change in European schools. *European Journal of Education*, 55(4), 572–587.

Walko, Aquino, Ludmilla. (. (2022). Characteristics of the most efficient instrument design in the assessment of learning. *Academo (Asuncion)*, 9(1), 1–10. DOI: 10.30545/academo.2022.ene-jun.1

Warschauer, M. (2021). *Technology and Social Inclusion: Rethinking the Digital Divide* (2nd ed.). MIT Press.

Warschauer, M. (2022). *Learning in the Cloud: How (and Why) to Transform Schools with Digital Media*. Teachers College Press.

WEF. (2017). The travel & tourism competitiveness report 2017. Paving the way for a more sustainable and inclusive future. Geneva, Switzerland.

Weill, P., & Woerner, S. L. (2018). *What's your digital business model?: Six questions to help you build the next-generation enterprise*. Harvard Business Press.

Wenger, E., & Traynor, B. (2023). *Learning to Make a Difference: Value Creation in Social Learning Spaces*. Cambridge University Press.

Westerman, G., Bonnet, D., & McAfee, A. (2014). *Leading digital: Turning technology into business transformation*. Harvard Business Press.

Wiley, D., & Hilton, J. L.III. (2024). *Open Educational Resources: Foundations and Futures*. EdTech Books.

Williamson, B. (2022). *Big Data in Education: The Digital Future of Learning Policy and Practice*. SAGE Publications.

Williamson, B. (2023). *Datafication of Education*. Routledge.

Williamson, B. (2024). *Learning Analytics Futures*. Routledge.

Williamson, B., Eynon, R., & Potter, J. (2020). Pandemic politics, pedagogies, and practices: Digital technologies and distance education during the coronavirus emergency. *Learning, Media and Technology*, 45(2), 107–114. DOI: 10.1080/17439884.2020.1761641

Williamson, B., & Macfadyen, L. P. (2023). *Critical Perspectives on Learning Analytics*. Routledge.

Wiśniewska-Sałek, A. (2021). Change Management: Agile Business Transformation in the Hybrid Education System Management. *Proceedings of the European Conference on Knowledge Management*, 821–829. https://doi.org/DOI: 10.34190/EKM.21.179

Wong, K. V., & Robles, D. R. (2024). Barreras que afronta el alumnado con discapacidad visual en los servicios de apoyo para la inclusión en educación superior en México. DOI: 10.1590/SciELOPreprints.7967

World Economic Forum. (2024). *The Future of Jobs Report 2024*. World Economic Forum.

World Economic Forum. (October 20, 2020). The future of job report 2020. https://www.weforum.org/reports/the-future-of-jobs-report-2020/in-full/infographics-e4e69e4de7

World Economic Forum. (WEF, 2018). *Temas claves de la agenda global.* https://toplink.weforum.org/knowledge/insight/a1Gb0000000LPFfEAO/explore/summary

World Economic Forum. [WEF]. (2017). *Project Plan Overview: 21st Century Curriculum Project.* Sydney, Australia: World Economic Forum.

Yang, Y., Saladrigas, H., & Torres, D. (2016). The process of the communication in the step of knowledge. A theoretic analysis of your behavior as from two typical models. *University of Havana, 8.*

Ynzunza, C., Izar, J., Bocarando, J., Aguilar, F., & Larios, M. (2017). El Entorno de la Industria 4.0: Implicaciones y Perspectivas Futuras. *Conciencia Tecnológica,* 54, 86-98. Retrieved from https://www.redalyc.org/jatsRepo/944/94454631006/94454631006.pdf

Zapata, J. C. M., & Yepes, P. D. E. (2024). Representation of some principles of the Agile Manifesto in the Semat Essence Kernel. *Scientia et Technica*, 29(1), 41–48. DOI: 10.22517/23447214.24241

Zawacki-Richter, O., Marín, V. I., Bond, M., & Gouverneur, F. (2019). Systematic review of research on artificial intelligence applications in higher education – where are the educators? *International Journal of Educational Technology in Higher Education*, 16(1), 39. DOI: 10.1186/s41239-019-0171-0

Zhao, Y. (2021). *World Class Learners: Educating Creative and Entrepreneurial Students*. Corwin.

Zhao, Y. (2023). *Reach for Greatness: Personalizable Education for All Children.* Corwin.

Zhao, Y. (2024). *What Works May Hurt: Side Effects in Education*. Teachers College Press.

Zhao, Y., & Lei, J. (2023). *Teaching for innovation fatigue: Understanding and addressing burnout in educational technology integration*. Teachers College Press.

Zhao, Y., & Watterston, J. (2024). *Making Schools Work: A Vision for Innovation in Education*. Routledge.

About the Contributors

Edgar Oliver Cardoso Espinosa is Coordinator of the Doctorate Program in Administrative Sciences of the Instituto Politécnico Nacional, México (2020-2026). PhD, is Professor - Researcher since 2009 on Division of Postgraduate Studies and Research of the Superior School of Commerce and Administration (ESCA) of the Instituto Politécnico Nacional (IPN), Mexico City. His research includes evaluation of educational programs and executive education. He belongs to the National System of Researchers with the level II distinction (2024-2028) and level I (2012-2023) distinction in the CONAHCYT of Mexico. He has directed several research projects in the area of educational management. He has conducted thesis addresses at the master's and doctoral level in the educational area.

***

Marlett Blas Rivera is a Teacher in Administration in Management and Development of Education, currently a student of the Doctorate in Administrative Sciences taught in the Postgraduate Studies and Research Section of the Higher School of Commerce and Administration, Santo Tomás Unit of the National Polytechnic Institute (IPN), Mexico City. Topics oriented to educational management, school leadership, styles and models of educational leadership and ethics in educational organizations.

Maria Cerecedo Mercado is a professor and researcher at the Postgraduate Studies and Research Section of the Higher School of Commerce and Administration (ESCA) of the National Polytechnic Institute (IPN) since 2002.

Sandra Ruiz is a PhD student in Administrative Sciences.

Cristina Cuevas Hoyos egresada de la Universidad de Sonora en Ingeniería Industrial y de Sistemas, posee Maestría en Ingeniería en Sistemas y Tecnología, así como en Administración. Actualmente cursa el Doctorado en Ciencias Administrativas en el Instituto Politécnico Nacional. Con 15 años de experiencia en la Universidad de Sonora, se desempeña como asesora en procesos de evaluación y acreditación en la Dirección de Apoyo a Programas Educativos.

Mario Muñoz Mercado is a PhD student in Administrative Sciences.

Erick Nava Meléndez has a Master in Business Administration for Sustainability, currently a graduate student in the Doctorate in Administrative Sciences at ESCA Santo Tomás unit, IPN.

Claudia Cruz is a student of the PhD program in administrative sciences at ESCA, Santo Tomás, from the National Polytechnic Institute (IPN).

Silvia Daniella Pérez Muñoz, nació en la Ciudad de México. Estudio la Licenciatura en Educación Primaria en la Universidad Normal La Salle. Ha sido tutora de docentes recién egresados al Sistema Educativo. Ha concursado en dos ocasiones para la plaza de Dirección Básica. Asimismo, presento el examen de la Evaluación Permanencia Docente, el cual acredito y consiguió la basificación. Estudio la Maestría en Educación en la UNID sede Taxqueña. Ha trabajado como docente frente a grupo por 19 años; tanto en institución privada y pública. Actualmente, esta cursando el segundo semestre del Doctorado en Ciencias Administrativas.

Rosa Rivas García is a doctorado en Ciencias Administrativas Instituto Politécnico Nacional (IPN), Mexico.

Martin Sposato is an Associate Professor at the College of Business, Zayed University, Dubai, UAE. He holds a PhD in Leadership. His research interests include leadership, artificial intelligence in organizations, postcolonialism as a theoretical lens, Indigenous (Chinese) theories and conceptualizations of Human Resource Management (HRM), gender in organizations, and reflexivity in research.

Maria Trejo Carrillo is a PhD student in Administrative Sciences.

María Zepeda Hurtado is a n Investigador-Docente del IPN. Pedagoga, maestra en Administración y desarrollo educativo. Certificada en competencias docentes por la ANUIES. Experiencia en capacitación y diseño de acciones formativas de actualización, capacitación y formación docente así como en diseño curricular: elaboración y actualización de planes y programas de estudio.

Index

R

S

T

U

www.ingramcontent.com/pod-product-compliance
Lightning Source LLC
LaVergne TN
LVHW081345300926
849161LV00008B/2068
* 9 7 9 8 3 6 9 3 7 0 8 6 5 *